BALKAN FABRICATIONS

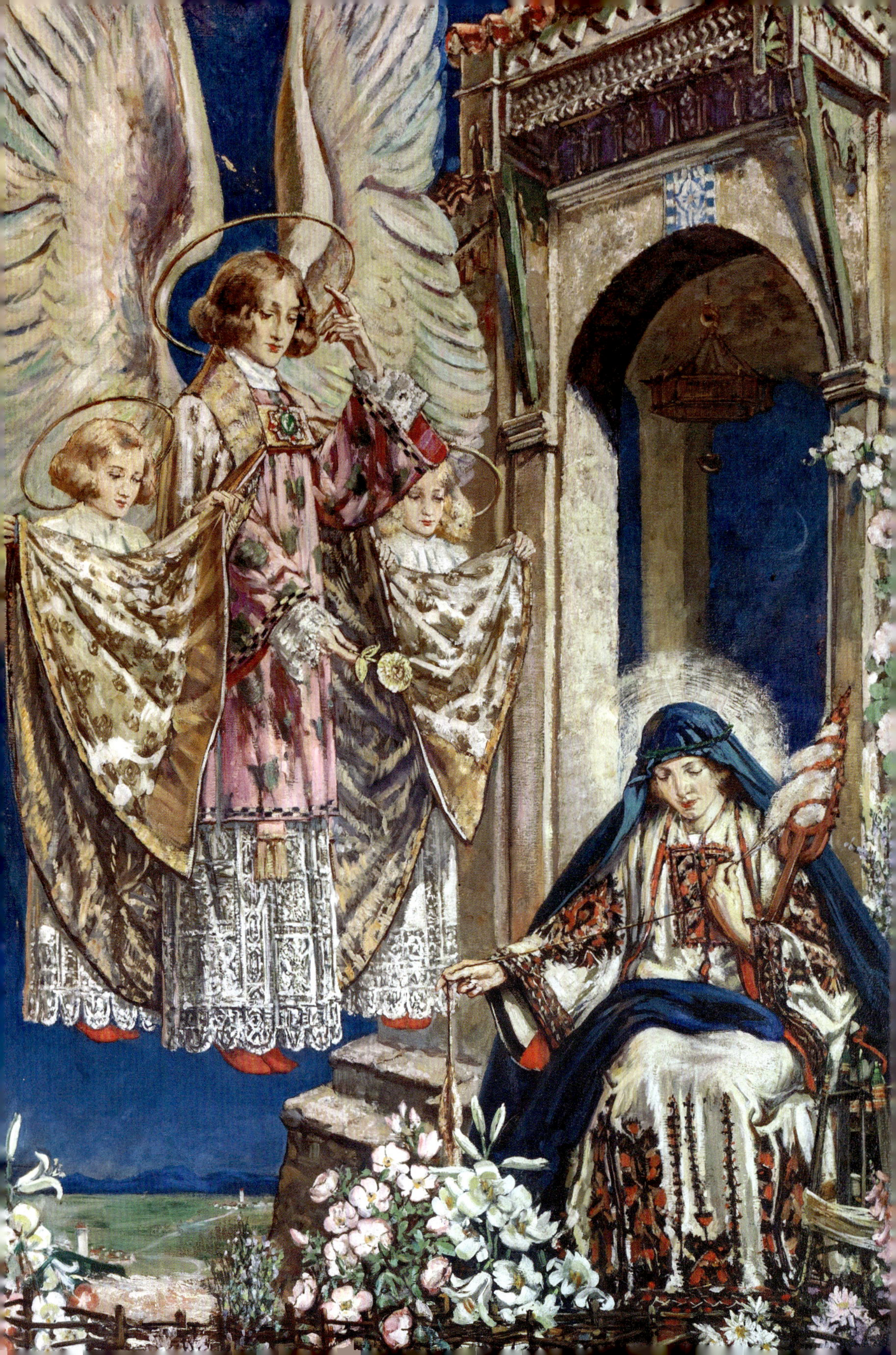

BALKAN FABRICATIONS

From Fra and Jessie Newbery's 'Serbian' Turn

Jeremy Howard

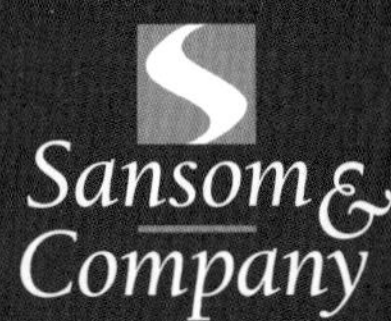

Sansom & Company

In memory of Robin Spencer (1944–2017),
a great friend and mentor

First published in 2022 by Sansom and Company,
a publishing imprint of Redcliffe Press Ltd.,
81g Pembroke Road, Bristol BS8 3EA
www.sansomandcompany.co.uk | info@sansomandcompany.co.uk

ISBN 978-1-911408-84-0

© Text: Jeremy Howard
© Images: artists/artists' estates

British Library cataloguing-in-publication data:
A catalogue record for this book is available from the British Library.

Design and typesetting by E&P Design

Printed and bound by Cambrian Printers Ltd

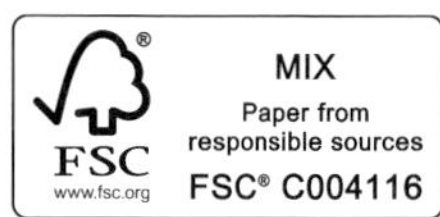

Sansom & Co is committed to being an environmentally friendly publisher.
This book is made from Forest Stewardship Council® certified paper.

Front cover: Fra Newbery, *Serbian Women*, *c.* 1929–30, oil on canvas, 90 x 115 cm
(Dundee Art Galleries and Museums, Dundee)
Back cover: Kathleen Mann, 'Yugoslavia: Serbia', from Kathleen Mann,
Peasant Costume in Europe, Book 2 (London: A. & C. Black, 1936), pp. 95
Frontispiece Fra Newbery, *Annunciation* [detail], 1930, Church of the Holy Spirit
[formerly Holy Ghost] and St Edward, Swanage, oil on canvas, 304 x 162 cm
(photograph: Simon Parvin)

CONTENTS

PROLOGUE

This book does not fit (which means it fits somewhere I have not thought of). It is not about being *per se* or p.c. Or being comprehensive. So it is not a book about Scottish art. Nor is it about English art. Or British art. Or Serbian, Croatian, Dalmatian, Macedonian, Bulgarian, Yugoslavian, Romanian, or Balkan art. It is not about national art. It is not about European art. But it is about artworks that relate the ties between these. And it delves into aspects of their histories, their coming together and their estrangement. And it is about an artist who was Scottish who worked in Scotland and England, and an artist who was English who worked in England and Scotland. And it is about the two artists, Francis and Jessie Newbery, going on European tours that were not grand – British conventionally grand that is. As this couple lead us through, the book zigzags and has a rough symmetry, its progress in keeping with the embroidered motifs on the costumes Jessie buys and adapts and that Fra paints and reinvents. It accepts that what it omits can be conceived as gap: there is no Montenegrin art. Barely any Slovenian, Bosnian, Herzegovinan, Albanian, Kosovan, Romani, Turkish, Muslim, Jewish art. There is also little Christian art. And, while probing mutable identity, it often elides Serbian with Macedonian, Croatian with Dalmatian, and all of them with Yugoslavian and Balkan. Plus Bulgarian shows a south Slav face. And Romanian appears alongside.

Not being about global art, local art, well-known art, neglected art, or about centres or peripheries, and yet with an underlying concern with all of these, this book also accepts that there are places the author has not been and does not go, folk that have not been met, archives that have not been used, images that have not been viewed, texts that have not been read, colleagues that have not been consulted, artists who have not been linked. And that some of these, at least, and ideally, should have been touched upon. Instead it relies on those visits, folk, archives, images, texts, colleagues and artists that are referred to, contemplates perspective and makes things up. In its fabrications it attempts not to be fanciful.

This book is not specifically about painting. Or embroidery, dress or other textile art. Or individual crafts. Or peasant art. Or outsider art. Or sculpture. Or performance. Or photography. Or collecting. Or ideas. But it is about these collectively, with art as craft, craft as art and art as creative act. With artist as craftist, and vice versa. At the same time it is not about style or fashion. And it is certainly not about -isms. It is not about originality, being pioneering or genius. It is not about ethnographic art. It is not about popular art. Nor is it about high, low, major or minor art. For it denies these as concepts. But it is about what are construed as these, as well as about makers being sedulous, inquisitive, generous, fair, bucking trends … into old age. It is anti-hagiographical and anti-hierarchical. In being this it, surely, is both.

This book is not about art of the 1920s and 1930s. Or 'interwar' art. Or the 1890s, 1900s, 1910s. But it is about all of these and what links them beyond concepts of time. It is not about women artists. Or men artists. Or queer artists. Or young or old artists. But it is about artwork of all of these. And it is about perceptions of womanhood (more than manhood), as well as the personhood of art, its biographical and social nature. And it is about hybridisation. So it is not about Fra Newbery. Or Jessie Newbery. But it is about them both, the colloquy of their art, and fragments of their practice, ideas, lives, correspondences.

This book is not art history. Nor is it political, economic, social history. Or philosophy of art. Or anthropology of art. Nor is it a treatise on expert or amateur art, beauty or utility. It is neither easy reading nor academic. But it may be a little of some of the foregoing. It has its look-and-read approach: this is its fabric and Balkan themes, its weaving format, its attention to detail, its references. It also tries to prioritise contemporary voice, from different cultures, over subsequent scholarly argument. Likewise its critical mass commences from the selected artworks and artists' words and only supplements these with later pontifications to open up enquiry. Essentially, its starting point is the Newberys' visual and material art, and its end point is their art theory. In between it conjures relations with Balkan and other European cultures. In so doing it also explores women-with-distaffs iconography and reapplies original, uncorrupted, meaning to the term 'spinster'. So, it is not historically sequential, though individual chapters contain some chronology. And it does not seek to expand 'the canon' since it does not recognise there is a set canon. Despite this, its aim is to challenge and stimulate, to question belonging and becoming, to push at boundaries while refuting their existence and rebutting the shenanigans of discipline. Hence, it has its method, its research, its threads, its needles in haystacks. And, while trying to be objective it pulls many punches, has its bias, its distaff (female) and spear (male) sides, its occasional expressions of truculence.

So in this book we explore what I perceive as networks of correspondences. And fractals, as I come to call the artworks of these networks and the networks. Bits and pieces, or better, pieces and bits. And thus we also explore written, posted and unposted, correspondence. And the play of such small signs of creativity and thought as part of bigger ones. With all this we move from painting and lectures in Dundee, to postcards from Sicily and Dalmatia; letters from Serbia; exhibitions in Kirkcaldy, Paris and Belgrade; sculpture in Dalmatia, a museum in Zagreb, performance in Dorset, costumes in Croatia and Macedonia; textile and other crafts handed down through Newbery generations; constructs of modernism, modernity and edge; publications in London and Skopje; people in Edinburgh, Swanage and Niš; schools in Glasgow and Travnik; Balkan design and British Balkanist art engagement. Getting ugly, if we were not already, we could say it is a book about intermodernism and interculture. We could say its jigsaw should have been made long ago but that multiple strictures and givens have conspired to prevent its thought. Which, while understandable, is odd, since we could say it is about the stuff of art. With feet on the ground, highfalutin head in the monitor and fingers on keys rather than buttons, it weaves together tales of sandals, scarfs, sleeves and aprons, as well as copies of photographs of paintings, words about vanished art and an actual altarpiece. This then is a book about the art of Balkan fabrications and forgotten distaff sides.

NB: All translations into English are by the author.

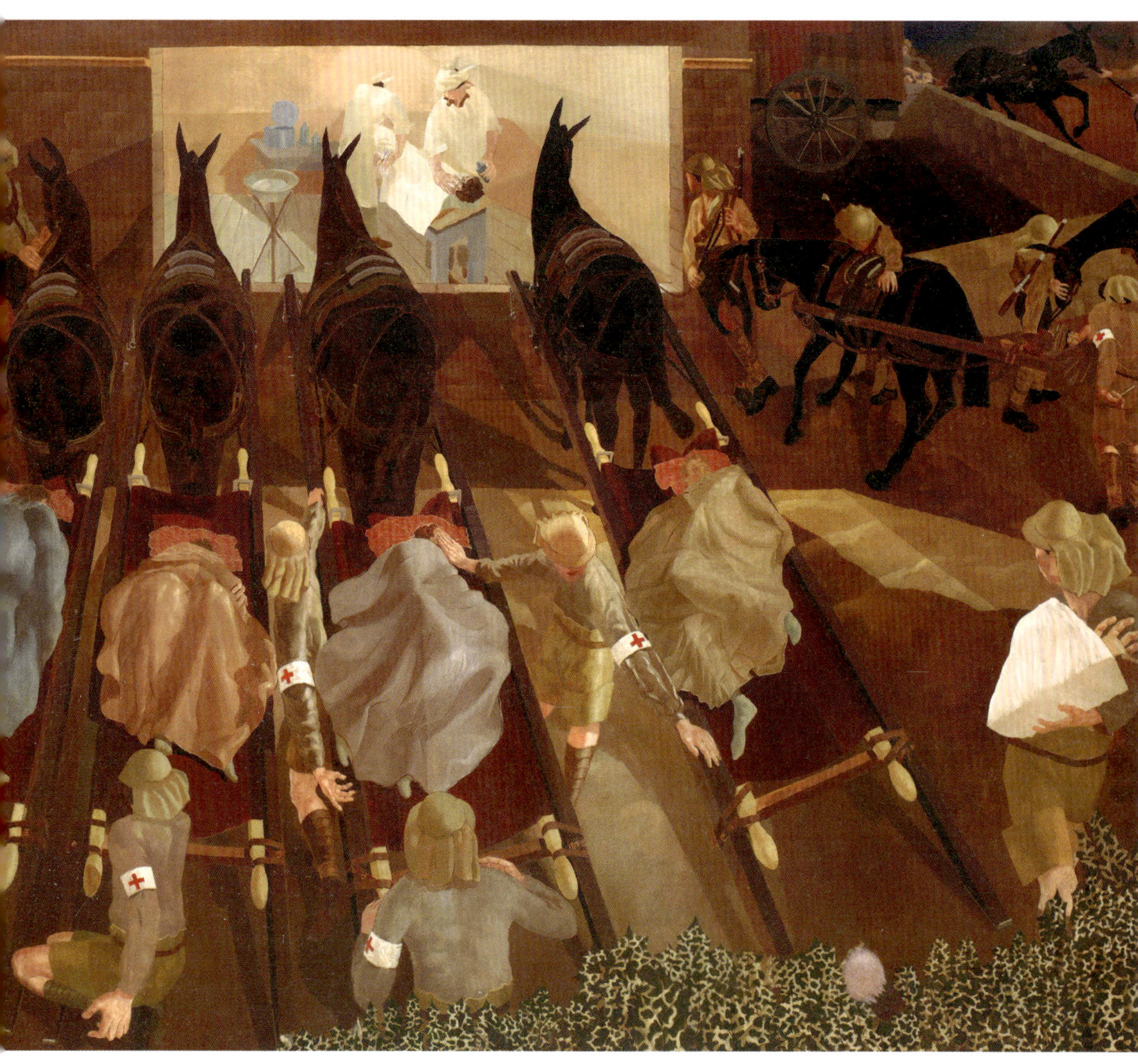

0.1 | Stanley Spencer
Travoys Arriving with Wounded at a Dressing Station at Smol, Macedonia, September 1916
1919, oil on canvas, 183 x 218.5 cm

PRELUDE

On Stanley Spencer's *Travoys Arriving with Wounded at a Dressing Station at Smol, Macedonia, September 1916*, 1919. A UK Ministry of Information commission.

Vardarec, Vardaris

Dear Stan

We write to take you out of that zone of yours into ours,
That which you entered, oh so briefly, in your Sixteen
And which you sought to capture with your brush for ever more.

To Yockney you wrote of depicting the scene at Smol
Without, as you said, 'truthfully representing' what you'd seen.
Oh, how we admire your honourable artistic goal.

Let us tell you first, that wounded are still arriving … and departing
At our place, which shortly after your time here
Greek officials renamed Mikro Dasos, your Little Wood.

Stan, we've admired your icon with its order but no stasis
You are right to have placed us in the dress circle of your theatre
For from in, and as, the gods, we, like you, see further than stalls,
*   wings and stage.*

Indeed we safely observe the enigma of arrival in your thanatopolis
Because you've also put us out, above and beyond the phrygana
That trails across your eery elision of interior and exterior.

Just remember, for all your record of noble, peaceful, pain
That muleteer you moaned of arms that ached from lugging
And cried out for moving, materials, change.

You call the Battle of Machukovo an attack on Machine Gun Hill,
While the 'never ending stream' of casualties you noted
Were more than two battalions lost to German force … and history.

Your colours and lines bleat redemption, offer hope
But since you're working for the Ministry we'd like some faces,
Please give us names, if not of those who sent and went,
*   at least of those so rent.*

For all your invaluable recollection, we know but one:
Dear Ernest Grace, a young private of the Lancashire Fusileers,
Killed in Evzonoi action beneath us, Vardarec-Vardaris.

Meanwhile, we'll give you a taste of our domain of river, knoll and air
With its vast necropolis of duo kiloyears past
And Hellenist idol of the ancients' god of archery, art and poetry.

Bulgar Smolikas was Ottoman, the Smolioti under a Turkish bey.
As the Sick Man weakened and other Sick Men meddled
Our place became a beating heart of Macedonian being and becoming.

Still its aorta was severed, first by the Sionidis gang, then the Bashibazouks.
Here, just before your dressing station days, were dozens of cheta slaughtered
And Apostol, liberation leader, among the few left wounded.

Then, after you'd gone, this place turned Hellas
With Sarakatsani set and Pontics resettled, the last
Survivors of Young Turk wipeout policies further east.

Now in your dressing place are temples of Pantaleon and Taxiarchis
And nearby is a border, with Bogoroditsa on the other side,
*   Idomeni on this:*
Great Healer, Bodiless Commander, Mother of God, Seer of Force.

Alas, in our Sixteen, we're back to soldiers and stretchers a-coming,
Doctors, nurses, volunteers and camps of caught-up multitudes:
The fare of far-off major wars of more Sick Men's making.

In ending, Stan, we thank you for your vision of sacrifice, deliverance.
You've harkened folly, violence and compassion.
Through your artifice travoys, table, actors carry moment.

We call on those who know and love you
To read beyond your orderly lines and repetitions
So that all may comprehend the cycles of man's waging.

Stan, for the sake of puny man, hear, be touched by, and feel us.
All around you and yours, we are the wind of all … and nothingness.

¶

Written by the author at the 2016 commencement of the ongoing refugee crisis in the Balkans; first published in Jane Draycott, Carolyn Leder and Peter Robinson (eds), *Stanley Spencer Poems: An Anthology* (Reading: Two Rivers Press, 2017), pp. 36–37.

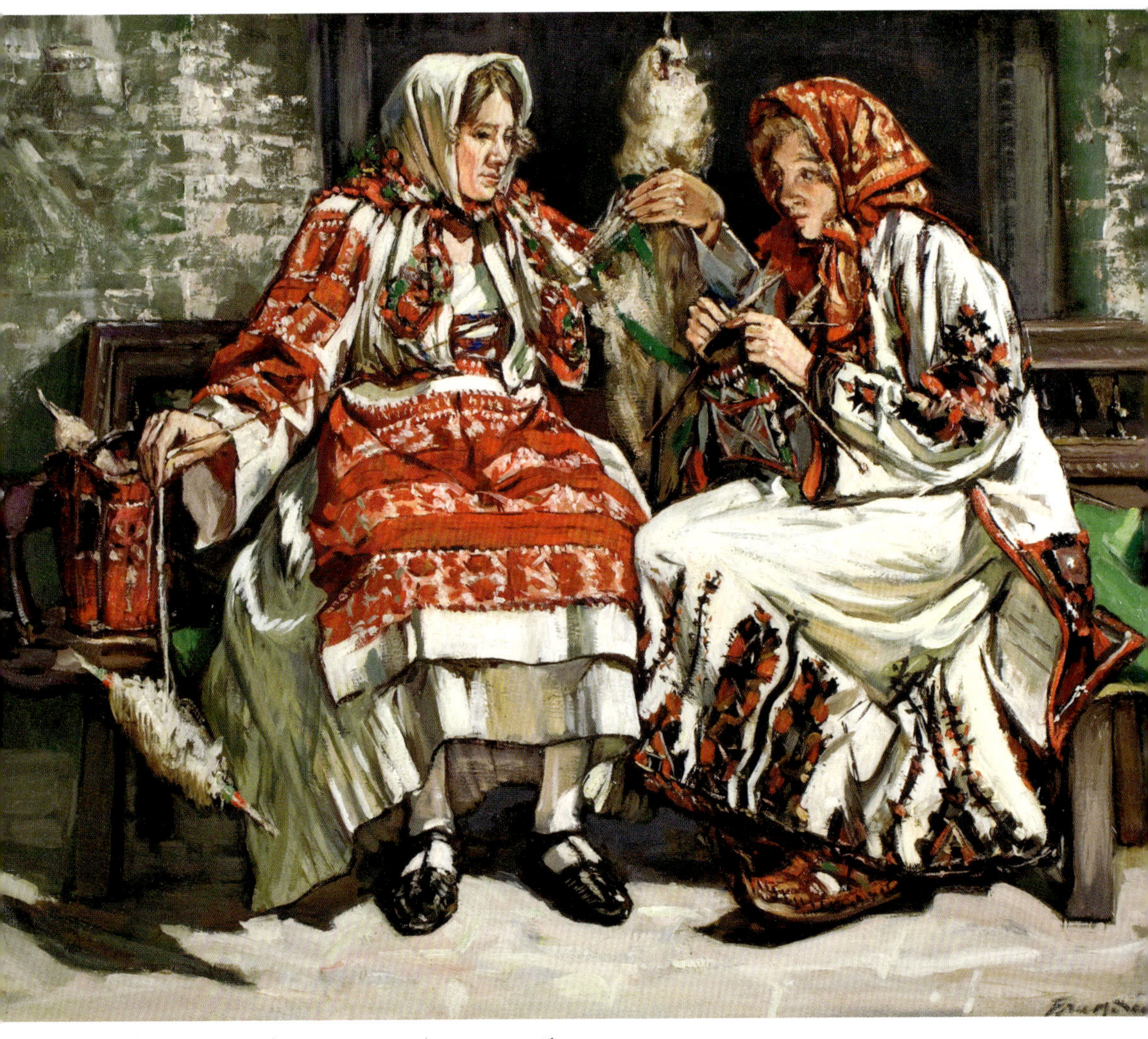

0.2 | Fra Newbery | *Serbian Women* | *c.*1929–30, oil on canvas, 90 x 115 cm
DUNDEE ART GALLERIES AND MUSEUMS, DUNDEE

INTRODUCTION

The fibrous stuff: Picturesque and congenial art

In the collection of the McManus art gallery and museum of Dundee, Scotland, is an oil painting from around 1929–30 by Fra (Francis) Newbery, the artist who, as director of the Glasgow School of Art from 1885 to 1918, transformed that institution into a leading centre of modern art and design [fig. 0.2]. Entitled *Serbian Women*, it features two women in elaborately embroidered, ample yet loose, folk dress seated on a bench with green cloth. One winds fibre, the other knits. A distaff with wool or flax rises vertically between the women, grasped loosely by the spinning figure on the left. The diagonal of her yarn leads across her body to a decorated red basket in which a yarn-laden spindle is visible. She appears dexterous and experienced in drafting the fibre from the distaff and spinning it onto the hanging spindle. Likewise her companion manipulates her long needles (at least four are visible) as she completes an intricately decorated garment, probably a woollen sock. Despite looking relatively young and serious, both women seem at one with their place and work without looking at their hands. Their bench may be Balkan, but similar vernacular types are also known in Brittany and in English pubs. It could, of course, be Fra's imaginary mixture of these. In any case, it fills the width of the painting and blocks, together with the women, the view of the wide entrance to a stone- or brick-built house behind them. The strip of visible ground seems to be made of flat rectangular flagstones. Strong shadows suggest the women are working in the middle of a sunny day. Covered from head to toe in their costumes, only their faces and hands are exposed to the sun and the viewer. Inclined towards one another, with knees almost touching, the women gaze beyond their work as if in deep thought, their busy hands frozen in time.

For all its being on display, its viewer-friendly dimensions (90 x 115 cm), obvious subject matter and figurative style, *Serbian Women* has been overlooked. Here, we reveal at least something of its mystery, and with that the draw that Serbia, the 'Balkans' and folk art had for Fra and his wife Jessie.[1] For the painting is really a product of both of their interests, Jessie having led, between 1894 and 1908, the advance of the embroidery department at the Glasgow School of Art, before continuing to work as an embroiderer, clothes designer and maker well into the 1930s, if not beyond.[2]

Jessie was the daughter of William Rowat, a shawl manufacturer in Paisley, a Renfrewshire town with a strong weaving and textile tradition, the renown of which was associated with 'the Paisley pattern'. Undoubtedly the variants of this decorative fabric design using a repeated hooked tear (*buta*) motif derived from Persia via India and her family involvement in their development informed Jessie's artistry. She not only developed her own 'Glasgow' style of fabric design but also designed and made practical, delicately embroidered and stylish dresses for herself and her two girls. In addition,

> *[f]rom the time of her first visit to Italy [in 1882], she was deeply interested in peasant crafts, especially textiles and pottery. The indestructible handwoven linen and the embroidery which is so often a part of the construction, made her study and collect examples from Italy, the Balkans and Russia.*[3]

Thus the objectification of women in the painting is complicated, and this complication is also our subject. For all our departure point being *Serbian Women* we also examine: its genesis in the Newberys' European travels and artistic interests; associated works that the couple created, collected, wrote about; and its wider context and legacy. Hence we also consider why the painting is in Dundee, in the course of which we assess Fra's hitherto neglected relationship with the city as well as with that of another textile industrial port to its south, Kirkcaldy. Plus we introduce the thorny issue of how the Newberys' 'Serbian' works may be interpreted apropos fluid and contested conceptualisations of 'Balkan' and 'Yugoslavian'. Through the compilation of these facets of our enquiry we posit a critical reassessment not just of Fra and Jessie's art, but also of how this aligns with fresh appraisals of early-twentieth-century, pan-European, artistic and socio-political trends.

In the course of the enquiry we consider what I have come to term the art of Balkan fabrications and forgotten distaff sides. These conjoined concepts involve placing the Newberys' Serbian turn within a setting of synthetic Balkanism and work by neglected or undervalued artists who were female (the two aspects also bringing to the fore some male, 'spear side', counterparts). This Balkanism contains features derived from the identity of its creators, who, principally, can be described as British, Balkan or a British-Balkan hybrid. These are supported by some French examples. Much attention is given to textile art, costume being given first place. Yet as an expression of identity, be that gendered and/or national, the focus on fabric is balanced by studying Balkan trends that override it, revealing an alternative, often transnational, modern visual language. What emerges is a form of pattern composed of multiple elements, or units in a network of correspondences. In some respects, the journey undertaken is underpinned by the notion of Jessie being a co-creator of Fra's *Serbian Women* even though we can assume that her hands did not touch the brushes, oil paint, canvas or easel involved in its making. For it was her eye, mind and money that captured the costumes, that led to their acquisition and cultural translation. In so doing Fra and she are joined in creative quest.

With Jessie and her keen sense of applied design coming to the fore, we also begin to introduce a selection of others whose creative worldviews draw upon similar sources. Some of these are itinerant – but for key periods Glasgow-based – women (including Ann Macbeth, De Courcy Lewthwaite Dewar and Kathleen Mann). Others are likewise itinerant, and had Scottish-, English- and/or Yugoslav-heritage/bases (for example Nasta Rojc, Ivan Meštrović, Nadežda Petrović, Lena Jovićić, Annie Dickinson, Ethel Mairet, Jean Milne and Rebecca West).

For many (but not all) the artistic associations and empathies they enunciate spring from an allegiance that began with the horrors inflicted upon the Serbian peoples by the Central Powers during the First World War. It was this conflict that was captured in a poignant and powerful, yet one-sided British 'Ministry of Information', way by Stanley Spencer in his *Travoys Arriving with Wounded at a Dressing Station at Smol, Macedonia, September 1916* (1919) [fig. 0.1]. While the import of this is deconstructed in the poem of our prelude, much of the work considered here expresses a different trajectory, one forged through co-operation, respect and the inventive reaction that the war and its wake invoked. Nevertheless, alternatives abound within our network of correspondences, including Croatian, Serbian, Bulgarian and Romanian images that, for all their commonality, derive from different political wellsprings.

Serbian Women was exhibited at the Paisley Art Institute's 55th annual exhibition in early 1931.[4] In all likelihood it was painted in 1929 or 1930. *The Scotsman* reported that 'F.H. Newbery has found picturesque and congenial material for colour and design in his Serbian women subjects.'[5] Despite the suggestion of this and its title the painting was physically created in Dorset, England, and depicts two local women. Hence, in order to comprehend its and its associated artworks' evolution, excerpts from letters that Jessie sent to her daughters Elsie and Mary from Serbia can serve as an introduction:

> *Palace Hotel: Nisch: Serbia: 29 Sept. 1926 … A day in this queer little borderland town between the West & the East … fascinating orangy/brown sheepskin coats with the fur inside & appliqued with thinner black leather & bright green pink yellow blue red shewing through punch holes in the back … prototypes (very primitive) of our Lilley & Skinner sandal – a whole street where they are made – peasants not so thrilling – some of them in Turkish trousers – just women. In Belgrade we had 'Jaoort' a kind of curdled milk … with sugar – delicious …*
>
> *Belgrade. 25 Oct 1926 … we are here – which we didn't expect to be but which I am very pleased about – as with the museum & the market & the view of the great plain from on high … it is a fine place to be in – & the small 2 story Belgrade houses that remain are very attractive, the handmade carpets about here are very interesting … chelems.* **I bought 2 articles of apparel** *– which you will see when you and Alick come to Corfe! I would like to buy more but they are dear even with the exchange in our favour … in Sofia we acquired braid in emerald, cobalt, yellow & scarlet, & some bowls – are you pleased? … Then Nisch – we found was selling that black pottery with gold encrustations … I got one [jug] … a lovely coat – Rodier fabric, camel hair coloured & stiff – with a little diaper of real gold – hardly tailored. The scarf goes through a slot & one end hangs down behind. Very long – no fur at neck …*[6]

With her eye clearly attuned to the material, colour and nature of dress, Jessie added two pencil drawings: the first of the Bulgarian braid bought in Sofia, the second of the coat she acquired in Niš, the capital of the Morava Banovina province of eastern Serbia, then in the Kingdom of Yugoslavia [fig. 0.3].[7] The golden diaper she mentioned

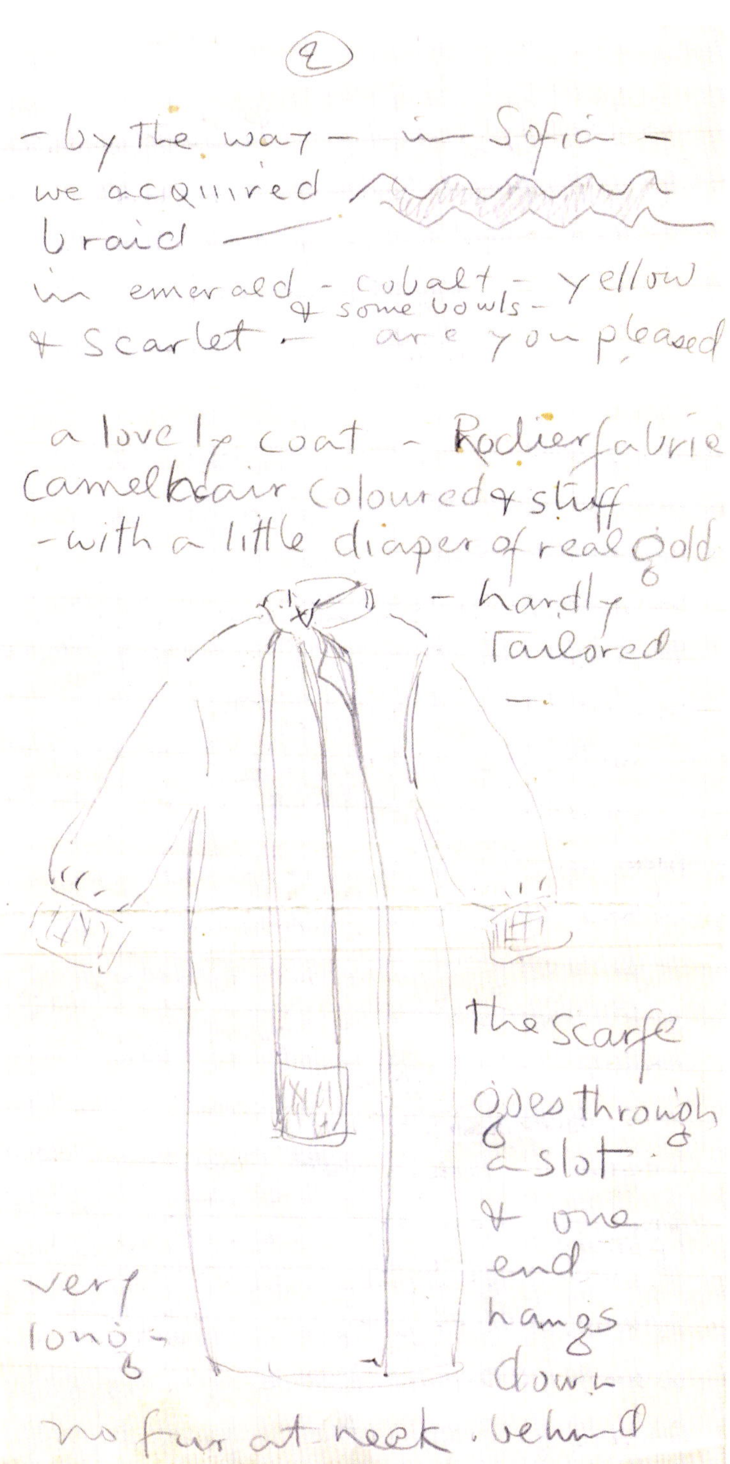

0.3 | Jessie Newbery, 'Bulgarian braid' and 'Serbian coat', pencil sketches in letter to Mary Newbery Sturrock, October 1926

would seem to be in the cuffs and scarf ends, hatched with lines suggesting embroidered geometric patterning (such work being a rarer usage of 'diaper'). In all probability this 'coat' appears in another painting by Fra (see below), while the two costumes Jessie purchased in Belgrade are those in *Serbian Women*.

Fra and Jessie Newbery's mutual sensitivity to Serbian artistry, their eyes for life-enriching colour, line and craft, as well as their collection and reinvention of Balkan artefacts, derive, in many respects, from the artistic credos and practices they developed in Glasgow in the 1890s and 1900s. Then, Jessie had begun her embroidery experiments, tracing, as noted in *The Studio* magazine, her modern British needlework 'back through continental ancestors to the mystic East, so that it cannot be considered an exotic, but a fully acclimatised growth.'[8] Five years later, in the same London journal, Fra was to note:

> *the dress of the modern Occidental man knows no art in its composition, nor can decoration, however added, redeem it from its state of sad monotony. But happily … in the hand of the woman … the work of the needle makes its appeal in poetry and has its place in art … we have in these latter days lost sight somewhat of that traditional use of the needle which in not very remote days brought a personal element to bear upon the beauty of household surroundings.*[9]

These sentiments were expressed about the same time that Fra began to write and direct masques.[10] Imaginatively probing history and identity, as well as the substance and evolution of art, this turn to textiles, costume and performance was to find particular resonance in his Serbian-related work of the late 1920s–early 1930s. In many respects then this book posits a form of Glasgow Style afterlife. As, post-1914, the style's leaders Charles Rennie Mackintosh and Margaret Macdonald removed to Suffolk and then Catalan France, and thereafter Mackintosh's creative language essentially moved to stylised watercolours of French Mediterranean built environments and textile designs, so its other main protagonists turned to country life.[11] In so doing, as we shall see through our examples taken from the Newberys and their Glasgow colleagues, Macbeth, Dewar and Mann, the Newbery-instigated Glasgow art initiative of *c.*1900 morphed into alternative forms of creative expression, the enriched vocabulary of which stressed broadened knowledge and an enhancing of the network of correspondences.[12]

In giving the painting the title *Serbian Women* Fra conveyed much about his artistic concept. First, the work, for all the proximity of viewer to subject(s), is not to be considered a portrait of individuals. Second, the anonymous women are identified by the demonym 'Serbian' rather than the ethnonym 'Serb', the implication being that they are native to or resident in a place called Serbia, but not necessarily of Serb ethnicity.

Finally, Fra's title denotes representation of type, as if his pair are norms for Serbian females, their activity and dress memes for Serbian culture. Here, in unfurling some of the issues concerning such identification, we also find, beyond the title, that in their joint production of *Serbian Women* Fra and Jessie catch the enduring association of womanhood with the bedrock of Serbian society as expressed in the myths of Serbian epic poetry. In so doing they offer a glimpse of that described by sociologist Mira Crouch:

> *… the poems seem to suggest that women … at all times circumscribed within the quotidian … are society's fundament, the entrenched inhabitants of institutions for which they are – and are made to be – responsible. Their roles are much more profound than are the tasks of the variably present, albeit more conspicuous, men … in these poems men appear as* phenomena *of history, but women are the* noumena *of life, of the ineffable nature of the world … here men are the Other(s) who tug and pull at the threads of the dense fabric of everyday existence.*[13]

Fra's painting was preceded, some fourteen years earlier, by another British performance of Serbian womanhood and it is this which sets the tone for his and Jessie's fabrications. For then, the hastily organised Kossovo [sic] Day Committee arranged a series of meetings to urge support for the Serbian peoples being horrifically crushed by the Habsburg military forces which had invaded their lands. At one such meeting, on or just after 28 June 1916, Fanny Copeland, a polymath who by then was a veteran singer, borrowed 'a genuine Serbian peasant costume' and wore it while delivering a lecture entitled 'The Women of Serbia'.[14] While no images appear to have survived of the event, Copeland published her talk and is to be seen wearing 'Serbian national dress' in a later photograph. Her paper is remarkable not just for its evaluation of the role played by women across Serbian history, but also, for us, for its appreciation of the artistry and significance of their needlework:

> *… from the 12th to the 15th century, Serbia was a flourishing State – young, strong, and with a well-developed civilisation … influenced by both Bysance and Rome … that short-lived period of prosperity has bequeathed … a wonderful school of design, which to this day expresses itself in lovely embroideries and textile fabrics …*
>
> *Lady Jefimia … one of the most accomplished women of Serbia in her day … retired into a convent, there to devote herself to commemorating the martyrdom of her sainted kinsman [Tsar Lazar at the Battle of Kosovo, 15 June 1389] by embroidering a pall for his coffin. First she thought to embroider a beautiful, fanciful design –*

but when she began her work, it seemed false and inadequate, and so she composed an In Memoriam *poem instead, one of the pearls of Serbian history; and this she embroidered in threads of gold on fair white silk for a pall on Lazar's coffin. …*

Till recently, all home industries in Serbia were in the hands of the women. Every scrap of stuff in a Serbian home was spun and woven by the women of the household, and the exquisite embroideries on the national peasant costumes bear witness to the skill and good taste, no less than to the patience of the embroideresses.[15]

Copeland's insights into the place of women and textile art in Serbian culture were published shortly after her 1915 translation of Srđan (Srgjan) Tucić's *Slav Nations*, a volume which bemoaned the widespread ignorance and derogatory conceptions of southern Slav identities. The book was rounded off with an epilogue entitled 'Buried Treasures' by Dimitrije Mitrinović, an art historian dedicated to furthering inter-cultural understanding. In it Mitrinović prioritised, alongside southern Slav national poetry, a new appreciation of Balkan music and 'the national textile art of Old Serbia, Dalmatia and Croatia', the beauty and nobility of these being impossible to value since they are 'unknown'.[16]

As if taking her lead from Tucić and Mitrinović, and sparked by the suffering inflicted upon the Balkan nations by outside, bloody, assumptions of hegemony, Copeland dedicated the remainder of her life to Yugoslavia, settling in Ljubljana, where she was employed in the university's English department for more than two decades from 1921. It was presumably early in this period of Slovenian living that she appeared on a balcony in national costume to have her photograph taken [fig. 0.4]. With her right hand supported on a wooden fence she looks straight at the lens, her gaze confident, body erect. Adorned with head-scarf, necklaces and tasselled apron, her skirt and dress appear white with bands of rich embroidery above their hems. Behind her, across a wide straight street, are tall, relatively modern, blocks of city housing. Her faux Serbian personhood at once anticipates and contradicts Fra's painted fabrications. Recent publications that have included this image have captioned it 'in Serbian national dress', 'in Croatian national dress – 1927' and 'in "traditional costume"'.[17] Probing such identity ambiguity and the hybridisation it masks is at the heart of this study into neglected southern Slav visualisations.

If there is an overarching point to all this it is to illuminate some of the vital forces and relations of European visual language in the early twentieth century, these arising against a changing backdrop of war and peace, liberal and conservative gambit, and trends in material culture or art historical enquiry that have contrived to obscure, if not deny, their significance. Thus our enquiry can be seen as a rearguard action to bring these buried networks, if not to the fore, at least out into

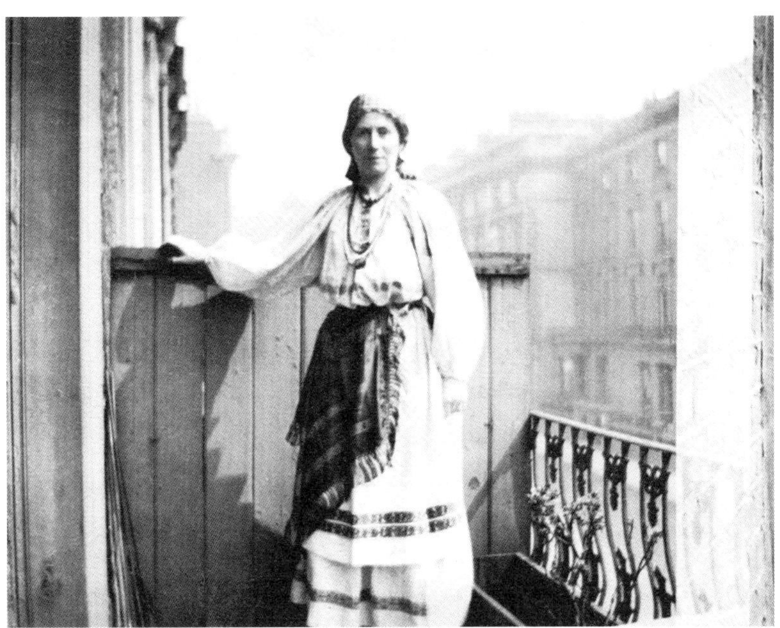

0.4 | Fanny Copeland in 'Serbian national dress', *c.* 1927

the open where they can complement conventional pantheons of centres, greats and relationships. For we posit our works and their creators as important signifiers of worldview. Their articulation of identity deserves recognition, both in terms of aesthetic merit and as a reaction to socio-political drivers of the modern age. Their virtual exclusion from, or at best obfuscation within, corporate anglophone art history, including that which considers itself to be championing 'global modernism', reveals the power interests and dynamics which control wider discourse and which, thereby, limit understanding, mutual or otherwise.

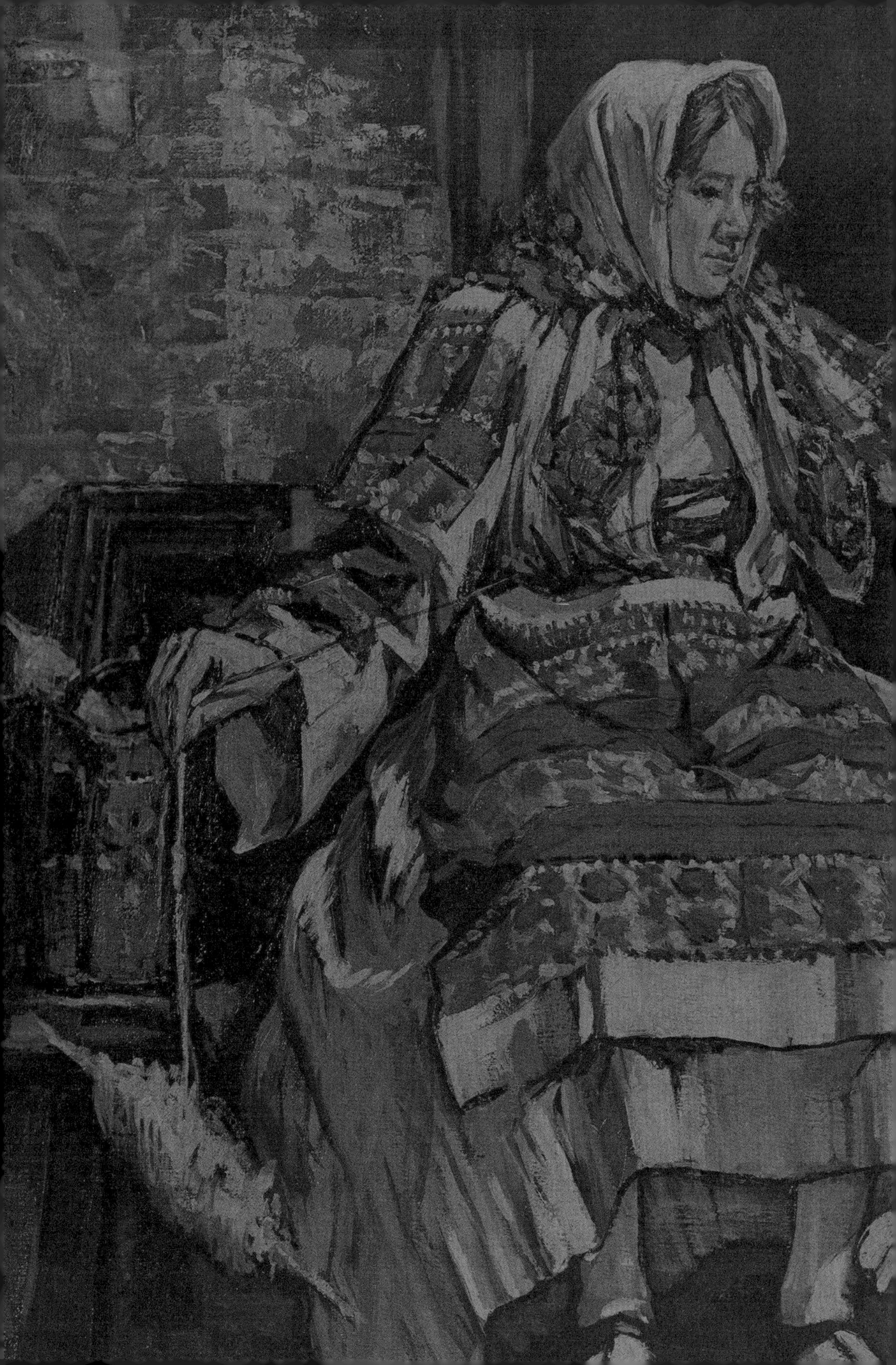

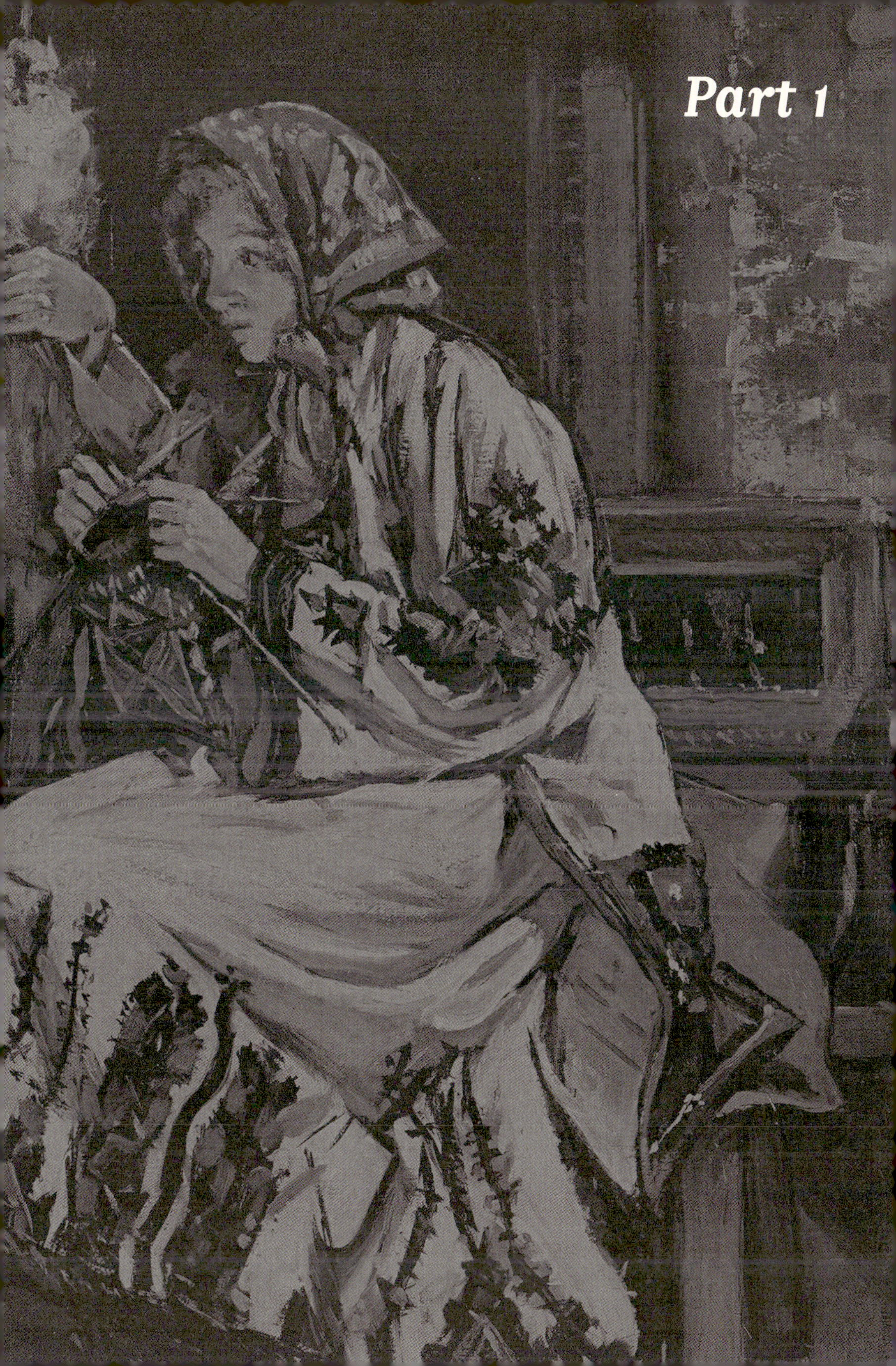
Part 1

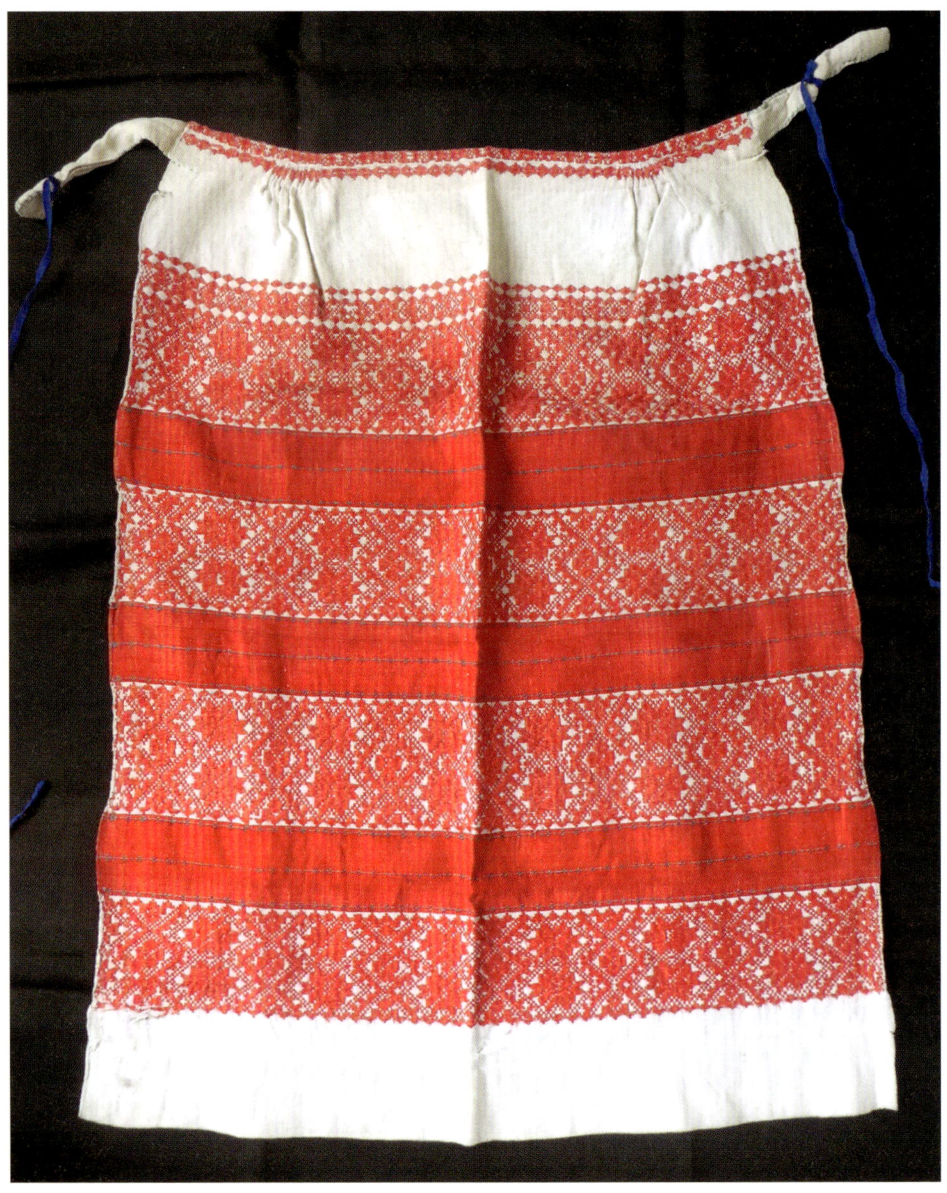

1.1 | Apron, Upper Vardar region, Macedonia, linen and wool, *c.* 1920s
PRIVATE COLLECTION

1 INTERWEAVING THE POSTCARD PROBLEM

Sewing together Jessie's cards: from Dalmatia, Sicily, Aveyron, Madrid

Serbian Women [fig. 0.2] features two costumes from neighbouring areas of 'Old Serbia' (northwestern Macedonia), one from Kumanovo (on the left of the painting) and the other from Blatija or Vodna in the Upper Vardar region, some 160 kilometres south of Niš.[1] Evidently Jessie had purchased some fine examples of 'Old Serbian' dress, including the linen or hemp *košula* (chemise), *zubun* (vest), *pregača* (apron) and a pair of *opanci* (moccasin type sandals).[2] The dress of the woman on the right, which is to reappear in other Newbery works, features a painterly interpretation of the 'nine-flower' motif that characterises much Macedonian chemise-sleeve embroidery (see below). With this and the other embroidered parts of the dress – cuffs and hem, as well as their aprons – Balkan women were said to gain protection 'against the entry of evil spirits'.[3] The intricate and extensive needlework is comprised of mainly red and black threads (with accents of green) whose colour would initially have derived from locally sourced vegetable dyes. The actual apron of the woman on the left has remained in the Newbery family [fig. 1.1], its thick red woollen bands and rows of intricate red zigzag and star forms, which stand out from the bleached linen, being rendered with a painterly flourish in Fra's oil-on-canvas interpretation.

Fra adopts a close-up, low-level, frontal viewpoint towards his harmoniously arranged and adorned women. As such he copies, whether consciously or subconsciously, examples of postcards that the couple had bought on their Balkan travels of the late 1920s. One such is the politicised, sepia-toned black-and-white view of two women in folk

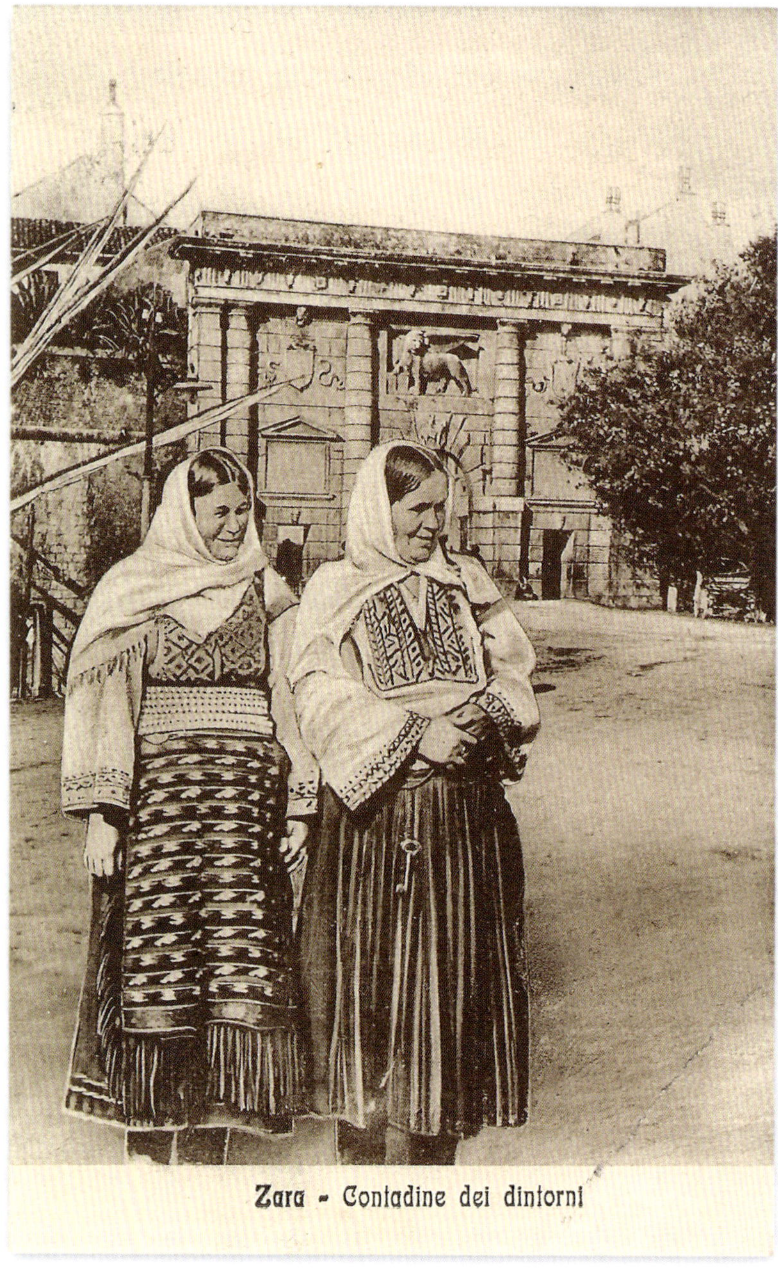

1.2 | 'Zara – Contadine del dintorni', postcard (A. Gilardi e Figlio, Zara, *c.* 1926)

dress standing before the Venetian Porta Terraferma of Zara, Dalmatia – now the Kopnena vrata, Zadar, Croatia; Zara became Zadar in 1947 [fig. 1.2]. In October 1929 Jessie sent this to her young Dorset neighbour and friend, the sixteen-year-old performance artist and future sculptor Mary Spencer Watson.[4] The women wear white headscarves (one tasselled, the other not), blouses and vests that are richly embroidered with bold, dark-coloured geometric patterns, and knee-length pleated skirts.[5] While the woman on the right has a large key dangling on a cord below her waist, her companion has a lively striped apron over her skirt. They are further distinguished by the latter's hands hanging by her sides and the former's being brought together in front of her. These elements, with the individual being anonymised and turned collective, bear much in common with those of Fra's *Serbian Women* figuration.

Despite the costumal and compositional similarities between the two images, the Dalmatian women are more evidently middle-aged and well built, and they have their feet cropped by an Italian caption: 'Zara – Contadine del dintorni' [Zara – Peasant Women of the Neighbourhood]. With Zara having become Italian territory in the wake of the First World War, written mention of ethnicity is avoided. The obfuscation accords with their north Dalmatian identity being assimilated into Italian. Furthermore, the Zara peasant women are cutouts from another (currently unidentified) photograph that have been super-imposed upon the backdrop of the gate to make the collaged postcard. By so doing, the image-makers, Zara-based photographers/publishers A. Gilardi e Figlio, make them seem as if smiling towards something off-right – that is, to the southeast, in the direction of the city's first city park, set out a century earlier by the Austrian military administrator of the city, Baron Franz Ludwig von Welden, on the site of a former Italian bastion. Thus their fabricated contented look joins the gaze of the gate's highly visible carved winged lion, the (St Mark's) symbol of the Republic of Venice, this being centrally placed above one of the women. The viewer's eye is led to this, and the Venetian coat-of-arms beside it, by the pointing diagonal of a spar from a ship moored, out of sight, in the harbour off-left. Having built the gate in 1543 and ruled over Zara for over five hundred years before the Austrians took over in 1797, the Venetians are thereby recalled through presence and absence. Hence, for all the similarities, the sepia women become part of an 'Italian again' propaganda trope that overrides nationality, this in keeping with contemporary Fascist policies directed against minority rights and in contradiction to Fra's colourful and ethnically identified (albeit somewhat spuriously) *Serbian Women*. The fact that the Zara women stand with their feet cut off by the caption while Fra's women are seated with clearly visible feet in local sandals planted firmly on the ground epitomises the variant intentions of the respective image-makers.

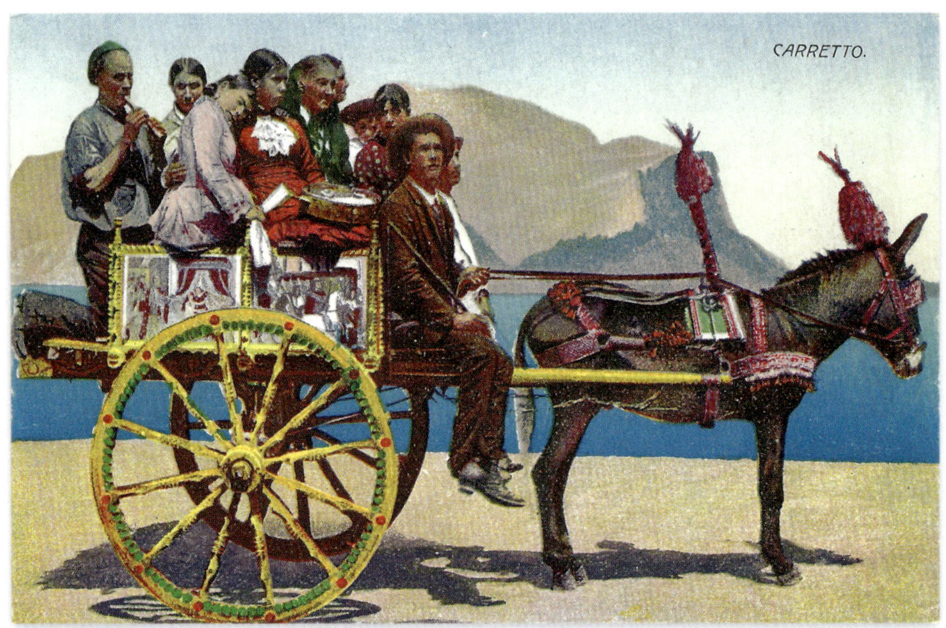

1.3 | 'Carretto', postcard (Guiseppe Attanasio, Taormina, *c.*1924)

'Zara – Contadine del dintorni' is the last in a set of five known postcards Jessie sent to her young friend Mary Spencer Watson and her mother Hilda between 1924 and 1929, with two others also featuring local folk in traditional attire, posed for the tourist. All reveal Jessie's great sensitivity to artistry, and with that her desire to foster or enhance similar sensitivities in others. The first card, which Jessie dated 19 March 1924, was published by Guiseppe Attanasio of Taormina, and is captioned 'Carretto' [fig. 1.3]. It depicted a hand-tinted, static Sicilian donkey and cart (*'carretto siciliano'*) loaded with ten people. These are cut out and collaged with a simple coloured backdrop of sea and mountain, this representative of the bay of Palermo and Monte Pellegrino. Their varied dress, age and gender, together with the intricate, brightly decorated side panels and wheels of the cart, as well as the tasselled mane of the donkey, make the folk scene picturesque. Jessie noted on the back:

> *Nearly all the carts in Sicily are like this one – and the donkeys wear long tassels at their ears and are very attractive. My Mary and I carry crusts in our pockets to tempt the donkeys to make friends with us.*

Numerous versions of the Attanasio 'Carretto' postcard exist. Their replication and modification from the 1890s, when the first seems to have originated from a photograph of the taxi-cart taken on Via Filippo

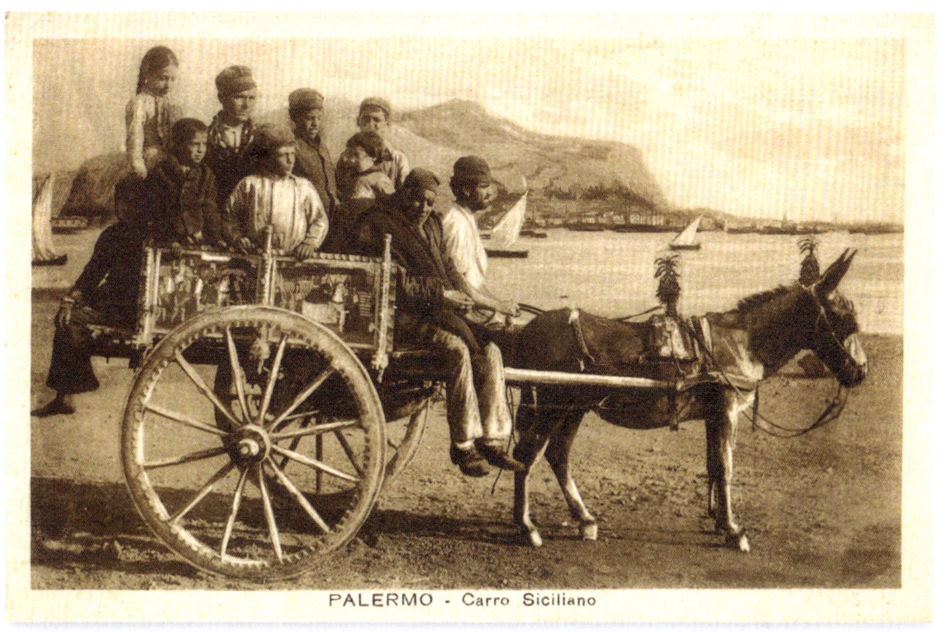

1.4 | 'Palermo: Carro Siciliano', postcard (Ediz. Francesco Verderosa, Palermo, *c.*1924)
PRIVATE COLLECTION

Turati in central Palermo, indicative of the carts' popularity, not just for the tourist eye but also as genuinely useful objects of Sicilian folk art. Furthermore, the Newberys kept a very similar postcard for themselves, the composition and 'location', now identified as Palermo, being identical [fig. 1.4]. While the donkey, driver, nine passengers and cart are evidently different, and the setting is more detailed and realistic, this sepia-toned version lacks the picturesque gaiety of the coloured card sent to the then eleven-year-old Spencer Watson.

Soon we will come to Jessie's second postcard to Mary Spencer Watson. However, before doing so we should look at two further cards, that survive from the Newberys' sojourn on Sicily. The first of these, also sepia-toned, can be seen to have a certain relationship with Fra's *Serbian Women*. The picture on this card is captioned: 'Piana dei Greci: Gruppo di giovani donne', or 'Plateau of the Greeks: Group of Young Women' – Piana dei Greci was the actual name of the featured young women's community until 1947 [fig. 1.5]. The card was produced by Francesco Verderosa of Palermo, a publisher who made sets of cards featuring manipulated photographs of local folk as Sicilian 'types' and 'costumes'. As with 'Zara – Contadine' specificity of type or costume is avoided. However, by mentioning the Piana dei Greci community, the three young women on the Newberys' card are identifiable by association, that is they are Arbëreshë, these being the Albanians of Sicily. The identification of the commune that they represented as being

Greek (because of their use of ancient Greek, due to their observance of the Byzantine rite) was a state-applied misnomer, corrected officially in 1941 when the town became Piana degli Albanesi. Inhabitants refer to it, in Albanian, as Hora e Arbëreshëvet, or Plain of the Albanians. It is situated on a high plateau between mountains some twenty-five kilometres south of Palermo.

The young women of this card are cut-outs pasted onto a photographic backdrop of hilly countryside. They are posed, two standing to the sides of a centrally seated one. They gaze intently and directly at the camera. Pictured frontally, full-length and close-up, with the seated teenager twisting her upper body around, such compositional traits anticipate those of *Serbian Women*. Furthermore, the lens picks out the variety of design and embroidered detail of their dress just as Fra's eye and brush does. Here, however, the young women are idle, their hands held close to their waists, with the two standing having fabrics of distinct kinds folded over their right lower arms. Arbëresh women were renowned for their richly worked costumes, often created to mark significant points in their lives as well as religious holidays. The bold floral designs visible in 'Piana dei Greci – Gruppo' are actually key signifiers of Arbëresh identity, so much so that a local contemporary painter, Ettore De Maria Bergler, unwittingly followed Fra's *Serbian Women* lead with his oil *Sicilian Woman in a Piana degli Albanesi costume* (*c.*1933, Galleria d'Arte Moderna Sant'Anna, Palermo). Bergler's

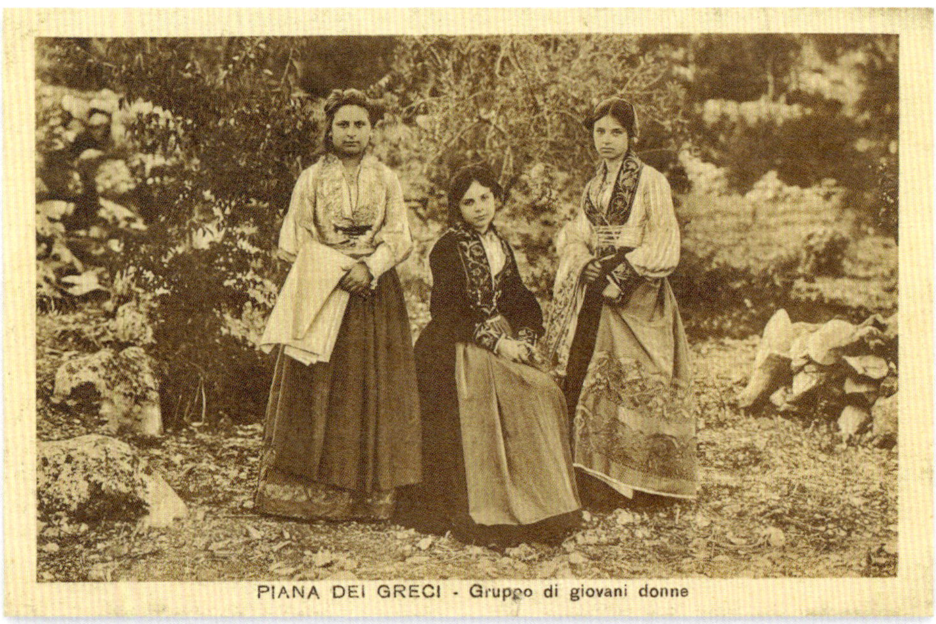

1.5 | 'Piana dei Greci: Gruppo di giovani donne', postcard (Francesco Verderosa, Palermo, *c.*1924)
PRIVATE COLLECTION

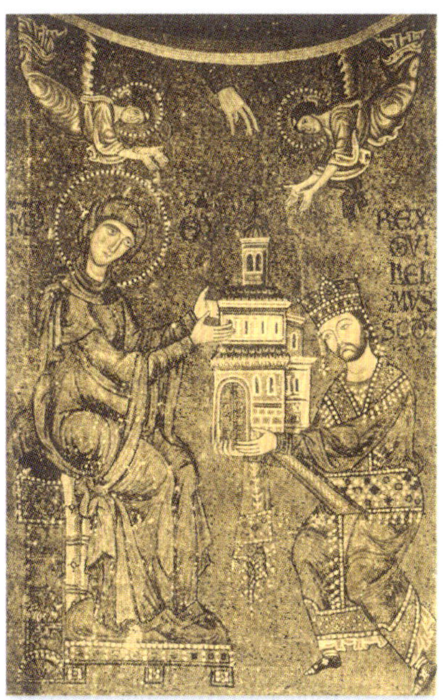

1.6 | 'King William II of Sicily presenting a model of the cathedral to the Virgin Mary', apse in Monreale Cathedral, near Palermo, postcard (GBP, *c.*1924)

sitter wears a costume whose embroidery very closely resembles that of the standing (right) girl in the postcard. The similarity continues through the facial features, centrally parted dark hair and hair bow delicately placed towards the back of the skull. That the Newberys should have collected an image of tradition-bearing young Arbëresh women in advance of Fra's painting *Serbian Women* was no random chance. They, and particularly Jessie, were looking for such articulations of artistry in order to reinterpret and share what they perceived there through their own modern yet convention-indebted artworks. Presumably, in Sicily, Jessie found no Arbëresh dresses for sale (at least not at a price she could allow), hence, unlike in Serbia, she contented herself with the postcard …

The third of the cards acquired by the Newberys on their visit to the Mediterranean's largest island also captures a major tourist object, but it is significant because it offers a contrasting form of local Sicilian art: the twelfth-century Byzantine-style mosaic panel of King William II of Sicily presenting a model of the cathedral to the Virgin Mary, from an apse in Monreale Cathedral, near Palermo [fig. 1.6]. Possessing a representation such as this coincides with Jessie having gained an abiding interest in mosaics following her first Italian tour of 1882 (when, among others, she saw the Byzantine mosaics of Ravenna).[6]

We now come to Jessie's second postcard to Mary Spencer Watson, sent from Rodez in southern France and dated 19 November 1925 [fig. 1.7]. Here, rather than Sicilian horsecarts or Dalmatian peasant women, Jessie has selected 'Types Aveyronnais', a postcard published by the shops of the 'Bazar à La Ménagère' in Rodez. She makes no comment on the image, though does note: 'This is a town high up on a hill – we see far away over lovely countryside.' Yet the picture is another of static wooden carts, this time one ready to be pulled by two oxen and the second, empty and cropped by the picture edge. Between them stand two bearded peasant men. Wearing the broad-brimmed hats used by Aveyron menfolk to protect them from sun and rain, one is dressed in a smock and holds a long stick for guiding the oxen, while the other wears a loose jacket and has what seems to be a characteristic Aveyron knife (possibly two) attached to the belt above his trousers. They pose in front of a tall, rough rubble wall. Black-and-white, they

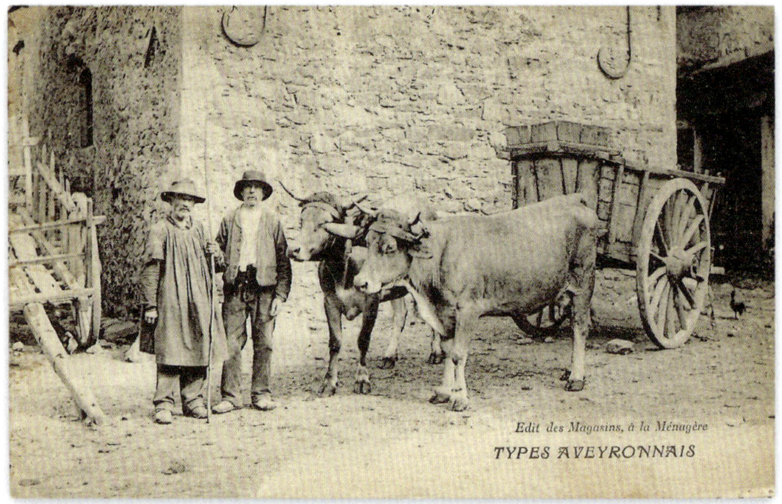

1.7 | 'Types Aveyronnais', postcard (Bazar à La Ménagère, Rodez, *c.*1925)
PRIVATE COLLECTION

form a pair with the 'Zara – Contadine', though the Aveyron hill farm-ers have their leather-shoed feet visible and firmly on the ground, their representation of type and setting containing more truth than if they had been superimposed from another place and source. At this point it is also worth noting another postcard from the Newbery family col-lection that Jessie or Fra must have bought in Rodez (or nearby) but did not send [fig. 1.8]. This is a close-up of the Christ in Majesty and

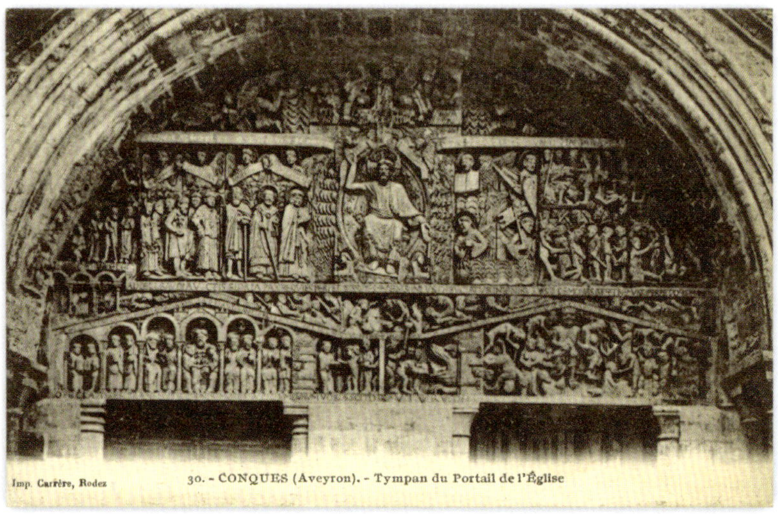

1.8 | 'Christ in Majesty and Last Judgement', carved relief tympanum, Abbey Church of Sainte-Foy, Conques, postcard (Carrère, Rodez, *c.*1925)
PRIVATE COLLECTION

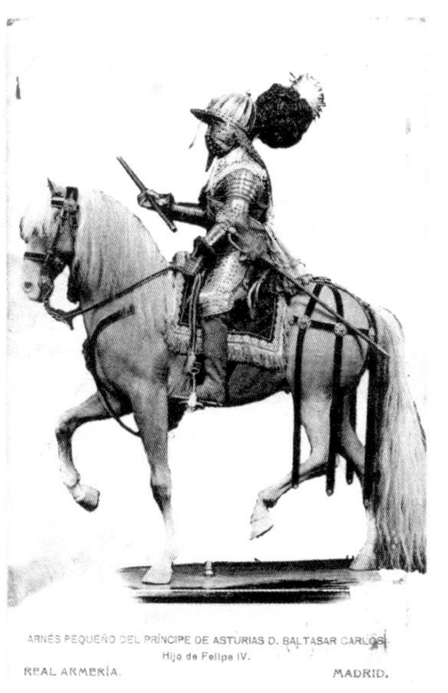

1.9 | 'Arnés pequeño del Príncipe de Asturias D. Baltasar Carlos', postcard (Hauser y Menet, Madrid, *c.*1928)

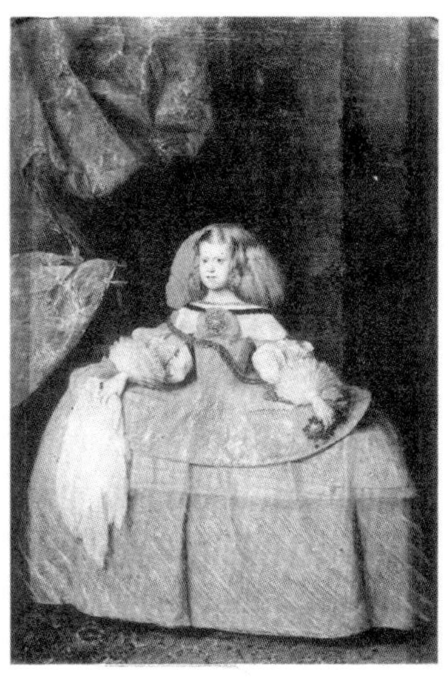

1.10 | Diego Velázquez/Juan Bautista Martínez del Mazo, *La Infanta doña María Teresa de Austria/Margarita de Austria*, postcard (Hauser y Menet, Madrid, *c.*1928)

Last Judgement carved relief tympanum above the western entrance of the pilgrim Abbey Church of Sainte-Foy in the Aveyron village of Conques, forty kilometres north of Rodez.[7]

Drawing Mary Spencer Watson's attention to the mutually bene-ficial close relationships of humans and beasts that the youngster ap-preciated from her life in the Purbeck countryside, the norm in her cards was for Jessie to pick out idiosyncratic creative aspects. Thus her third postcard featured a black-and-white photograph of an equestrian armoured mannequin of the child prince of Asturias, Baltasar Carlos, the prematurely deceased heir to Felipe IV, the seventeenth-century Habsburg king of Spain [fig. 1.9]. Sent from Madrid, where she and Fra evidently visited the Royal Armory during an Iberian tour in autumn 1928, on the reverse Jessie complemented the image with the following description of a related work in the collection: 'Even we [sic] saw a dog in armour with a velvet caparison under the steel – & a bunch of ostrich plumes on his head. He looked very pround [sic] & a pet ...'[8]

Around the same time as she was alerting Mary Spencer Watson to the armoured costuming of dog and child, Jessie sent another pic-ture postcard to Mary's performance-artist mother Hilda, this time with a representation of a young sister of Prince Baltasar Carlos [fig. 1.10]. Previously considered to be of a painting by Velázquez of María Teresa (of Spain, Portugal and Austria), the image is now ascribed to

Velázquez's son-in-law Juan Bautista Martínez del Mazo and said to be of Margarita Teresa (of Spain and Austria). Issues of identity and history were not Jessie's concern. Instead she conveyed to Hilda her relish of what she termed 'shorthand' – the quick, evocative mastery, as expressed in the oil-painted light, colour and material of dress:

> *No doubt you have seen a reproduction of this – but the shorthand in producing the shimmer of grey silver brocade shot with silvery rosy scarlet is very exciting – we have spent 2 forenoons in the prado.*[9]

Spinning a people's world of art, with dress to the fore

The archive of Fra and Jessie's picture postcards in the Newbery family collection consists of twenty-two cards, nine of which were purchased in Zagreb, presumably on the same Balkan trip of 1929 as the 'Zara – Contadine' card. Taken as a whole the archive reveals acute, inter-cultural, aesthetic awareness that leads to and informs *Serbian Women*. The varied nature of the selection suggests both Fra and Jessie contributed to the acquisitions. Before coming to the Croatian cards, a survey of the remaining non-Balkan images serves to contextualise where the Newberys' artistic interests lay as they travelled across southern, central and eastern Europe in the 1920s.

The earliest cards actually appear to predate the Newberys' 1920s European sojourns, as they are reproductions of *ukiyo-e* woodblock prints, seemingly representative of two key strands of these Japanese 'floating world' images: refined landscape and female form.[10] The first of these is entitled *View of Mount Akiha in Enshū* [fig. 1.11]. From an elevated viewpoint, it represents a wooden trestle-bridge over the Keta River in the Akaishi mountains area of the old Tōtōmi (Enshū) province of central Honshū. The scene is screened by a group of trees and a cropped *torii* gate of the Akihasan Hongū Akiha Jinja, the head Akiha Shinto shrine. Several diminutive people head towards, over and away from the bridge, indicating the temple's significance on pilgrimage routes. In fact both bridge and *torii* had appeared as the twenty-seventh station, Kakegawa, in different versions of Hiroshige's popular *ukiyo-e* series *Fifty-Three Stations of the Tōkaidō* (from 1833–34). As a detour off the main Edo Period road, a key artery of old Japan, the Akiha shrine also marked the halfway point between the shōgun and military capitals. Cropping the shrine's gate suggests that the threshold between profane and sacred realms that it marks is reiterated by picture edge and empty surrounds. Were Fra and Jessie alert to such spiritual issues? Or were they guided by the qualities of aesthetic harmony and stylisation that

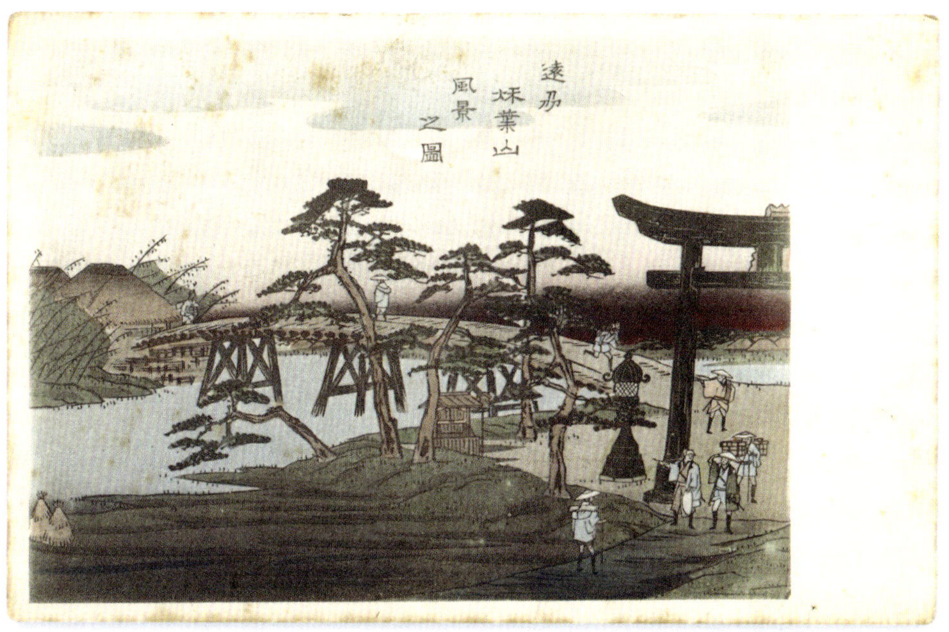

1.11 | 'View of Mount Akiha in Enshū', postcard (*c.* 1898–1912)

the image possesses? Perhaps, due to their own many years' questing after beauty and understanding, the answer is something of both.

Similar issues beset the choice of the Newberys' second Japanese card, though, by contrast, this is based on Utamaro's series of twelve sericulture prints, *Joshoku kaiko tewaza gusa* (Women's Work in Silk Culture) (*c.*1802) [fig. 1.12]. Derived from the seventh print, it shows three women, one of whom holds a thread with which she steers two domestic silk moths so that they may lay their eggs on a sheet of paper. More sheets and a box are ready for the continuation of the process, all this in preparation for the harvesting and subsequent winding, spinning and weaving of silk from the cocoons of the eggs' larvae. The women are seen close-up, their triangular grouping and traditional dress of ornate kimonos and *kanzashi*-held hair anticipating similar objectifications in the Arbëreshë card. Here, however, there is a certain looseness to the kimonos and an extra display of female flesh, in keeping with Utamaro's preference for the visual melding of performance with prostitution. Despite this the Newberys have chosen a depiction of idealised feminine craft, its formal qualities in keeping with those adopted en-masse by japonising Western artists, including Whistler, Mackintosh and the Macdonald sisters, all of whom connected with the aesthetic reforms Fra introduced during his tenure at Glasgow. That this craft was textile in nature and Utamaro's women were engrossed in its evolution signals Fra's and Jessie's own concerns as expressed in *Serbian Women*.[11]

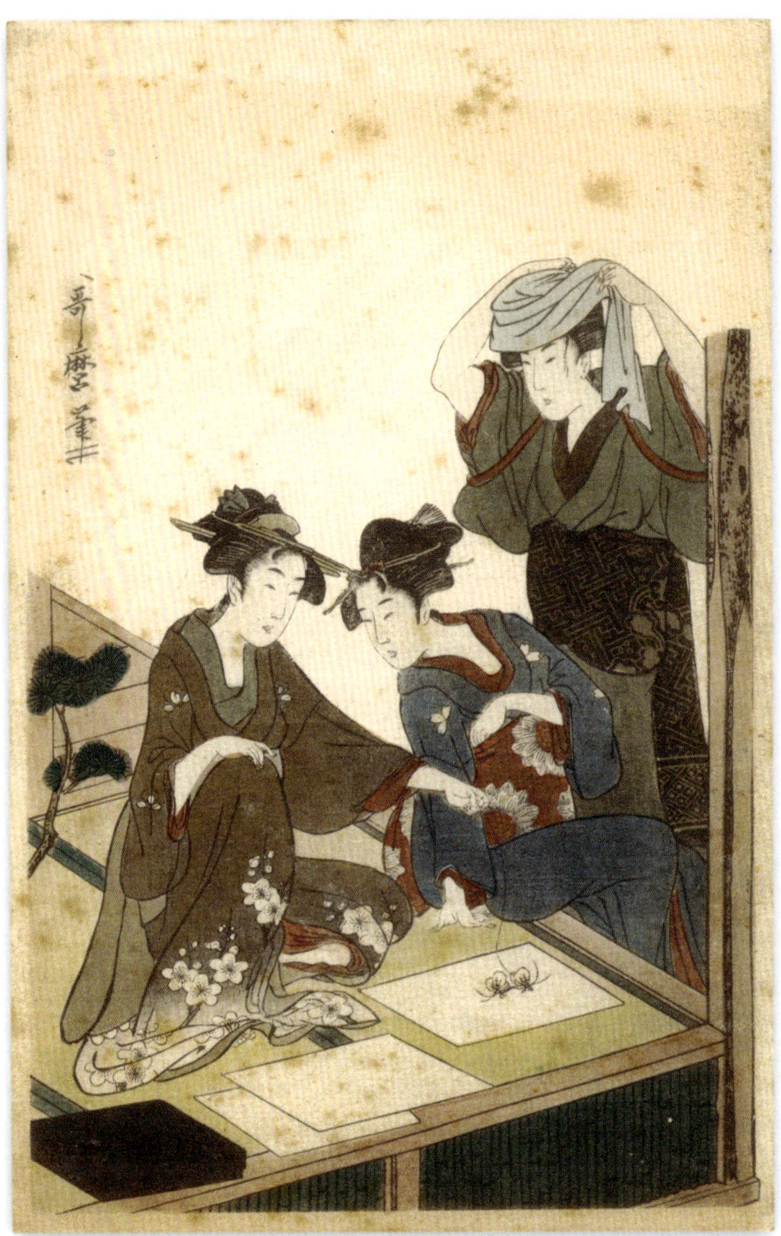

1.12 | 'Joshoku kaiko tewaza gusa' [Women's Work in Silk Culture], postcard (*c.* 1898–1912)

PRIVATE COLLECTION

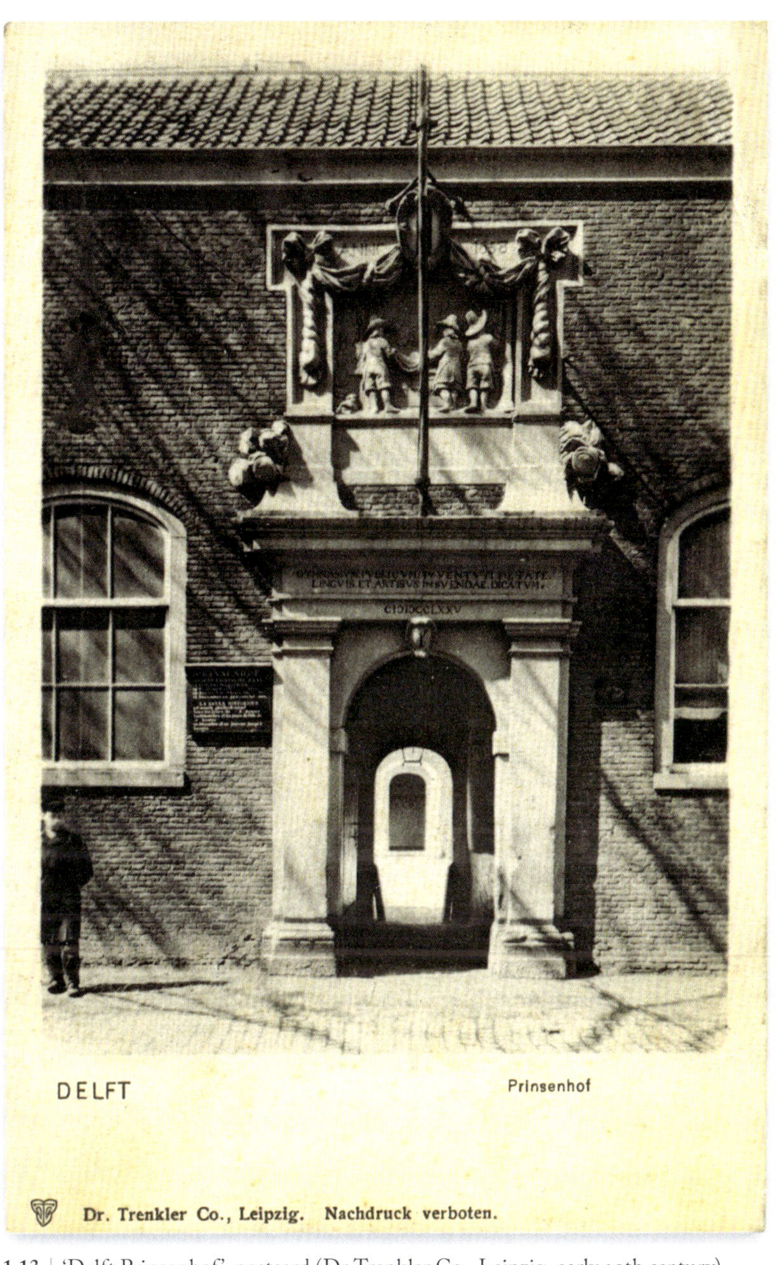

1.13 | 'Delft Prinsenhof', postcard (Dr Trenkler Co., Leipzig, early 20th century)
PRIVATE COLLECTION

Because Fra and Jessie saw all the arts as one, undivided by medium or category, it is no surprise to find in their card collection an image that, on first glance, looks to have nothing whatsoever to do with that of *Joshoku kaiko tewaza gusa*. For this is a black-and-white reproduction of a photograph labelled 'Delft Prinsenhof' [fig. 1.13]. It shows a narrow portal through a brick wall to one of the courtyards within the former St Agatha Convent. The modesty of the setting is overridden by a large garlanded and ribboned relief panel above the arch. Fra and Jessie must have been alert to the visual symbolism of the relief, for it announced the entrance to Delft's seventeenth-century cloth hall. Known in Dutch as the 'Saai, Grein en Stoffe Hal' (Serge, Camlet and Fabric Hall), its title alone links it to the silk trade envisaged by Utamaro. Now, however, instead of the triangle of forward-facing, flattened and graphic oriental courtesans we have a line of three men sculpted in high relief, their backs to the viewer as they inspect the cloth between them and to the side. Their large conical, broad-brimmed hats, coats and breeches form a display of contemporary Dutch male drapery styles. With three more figures, one artisan and two traders, in low relief in the background the Delft image acts as a fitting counterpart to the *Joshoku*, thereby stressing the global nature of the textile trade.

Two further Dutch postcards, possibly acquired on the same trip to the Low Countries, reveal more interest in the products of this trade. The pictures shown on these are sepia-toned photographic copies of two marriage paintings in the Rijksmuseum, Amsterdam: Anthony van Dyck's *William II, Prince of Orange, and His Bride, Mary Stuart* (1641) and Frans Hals' *Portrait of a Couple, Probably Isaac Abrahamsz Massa and Beatrix van der Laen* (*c.*1622) [figs 1.14, 1.15].

For all their posed celebration of the nuptials of two individual couples both of these are vivid visualisations of high fashion based on silk (with lace support). That Massa should also have been a silk merchant and Dutch diplomat involved in negotiating a silk trade route from Persia through Russia to the Netherlands would have passed the Newberys by, not least because the portrait was, at the time of purchase, misidentified as being a self-portrait with wife by Hals. Irrespective of such misattribution, Fra and Jessie collected images that highlighted the extreme ends of silk

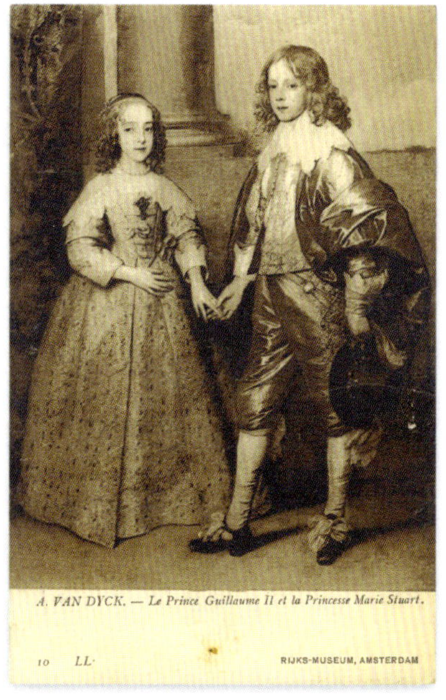

1.14 | Anthony van Dyck, *Le Prince Guillaume II et la Princesse Marie Stuart* [present-day English title: *William II, Prince of Orange, and His Bride, Mary Stuart*], 1641, postcard (Rijks-Museum, Amsterdam/10 LL)

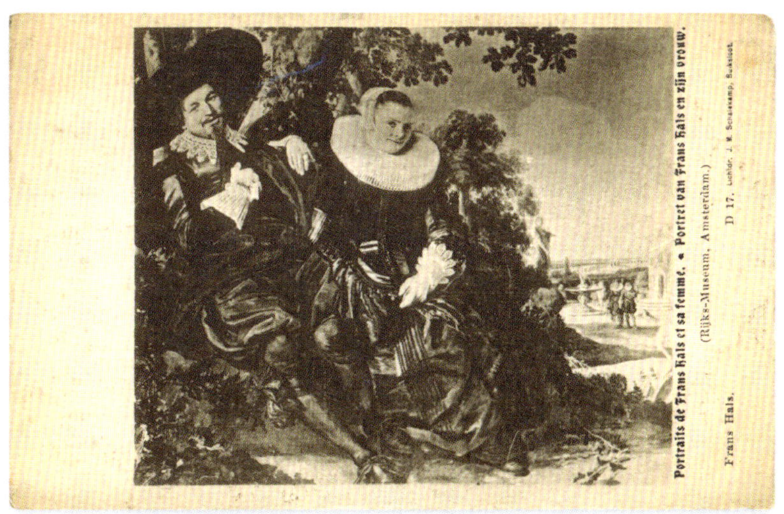

1.15 | Frans Hals, *Portraits de Frans Hals et sa femme/Portret van Frans Hals en zijn vrouw* [misattrib; present-day English title: *Portrait of a Couple, Probably Isaac Abrahamsz Massa and Beatrix van der Laen*], *c.*1622, postcard (Rijks-Museum, Amsterdam/ D.17 Lichtdr. J.M. Schalekamp, Buiksloot, *c.*1893–1912)

production. And, in so doing, once again focused on close-up costume pieces that evidently relate to *Serbian Women*.

The eclectic nature of the Newberys' postcard collection is rounded off, before we reach the Croatian set, by four divergent images: two further pictures of 'high' art and two of folk types. The first pair comprises black-and-white photographic reproductions of well-known Florentine Renaissance paintings: Perugino's *Madonna with Child Enthroned between Saints John the Baptist and Sebastian* (1493, Uffizi Gallery) and a detail of the face of Giovanna degli Albizzi from Ghirlandaio's *Visitation* fresco in the Tornabuoni Chapel of Santa Maria Novella (1486–90) [figs 1.16, 1.17]. The composite nature of the represented paintings undoubtedly attracted the Newberys. Perugino's mature Mary, dressed in embroidered silk, is seated on an ornate throne in front of an architectural and landscape setting. Meanwhile Ghirlandaio's noblewoman Giovanna is turned into a serenely beautiful profiled bust, her simultaneously elaborate but restrained hairstyle an artwork in itself. With hints of her richly embroidered gown, and her placement on the threshold of a building, she watches, out of sight, the meeting of Mary and Elizabeth. That both paintings were created for mortuary chapels is felt in the sombre gazes of their women.

If feminine grace is centre-stage in the two Italian cards, as it is in many of the others, this is also the case, for all their variety, with the two remaining non-Balkan postcards. Both represent 'regional' folk, this time from further west and east in Europe. Both are also based

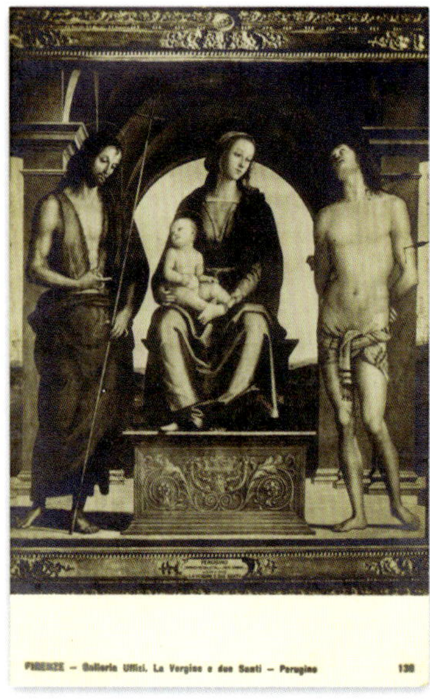

1.16 | Pietro Perugino, *La Vergine e due Santi* [present-day Engl. title: *Madonna with Child Enthroned between Saints John the Baptist and Sebastian*] 1493, postcard (Ed. Montinari & Albucci, Florence)

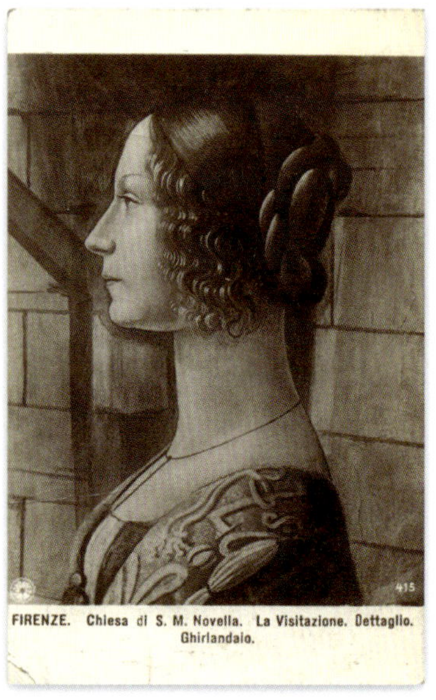

1.17 | Domenico Ghirlandaio, *La Visitazione/Visitation* (detail of Giovanna degli Albizzi), fresco, Tornabuoni Chapel of Santa Maria Novella, Florence, 1486–90, postcard (NPG)

on posed photographs. The first was actually sent by Jessie to her Scottish grandson Fred Lang [fig. 1.18]. While the frank date is unclear its stamp shows King Alfonso XIII of Spain and is the same as those on Jessie's 1928 cards to the Spencer Watsons. Given that Fred was born in 1918 and Alfonso ceased being king in 1931 the card could well have been sent during the same 1928 Spanish visit and in any case it dates from a year or so either side of the Newberys' *Serbian Women*-sparking Balkan tour. Captioned 'Al mercado' (To the Market) it is the sixth in a series of hand-tinted cards called *Tipos y Escenas Vascas* (Basque Types and Scenes) published by San Sebastián (Donostia) photographer Gregorio González Galarza. Once again Jessie has identified with a small nation on the rural fringes of a minority-repressing state, in this case that of the late Spanish monarchy. 'Al Mercado' shows a picturesque scene of a peasant couple in front of a donkey, cart and girl. A mountain ridge forms the horizon line behind them. Bathed in sunlight it is the woman who is made to stand out. Her clothes, including headscarf, embroidered jacket and long skirt, are brightened with colour. She and the stick-bearing man gaze at what seems to be poultry in her hands and a wicker egg basket on the grassy ground. For all its manipulated performance of ethnicity the image's pyramidal composition of donkey, man and woman creates a classical sense of balance and harmony in keeping with Galarza's place as the outstanding Donostia photographer of his era.

Constructed ethnic performance reaches a certain apotheosis in the Newberys' final non-Balkan card [fig. 1.19]. For, while moving us geographically closer to the southeastern European peninsula through its depiction of eleven Carpathian highlanders, here we are being presented with a troupe in Paris, at the 1925 Exposition Internationale des Arts Décoratifs et Industriels Modernes. The collection of this card rather than one depicting any of the modernist and Art Deco architecture, interiors and furniture or fittings on show (and for sale through exhibition souvenirs) is highly pertinent to our enquiry. Hence rather than focus on the static pavilions, Jessie's (and possibly Fra's) eye has been drawn to the people. In the vast majority of literature on the exhibition this medium of display is overlooked. Furthermore, the Newberys' card obscures the architecture behind it, this being the main entrance to the prize-winning Polish pavilion designed by Warsaw architect Józef Czajkowski. The doors are closed on the lavish blend of modernity and national tradition of the spaces within. Only the rhomboidal lace drapes in the windows give a hint of the geometric motifs that predominate in the design.

The Parisian card, number eighty-seven in an exhibition set issued by Braun & Cie, is captioned: 'Montagnards Polonais de Zakopane

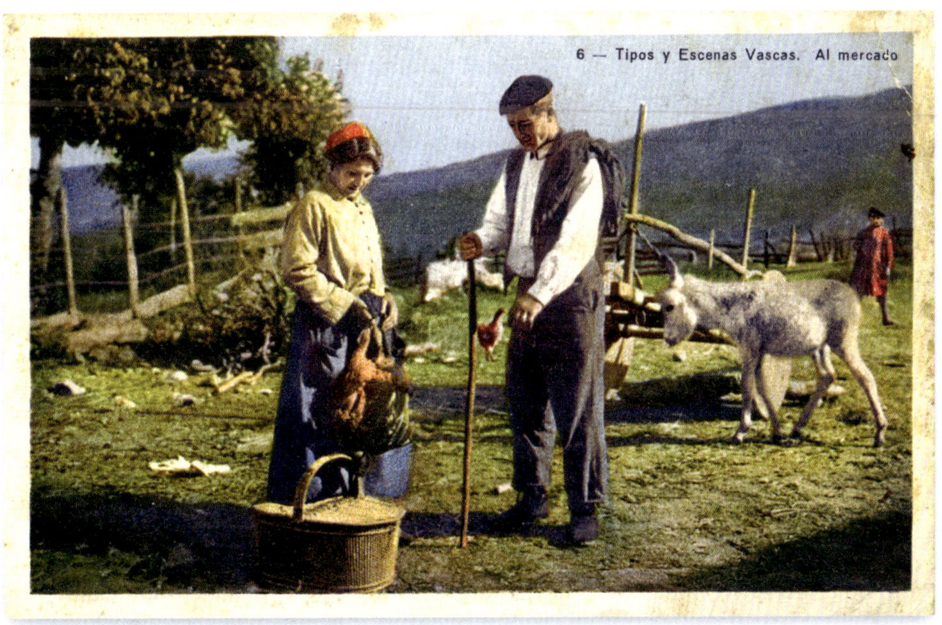

1.18 | 'Al mercado' [To the Market], from the series *Tipos y Escenas Vascas* [*Basque Types and Scenes*], postcard (Gregorio González Galarza, San Sebastián (Donostia), *c.* 1928)

(Mont Tatra dans les Carpathes Polonaises)' (Polish Highlanders of Zakopane (Tatra Mountain in the Polish Carpathians)). That the word 'Polish' was used twice reinforces the assimilation into the new Polish state of those represented, this despite them not being ethnically, linguistically or culturally Poles. For this is a troupe of Górale (Highlanders), a west Slavic people settled on the northern slopes of the Carpathian mountain range, in this case within Polish territory in an area known as Podhale, although their homelands and those of their closest ethnic kin are also in present-day Slovakia, Ukraine and Romania. Irrespective of their political assimilation Jessie (and/or Fra) bought the card because of its manifestation of folk dress.

Despite the card being black-and-white, the posing of the three women and eight men on and in front of the pavilion's steps means that its photograph offers us a rather full yet intimate frontal view of the national collective. The male highlanders wear elaborately *parzenica*-embroidered rough white woollen jackets (*cuchas*) and trousers (*portki*), leather vests (*serdaki*), round, narrow-rimmed black felt hats adorned with feathers, and strapped leather moccasins (*kierpce*). The front sides of their jackets are joined by a variety of ornate clasps. The women cover their heads with scarves and wear a combination of loose sheepskin and woollen jackets, bodices and blouses, long patterned percale skirts and strapped moccasins. All of the attire on display is character-

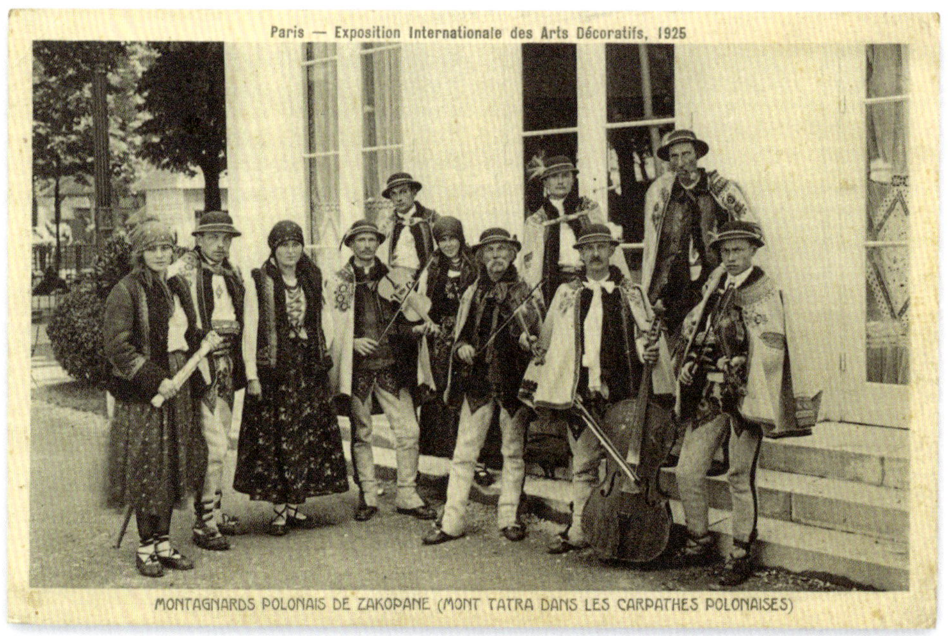

1.19 | 'Montagnards Polonais de Zakopane (Mont Tatra dans les Carpathes Polonaises)' [Polish Highlanders of Zakopane (Tatra Mountain in the Polish Carpathians)], postcard (Braun & Cie, Paris, 1925)

istic, celebratory and yet essentially modern Górale. The *parzenica* embroidery, for instance, had only been introduced into the men's dress through conscription into the Royal Hungarian Honvéd after 1867, the parade uniform of the regiments featuring such designs. That the group is a contemporary dance-music ensemble is further emphasised by the front-row display of modern violins (not *zlobcoki*, the older, more primitive, equivalent) and cello (equivalent of the older *basy*) with bows at the ready. It is also hinted at by the stick seen behind the man on the left, this being the shepherd's stick-cum-axe (*ciupaga*) that had become incorporated into Górale performance. The exploitation of the Górale as something distinctly 'Polish' had commenced in the late nineteenth century as middle-class Poles headed to the hills, particularly those of the Zakopane region south of Kraków, to reinvent themselves and their own national identity through contact with the apparently pure, uncorrupted peasant culture to be found there. Preservation, promotion, assimilation and reinterpretation as something 'greater Polish' went hand-in-hand. Through their acquisition of the card Jessie and Fra joined in this rustic celebration.[12]

Embroidering Croatian identity

By male brush

The assumption that the Newberys visited the 1925 Paris exhibition may be wrong, but it is highly likely they did, not least since they had been actively involved, Fra in particular, in European international exhibitions from around the turn of the twentieth century. Furthermore, we know that they visited the 1937 successor to the 1925 show, the Exposition Internationale des Arts et Techniques dans la Vie Moderne, following which, through their encouragement, Mary Spencer Watson was taken there by her parents – this, in turn, leading to Mary's tutelage in Paris under Ossip Zadkine.[13] While Paris 1925 might have been the closest the Newberys came to witnessing the folk art of the Górale, they certainly immersed themselves more directly and deeply in that of Croatia, through a visit to Zagreb on their Balkan tour of 1929. So having commenced our postcard survey with an image of Dalmatian dress, we conclude it with a deconstruction of the nine Croatian cards they left to their family. These represent folk costume through reproduction of painted and drawn pictures by six artists (three male, three female). And while one is also a major painting by a man of women's folk ritual, two, by women, subtly reveal that the distaff and spear sides are not fixed.

Vladimir Kirin was the artist of four of the Newberys' Croatian cards, the images on these belonging to a large set of watercolours depicting

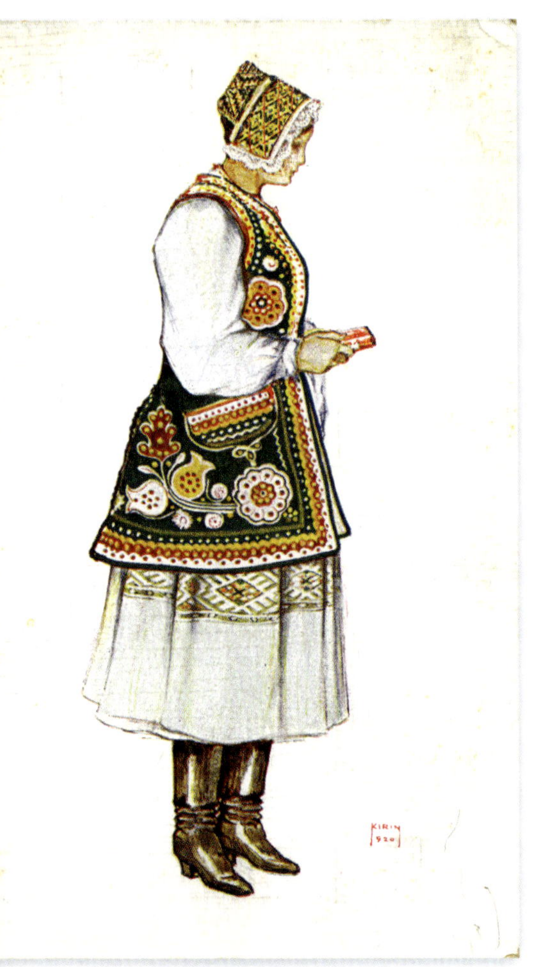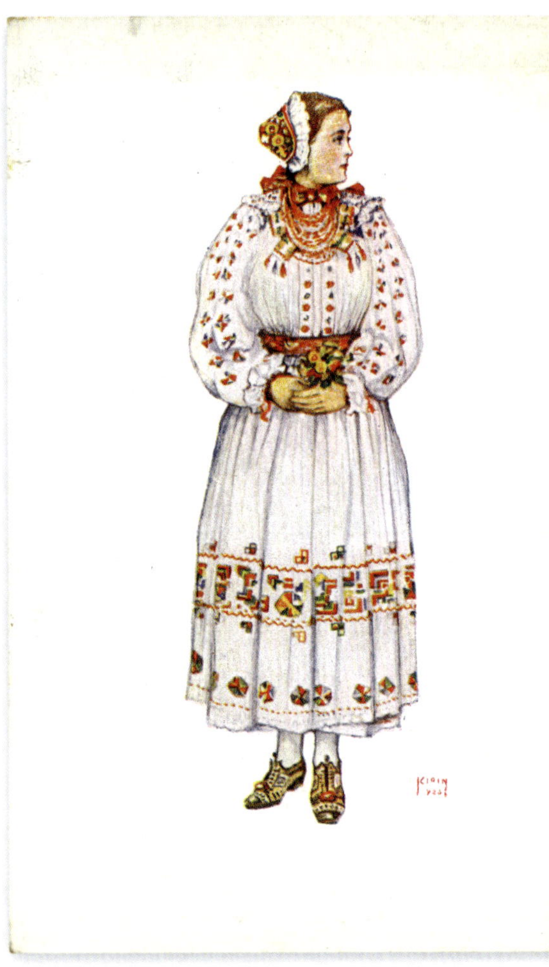

1.20 a–d | Vladimir Kirin, 'Croatian National Wear', 1920 [a. Zagreb environs; b. Martinska Ves (Sisak district); c. Sunja (Petrinja district); d. Otok (Vinkovci district)], postcards (Drava, Zagreb, late 1920s)

'Croatian National Wear' and created in 1920 [fig. 1.20 a–d].[14] Three of the Kirin works are of individual peasant women, or rather female folk costumes, set against an abstract white ground. The fourth is of a man and costume in front of elements of vernacular timber architecture. Each carries a distinguishing prop, or two: book, embroidered scarf, posy of flowers, pipe and walking stick. They represent peoples from the following Croatian localities (respectively, from a to d): Zagreb environs, Martinska Ves (Sisak district), Sunja (Petrinja district) and Otok (Vinkovci district) – that is, from the northwest through the central south to the east (Slavonia). Turned into fashion models the figures are seen full length, in profile, full frontal and three-quarter frontal. Their embroidered costumes highlight regional as well as gender varieties and while the women appear young, the man is old (his age, broad

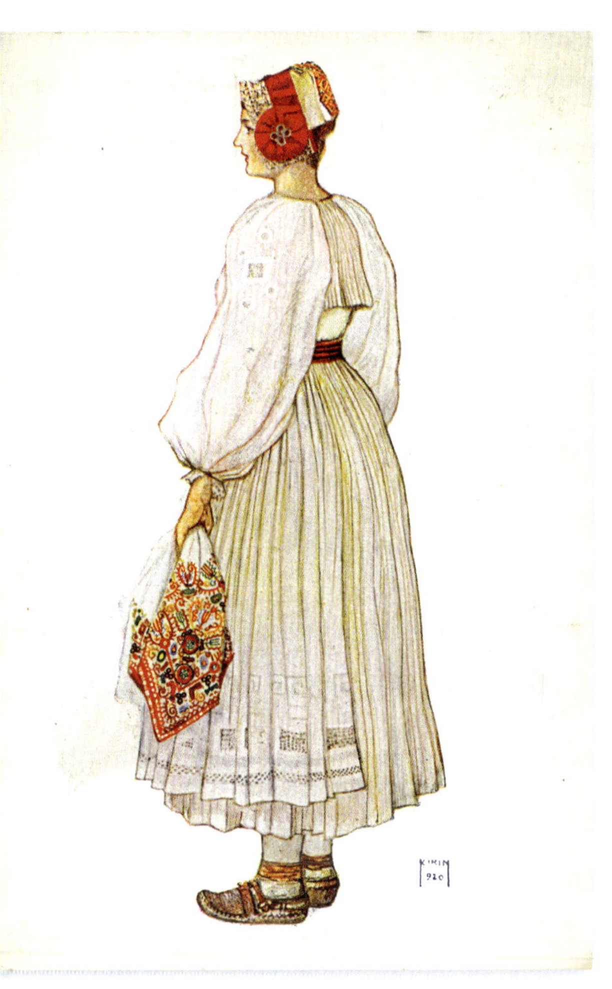 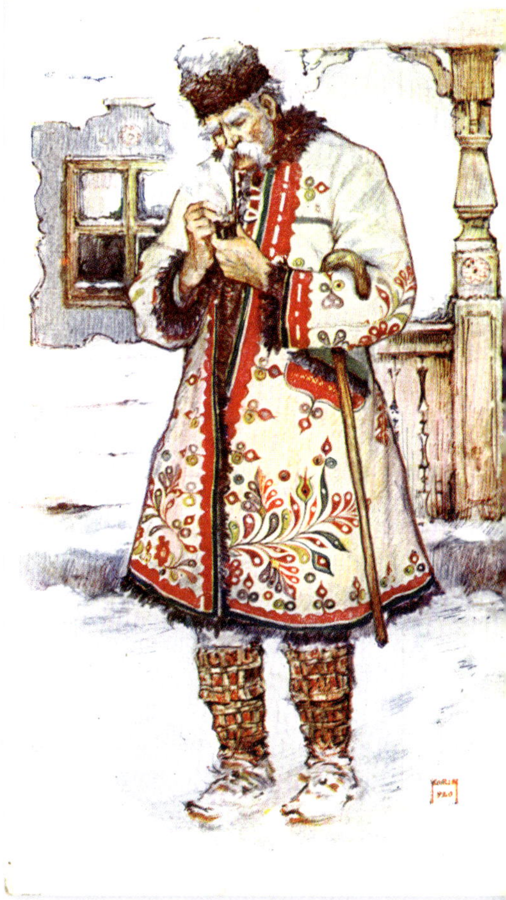

body, bushy white moustache and intent expression not dissimilar to Fra's in several photographs).

The predominant (non-)colour in the Kirin images is white, two of the women's white dresses being decorated with colourful embroidery, much of it stylised floral or geometric designs. Though each woman wears an intricately worked bonnet, only the woman from the Zagreb vicinity is adorned with a long sleeveless jacket (which is covered in bold designs) and shiny leather knee-length boots, while also carrying what seems to be a book. As the women move away from the Croatian capital (towards the south), the look gets simpler, from the flower-bearing Martinska Ves woman with her ornate neckwear, sash and shoes, to the Sunja woman, who wears strapped sandals (*opanci*) and whose main accoutrement is a red rosette on her bonnet and the vivaciously embroidered scarf in her hand. The well-covered flesh (apart from hands, neck and face), upright modest poses and averted gazes of the women turn them into epitomes of feminine propriety. Their white grounds offer further associations with purity. By contrast the Otok man is elderly, more bent into himself, and is contextualised, spear-side wise, by the ornately carved wooden portico and window surround to his rear. His long woollen coat, with its wealth of bright stylised floral motifs and decorative red edging, is accompanied by an elaborate hat and stockings both made of thick material, the latter joining with his *opanci*. Dressed for the cold he shows vulnerability through needing to smoke and walk with a stick. So if the women are nubile and represent spring and summer, the old man, for all his vigorous attire, indicates the passing on of tradition and the need to survive autumn and winter.

The aim of the Kirin images is to document abiding national features, and such concern can be considered part of a Croatian revivalism begun in the nineteenth century when Croatians were negotiating their way to a heightened manifestation and consciousness of their nation with their Habsburg, and particularly Hungarian, overlords. Kirin's work, like the other Croatian images possessed by the Newberys, harkens to the invigoration of such revivalism in the wake of the Habsburg empire's collapse, post-First World War, and with the establishment of the Yugoslav Kingdom of Serbs, Croats and Slovenes in 1918. All five of the other Croatian postcards visualise significant aspects of this new drive for clear identity markers. All of them are products of the new generation of artists to whom Kirin belonged.

Four of the five remaining Croatian postcards were published by S. Marković of Zagreb. They possess a certain freedom of expression and sense of community denied the stiff, isolated figures seen thus far. In keeping with the field of the most imaginative and rich Balkan folk art, young women's attire dominates. The continuation of the Newberys' postcard realisation of this uneven male-female Croatian costume/art balancing act is felt even where the two sexes appear, and seemingly quite equally, as in Slavko Tomerlin's card of 'National Dress from Šestine-Gračane in the Zagreb region' [fig. 1.21].[15]

As with Kirin the garb is mainly white, this combining with an essentially white background. However, now we see two children, a boy and a girl aged about ten, seated on a long wooden bench playing a game of knucklebones. The ground under their feet is light green, and the shadows cast by their legs indicate a bright, sunny day. The boy straddles the narrow bench with his legs in wide, loose trousers. He wears a richly embroidered red, yellow and black sleeveless jacket (*lajbek*) and circular cap. The girl sits modestly with her feet crossed in front of the bench, thereby projecting out of the picture plane into the viewer's space slightly more than the boy. With a red and yellow patterned headscarf over her long plaited hair, she also wears an apron

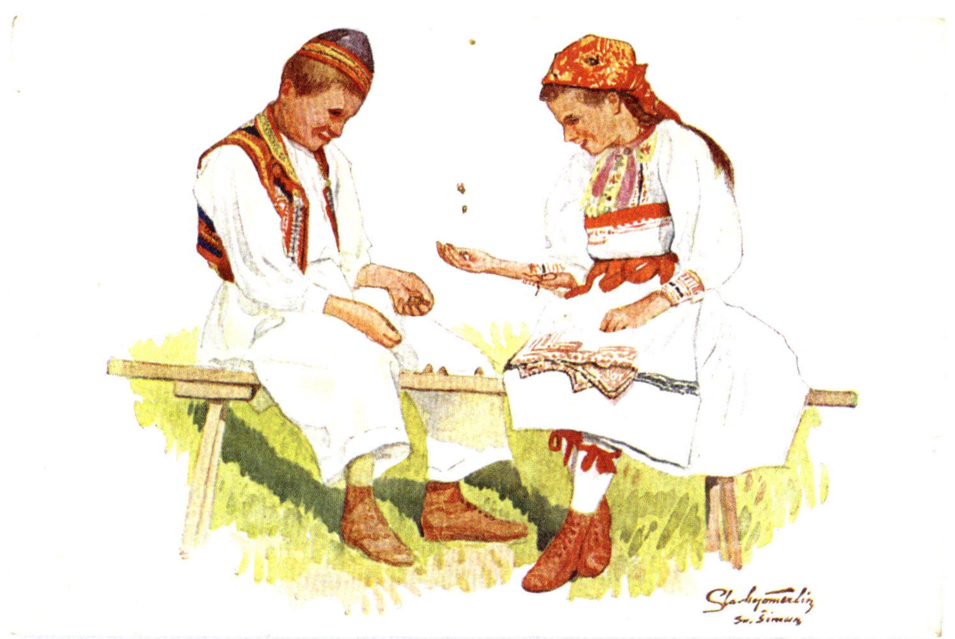

1.21 | Slavko Tomerlin, 'National Dress from Šestine-Gračane in the Zagreb Region', postcard
(S. Marković, Zagreb, 1926)

and has a folded cloth on her knees, each with red, patterned borders. Both wear laced boots. They lean their heads gently towards one another as they smile and watch the 'knucklebones' that the girl throws and attempts to catch with her right hand. More knucklebones are distributed between them on the bench and in the boy's left hand. Here then the Newberys have collected an image not just of Croatian folk costume but also one of a universal children's game, which many artists before Tomerlin had been drawn to as a subject. By turning knucklebones into an aspect of Croatian national performance, Tomerlin develops a visual line on the game inherited from his artist predecessors, be they ancient Greeks, Pieter Bruegel the Elder, numerous neoclassicists or, indeed, relatively recent observers of folk life, such as the sentimental Russian realist Vladimir Makovsky and the soft English Impressionist Philip Wilson Steer.[16]

The symmetrical grouping of Tomerlin's children along and around the horizontal line of their bench, with their knees almost touching, their hands and eyes engaged and an imagined vertical line supported by an outstretched hand midway between them, relates closely to Fra's pictorial means for the expression of communal identity in *Serbian Women*. Such simple conveyance of bond through craft and kindred interaction is made more complex in the second of the Marković cards in the Newbery collection. Simultaneously, the leadership of the

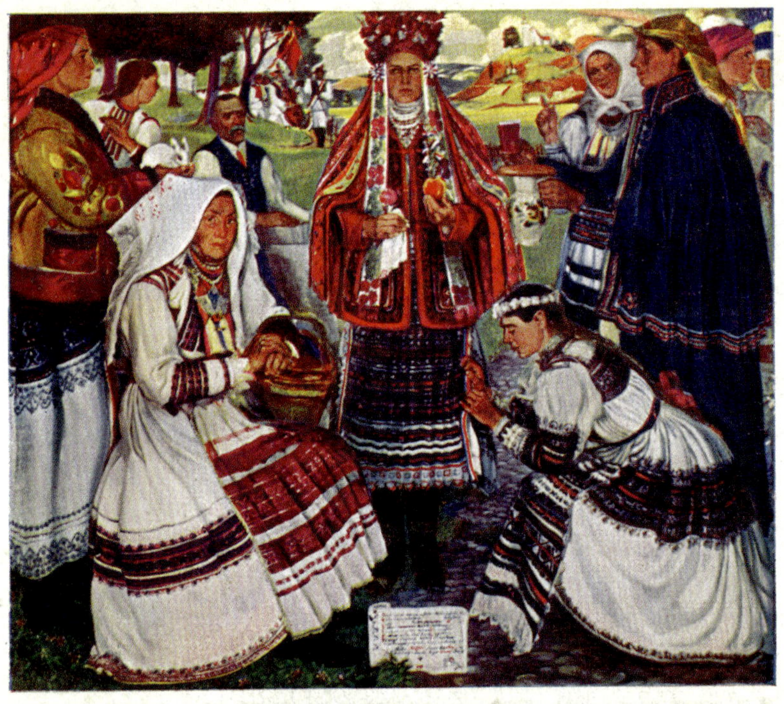

1.22 | Maksimilijan Vanka, 'Zagorje Bride', postcard (S. Marković, Zagreb, 1928)

female sex becomes more overt than that tacitly acknowledged in Tomerlin's image of Croatian knucklebones. The card in question features Maksimilijan Vanka's vision of the dressing of, according to the caption on the reverse, a 'Zagorje Bride' [fig. 1.22]. The image belongs to a set representing the folk customs and costumes of Croatia.[17] The original is actually a large oil painting entitled *Preparing the Bride for Her Wedding* (1925).[18] Owned by the City Council of Zagreb, it hangs in the Old City Hall. It rivals, if not surpasses, Tomerlin in its relationship with *Serbian Women*.

Preparing the Bride visualises a young woman, Dora Brezović, being prepared for her marriage to Stjepan Špoljar close to her home village of Donja Bistra in the eastern foothills of Medvednica mountain. 'Zagorje' refers to the rural cultural region 'beyond the hill' from Zagreb. Vanka places Dora in the centre of his composition dressed in her bridal costume, replete with tall, lavishly bedecked, wreath crown with long embroidered ribbons. Full figure and frontal she stands stiffly upright, holding a flower, fruit and handkerchief (the gift of bride to groom that becomes a wedding invitation for the whole village) before her. Beneath her feet is a tablet covered with hard-to-decipher handwriting which must relate to the oath and occasion of marriage.

Dora and her mother, who is seated to the left, both wear traditional *kraluš* beaded necklaces. They are the only figures who gaze directly, and without emotional expression, at the viewer. Dora is attended by her cousin and other womenfolk, and also by the somewhat diminutive, slightly distant, figure of her father, who is half-hidden behind her mother. To the right her cousin adjusts her dress, completing a central compositional triangle with Dora and her mother. The other women bear tokens of folk blessing: white rabbit, ceramic jug, wicker basket. The group of seven main figures fills much of the picture space, their play of rich reds, blues and whites dominating the florid surface. They are joined on their fringes by a few more women who look elsewhere, one towards the band of male musicians heading out from behind the trees at top left. The bride's upper body is surrounded by the lush green and yellow pastureland and blue mountains of her district. She stands on a cobbled track facing away from the distant white church, where her vows will be taken, atop the hill in the background.

Preparing the Bride possesses a spiritual primitivist quality. Since he was brought up in the nearby Zagorje village of Kupljenovo and frequently returned there, Vanka's treatment of tradition and place contains, for all its contrived painterliness, authenticity. It is, therefore, a somewhat more genuine reflection of folk and folk convention than Fra's in *Serbian Women*. Nevertheless, a romantic colourist persuasion, the visualisation of dress as the chief bearer of peasant craft tradition and a close compositional accord, unites the two. The question remains as to whether Fra and Jessie could have been aware of the debt Vanka indirectly owed them. For, from 1910, Vanka, an illegitimate son of the aristocratic Fürstenberg and Salm families, had trained under Jean Delville in Brussels, shortly after the Belgian Symbolist painter had returned there following seven years' employment under Fra at the Glasgow School of Art. The tutelage of Delville and his Brussels colleague Constant Montald proved critical for Vanka, leading him in turn to become a professor at the Zagreb School of Arts and Crafts in the 1920s and subsequently a muralist. No records are known to exist or to have existed, but it is nice to speculate that, given Vanka's background and standing in the art world of the Croatian capital, Fra and Jessie met with him there. They certainly met with his work.

By female design

Vanka had imparted stylised qualities of 'primitive' religious painting and stained glass to the flattened, symmetrically organised figures, ambiguous space and strong coloration of his 'Zagorje Bride', as well as a sense of the monumental in the way Dora is posed above the 'pedestal' of the inscribed tablet. By so doing he transformed the bride into a static object of aesthetic veneration as well as a symbol of tradition. Among the cards featuring artwork by women that accords with such

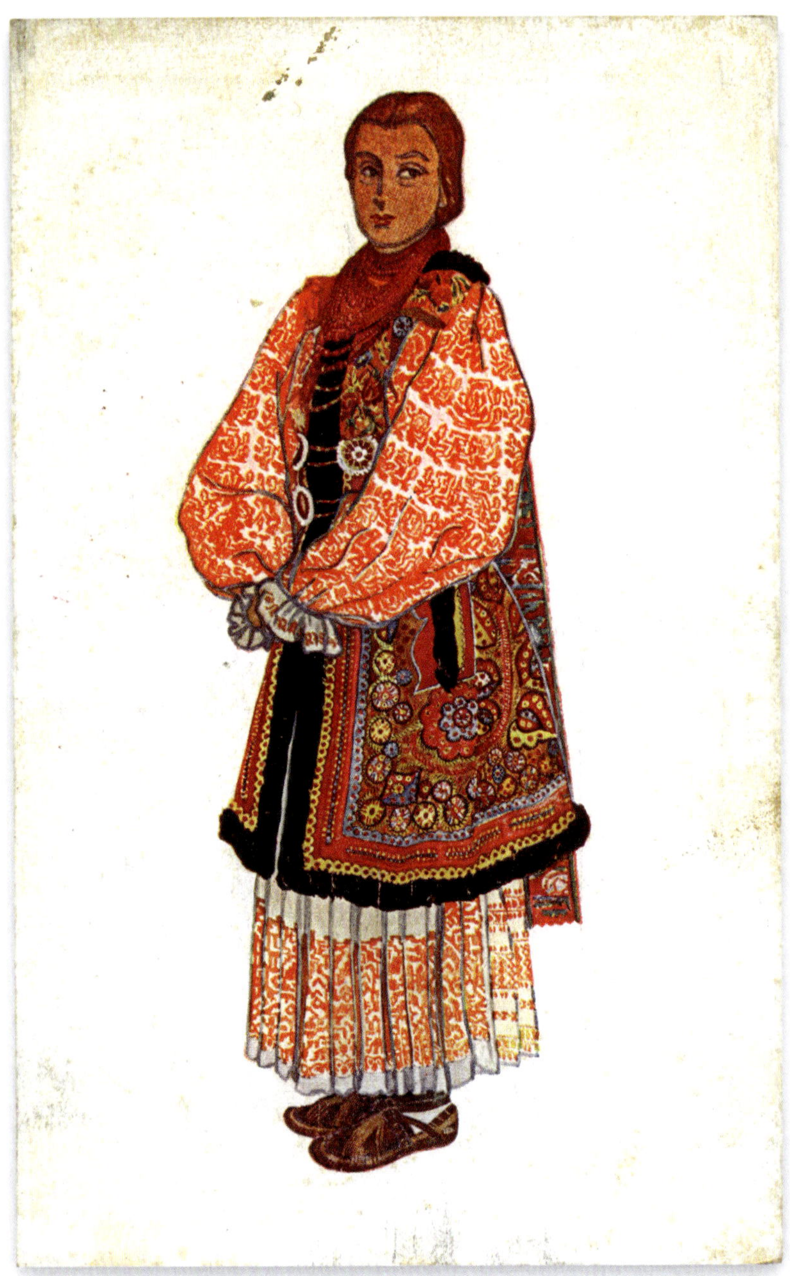

1.23 | Zdenka Sertić, 'Girl from Vukomerec in the Environs of Zagreb', postcard,
(Ethnographic Museum, Zagreb)

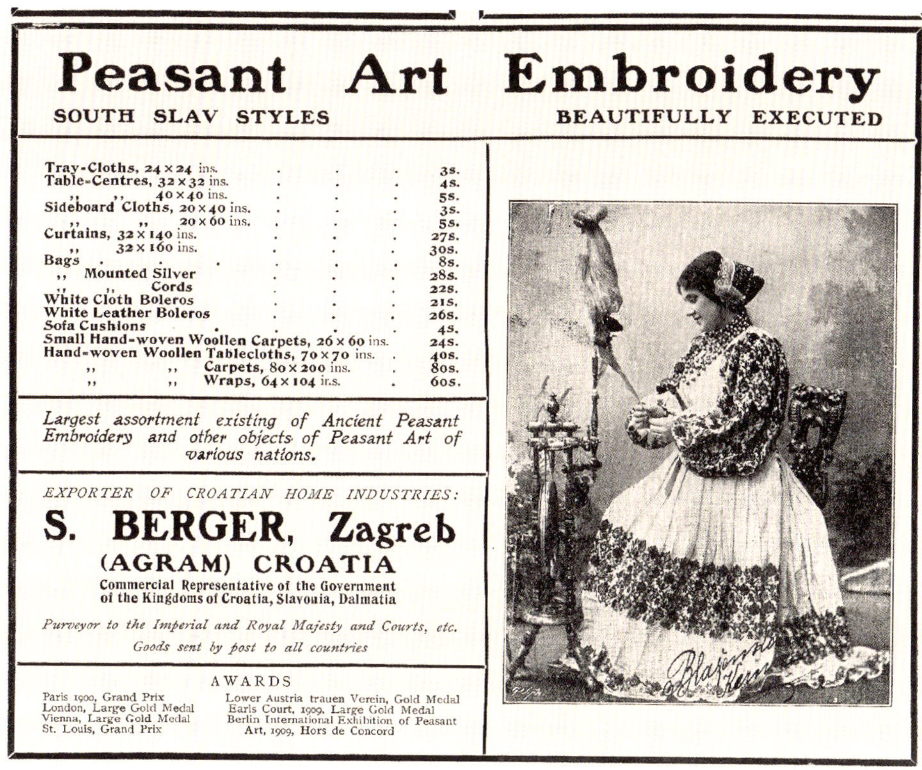

1.24 | Salamon Berger, advertisement; from Charles Holme (ed.), *Peasant Art in Austria and Hungary* (London: The Studio, 1911), p. vi

treatment is one with Zdenka Sertić's painted 'Girl from Vukomerec in the Environs of Zagreb' [fig. 1.23].[19] That said, being of a single figure against a white ground, iconographically, the image is closer to Kirin's work. The card was published by the Ethnographic Museum in Zagreb, this having been founded in 1919 by Jewish textile merchant and collector Salamon Berger. Berger was also a highly successful manufacturer of textiles, specialising in 'Peasant Art Embroidery' and particularly 'South Slav Styles' [see fig. 1.24].[20]

Sertić, the youngest of the Newberys' six Croatian artists, was employed as curator and artist at the museum from 1927.[21] Her painting is of a teenage girl, whose unmarried status is signalled by her lack of headwear. She wears the most richly adorned costume of all the cards. Full-figure and three-quarter frontal the girl looks past the viewer to the right. Her knee-length sleeveless jacket is an organised riot of colour-form, with the multi-coloured bands of braid enclosing a plethora of energised circular shapes, the variegation of which is complemented by that of the long embroidered scarf hanging down her back. Her dress is marked by intense red abstract patterning on the white linen while her attire is completed by decorative *opanci* and strings of red beads

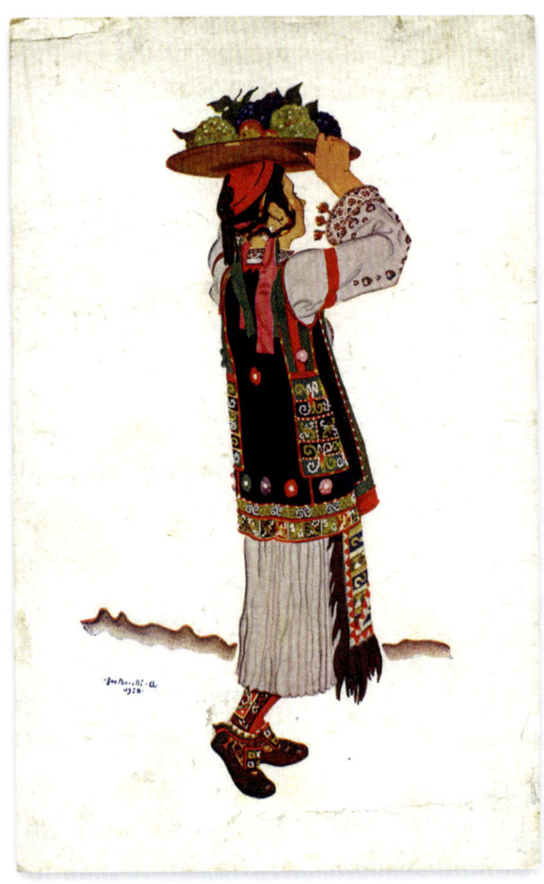

1.25 | Zoe Borelli, 'Peasant Woman from Northern Dalmatia' [1928], postcard (S. Marković, Zagreb, 1929)

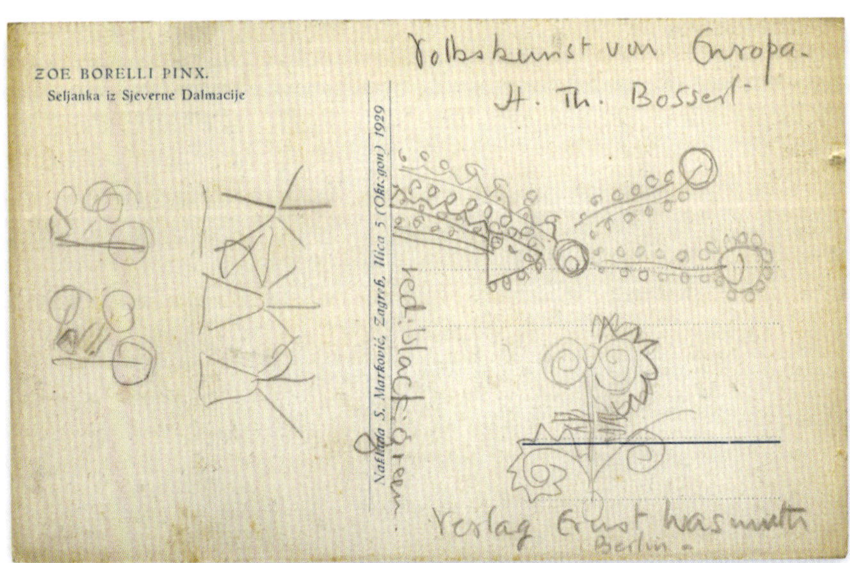

1.26 | Jessie Newbery, drawings and writing on the reverse of fig. 1.25

around her neck. In this ceremonious state, with her hands clasped invisibly in front of her waist and her steady gaze, which could be seen as both discerning and pensive, this girl is evidently on the brink of womanhood. Through such imagery Sertić announced the meticulous ethnographic approach that was to be a hallmark of her prolific artistic and museological career thereafter.

The defining of roles evident so far in the Newberys' Croatian postcards is challenged, to variant degrees, by the last two cards by women. For all the signs of generational, gender and geographic range in the cards we have already considered the main emphasis has been on relatively young female dress from locations not far from Zagreb, that is within a restricted part of what is known as the Pannonian ethnographic zone that covers the northern lowland parts of Croatia. This being the case, it is also now time to consider the work of an artist who extends the iconography to the south and who simultaneously conveys an alternative feeling of both life and artistry: 'Peasant Woman from Northern Dalmatia' by Zoe Borelli [fig. 1.25].[22] With this card we have a hybrid example of a woman studying signs of womanhood for it contains not only Borelli's image but also, on its reverse side, pencil drawings and text by Jessie [fig. 1.26].

Arguably Borelli was the most talented and imaginative of the Croatian artists featured in the Newberys' collection. Her extensive European education, coupled with her experience of life in Vienna, Rome and Florence, as well as her visual probing of the paranormal (she was an early exponent of automatic writing), led to a highly sensitive aestheticism in her work. That she was also from Zara, the scene of our first postcard, also meant that she was inclined to explore northern Dalmatian folk art. In contrast to the static artificiality of the feet-deprived figures in the sepia photographic card Jessie sent to Mary Spencer Watson, Borelli's Dalmatian peasant woman is colourful, younger and on the move. Furthermore we now have a three-quarter back view of a young woman or teenage girl actually doing something rather than acting as an example of stiff ceremonial type. For, with the heel of her right foot raised, she is making steps in her brightly coloured *opanci* and embroidered stockings. And she does so while carrying on her head, supported by strong arms, a large round tray filled with thick bunches of black and green grapes plus a couple of apples. Wearing a tasselled red cap, her dark hair is woven in braids and adorned with red ribbons signifying that she is unmarried. Over her white skirt and embroidered blouse she wears a long, dark blue sleeveless jacket and tasselled apron, both richly, but not overabundantly, decorated with abstract curvilinear and geometric motifs. The white space around her is broken by a curvy thick line cutting across her body around knee height and thereby giving a hint of space. The informality of Borelli's painted image accords with that of Tomerlin. The impression is of a waitress serving a feast, one who is a model of balance and poise, a purveyor of local viticultural and costumal sustenance. Her food-laden platter becomes a gloriole elevating her being above the physical labour she represents, in a mirror-like reflection of Fra's *The Nimbus of Toil* (1897) [fig. 4.1] completed three decades earlier (see chapter four).

Borelli's card is important because it also leads us to contextualise what we are being shown by reference to contemporary and recent research into folk costume by inquisitive outsiders bent on learning from its language. For Jessie's study of Borelli's northern Dalmatian female dress is confirmed by her use of the back of the card for visual and literary jottings. From these it is apparent she is referring herself, no doubt with potential embroidery design of the future in mind, to the recently published thesaurus of European folk art by Helmuth Theodor Bossert, *Volkskunst in Europa* (Berlin: Verlag Ernst Wasmuth, 1926). While she notes 'red: black: green', her lead pencil drawings of sprouting linear patterns are hard to identify with particular images from Bossert, his Yugoslavian and Bulgarian examples (as well as others) offering similar but not identical designs. Of course it could also be possible she was making notes from exhibits in the Ethnographic Museum or costumes seen elsewhere on her 1929 Balkan trip. But the fact that she was directing her own attention to Bossert, who illustrated his huge thesaurus with numerous colour images of textile work in the Zagreb museum's collection, makes it worth pausing here to consider and contextualise the German author's contribution.

Essentially, the Bossert volume was the most comprehensive pan-continental visual survey (with some 2,100 images, many in colour, of objects and motifs) of peasant artwork to date, in accordance with its author's campaign to record what he saw as a vital but dying realm of art. His call for museums to be cornerstones of new understanding in this respect came:

> [b]ecause every European country has, or used to have, a distinctive, self-willed folk art that essentially helps the state gain a certain independent validity and value. This because it is precisely in folk art, in contrast to prevalent stylistic trends, that a uniform European spirit is to be found. As such it reinforces and bears witness to the close common bonds of the European peoples.[23]

As we reveal below Bossert included embroidery motifs (Macedonian, from the Zagreb museum collection) that are very close indeed to those seen in Fra's *Serbian Women* and other 'Serbian' paintings.

Bossert's defence of folk art would have struck a chord with Jessie, but it is likely that another author's work was of equal or greater importance for her – that of Amelia Levetus. For it was the latter who had, as far as the modern British public was concerned, first drawn attention to the importance of embroidery in central European folk culture. In 1911 Levetus was the main contributor of essays to *The Studio*'s volume *Peasant Art in Austria and Hungary*, a lavishly illustrated compendium of folk art from the Habsburg empire presaging Bossert's broader European version. In her introductory article, 'Austria', and in 'Croatia and Slavonia', Levetus highlights the unrivalled importance of women's embroidery and lace work in the folk art of the region.[24] Even a small selection of excerpts from her text reveals an aesthetic stance akin to Jessie's (and Fra's), yet more informed with regard to the Austrian-controlled territories (in which Levetus had settled). In this she goes considerably beyond what Bossert had offered:

> *For in the peasant woman, in a still higher degree than in the peasant man, an inborn feeling for art exists. One need only take a glance at the exquisite specimens of lace and embroidery here reproduced to realise the inventiveness of their minds, and with what pride and skill they have performed their self-imposed tasks. Their art has passed from generation to generation … embroideries offered the peasant woman full scope for her inborn love of the beautiful …. To describe even a few of the head-shawls, head-scarves, and caps would require more space than we have at our disposal, so fertile are the imaginations of the women, so rich their fantasy. These articles vary considerably … Often between the lines of embroidery beautiful drawn-thread work is to be seen … older specimens are always on home-spun linen, and the dyes are purely vegetable ones, extracted from the plants by the woman herself … Some of this work baffles description, it is so intricate and so beautiful, the designs in the eastern countries reminding one of those of the Orient or of the ancient Egyptians.[25]*

If the Newberys had known Levetus' text and its accompanying illustrations, as they surely did, then they would have arrived in the Balkans alert to the intrinsic value of the folk art they saw and purchased examples of there. We have already established that far from simply signifying the vogue for casual tourist souvenirs their postcard collection acts as a record of life-long interest in the stuff of artistry. That said, they clearly had no time to delve as deeply as Levetus into defining specifics of individual peoples, hence it is left to her to convey something of the idiosyncrasies of place and type of design that underlie their Balkan acquisitions. Several excerpts of her text are worth collating here in this respect:

> *… the South Slav group of Austrian* Volkskunst*: the further south one goes the more apparent is the peculiar character of* Volkskunst *which has come under different influences – that of the Slavs of the Balkans, and of the Italians, chiefly Venetians. Dalmatia stands*

alone, for in addition to these elements the people have also been strongly influenced by Byzantine and Turkish art. This is chiefly to be seen in their homes and in the decorations of their persons. The Dalmatians can boast an extremely rich and varied textile industry, which, like that of the other primitive races of Austria – the Goralians and Ruthenians – expresses itself in the ancient designs and in the technique in which they are executed. The bridal blouse is most elaborate in design and workmanship, being literally incrusted with embroidery. The women of Croatia and Slavonia excel in spinning, weaving, embroidering, drawn-thread work, and, to a certain extent, in lace-making … even before the needle came into use there was nothing these peasant women could not weave on their looms, no manipulation so difficult but that they could master it. In no country, except perhaps Sweden, can they boast of such traditions in weaving as in Croatia. The reason is not far to seek if the geographical position of the country be taken into consideration. Both Croatia and Slavonia lie on the threshold of the Orient, and the latter country has been mainly influenced by Byzantine culture, the former by that of the western countries … thanks to the exertions of Herr Berger, who rescued it from oblivion … the [weaving] craft has been handed down to this day … The Croatians and Slavonians still keep to the peasant dress. It is always interesting and in good taste and of the women's own spinning. But by far the most beautiful and most interesting is that worn by the women … The women of Slavonia are more lavish in their designs, which are essentially Byzantine in feeling, and prefer gold thread as a means of expressing this. They have a fine feeling for harmony of colour; and this may also be said of the Croatian women …[26]

Levetus' enquiry into the history, context and appearance of folk art in the Austrian-controlled parts of the Habsburg empire is indicative of her pioneering, outreaching place in both art criticism and the women's movement in her adopted home of Vienna. Her intellectual probing of intrinsic creative drive, which can be termed *Kunstwollen* (literally 'art and will' – the cultural concept enunciated around 1900 by Viennese art historian Alois Riegl), is provided with a visual and living counterpart in the image and artist of the final Newbery postcard. Entitled 'Good Shelter' (Dobar zaklon) the card's painting is by Nasta Rojc [fig. 1.27]. It belongs to a set of at least five paintings of peasant life and costumes of Šestine that Rojc published as postcards in the late 1920s (this one is dated 1927).[27] As a result of the location these correlate with Tomerlin's knucklebones painting but they also go further in their capture of a female leading role, with four of the five images foregrounding women in national dress, and three of these showing particularly active, poised women. The Newberys' card is the one from the set which,

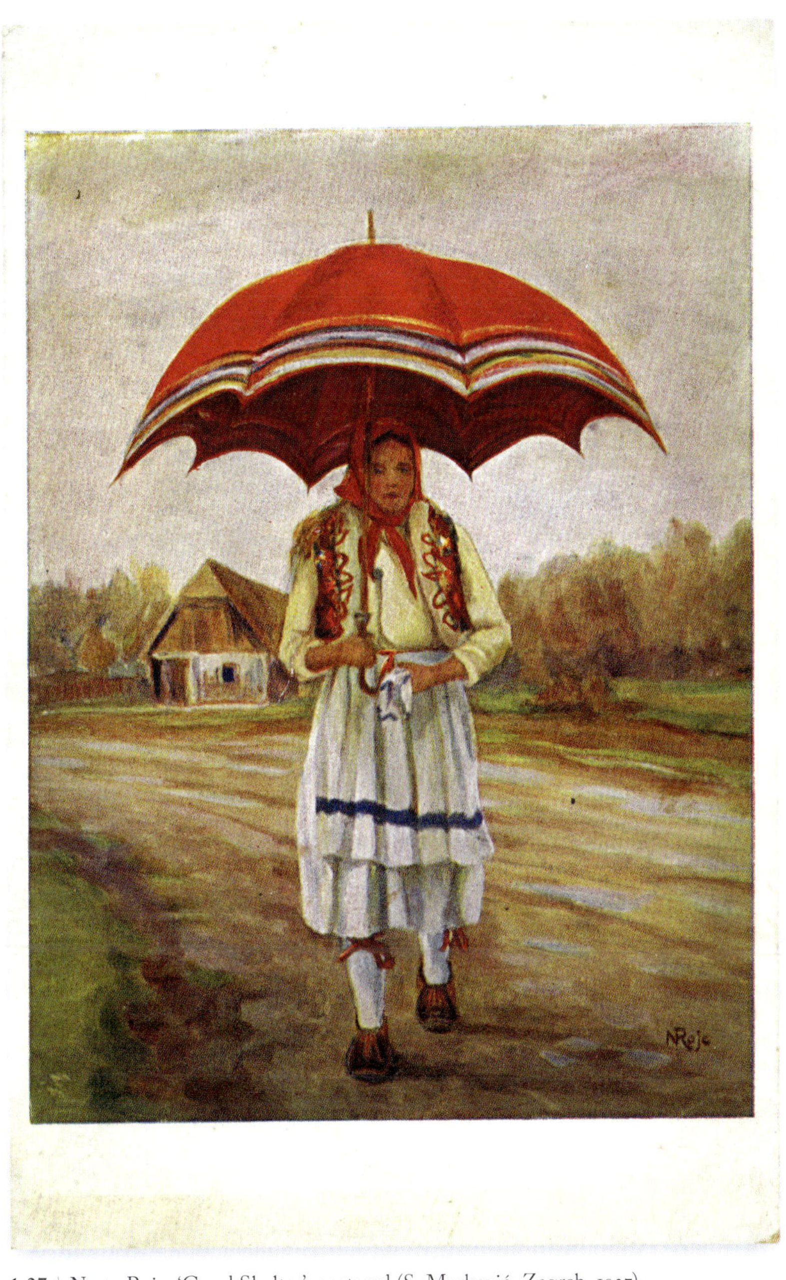

1.27 | Nasta Rojc, 'Good Shelter', postcard (S. Marković, Zagreb, 1927)

while focusing on an individual figure, adds a hint of narrative beyond her objectification as a piece of a peasant jigsaw. So while the figure is, like Borelli's, a young woman or teenage girl in local costume stepping forward, now the step is more decisive. Furthermore, the step is away from the timber cottage-barn of the background and along the curve of a road that leads directly towards the viewer. Instead of the steeply pitched roof of the country homestead (or indeed Borelli's tray of fruit) the girl is protected from the elements by a large open umbrella, red with multi-coloured stripes. This outsized, upward pointing, portable canopy draws attention away from the dress, becoming instead a modern, secular nimbus for the woman. Though she may be caught frozen in time, her gait, the signs of sunlight crossing her body and steady gaze, plus her grasp of both handkerchief and umbrella handle, suggest at least an element of self-determined advance.

Yet radical the woman of 'Good Shelter' is not. For Rojc's substituting of distaff (as well as halo, bridal crown, basket, and so on) with the seemingly incongruous accoutrement of a modern umbrella is not quite the statement of aspiration it could appear. This because what she is bearing is a Šestine umbrella whose large size, wooden handle and red canvas with rainbow stripes had come to be seen as a key element of local folk costume. Furthermore, it was to appear numerous times in another Šestine card by Rojc, its size allowing protection for two as well as the loads carried on women's heads. With its red colour symbolising love and the sun, the addition of the umbrella's multi-coloured border was a Šestine attempt at warding off the drear effects of rain, both physically and metaphorically. It is possible to speculate as to why Jessie (and/or Fra) bought and kept this particular, single-figure card rather than any other by Rojc, but what is clear is that in it we find an artist expressing a move towards the naïve, kitsch and rustic from a privileged, unconventional and bohemian starting point. That Rojc's personhood and making of art led her to explore relationships outside of those perceived as the norm by socio-political powers-that-be would have been very much supported by the Newberys, had they known about her. Actually Rojc's outlook was informed by both her homosexuality and her integration into Croatian as well as British society, a fact which adds to her merits for further exploration.[28]

The winding of distaff-side romanticism

Detailed study of the Newberys' letters and postcards unearths purposefully directed ways of seeing that underpin the vision of female craft and community presented in *Serbian Women*. Yet, for all the

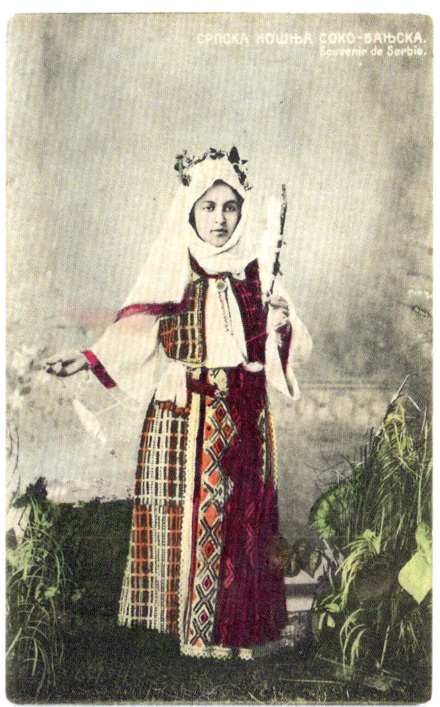

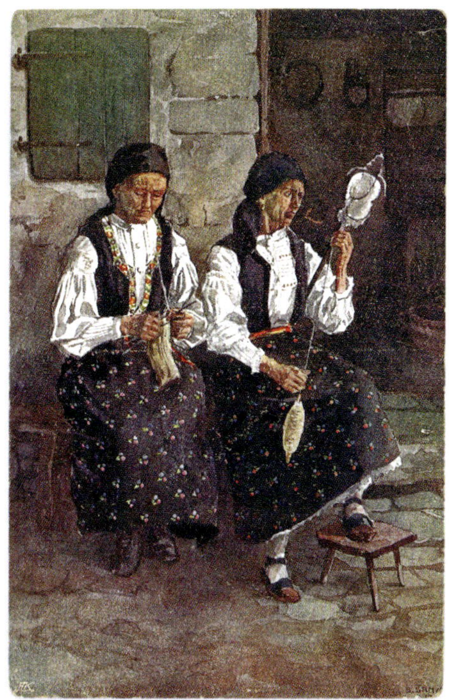

1.28 | 'Serbian National Dress, Sokobanja', eastern Serbia, postcard (Rajković & Ćuković, Belgrade early 20th century)

1.29 | Saša Šantel, *Women from the Istrian Coast*, postcard (Edition Čaklović, Zagreb, 1920s)

correlation of subjects, composition and thinking, we have nowhere encountered a peasant distaff or spindle. For these we need to turn beyond Fra and Jessie's works, to other postcards of the same period. A trawl of Serbian and Croatian cards reveals a good number featuring pictures of women holding distaffs and spindles. Some are from studio photographs, such as that of a girl from Sokobanja, eastern Serbia; others are from paintings, for example Saša Šantel's watercolour of two women from the Istrian coast of Croatia [figs 1.28, 1.29]. While the dress of the Belgrade-published former resembles that of the woman on the left in Fra's painting, the composition and setting of the Zagreb-produced latter are closer to *Serbian Women*, with the two women seated on a bench in front of an open cottage door – one knitting, one winding yarn.[29]

In fact, the image of woman with distaff and spindle was extremely widespread, with any number of precedents, from postcards to paintings and other media, and from around the globe, that Fra could have drawn upon, had he so wished. We cannot tell precisely how much he was aware of this iconographic convention but since he returned to the subject on numerous occasions he surely studied it to some degree. One

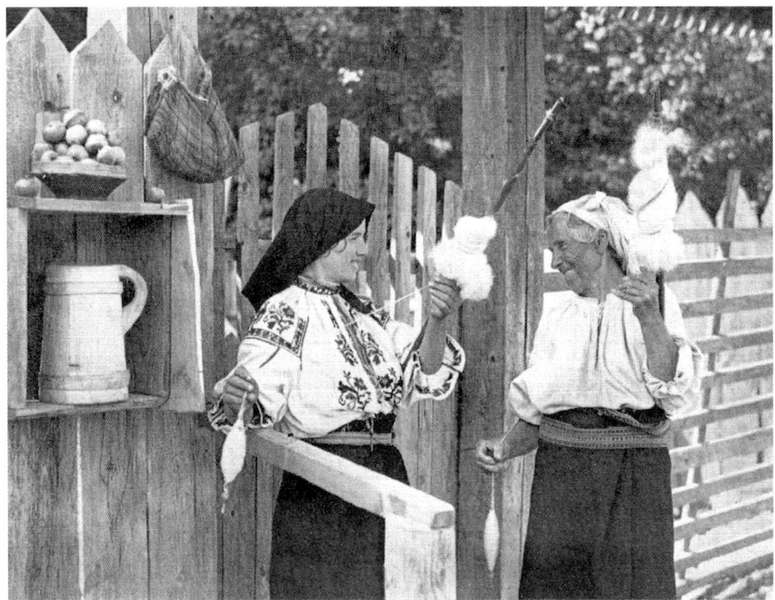

1.30 a–d | Iosif Berman, photographs of women spinning [a. Wayside water and fruit stall, Vrancea, Moldavia; b. Farmyard scene showing the Wallachian style of dress; c. Roadside gossip, Bukovina; d. Peasant woman spinning, Bukovina]; from *Oprescu, Peasant Art in Roumania* (London: The Studio, 1929)

Balkan source that he almost certainly saw shortly before painting *Serbian Women*, not least due to his and Jessie's long-time close relationship with the magazine, was Iosif Berman's photographs of women spinning from distaff to spindle as published in a special issue of *The Studio* in autumn 1929 [fig. 1.30 a–d].[30] Entitled *Peasant Art in Roumania*, this was a monograph authored by George Oprescu. As is shown below (chapter three), we know that one of Jessie's successors as head of embroidery at Glasgow, Kathleen Mann, utilised Oprescu's book for advancing her own art, particularly as a paradigm for others to follow. Dominated by a detailed visual and literary survey of Romanian textile art, the tome included four images of spinsters taken in the mid–late 1920s when Berman was collaborating with sociologist Dimitrie Gusti on a study of Romanian folk life.[31] As such, and with Oprescu's intention being the conveyance of the wealth, diversity and place of Romanian artistic tradition (in the face of adversity), the photographs represent women from three different Romanian regions: Moldavia, Wallachia and Bukovina. These were to find significant counterparts in images of spinsters from a fourth Romanian region, Transylvania, created in the 1920s and 1930s by three British artists: Denis Galloway, De Courcy Lewthwaite Dewar and Henry J. Howard (see below and chapter three). For Oprescu and his *Studio* editors, there was no need to mention the spinster images in the text. Instead, they are sprinkled

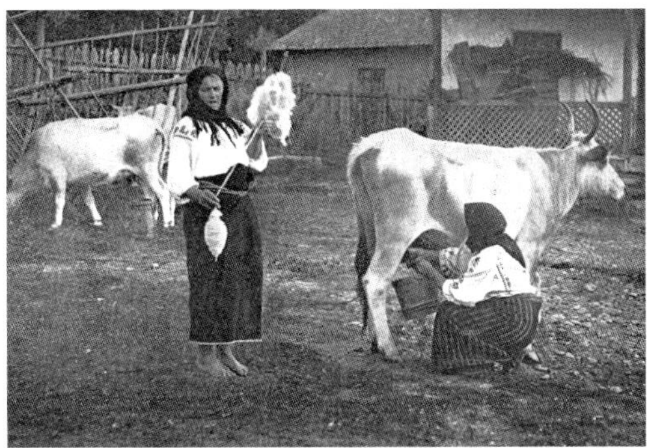

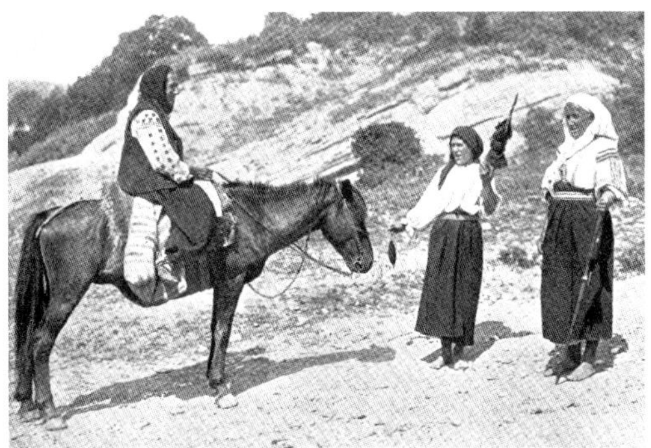

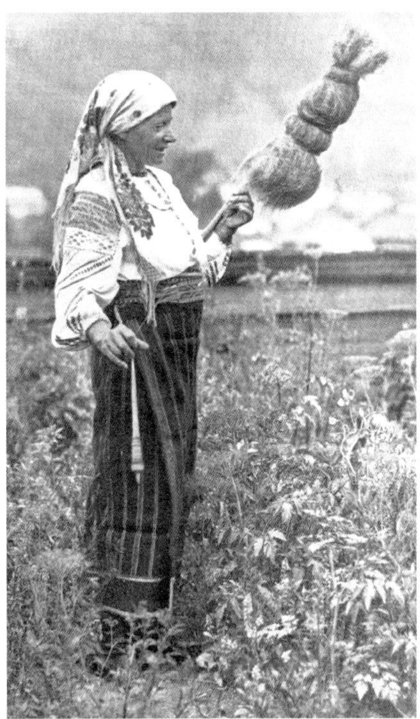

around, becoming key signifiers of the fundamental role of women in the making and preserving of the fabric of Romanian life.

Berman's photograph of Moldavian spinsters possesses striking similarities with Fra's *Serbian Women*. Captioned 'Wayside Water and Fruit Stall (Vrancea, Moldavia)', the image is a close-up of two women, both winding wool from distaff to spindle, in front of a rustic background. They form a central symmetrical group bonded by their intimacy, distinguished by their diversity of age and dress, with the younger woman on the left wearing a heavily embroidered chemise and dark headscarf as opposed to her companion's plain white blouse and headscarf. Their placement, smiles and eye contact suggest a degree of posing for Berman's lens. His three other photographs of spinsters also show the women spinning while otherwise occupied in the open air. Two of them, 'Farmyard scene showing the Wallachian style of dress' and 'Roadside gossip: Bukovina', appear more spontaneous with their spinning women, both of whom are barefoot, forming part of groups engaged either with milking cows or meeting others on a track. Unusually, the latter not only shows black rather than white wool on distaff and spindle but also has one of the women using her distaff as a walking stick, her spindle with spun yarn being neatly and conveniently attached to it. The final Berman image, 'In the fields: peasant woman spinning: Bukovina', is presented full-page as a division between

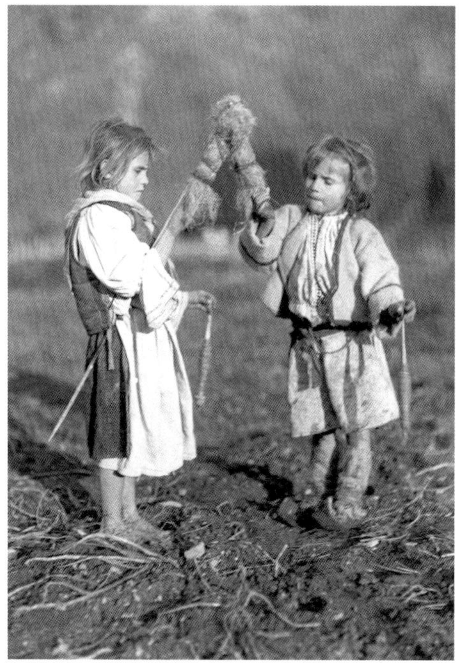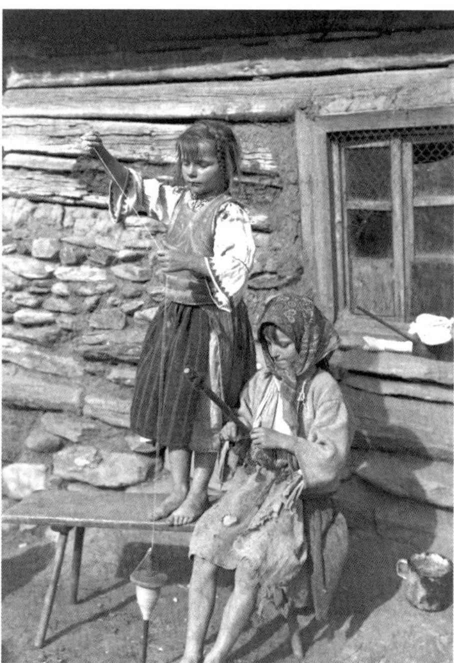

1.31 a–b | Denis Galloway, two girls spinning yarn in field [left], and two girls spinning yarn outside cottage [right] (Lunca Cernii de Jos, Transylvania, *c.* 1929–31)

Oprescu's 'Peasant Dress' and 'Embroidery' sections. As a full-length solitary figure in elongated vertical format she possesses more in common with Fra's *A Serbian Woman* (fig. 2.10). With its profiled view of the woman in richly embroidered blouse and girdle, floral-patterned headscarf and linear-patterned skirt, the loaded distaff and empty spindle suggest she has just arrived in the meadow which surrounds her, having walked there from the hillside village seen in the out-of-focus background. The diagonal of her distaff intersects her upright body at its visual juncture with the horizontal band of the field's fence behind her, the three lines of these thereby dividing the picture space in a way that suggests creative fabrication.

That the spinning of yarn was embedded from a very early age in the quotidian existence of peasant women across the Romanian regions was captured in two photographs of pairs of spinning girls by Denis Galloway taken almost simultaneously with Berman's and Fra's works [fig. 1.31 a–b]. A Scot, born in Wales and trained at the Slade School of Art in London, Galloway had settled in Cluj-Napoca in 1926, working as an artist and photographer for the city's new Ethnographic Museum of Transylvania.[32] Spending months living among the people of the Transylvanian provinces, Galloway took these two photographs in Lunca Cernii in the hilly countryside of the region's southwest (just

150 kilometres from the Serbian border). With their depictions of girls between about five and ten years old he reveals how early their dexterity with distaff and spindle begins. Furthermore, the two pairs show accord with Fra's *Serbian Women* composition, not least through their close-up viewpoint, centrality and play of vertical, diagonal and horizontal lines. That they also convey, whether in the field or on the bench outside the cottage, independence and complete engagement in their activity harkens to the bonds of community they represent.

Taking all of these together with Fra and Jessie's Balkan fabrications we are presented with a set of images where a signifying of commonwealth gains precedence over a nominal recognition for those featured. As such, individuals become at once carried and carrying precipitates of integral relationships (fractals).[33] How appropriate, then, that Oprescu (who found more meaning in 'progress'-threatened folk art than in modernist trends) should point out:

> *In Roumanian … embroidery bears the very picturesque name of 'Rîuri', which would be literally translated as 'rivers'. Here is a 'river'-sewn (or 'river'-trimmed) smock, a peasant woman will say … the intention in the popular mind has clearly been to compare the sinuous, frequently parallel lines running along the material with the winding course of the rivers in the valleys.*[34]

We can go further and suggest that Romanian 'rîuri'-work alludes to the interweaving of multiple streams of human craft that Fra and Jessie dedicated their lives to navigating.

The rivers of folk textile art, and concomitant representation of women as fount, flowed far beyond the Balkans. For our sake, we can conclude this section with two examples of painted spinsters, one from close by and one from further afield. First, the timing of Fra's creation of *Serbian Women* accords with that of a comparable watercolour by the Czech artist Jan Hála: *Woman from Važec, Spinning* (1929) [fig. 1.32].[35] Hála dedicated his mature years to depicting folk life in the mountainous Liptov region of central Slovakia where he settled in the mid-1920s. Thus his representation of the rural distaff side was, similar to Fra's, about capturing and cherishing surviving, yet threatened, craft and folk traditions. While Hála focuses on one woman spinning yarn, the similarities in dress, pose, composition and setting are remarkable. Evidently Fra's work has a contemporary relevance considerably beyond the Balkan peninsula and its Yugoslavian, or Serbian, peoples with whom he identified.

Given Fra's and Jessie's background, one final card is worthy of comparative analysis: R.R. McIan's 'Spinning with the Distaff' [fig. 1.33].[36] Published in the early twentieth century, the card's image was a painting from McIan's series, done in the 1840s, showing scenes of life in the Scottish Highlands. Though McIan was partially inspired by Walter Scott's romantic views of Scotland's cultural traditions, his picture does also visually document folk life and material culture in the north of the British Isles. As with Fra, two women are placed centrally in front of an open cottage door. One is seated on a low wooden stool and uses distaff and spindle to wind wool. The other stands looking on. Both appear quite young and well-dressed in complementary clothes. Their bare feet enhance the feeling of homeliness. On the left is a cooper's wooden tub and a triangular fish-drying rack. The cottage is made of stone with a low thatched roof. A lucky horseshoe hangs, ends-down, above the door. McIan's viewpoint is not quite as central or close-up as Fra's but it is at a similar level. Both represent women's craft

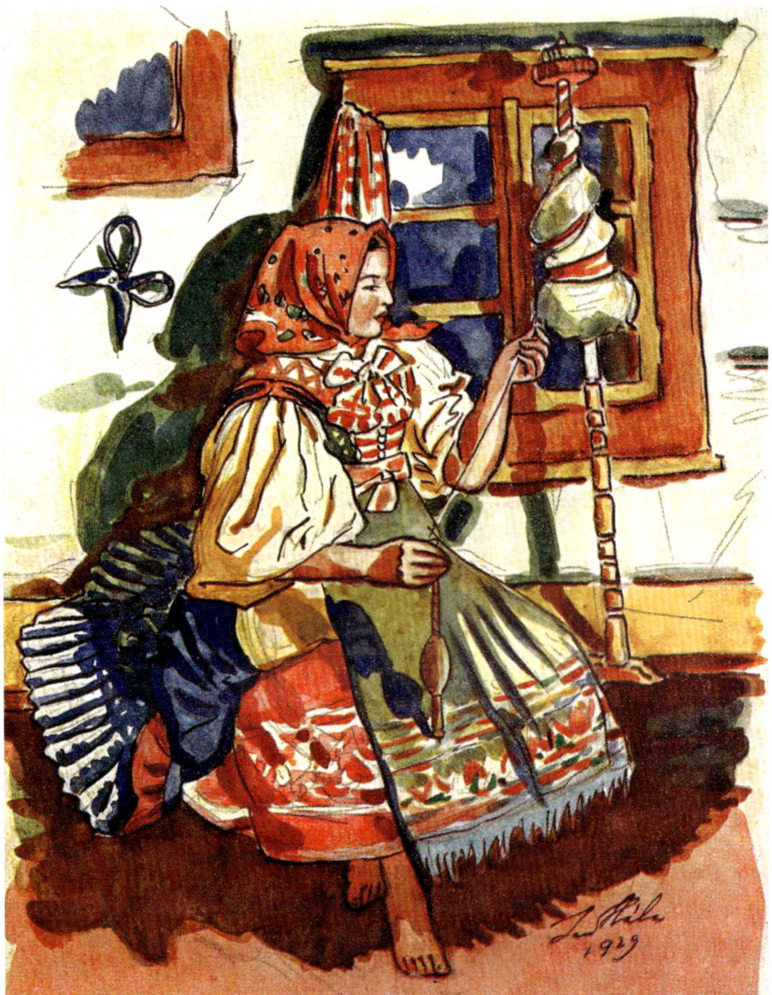

1.32 | Jan Hála, 'Woman from Važec, Spinning', 1929; from L.W. Rochowanski, *Columbus in der Slovakei* (Bratislava: Eosverlag, 1936), opp. p. 380

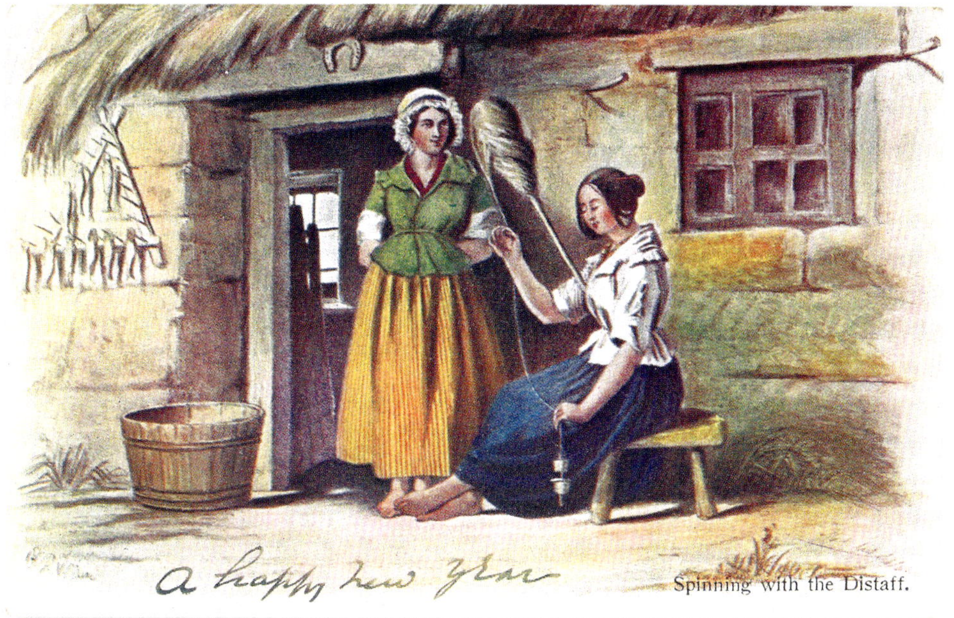

1.33 | R.R. McIan, 'Spinning with the Distaff'; from 'McIan's Highland Series', postcard (D.B. & S., n.d.)
PRIVATE COLLECTION

and togetherness outside in good sunlight and air, before the threshold of a dark interior, in keeping with the best and most sociable place to work when weather permits. But therein, as with the other cards, lies the problem … Is *Serbian Women* a painterly pastiche of a picture post-card, itself a cheap, manipulated memento of place and people? Is it a product of folksy tourism? A superficial souvenir of brief holidays that were about escape and illusion rather than understanding and reality? The answer is yes. But this makes it all the more significant. How else could or should a seventy-five-year-old painter and retired art educationist find and represent subjects which conveyed his wider empathies and concerns? That *Serbian Women* uses Dorset women as models and is almost certainly painted in front of the double doors (now French windows) and Purbeck stone walls of the seventeenth-century house (Well Court, at 22 West Street, Corfe Castle) that the Newberys had bought in the early 1920s, is an intrinsic part of the creative deceit. In fact, the doors open onto a courtyard enclosed on its southwest side by an old chapel that Fra converted into his studio. By touring abroad, aesthetically and physically, both Fra and Jessie shed light on what comprised, or was conceived as, home … and not just for themselves.

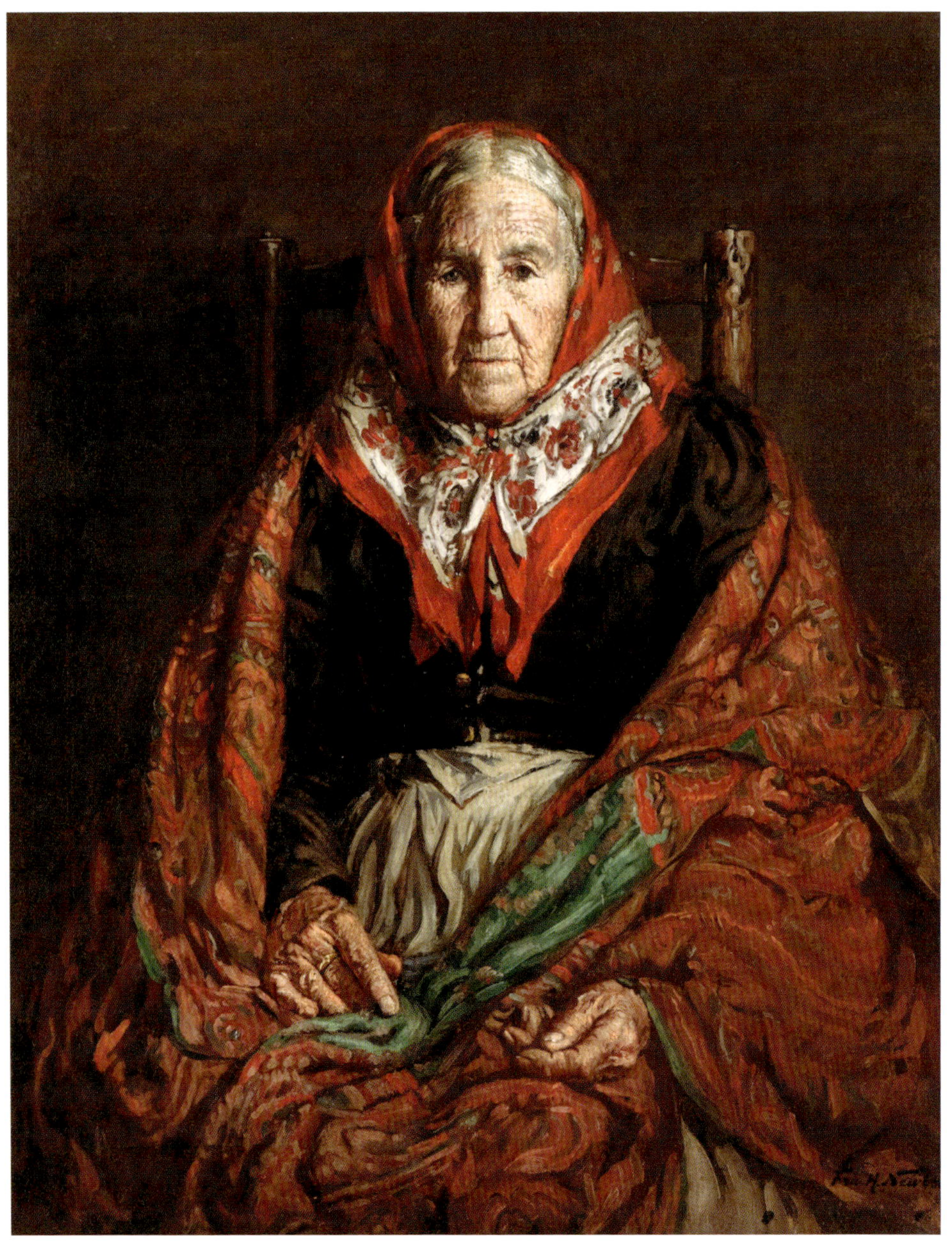

2.1 | Fra Newbery | *The Paisley Shawl* | *c.*1907, oil on canvas, 101 x 81 cm

2 MATERIALISING BALKANIC DORSET AND MORE

Painting needlecraft

Their art, like that of other peasants, is a spontaneous one, arising out of man's first idea for ornament, a desire to bring something bright into their daily lives, a natural longing to possess comely homes and comely dress. It is something their very own which they cherish as such. Only those in true sympathy with the peasant can rightly measure it.[1]

It would be easy to dismiss *Serbian Women* as a one-off, Western mélange in which an out-of-step, romantic English painter exoticised 'distant' peoples and customs. Yet, it was part of a very real connection the untrammelled Fra and Jessie felt to the power of textile art and with it the wealth of rural traditions and their benefit to the modern era. As such it can be taken as a criticism of the contemporary 'Western' machine age, whose capitalist urban industrial basis was, in many respects, a process of alienation and self-destruction, as predicated by Karl Marx in the 1860s. Fra and Jessie were known to have 'socialist sympathies', their own work being informed by, representing and encouraging respect for 'the dignity and hardship of the labourer's life'.[2] Thus, though they may have reaped some of the rewards of bourgeois living, their artistic championing of the folk, including reform and re-invention through things and ways folkish, went hand-in-hand with retreat from the rule of city, machine and empire. Furthermore, they were by no means alone in their campaign and approach, for, as we have just seen through the examples of postcards they gathered, they actually were part of a widespread (if underacknowledged) creative alternative to, or indeed adjunct of, modernist trends.

Serbian Women belongs to a line of Fra's paintings which concentrated on fabric production and dress design as a worldwide mover and

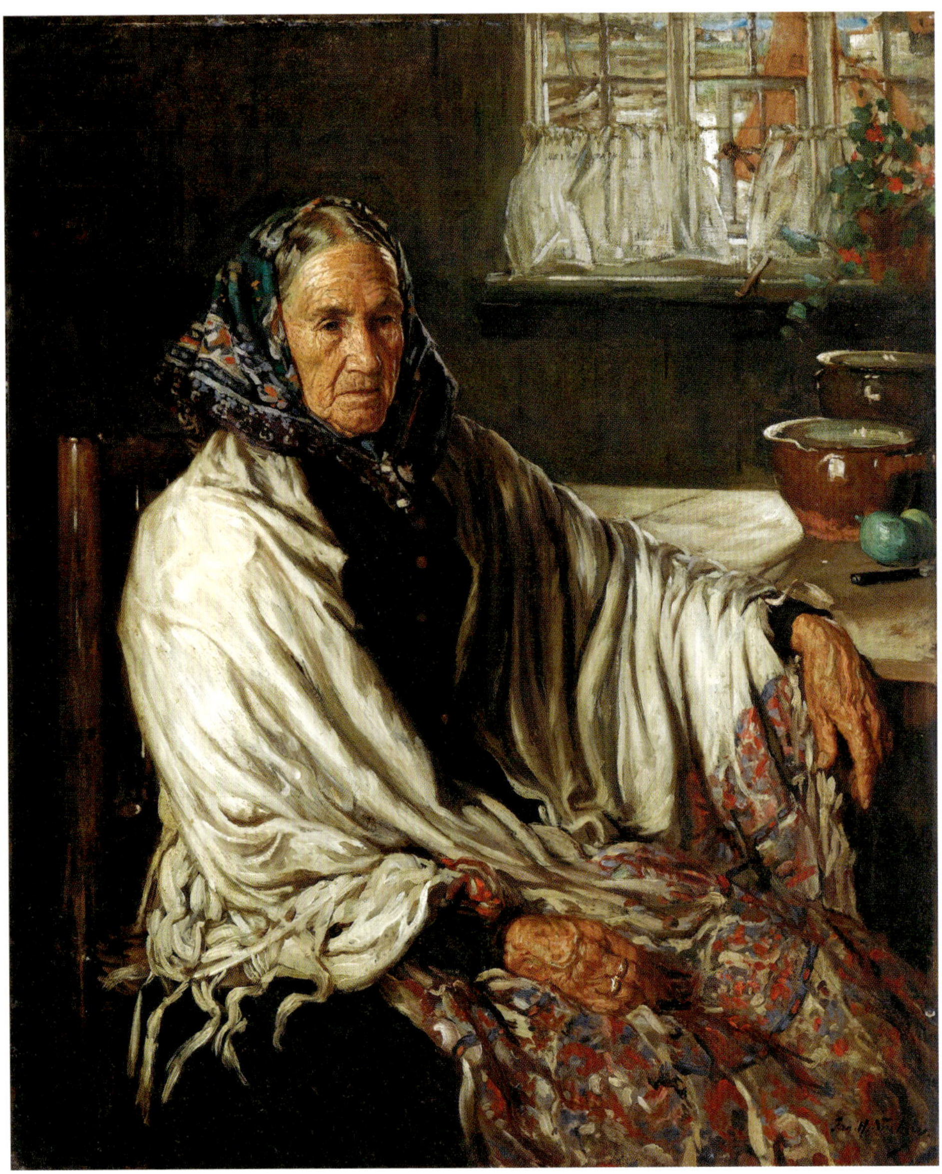

2.2 | Fra Newbery | *Portrait of a Devonian* | 1908, oil on canvas, 114.5 x 95 cm

2.3 | Fra Newbery | *The Lady of the Carnation* | c.1916, oil on canvas, 163 x 73 cm

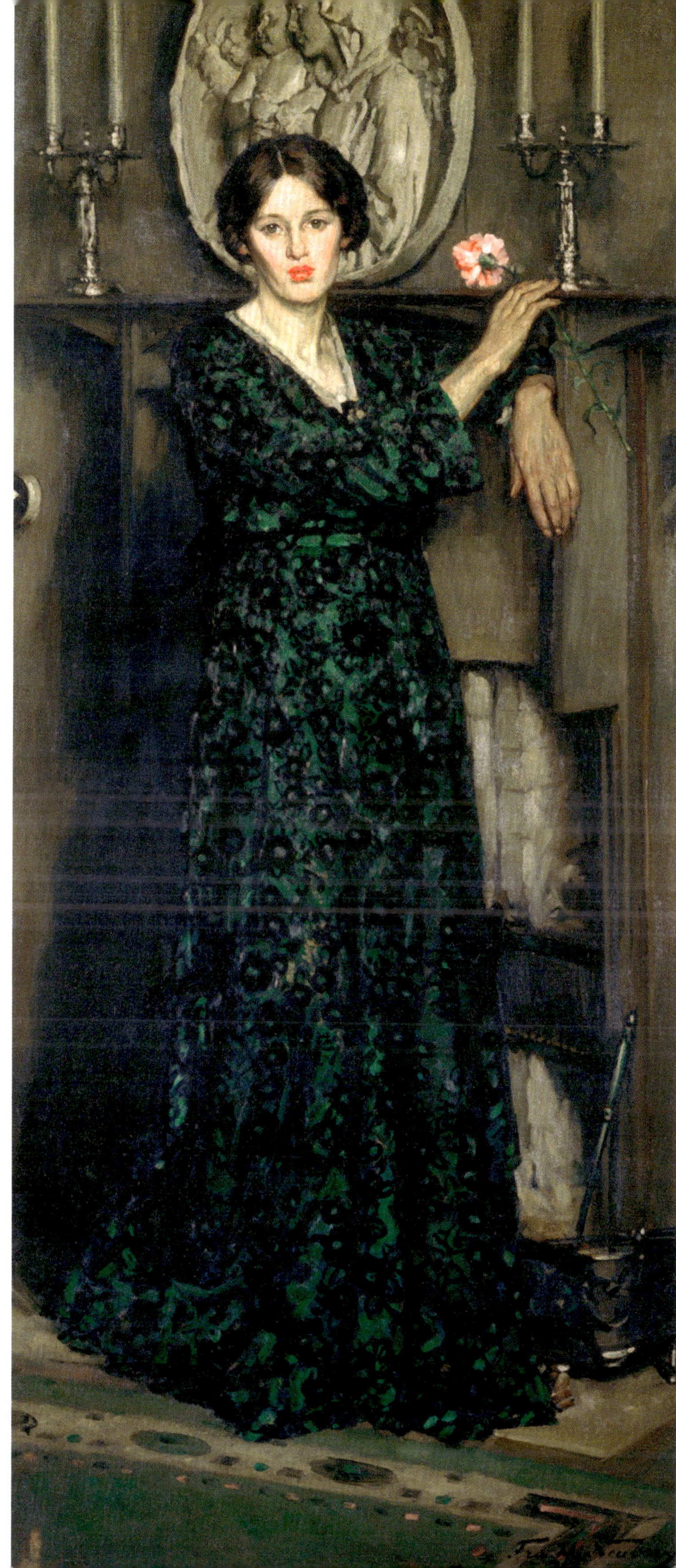

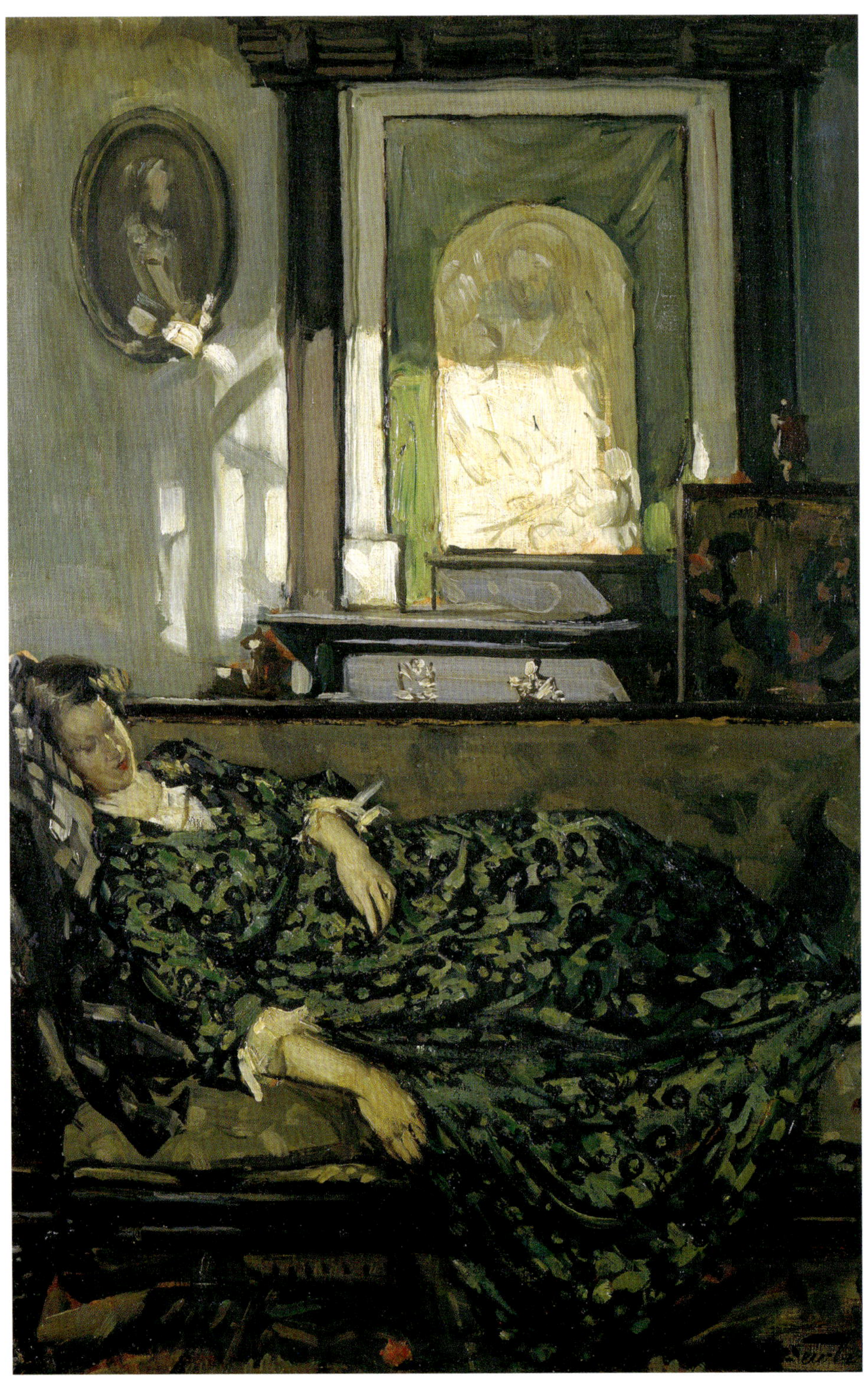

2.4 | Fra Newbery | *Daydreams* | *c.*1927, oil on canvas, 82.5 x 51 cm

keeper of convention. While turning his women models into accoutrements of clothing and painterly style, his objectification, far from reducing them to stereotypes, still brought out their individuality. This can be seen in numerous works, including *My Lady Greensleeves* (*c.*1905), *The Paisley Shawl* (*c.*1907) [fig. 2.1], *Portrait of a Devonian* (1908) [fig. 2.2], *The Mirror* (*c.*1911), *The Spanish Shawl* (*c.*1916), *The Lady of the Carnation* (*c.*1916) [fig. 2.3], *Daydreams* (*c.*1927) [fig. 2.4].[3] In such paintings he held back from naming his subjects in the works' titles and instead used more general descriptors. *Paisley Shawl* and *Devonian*, which both use a Mrs Cleeve from the Bideford area of north Devon as their model, betray a debt to Rembrandt in their evocative treatment of elderly figure in darkened interior. They also harken to particular place and textile tradition.

Such tendencies then make way for touches of James McNeill Whistler's aestheticism, Fra's relish of visible brushstroke, colour and composition combining with a cropped, 'feminine' interior space, as witnessed in *Lady of the Carnation* and *Daydreams*. The former was painted while the Newberys were still based in Scotland. It has a slender vertical format and symmetrical composition focused on a central full-figure: a tense young woman in long, modern, richly patterned green-and-black dress designed and made by Jessie around 1912. She stands in front of a Glasgow Style fireplace, her head enhaloed by a mother and child plaster relief, the pink carnation in her right hand adding to the aesthetic effect while symbolising Marian love and gratitude. By the time Fra painted *Daydreams* in Dorset, though his abiding preference for shades of green is still evident, now his model reclines on a sofa in the lower half of the painting. Above her, in dappled sunlight, is a diagonal of three loosely rendered images of women, from an oval-framed society portrait, to 'plaster' Madonna and child 'altarpiece', through to square, possibly oriental, recumbant figure. Fra borrowed the dress from Jessie, she herself wearing it before passing it on to her daughter Mary. It was to become key for the most informative article to date on Jessie's practice and aesthetic principles: Margaret Swain's 'Mrs Newbery's Dress'.[4] Informed by an interview with Mary and study of the actual 'silk cut velvet' dress, Swain not only revealed its use in *Daydreams* but also the following details, thereby indicating Jessie's mastery and vision:

> *The skirt is softly gathered, but by no means full, so that the design of the material may still be appreciated. The bodice is cut in one with the slightly bell-shaped sleeves, and crosses over at the front, held in place by a belt of self material. The V-neck is lined with Mrs Newbery's very characteristic white lace inset gathered by narrow black velvet ribbon. The sleeve is lined with an inner frill of lace, only to be glimpsed when the arm is raised. The Russian pendant … of gilt metal inset with coral … worn with it, was a favourite ornament.*

One of the earliest of Fra's paintings to play with the power of women's textile work, and thereby also anticipating *Serbian Women*, is *The Embroideress* (1903) [fig. 2.7]. For this image reveals the Newberys' mutual persuasions for female dress as signifer of both reform movement and local tradition. Significantly, *The Embroideress* was actually a portrait of their German friend, the singer Anna Muthesius, painted at the height of her campaigning, in both written word and material art, for life reform.[6] It was not coincidental that a colour reproduction of Fra's painting was turned into the front cover of the leading Munich arts magazine *Jugend* in August 1904, this appearing after Muthesius had published *A Woman's Personal Dress* [*Das Eigenkleid der Frau*] in Krefeld the previous year.[7] The book was her call for each woman to clothe herself in keeping with her own style and life needs, and to do so by taking up dress design and making, thereby avoiding being a slave to the inhibiting strictures of mainstream fashion, convention and economics. The volume featured a Frances Macdonald McNair cover of three graphic Glasgow Style Graces in loose teardrop- and wing-shaped

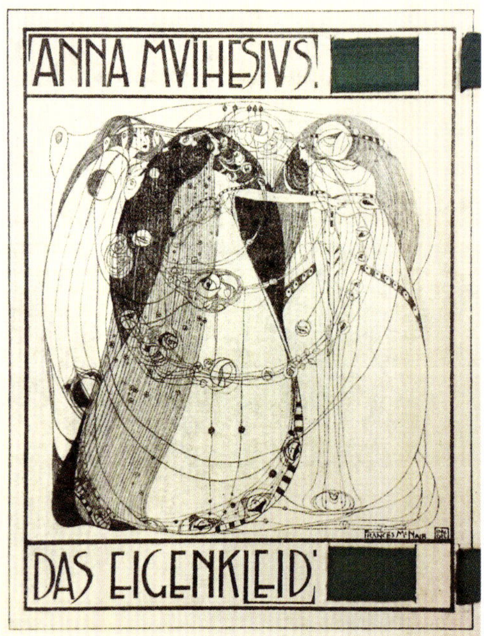

2.5 | Frances Macdonald McNair, illustration; from Anna Muthesius, *Das Eigenkleid der Frau* (Krefeld: Kramer & Baum, 1903), cover

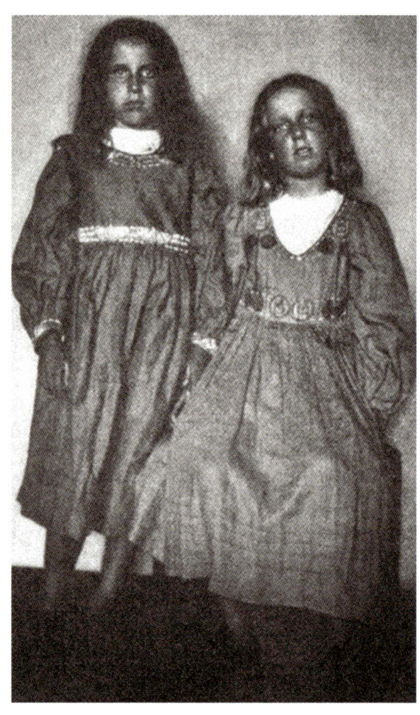

2.6 | Two linen dresses worn by Elsie and Mary Newbery [photo by Jessie Newbery], from Anna Muthesius, *Das Eigenkleid der Frau*, (Krefeld: Kramer & Baum, 1903), p. III

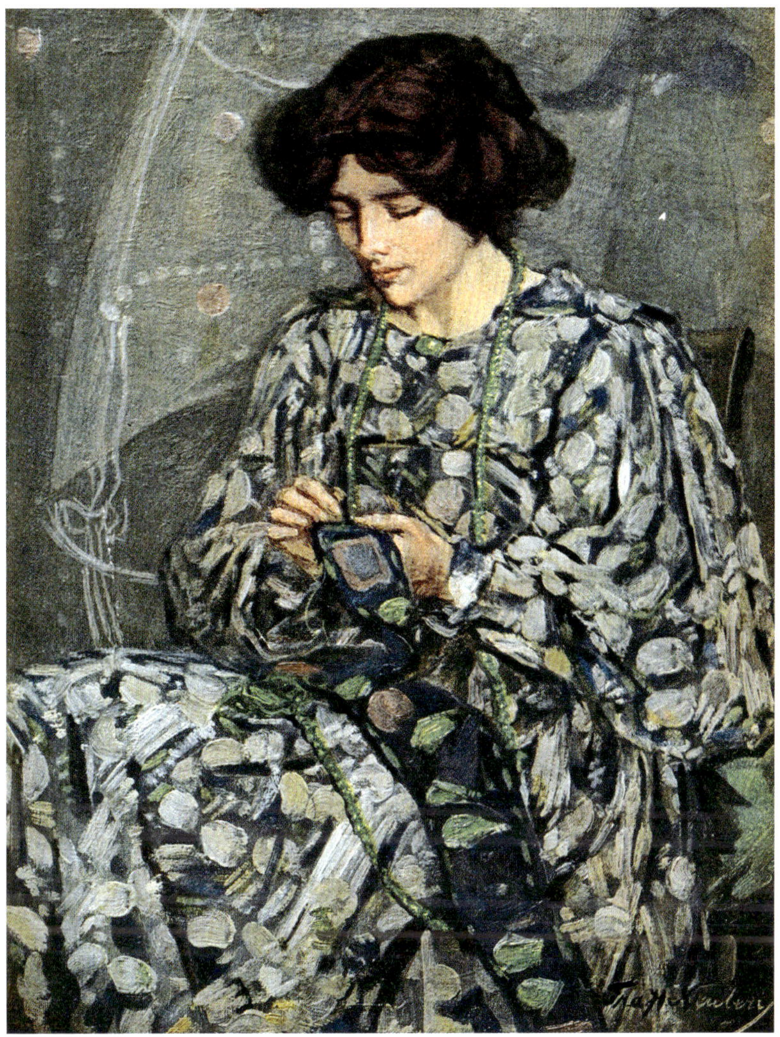

2.7 | Fra Newbery | *The Embroideress* [Anna Muthesius] | 1903
from *Jugend*, vol. 9, no. 33, 1904, cover

dresses, their flattened, organic forms woven together and comprising a flowing, energised linear web replete with symbols of abstract roses [fig. 2.5]. It was concluded by fourteen associated black-and-white photographs of women in a variety of modern dress, the final one of which was of two comfortable knee-length green linen dresses replete with appliqué and embroidery by Jessie, these being modelled by her daughters Elsie and Mary [fig. 2.6].

In Fra's painting of Muthesius she is depicted seated, three-quarter frontal and very close-up. She appears at ease in the abstract green cocoon of flattened space around her, which contains hints of a standing female figure in a long loose dress above her left shoulder and some

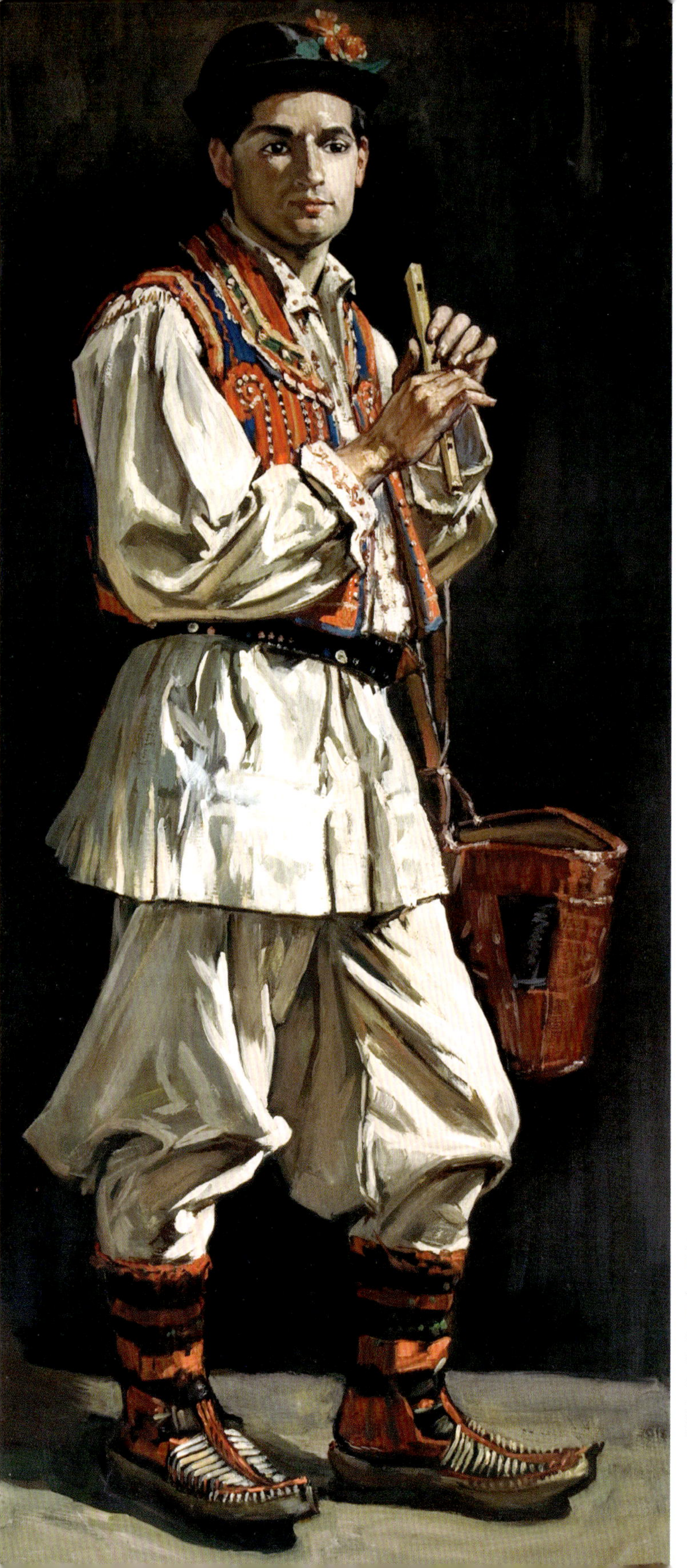

2.8
Fra Newbery
A Serbian Musician
[David Brynley]
1927, oil on canvas,
163 x 74 cm

curving dotted and unbroken linear borders to her right. Wearing a vividly patterned, flowing modern dress with generous loose sleeves, she devotes all her attention to the handiwork going on above her lap.[8] Her neck and face with downcast eyes appear pale under her thick mop of dark hair, held up gently by a dark ribbon seen on her forehead. She is embroidering a girdle, stitching a hem near its clasp, and the girdle and her arms overlap a long loose necklace of green beads. As such she becomes an icon of modern European womanhood and simultaneously (albeit around twenty-seven years in advance) a counterpart to *Serbian Women*. In fact, for all their apparent conservatism, the figures of *Serbian Women* likewise wear loose, ample clothes that, far from inhibiting their craft and daily activities (as dictated in constraining, corseted metropolitan fashion worlds), were at once pragmatic and personally made beautiful items. Notice, then, the similarities in pose, activity and convenient dress between Muthesius and the woman on the right in *Serbian Women*.

Painting 'Serbian' folk

Serbian Women was but one of a set of Balkan-influenced artworks that the Newberys created in this period. First, from 1928 Fra began to exhibit (in Glasgow, Paisley and Edinburgh) oil paintings with Serbian titles: *A Serbian Musician*, *A Serbian Woman*, *A Serbian*, *Serbian Folk*.[9] It would seem that he altered some titles as the works moved between exhibition venues. *A Serbian Musician* survives, this being an almost life-size portrait of David Brynley, a flamboyant young tenor singer and resident of Woolgarston, a hamlet neighbouring Corfe Castle [fig. 2.8]. Brynley was known to be a special favourite of the Newberys and was often to be found in their company.[10] He is shown full-length and turning towards us from a three-quarter frontal position. He wears Croatian dress, replete with embroidered *lajbek* waistcoat, *skrlak* hat and *frula* (or *jedinka*) pipe, and most probably from the Prigorje vicinity of Zagreb, but with Serbian *opanci* (sandals).[11] His shepherd-like appearance is completed by his satchel, which looks very similar to the basket holding a spindle of wound wool on the bench in *Serbian Women*.[12] Brynley's attire derived from the collection of peasant art purchased by the Newberys on their 1926 Balkan tour. The *lajbek*, linen tunic and pantalones have been passed down through the family generations. Of these it is the *lajbek* which is the most eye-catching, its blue cotton being decorated with a plethora of red, white, green and straw-coloured embroidery [fig. 2.9 a–b]. This comprises a symmetrical arrangement of bold straight and curving lines formed of intricate waves, arabesques, loops. Covering much of the material surface the

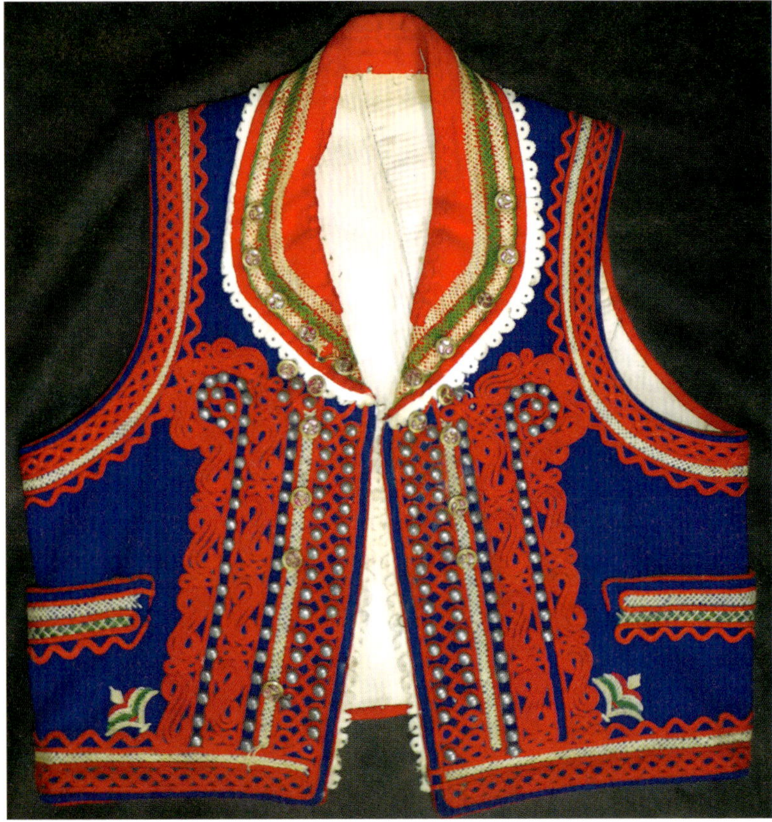

2.9 a–b | Croatian waistcoat [*Lajbek*], pre-1927, cotton, wool, sequins

lines are joined by floral, star and budding circle motifs on front and back.[13] The main verticals of the front, two of which on each side join in a fern-like curve to meet the shoulder hem, and the bands of the collar, are filled with multiple sequins and buttons that follow their course, and which stand out in *A Serbian Musician*. Brynley is caught in a moment of time, poised as if ready to take the pipe to his lips, and looking past the viewer with a somewhat dreamy gaze. Being an accomplished professional opera singer, his performance appears natural though his abstract, almost monochrome, surrounds betray the fact that this is a studio piece (as does Helen Muspratt's photograph of the painting – see below).

If the camp Brynley is Fra's Dorset deceit of a Balkan shepherd, in such performance it joins *Serbian Women* and two other known paintings of the period. That said, *A Serbian Musician*'s elongated vertical format and focus on a single figure means it more particularly resembles the two paintings which feature individual women in Balkan costume. The first has a young woman posing, with distaff and spindle, in

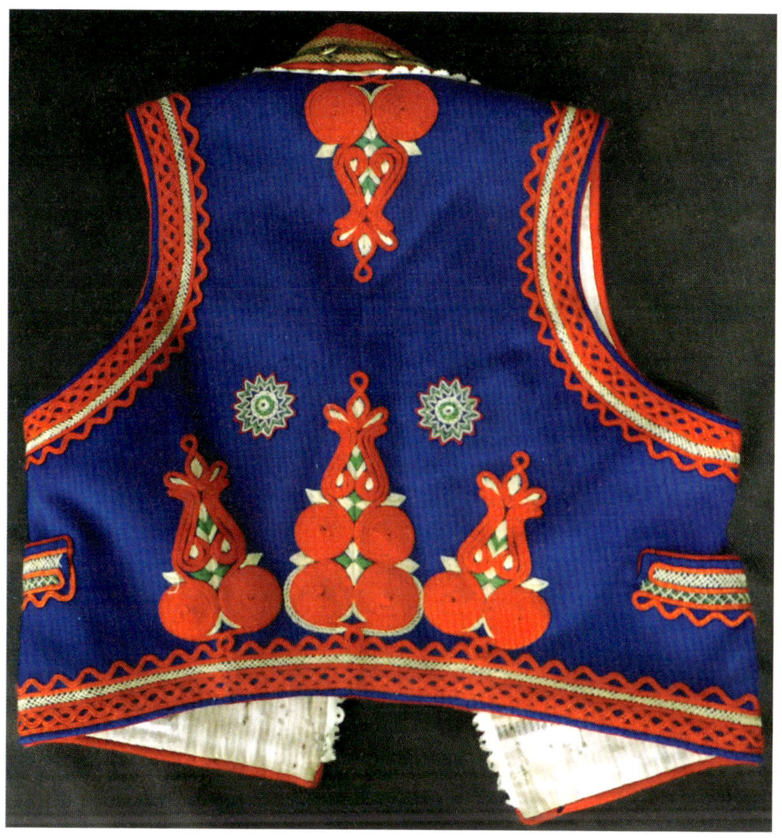

front of a mirror in Fra's Dorset studio [fig. 2.10]. It may well be that this was the painting titled *A Serbian Woman* that he exhibited at the Society of Scottish Artists' exhibition in Edinburgh in December 1928. An anonymous reviewer for the *Aberdeen Press and Journal* made pertinent associations:

> *Akin to the portraits are one or two fine figure subjects … the boldness of Mr F.H. Newbery's* Serbian Woman *and the exotic decoration of Mr* [sic] *M.R.* [Marjorie Rorie] *Caird's* In Xanadu *and* St Jean – *embroidery in oils … Colour and the older manner attract in … Mr Newbery's pyramidal* Corfe Castle.[14]

That the figure of *A Serbian Woman* is represented in the studio against a backdrop of a large framed figurative painting, cheval mirror and gate-leg table with large ceramic jug serves to highlight her artificiality.[15] Any semblance of make-believe, including the act of winding fibre, is deliberately undermined by such a setting. Furthermore, the

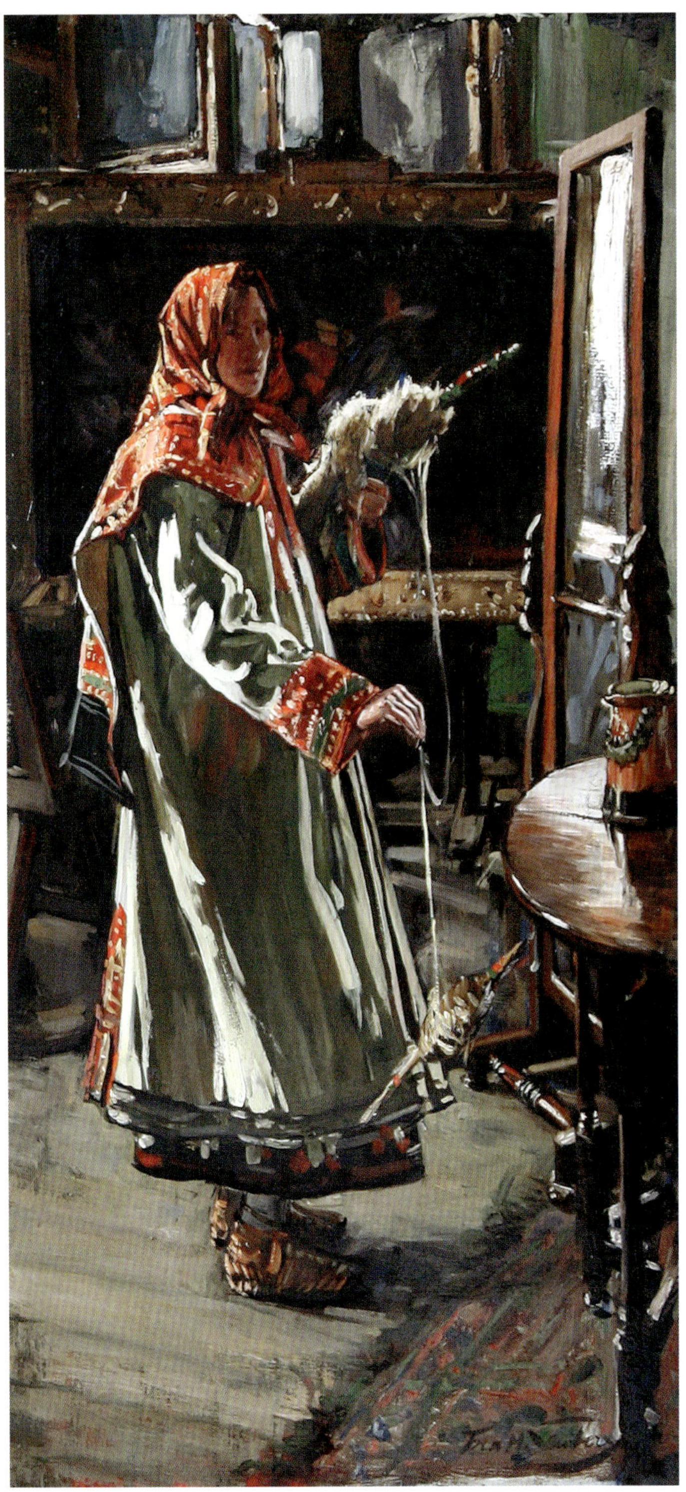

2.10 | Fra Newbery | *A Serbian Woman* | *c.* 1928, oil on canvas, 132 x 64 cm
PRIVATE COLLECTION

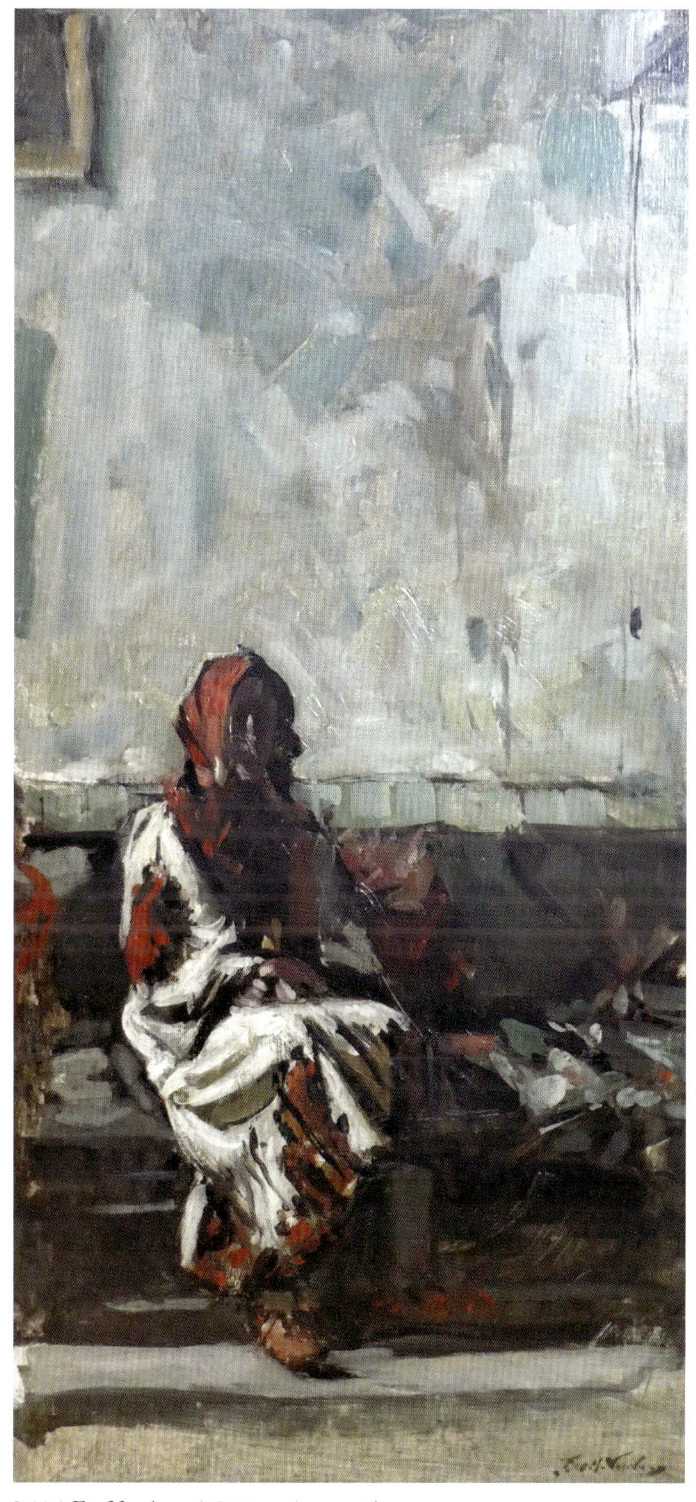

2.11 | Fra Newbery | *Patience* | 1930, oil on canvas, 92 x 45 cm

woman's body is now seen from the side, her costume lit from an external source of light behind her, and the mirror so slanted as to reflect light rather than the figure. So, although she turns her head to face the viewer, her features are in shadow, the embroidery on the red trims of her clothes blurred dabs of rich patterning. Nevertheless, from such elements of her headscarf, stole and cuffs, as well as from the loose tunic, hint of skirt and strapped *opanci*, we can read the woman as having donned authentic Balkan garb.

For all that *A Serbian Woman*'s face is shaded, what we can see of her features suggests she is probably Lucy Orchard, one of Fra's favourite Corfe models. Close comparison of his portrait of Lucy (1925, not shown in this book)[16] reveals not just similar studio setting and accoutrements (cheval mirror, round table, hints of background paintings) but also a young woman or teenage girl with dark hair, straight nose contours and cheek structures that resemble those of *A Serbian Woman*. Furthermore, these also correlate with the hair and face of the woman on the right in *Serbian Women*.

The second painting of a single 'Serbian' woman gained the title *Patience* when exhibited in 1931, although it may have been entitled *A Serbian* as a work with that title was shown by Fra at the Royal Glasgow Institute in 1929 [fig. 2.11]. It is much freer in its brushwork and more abstract in its definition than any of the other known 'Serbian' pictures. It appears to show a figure in the same garb as the younger woman in *Serbian Women*, with which it was shown at the 1931 Paisley exhibition. Now, however, the passage of time that the woman represents leads to indistinction. So although she also is seated, and directly facing the viewer, she becomes blurred, as if in a photograph where the sitter has moved slightly while the aperture was open. The notion of her representing 'waiting' or 'patience' is made manifest by her inactivity and crossed leg. In addition, the cropping of the bench upon which she sits and the frame at the upper left corner, as well as the apparent blemishes and decay of the beige wall behind her, suggests that the world continues to move both in and beyond the picture while she remains in her place, left to look forward in anticipation from under her red headscarf.

Performing synthetic Balkanism

The 'Yugoslav' qualities of the four extant 'Serbian folk' paintings detailed above accord with two further, exceptional, collaborative artworks that follow a similar vein. On 2 July 1927 Newbery organised a pageant in his home village of Corfe Castle. Having created, together with local craftsmen, a new village sign dedicated to Saint Edward the Martyr, the teenage king of Wessex who had been murdered close

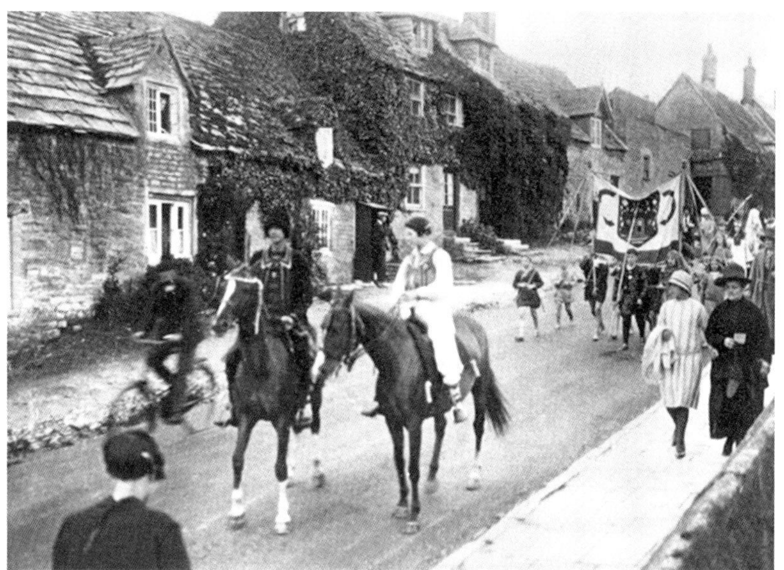

2.12 | Hilda and Mary Spencer Watson as 'Amazons', Corfe Castle, 2 July 1927

to the castle in 978, he turned its inauguration into an event of syncretic performance.[17] In so doing he garnered as much creative force from within the community as was possible: his martial, festal, historicist and parochial songs and recitations were performed by the parish schoolchildren, librettos set to music by Brynley, instruments of fiddles and drums played by eight youngsters. The children were led, by two 'Amazons' on horseback, in a procession from school to village square and back again [fig. 2.12]. The 'Amazons' were Mary Spencer Watson and her mother Hilda dressed, as surviving photographs show, in Balkan costumes, with Mary wearing the outfit, complete with *lajbek*, of Brynley in *A Serbian Musician* and Hilda adorned in the style of Vojvodina, northern Serbia. The new sign was unveiled by the village 'queen', in this case thirteen-year-old Edna Moss, dressed in a very similar costume (derived from the Upper Vardar region or nearby Kosovo) to the figure on the right in *Serbian Women*, only this time with crown rather than headscarf [figs 2.13, 2.14]. The children themselves were in costumes that could be called a loose interpretation of Balkan and Anglo-Saxon, these having been designed by Jessie Newbery and made by the village dressmaker Mrs F. Orchard. With Mrs Orchard's daughter Lucy seemingly the model for the right-hand woman in *Serbian Women*, it is quite possible that her yarn-winding companion is none other than her mother since, as we have seen with Brynley, Fra enjoyed romantic representations of his sitters in their professional roles.[18]

The photograph of the unveiling of the Corfe Castle sign also reveals a girl in some form of peasant dress holding a dressed distaff.

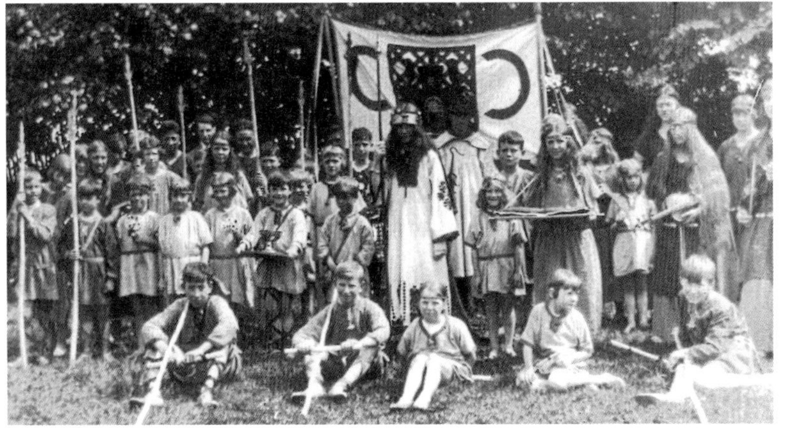

2.13 | 'Children and the Village Queen', Corfe Castle, 2 July 1927

This may have been the one acquired by Newbery when he and Jessie visited Sofia, Bulgaria in the autumn of 1926, though many of the girls in the pageant bore distaffs. She stands prominently before the 'Balkan Amazons', who themselves are neighboured by Fra Newbery (wearing a white hat with dark headband). Her pose is suggestive of a 'virgin and child' and this association may not have been coincidental given another of Newbery's late works: a large altarpiece named *Annunciation* (1930) that he produced for the Roman Catholic Church of the Holy

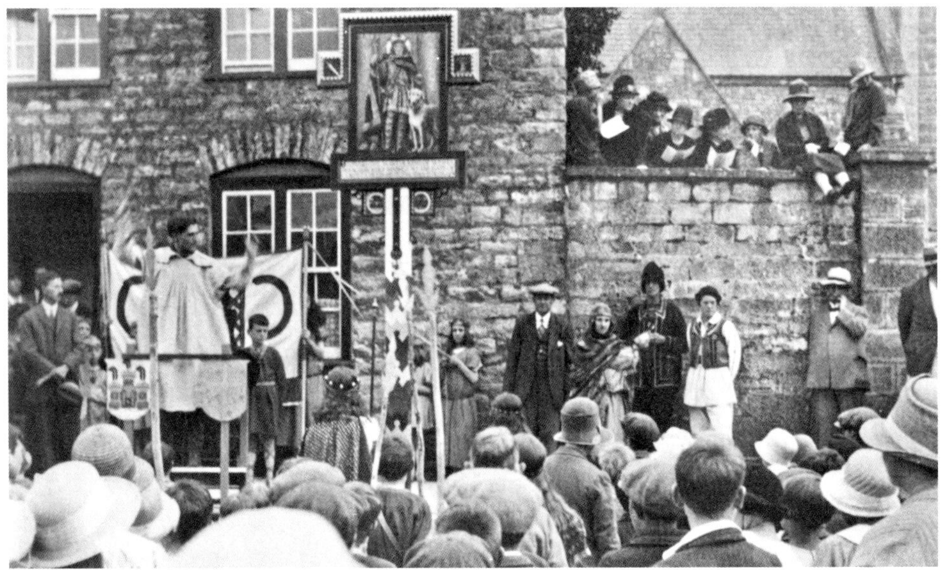

2.14 | 'Unveiling of the Village Sign', 2 July 1927

Ghost and Saint Edward, Swanage, the nearest coastal town to Corfe Castle [fig. 2.16].[19] This was part of a decorative scheme he and Jessie realised for the Lady Chapel in the west (liturgical 'south') transept of the church, adding to that which they had already produced for the sanctuary.[20] The scheme, replete with surrounding stencilled frieze of roses, lilies and the Annunciation text of 'Ave Maria gratia plena', was to be Fra and Jessie's last, and most important, work of such kind.

Annunciation is also the apotheosis of the Newberys' synthetic Balkanism. Attended by two child angels and in fine silk and lace clerical vestments, a celestial Archangel Gabriel makes his pronouncement of theotokos to the Virgin Mary. Simultaneously Gabriel points upwards in reference to the Holy Spirit (a barely visible visage with aureole appears in the sky above) and offers a white rose. Mary is seated in the bottom right corner of the image in a garden of blossoming flowers (white Michaelmas daisies, foxgloves, lilies and roses arranged along a low wattle fence).

She wears 'old Serbian', that is Macedonian (see below), robes akin to those of the pageant queen and the right-hand figure in *Serbian Women*, only now under a nimbus and dark blue mantle. Comparison with illustrations from Bossert [fig. 2.15 a–b] show a remarkable similarity in the embroidered hem and sleeve motifs of her vestments and those of a woman's costume from Vodna, near Skopje, Macedonia (and then in the Ethnographic Museum, Zagreb). Furthermore, she is seated before a ciborium of Balkan-oriental appearance, through which can be seen a waxing crescent moon, representative of generative power. The pantiles and wooden brackets recall such elements of vernacular housing in, for instance, Macedonia and Kosovo. In addition, Mary is winding red yarn, from distaff to spindle in a pose similar to that of the left-hand figure in *Serbian Women*. The 'third hand' of the distaff is ornate, its plentiful fibre held in place by red braid. In the bottom right corner is a warp mill dressed with some white yarn. As with the dark blue of her mantle, the spinning Virgin is a motif borrowed by Newbery from Byzantine sources, and in all likelihood, Balkan versions of these.[21] Here then we see an artist in interwar Britain referencing the idea of Mary as one of celestial motherhood and her spinning as symbolic of the act of (pro)creation: Christ's body is a fabric spun and woven by the Madonna.

The pale face of the *Annunciation's* Virgin might be archetypal but it is also likely to be from a Corfe or family model. In any case, it recalls, as does the seated, spinning maiden motif, that of Newbery's centrepiece, *The Spirit of Bridport* (1924–27), for his painted decoration of the town hall in the Dorset town where he had grown up and first studied art in the 1870s [fig. 2.17]. Uncoincidentally, not least given his and Jessie's beliefs in the vital efficacy of textile art as well as the town's previous economic reliance on the textile industry, this slightly earlier

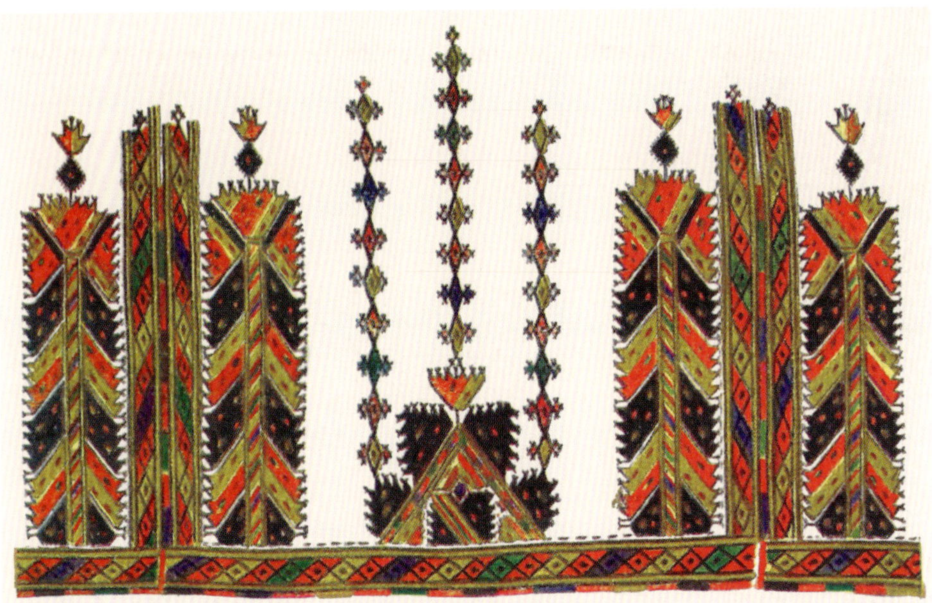

2.15 a–b | Drawings of hem and sleeve motifs, embroidery, Vodna, Macedonia; from H. Th. Bossert, *Volkskunst in Europa* (Berlin: Verlag Ernst Wasmuth, 1926), plate 85

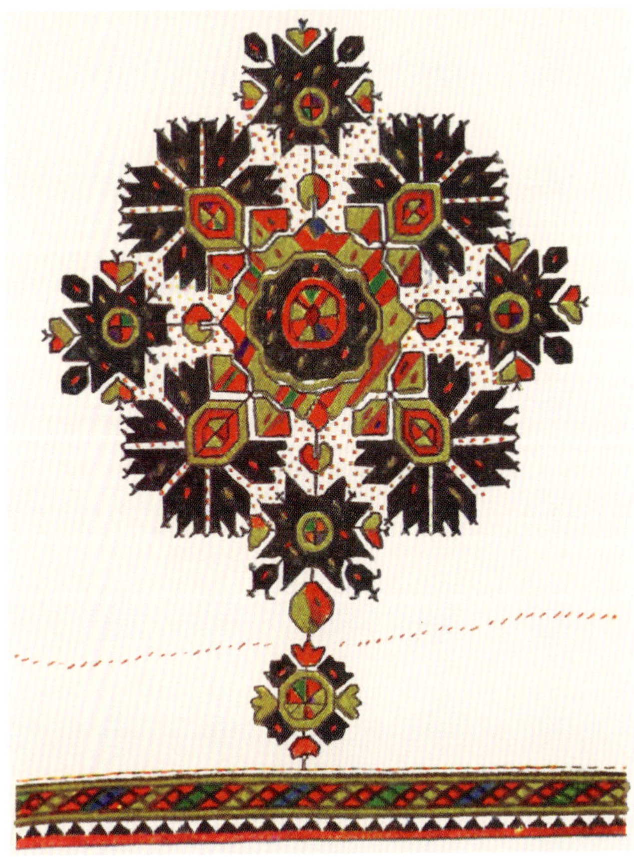

2.16
Fra Newbery
Annunciation
1930, Church of the
Holy Spirit [formerly
Holy Ghost] and St
Edward, Swanage, oil
on canvas, 304 x 162 cm

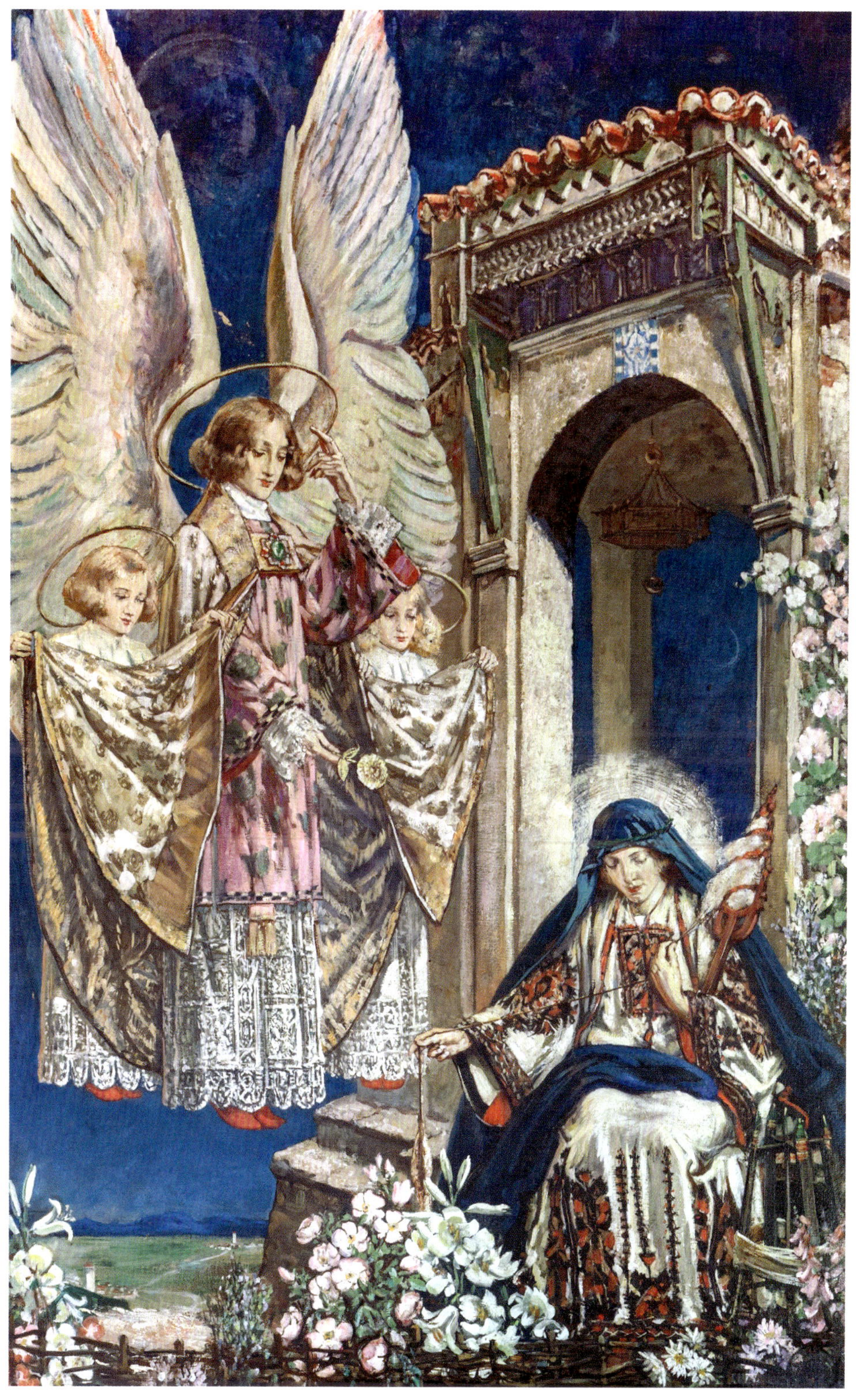

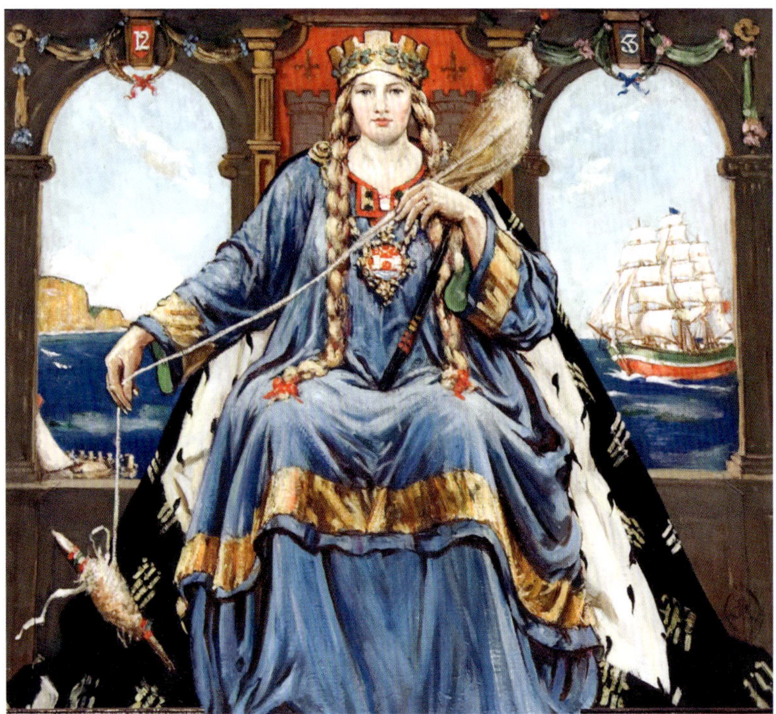

2.17 | Fra Newbery | *The Spirit of Bridport* | 1924–27
central section of mural, Bridport Town Hall, oil on panel, *c.* 90 x 104 cm

decorative scheme was also dedicated to the production of fabric. In this case we know that the Bridport *Spirit* is a local girl, Kathleen Reynolds, and as such it is she who acted as a prototype for the Serbian Madonna in the Swanage *Annunciation*. We can also see a clear relationship with an earlier mural painted in Dundee by the Scottish Symbolist John Duncan (see below, chapter three).

Entwining the Balkan spirit

Muspratt

The faces of the Swanage spinning Mary's three revelatory feminised visitors in the sky are based on two other Fra models: the young Swanage photographer Helen Muspratt as both Gabriel and one of his angel attendants and possibly Lucy Orchard (*Serbian Women*) as the second attendant. The collaboration and friendship of Muspratt and Fra was particularly productive around this time. For her part Muspratt took the best portrait photographs of Fra and Jessie from their Corfe years [figs 2.18, 2.19].[22] In addition, she photographed the *Annunciation* and *Serbian Musician* in Fra's studio, the first also comprising a portrait of the artist, since he stands beside the painting, palette and brushes in hand, in overalls and bow-tie, facing the camera [figs 2.20, 2.21]. Muspratt turned both into bromide prints, the dense silver areas of which have acquired, over time, a bluish sheen. That of *Serbian Musician* (which she mounted and signed) included, instead of Fra himself, a cropped view of his workshop, with its fragments of door, heating pipe, mug, papers, candelabrum and miscellaneous images appearing,

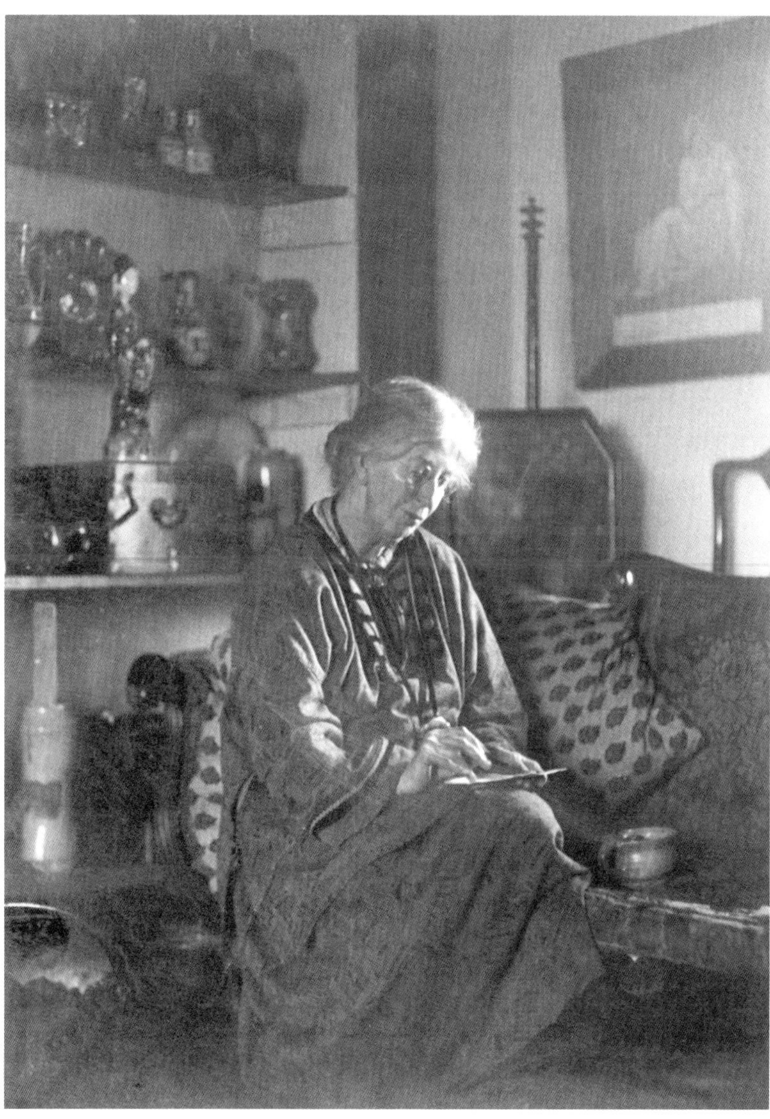

2.18 | Helen Muspratt, *Portrait of Jessie Newbery, c.* 1929

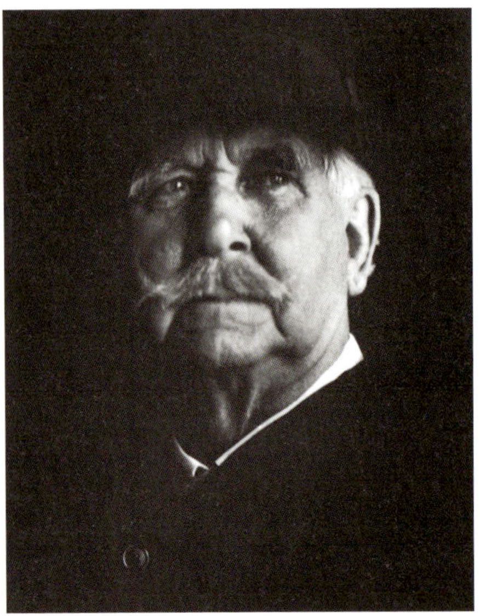

2.19 | Helen Muspratt, *Portrait of Fra Newbery*, *c.* 1929
PRIVATE COLLECTION

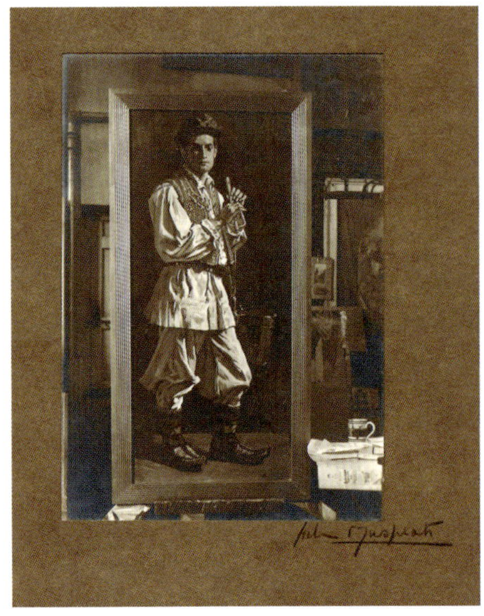

2.20 | Helen Muspratt, 'Fra Newbery's *Serbian Musician*', *c.* 1928
PRIVATE COLLECTION

together with the off-centre painting, like an abstract collage. One reason for such work by Muspratt was that Fra would send out copies of these as greeting cards to his friends. It is known, for example, that, appropriately, he turned Muspratt's rendering of him painting the *Annunciation* into a Christmas card, preparing one for his friend John Taylor Ewen in the year he completed the Swanage commission.[23]

In return, Fra painted Muspratt's portrait replete with camera and photographs, as well as designing the decoration and spaces of her two Swanage studios, her letterhead and shop signboard. She essentially became his last student, herself later acknowledging 'He taught me all I know about art.'[24] He gave her introductions and encouraged her further study. In this regard, their relationship also takes us back to the postcards with which we began our enquiry. For Fra sent Muspratt postcards from trips to Yugoslavia (1929) and Italy (1930). The latter, the chronological last in our series, may serve as an introduction to the former [fig. 2.22]. Sent on 16 October 1930, from a European sojourn made shortly after the completion of the Swanage *Annunciation*, Fra's (and Jessie's) greeting was, inevitably perhaps, both visual and literary: 'Here is the Saint (Gimignano) with his many towered town on his lap. The quaintest place we have ever been in. Regards from both to you and Mrs Muspratt.'[25] The picture was a black-and-white photographic reproduction of the central panel of Taddeo di Bartolo's polyptych of the life of Saint Geminianus (*c.* 1401) that was originally the reredos in the Collegiate Church of San Gimignano, Tuscany. Fra's attraction

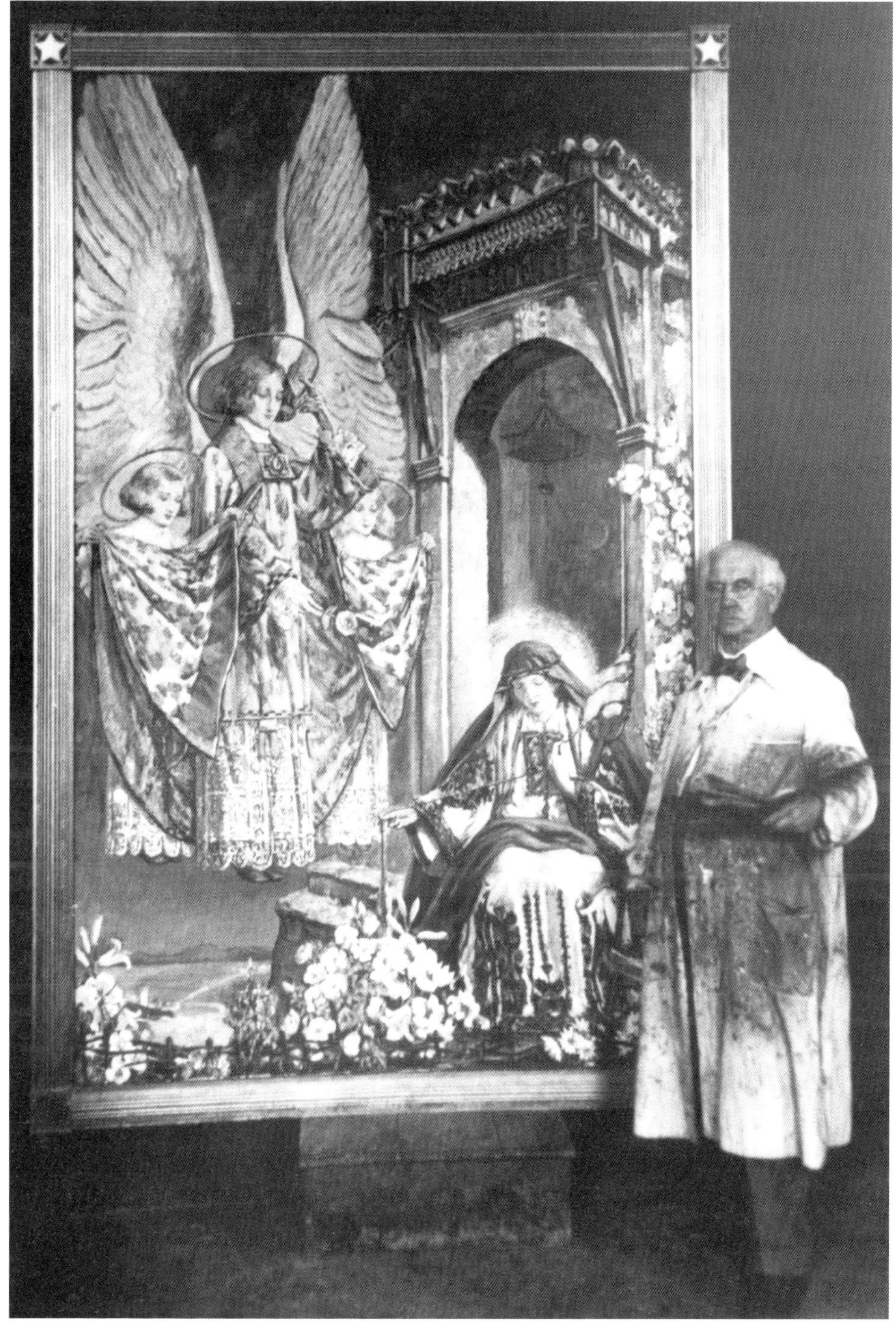

2.21 | Helen Muspratt, 'Fra Newbery painting *Annunciation*', 1930

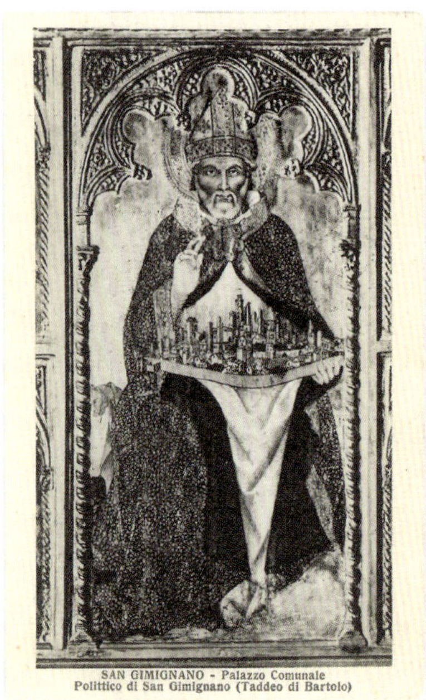

2.22 | Taddeo di Bartolo, *Life of Saint Geminianus*, *c.* 1401, central panel of reredos, Collegiate Church of San Gimignano, Tuscany, postcard (Edizione Logi Alessandro & Figli, San Gimignano (4-3175), *c.* 1930)

2.23 | Fra Newbery | *Saint Aldhelm* | 1926 altarpiece, left panel, Church of the Holy Spirit and St Edward, Swanage, oil on canvas, *c.* 240 x 70 cm

to the Gothic image of Geminianus, who, as Bishop of Modena, had become patron of the medieval Sienese hill town which received his name, can be related to the altarpiece he created in 1926 for the sanctuary of the Swanage Roman Catholic church. For the left panel of this triptych represented Saint Aldhelm, first bishop of Sherborne, Dorset, holding a model of the abbey for which he paved the way [fig. 2.23]. Thus, in choosing the card for Muspratt, Fra drew an historical thread and made a visual analogy between it and his own episcopal celebration, just metres from his model and student's incarnation as Gabriel in the Balkanist *Annunciation*.

Meštrović

Fra's first postcard to Muspratt was written eight days after Jessie had sent Mary Spencer Watson her card of the Dalmatian women 'in' Zara. Despatched from Dubrovnik, in keeping with Muspratt's profession Fra chose a card with a black-and-white photograph featuring a distant view of the coastal village of Cavtat. Given the way she was to turn his paintings into manipulated photographs it is no surprise that he addresses her as 'Artist Photographer'. Then, by way of introduction, he revealed his appreciation of Yugoslavia's most prominent modern artist: 'This little place contains the Račić monument, one of the greatest of Meštrović, the sculptor's work.'

In drawing Muspratt's attention to Ivan Meštrović, Fra was conveying his knowledge of the plastic master whose sublime monumental forms were at once powerfully mythopoetic, modern, timeless and, by 1929, of high renown. Often they were also distinctively Balkanic. Both Meštrović and Fra had shown at the Royal Glasgow Institute's 1915 exhibition, the Yugoslav's presence being the highlight:

> *On entering the first Court one is brought at once into contact with a great mind expressing itself in a large and grand manner. Each of the works of Ivan Mestrovic, the Serbian sculptor, is worthy of a notice itself. I mention only* Women Dancing, *a marble in low relief;* Head of the Artist's Wife, *also in marble;* Shepherd Boy, *a life-sized bronze; and the* Heroic Head, *lent by Mr Lavery. These are full of great beauty and nobleness – the work of a genius.*[26]

I have so far been unable to ascertain whether Fra and Meštrović were personally acquainted but, from 1911, 'Mr Lavery' – Fra's close friend and artistic ally, the former 'Glasgow Boy' painter, John Lavery – was in close contact with, and an ardent promoter of, the Yugoslav 'genius'. In 1915 Meštrović's one-man exhibition at the Victoria and Albert Museum turned into the most controversial art show of the year as far as Great Britain was concerned, not least for his expression of South Slav passion and suffering caused by outside forces.[27] Whether Fra and

Jessie saw the exhibition or not, they would have read and seen images of it, and, of course, they would have seen the Meštrovićs in Glasgow. Furthermore, Meštrović showed twenty-two sculptures at the Royal Scottish Academy exhibition in 1918 (where Fra also showed), including a bust of the recently deceased Dr Elsie Inglis, the doctor and suffragist who had set up the Scottish Women's Hospitals for Foreign Service (see Rojc above) that had played a major welfare role in Serbia during the First World War. Simultaneously Meštrović was elected an honorary member of the Academy. The amount of reviews, many illustrated, of Meštrović's English and Scottish exhibitions was unprecedented for a contemporary artist.[28] And not only did they analyse his creative work but they also dug into his biography, revealing an identity destined to appeal to Fra and Jessie; for example:

> *The son of a Croat peasant of North Dalmatia, Mestrovic was born in 1883 and spent his early youth as a shepherd boy amongst his native hills. While still only a child he had commenced wood-carving, for there that is what we call a peasant art, and when eighteen he was apprenticed to a marble-worker at Spalato … folk songs … have in-fluenced the sculptor profoundly.*[29]

The fickleness of British political-economic motivations, and the art-establishment concerns that follow in their train, meant that, after the First World War, Yugoslav art was suddenly no longer fêted. That said, the British support for strong monarchical Balkan states helped facilitate reciprocal 'friendship-society' exhibitions of British contemporary art in Yugoslavia and Yugoslav art in Britain in 1928–29 and 1930 respectively.[30] Though the Newberys' aesthetic interests would have been well represented by these, the exhibitions attracted little critical attention beyond Yugoslavia and it was not until the Second World War that, as far as the British powers-that-be were concerned, Yugoslavian art (still led by Meštrović) became noteworthy again.[31]

Fra and Jessie bucked such official trends by delving deeper into Balkan material culture in the interbellum period. As a result Fra's portrait of Brynley as a Croatian-Serbian shepherd not only engages with Meštrović's background but is also a painterly counterpart to the latter's sculpted *Shepherd Boy* (1913) [fig. 2.24]. The complementary nature of the two works is striking. Meštrović's *Shepherd Boy* is a monochrome bronze young male nude. As with Brynley, he stands upright and plays his flute. However, the shepherd's pipe meets his lips and he blows into it, closing his eyes and slightly inclining his head as he does. And unlike the more mobile, demonstrative Brynley, the shepherd, with his bare feet placed flat on the ground, appears motionless, rooted. If he is Balkan and autobiographical, Meštrović's *Shepherd Boy* is also universal. Likewise, the Yugoslav's *Annunciation* (1913) [fig. 2.25], also shown

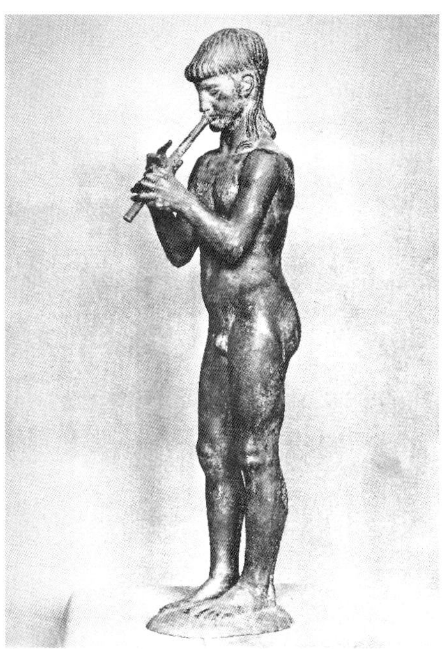

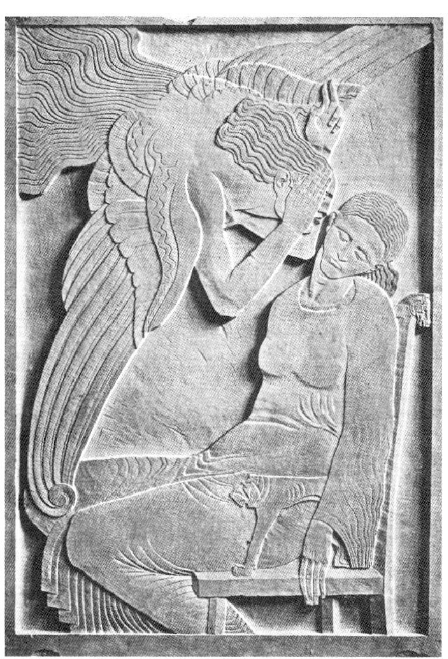

2.24 | Ivan Meštrović, *Shepherd Boy*, 1913, bronze; from *Milan Ćurčin, Ivan Meštrović: A Monograph*, (London: Williams and Norgate, 1919), plate xxviii

2.25 | Ivan Meštrović, *The Annunciation*, 1913, relief; from *Milan Ćurčin, Ivan Meštrović: A Monograph* (London: Williams and Norgate, 1919), plate 3

in Britain in 1915, can be read as a sculptural counterpart to Fra's altarpiece. Meštrović's relief possesses no obvious Balkan trappings and no auras. Mary appears asleep, slumbering in a chair at the bottom right as she is hailed by a celestial Gabriel, who points towards the heavens with his left hand. The vigour of the descending archangel and his proximity to the Virgin renders him far more assertive than Fra's ethereal, upright group. His announcement of divine favour appears more a demand for awakening and intercession, and by its virtue a cry for the messianic salvation of the downtrodden people of Meštrović's peninsula.

Irrespective of any artistic and personal relationship with Meštrović, the fact that Fra made his way to Cavtat to view the Račić family mausoleum, and that he was able to evaluate it in terms of high praise suggesting knowledge of the Croatian's oeuvre, is indicative of his continued acute awareness of the major forces in contemporary European art. That Meštrović had been awarded the Grand Prix of the 1925 Paris Exposition Internationale precisely for the Cavtat ensemble may have drawn Fra's attention. But he could also have been persuaded of its significance by the coverage it received in the arts media [fig. 2.26 a–b].[32]

The interpretation offered by Kineton Parkes, in the first issue of the then-new London journal *Artwork: An Illustrated Quarterly of the*

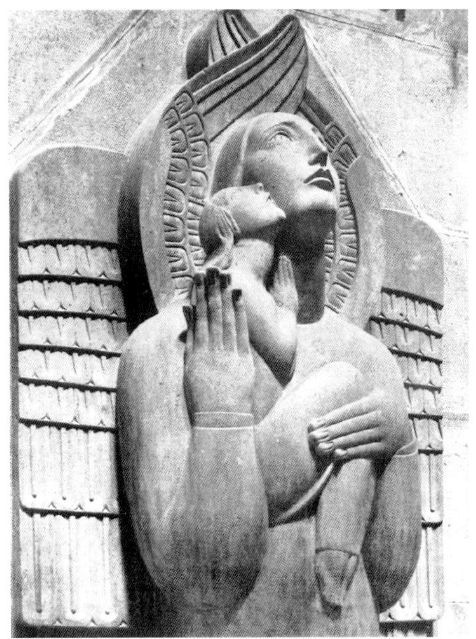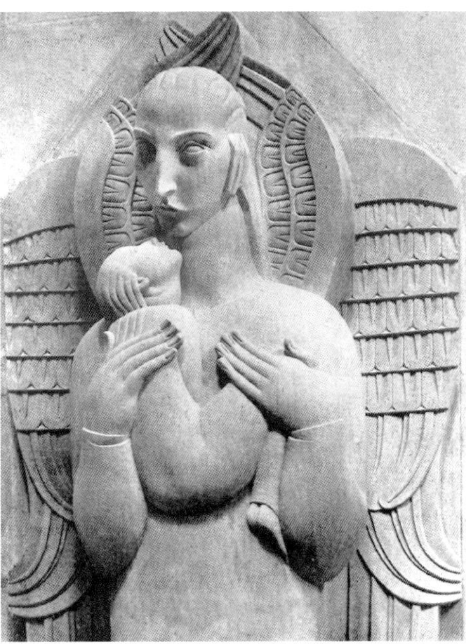

2.26 a–b | Ivan Meštrović, *Angels with the Souls of the Departed, c.*1922, two stone reliefs below the dome of the Račić family mausoleum, Cavtat; from *Deutsche Kunst und Dekoration*, vol. 52, June 1923, pp. 162–163

Arts and Crafts, is the most likely source for any prior knowledge of the mausoleum Fra may have had. Excerpts from Parkes' analysis of the coastal chapel and its appearance as an eclectic modern *Gesamtkunstwerk* that is a meditation – via angelic, saintly and human form – on existence, love and belief coincidentally suggest the ecclesiastical-decorative ensemble that is Fra's Swanage swansong:

> *A great monument not only to the art of Mestrovic as sculptor and architect, but to his religious zeal is the Mortuary Chapel at Ragusa, finished last year. A noble monument, it is simple and intimate, chaste and impressive, and its situation is one of the utmost beauty: its almost inland site on the Dalmation coast backed by magnificent mountains … The high altar includes a Pietà above, with the Lamb, flanked by six angels playing on musical instruments … a homogenous and impressive ensemble … the finest of Mestrovic's sculptural-architectural works, and one of the most impressive achievements of its kind that a century of years has produced. It will have its effect on all future work.*[33]

Practice, informed by broad contemporary and historical knowledge, as well as an understanding of design principles and technical means, and its intrinsic informing of future creative craft, was the driving force of Fra and Jessie's non-hierarchical approaches to art and life. In 1946, when Fra was aged ninety and close to death, Muspratt and her husband Jack Dunman visited the Newberys. Muspratt subsequently reported that Dunman was impressed by Fra's knowledge of the Yugoslav Partisan movement and his admiration for then Prime Minister Josip Broz Tito.[34] That a Balkan spirit was kindled in Newberyan Dorset was to be further evidenced by the career of Mary Spencer Watson, the Amazon in Croatian dress and recipient of Jessie's postcard from Split. For she was to come to regard her own visit to Yugoslavia in 1954 as a highlight of her life.[35] It is surely no coincidence that she is also regarded as having at least a touch of Meštrović in her sculpture.[36] While that cannot be the concern of our enquiry, we should just re-emphasise that the development of Spencer Watson's art, like that of Muspratt, owed most to the nurture of Fra and Jessie, and, with that, their Balkanist fabrications.

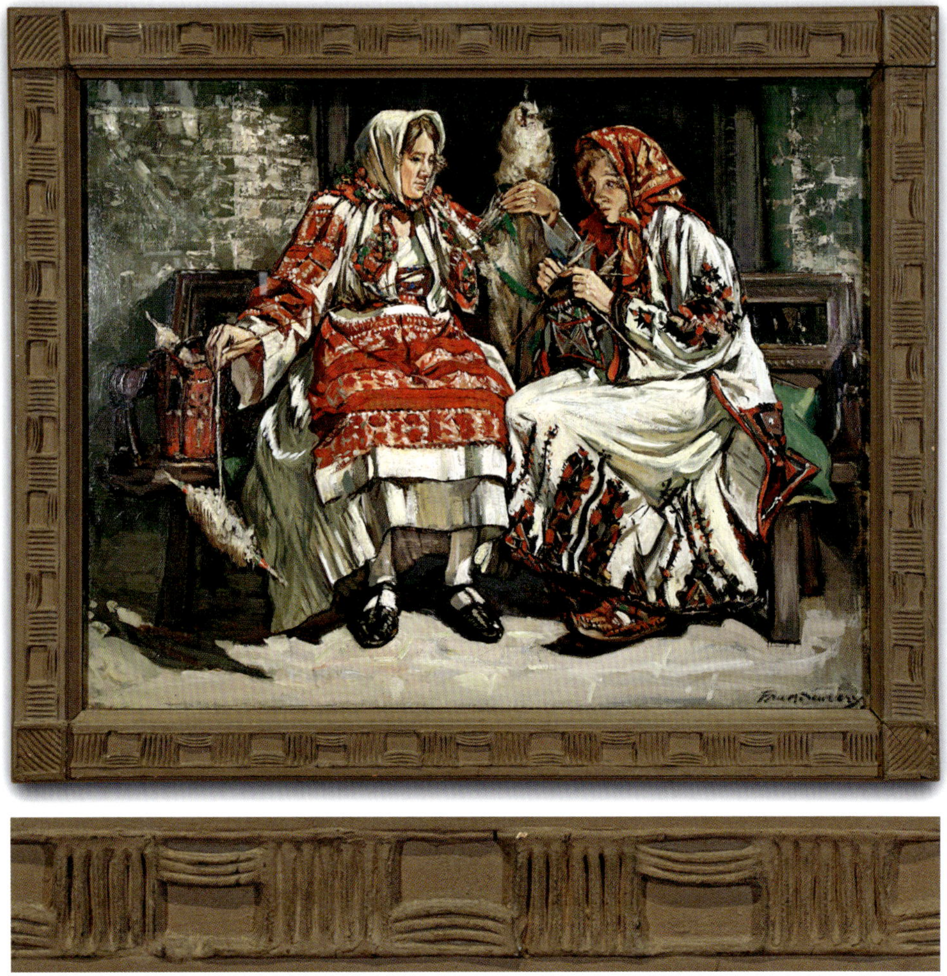

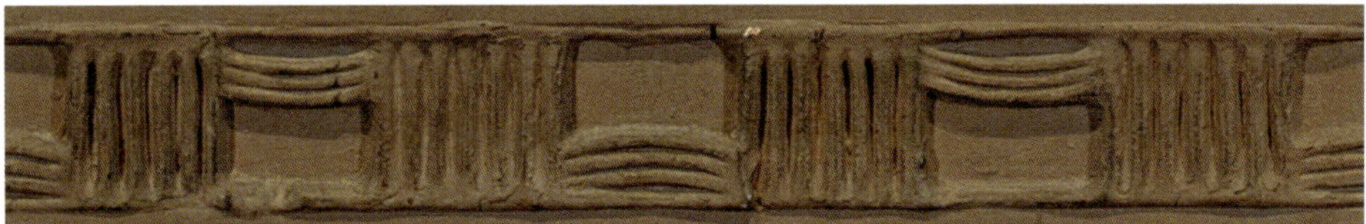

3.1 | John Gibson, frame detail of *Serbian Women* (fig. 0.1), *c.* 1920s/30s, Glasgow, wood

3 THREADS OF LEGACY
DUNDONIAN AND OTHERWISE

By the Tay:
The artist is nothing if not a worker

Fra died on 18 December 1946. Jessie died sixteen months later on 27 April 1948. He was ninety-one, she almost eighty-four. They passed away in their Dorset home and are buried together in God's Acre, Corfe Castle's main cemetery. The trustees of Fra's will, probably guided by Jessie, donated *Serbian Women* to Dundee's Albert Institute in the year of her passing. It presently hangs in the ceremonial Albert Hall in the permanent display entitled 'Dundee and the World', the institute having changed its name to The McManus: Dundee's Art Gallery and Museum. The wooden frame around the painting is not gilded or overly ornate. Rather its design suggests the weaving of threads, warp and weft, wattle [fig. 3.1]. An interplay of short bands of carved horizontal and vertical (and at the corners diagonal) strands alternate with one another. Each filament looks handmade or organic, their tiny irregularities and bends adding to the woven lattice effect. As such it possesses all the hallmarks of Fra and Jessie's craft sensibility. An almost identical frame surrounds Fra's *The Spanish Shawl*, which was first exhibited in 1916. The labels on the back of both bear the words: 'John Gibson carver, gilder, and picture restorer, 112 Bothwell Street, Glasgow. Picture Frames of any designs'.[1] Evidently by using a Gibson frame for *Serbian Women* and having it shown in, and ultimately left to, Scotland, Fra connected it with the land where his and Jessie's ideas on creativity had been most fully expressed.

The donation of the fabric-performing *Serbian Women* to Dundee was particularly fitting given the city's place at the heart of Britain's textile industry in the eighteenth and nineteenth centuries. That this trade, and with it Dundee's development and the wider economy, depended on international interchange is important. Furthermore, the prime source material for Dundee's linen was flax imported from Russia, a country whose convoluted Slavic and Byzantine cultural identity expresses a kinship with *Serbian Women*. Jessie bought textiles and metalware, including silver fastenings, from the 'Russian Peasants' Industries' sales organised across Scotland by Alexandra Pogosky in the 1890s. She may also have acquired Russian handicrafts from the Liberty store in London, and in any case it was 'from these she learned and developed the technique of needleweaving' which she passed on to her students.[2] Her own linen-based embroideries undoubtedly derived most of their material from Russian flax. Did she know that most of this entered Britain via Dundee?

It is also worth recalling that costume design and creation was in Fra's blood. The son of a Devonshire shoemaker and Dorsetian dressmaker, he had spent eight years (1877–1885) as a student then teacher at the National Art Training School. Attached to South Kensington (subsequently Victoria and Albert) Museum, this was the best college in the land for getting to know, learning from and aiming to master material techniques and forms from around the world. The first, and wider, consequence was Fra's transformation of art and design education in Scotland once he had been appointed headmaster of Glasgow School of Art in 1885.[3] The second consequence was Fra's own, long-nurtured, painting of folk identified with place, kin and profession (often textile-related), this interest finding fullest expression once he had retired to Dorset. Such direction is witnessed through his Bridport Town Hall murals (with their spinning, weaving, ropemaking and net-braiding subjects) as well as his studies of local agricultural workers and fishermen. His 'Serbian' or Balkan creations with Jessie should thus be understood in this context.

Fra spread his artistic principles and curriculum to Dundee via a course of twelve Friday evening lectures given at its recently founded Technical Institute (now Abertay University) in early 1892. It could be maintained that through these talks he attempted to counteract the pernicious effects of mechanised industry on the lives of Dundonians, not least its workers, though he did not subscribe to the view, often held by Victorian design reformers, that machine production necessarily meant deterioration in design quality.[4] More concerned with the origins of design, in his opening lecture he argued that art 'was an emanation of the human mind, and not the product of a machine'[5] for 'an artist was a meditative designer; a designer took nature and constructed out of it ornament. But no designer could imitate and no painter could conventionalise with safety.'[6] As such, in Dundee, he proclaimed his and Jessie's joint creed, one that was to be subsequently expressed in their Balkan fabrications. Ever an advocate for the role of good design and the breaking of falsely imagined boundaries between arts and crafts, he proclaimed, contentiously, that:

> *the artist was nothing if he was not a … worker. Mere picture painting did not form the bounds of art, although that seemed to be a popular notion. The public were not yet educated up to appreciate the art in designs. Art always led the way; the public slowly followed … Decorative art was the ornamental quality which men choose to add to articles of utility. An object which was not useful was never beautiful.*[7]

The fee for Fra's course was two shillings, with admission to his first lecture, chaired by Dundee Lord Provost Alexander Mathewson, offered for free.[8] While the full content of the talks is lost, a relatively detailed syllabus was published.[9] From it we can see how *Serbian Women*'s harmonised painterly treatment of composition, figure, object, light and space, as well as its study of textile- and embroidery-design variety, and even its frame, comprise a visual and material collation of the fundamental values he discerns in art. With this, and the other 'Serbian' works, in mind the programme is worth reproducing here.

*

PRINCIPLES OF ORNAMENT AND DECORATION

Mr FRANCIS H. NEWBERY, Headmaster, School of Art, Glasgow, will deliver a Course of Twelve Lectures on the above subject on Friday Evenings, at Eight o'clock, commencing Friday 15th January.

These lectures are primarily intended for painters, decorators, designers, wood and stone carvers, metal workers, and architects; but will also be of service to all those interested in the application of Art to Industry. Each lecture will be fully illustrated by Drawings and Practical Demonstrations on the Blackboard, together with suggestions as to Colour, Colour Treatment, and Application.

SYLLABUS

Lecture i. DECORATIVE ART – its origin, purpose and application.
Lecture ii. DEFINITIONS AND METHODS OF EXPRESSION. Definition of Ornament – Naturalism – Conventionalism – Naturalistic treatments not necessarily Ornament – Ornament has no existence apart from Nature – unsuitable enrichment not Ornament – Tempera or Distemper – Oil – Fresco.
Lecture iii. ELEMENTARY FORMS. Geometrical figures consisting of straight lines and their combinations – the stripe – the fret or key – the triangle – the square – the diamond – polygons – reticulations, etc. The same consisting of curved lines and

their combinations – the circle – the ellipse – the parabola – the hyperbola – the catenary – spirals – waves – meanders – scrolls – festoons – imbrications, etc.

Lecture iv. LAW OF ORNAMENT – COMPOSITION OF ORNAMENT.

Proportion – Repetition – Series – Variety – Contrast – Radiation – Tangential Junction – Symmetry – Balance – Stability – Subordination – Repose – Geometrical Arrangement – Growth – Superposition – Fitness – Unity – Composition – Ratios – Harmonic Proportion.

Lecture v. DIVISIONS OF SURFACES.

Division of plane surfaces, such as floors, walls, and ceilings, into panels of various shapes – diapers – treatment of curved surfaces, such as vaults and domes – borders.

Lecture vi. THE SETTING OUT OF ORNAMENT.

Geometrical basis – superposed ornament on planes – enclosure – subordination of parts – surface and its treatment – Texture – rough, smooth, polished, burnished – introduction of materials, such as tapestry and leather, woven stuffs, etc.

Lecture vii. CLASSES OF ORNAMENT.

Mnemonic or introduction of writing – Symbolic or endowed with a meaning – Aesthetic or purely sensuous.

Lecture viii. STYLES.

Realistic or Natural – Conventional or Abstracted – Naturalistic similar to those employed by Nature.

Lecture ix. THE HISTORIC STYLES.

Egyptian–Greek–Roman–Byzantine–Saracenic–Gothic–Renaissance – later developments.

Lecture x. ACCESSORIES.

Ships and boats – furniture – arms – armour and standards – musical instruments – utensils – festoons and garlands – dresses – hangings – fringes – ribbons, etc.

Lecture xi. ANIMALS etc.

Insects – reptiles – birds – fishes – quadrupeds – mythical forms, etc.

Lecture xii. THE HUMAN FIGURE and figure composition.

*

This syllabus expresses a direct connection with ideas concerning the core place that ornament has in art that were being expressed simultaneously by reform-minded artists and critics invited by Fra to lecture in Glasgow, for example William Morris, Walter Crane and Lewis F. Day. It also built on Owen Jones' formulation of ornamental principle, as expressed in his sourcebook *The Grammar of Ornament* (1856), with its great diversity of design. Furthermore, a copy of the syllabus is pasted into a press-cutting album compiled by artist and educationalist Henry Taylor Wyse. Wyse's apparent attendance on the course has led

Elizabeth Cumming to note that Newbery's 'ideas … had a profound impact on Wyse'.[10] Indeed, in many ways it was Wyse who thereafter took up Fra's mantle by playing a vital role in furthering the modernisation of art education in Scotland, not least through his manuals for making, his establishment of the art curriculum at the new Arbroath High School and by becoming Principal Lecturer in Art at Moray House College of Education in Edinburgh, and also by creating his own designs for furniture, ceramics and interiors.

Fra's deconstruction of ornament as an essential ingredient for art-in-life, for its uplifting, beautiful application to the built environment, and even as an end in itself, anticipates later theories of ornament. He categorises its functions and appearance in ways that determine distinct attributes. Occasionally, for example, it can be mnemonic, imbued with symbolic meaning, figural. In Oleg Grabar's terms this means it can be regarded as a carrier of 'iconophoric' message, that is it mediates meaning independent of its form by reference to something particular outside of itself.[11] Alternatively, it can be essentially formal, having no clear referent and comprising studies in combinations of shape, line and texture (surprisingly Fra's syllabus does not mention colour). And then it can be principally expressive, conveying, in accordance with Grabar, sheer sensuality. As such ornament becomes a mediator of 'aesthetic' beauty. Even this inkling of Fra's theory of ornament and decoration allows us to discern its ramifications for the visual language and meanings of his Balkan fabrications.

Initiated and sponsored by the philanthropical chairman of the Technical Institute, Martin White, Fra's lectures in Dundee coincided with both men – along with their mutual associate, the pioneering sociologist, biologist and arts patron Patrick Geddes – furthering the career of Dundee-born artist John Duncan. Hence, just as White was commending Fra for 'the best course that had ever been given in Dundee in technical instruction', Fra was giving Duncan the opportunity to teach art classes at Glasgow, these helping to set him on his path to becoming the leading light of Scotland's Celtic Revival movement.[12] Within a few years Fra and Jessie, along with Duncan, Mackintosh, Margaret Macdonald, George Walton, Phoebe Anna Traquair and several notable others, founded the Scottish Society of Art Workers to advance contemporary arts and crafts. Furthermore, by 1900 Duncan had executed murals for a new library wing of the Dundee mansion of the city's former Convener of the Nine Incorporated Trades and Lord Dean of Guild, George Brodie Paul. The intention was 'to beautify the new town house with paintings idealising the life and work of Dundee'.[13] While the murals have been lost, a description as well as a sketch by Duncan's assistant Nell Baxter survive [fig. 3.2]. These reveal that the centrepiece bore much in common with Fra's Bridport Town Hall murals and *Serbian Women*:

The iconographic similarities between Duncan's and Fra's work are
striking: their use of women spinsters – as allegories for history, tradition and places/communities as far apart as Dundee, Bridport and the
Balkans – relates to the prime role of textile manufacture in the making of those places' identities. That Duncan should have anticipated Fra
in his distaff-, yarn- and spindle-wielding seated female 'spirit' suggests, not least given their acquaintance, that Fra knew of the Dundee
murals. Furthermore, when the sketch for the centrepiece was published soon after the scheme was completed, the accompanying article
noted: 'Mr Duncan has achieved signal success as a decorative artist,
his decorative paintings … being excellent examples of decorative work
of high artistic import.'[15] Evidently Duncan's murals speak to his integration into Fra's decorative-artistic community, in terms of ideas
and practice, and particularly that which he championed in and for
Dundee.

There is one more seeming Dundonian legacy that is worth mentioning here, and it relates directly to *Serbian Women*. For it has a counter-

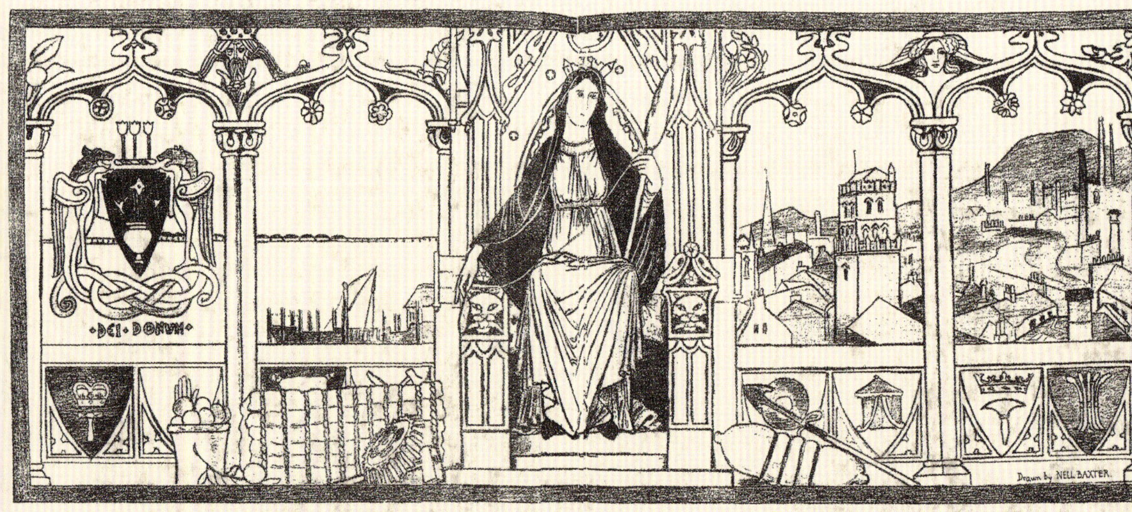

3.2 | Nell Baxter, 'The Duncan Decorative Paintings at Friarton Grove'; from *The Piper O' Dundee*, vol. 27,
no. 707, 23 May 1900, pp. 336–337

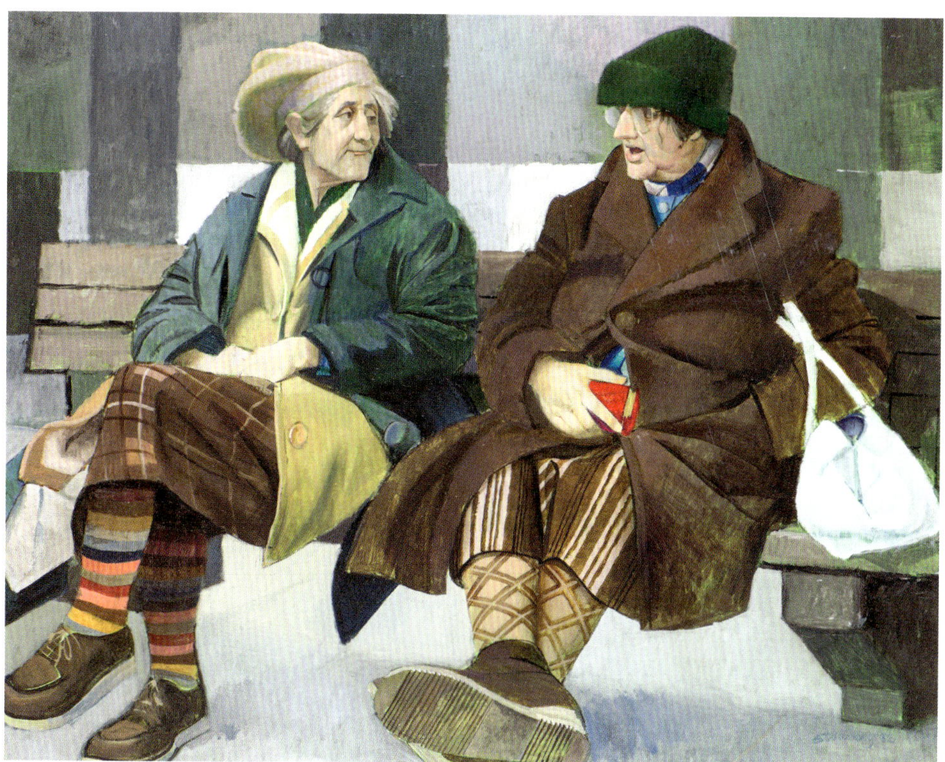

3.3 | **Ron Stenberg** | *Twa Auld Wifies, Dundee* | 1982, oil on canvas, 94.5 x 120.5 cm

part hanging in the McManus gallery: Ron Stenberg's *Twa Auld Wifies, Dundee* [fig. 3.3].[16] Painted in 1982 by the then head of Illustration at Duncan of Jordanstone College of Art, the image can be considered a late-twentieth-century local equivalent to Fra's work. The horizontal format, relatively close-up viewpoint, bench with two figures and cropped nature of the scene, all relate. Furthermore, Stenberg's *Auld Wifies* show signs of national dress (such as the tartan skirt of the woman on the left) and are engaged in a moment of togetherness on the street. And, as with *Serbian Women*, there is also a deceit and sense of generational passage. Here, however, this is due to the *Wifies* being Janet Isles-Denny and her son Alexander. Rather than being the working-class housewives Stenberg assumed them to be, Mrs Isles-Denny was one of Dundee's wealthiest women and a major local philanthropist, while Alexander, due to learning difficulties, was a long-term resident at the Royal Dundee Liff Hospital. Stenberg did not know their identity, but he captured them chatting on the corner of Reform Street as if wishing to convey a modern Dundonian reply to Fra's *Serbian Women*. Was it conscious? We may never know, but the uncanny signs are there.

By the Forth: There is only one art

Eleven years after his course on decorative art in Dundee, Fra was back on the east coast of Scotland, this time to be a judge and give a talk with the tellingly generic title of 'Art' at Kirkcaldy's inaugural (1903) 'Home Arts and Industries Association' exhibition. The 'Lang Toon' and port of Kirkcaldy, Fife, was Dundee's neighbouring textile-manufacturing counterpart, being situated fifty kilometres to the south on the banks of the Firth of Forth. And just as Dundee had (albeit not entirely) switched away from linen to jute, so Kirkcaldy (while maintaining a ceramics industry) moved to linoleum, the result being increased dependency on relatively unimaginative, mechanised factory production. Revival, innovation and improved living through craft and craftsmanship were therefore envisaged by the new association's founders, many of whom were connected with the textile trade.[17] With around 1,500 exhibits by eight hundred contributors, the display was divided into eleven sections, children being allotted subsections in some of these. Fra was judge of the two 'Fine Arts' (painting and drawing) sections and co-judge, with Jessie MacGibbon of the Guild of Women-Binders and Edinburgh Arts and Crafts Club, of the 'Needlework' section, the latter being the most extensive of all the sections. That he should have bridged the categories in such a way, and taken a lead in awarding women top prizes – be that in painting or needlework – is telling of his holistic conception of creative process. A review of his speech at the opening-cum-prize-giving ceremony is indicative of the thought (his and Jessie's) that went on to produce *Serbian Women* and its related works. For in it we discover Fra's appreciation of local tradition and derision of falsely conceived separate artistic categories:

Kirkcaldy Home Arts and Industries Exhibition …
Mr Fra. Newbery, Principal of the Glasgow School of Art gave an able address on 'Art', in the course of which he said they had been told by Lord Elgin that this institution had only been in existence for a few months, but he held that this institution had been in existence since the seventh century, and they were carrying on as Fifers the traditions of Fifers – and the most artistic county in Scotland was Fife – and it was not so much a credit as they believed. They had done good work, but it was their duty to do good work, and he could congratulate them on the very good show they had put before their judges that day. He would go a little further. The catalogue in hand bore the name of Kirkcaldy Home Arts and Industries Association. With the industries he had nothing to do, but he wanted to know what they meant by home arts. There were no home arts as opposed to other arts, and he would go further and say there was no such thing as professional art

and amateur art. There was the professional who got his bread and butter by the aid of art, but every piece of art done by any person that came up to a certain standard, whether at home or abroad, in cottage or in studio, was art and art only, and there was only one art, never mind its expression. (Applause).

He believed our art education – and he lived entirely by it – was absolutely and entirely on wrong and false lines, and till they got rid of the stringencies with which they viewed art they should never make any progress in spite of the schools and art and technical institutions. He saw around him very charming bonnets, hats, cloaks, and dresses on ladies' heads and shoulders. (Laughter and applause) Every lady who bought a hat has two processes, the process of choosing and the process of putting on. He did not know which entailed the greater of artistic skill, but every one when they choose a hat displayed their taste or distaste, and any lady who stood before a mirror to see that her hat was put on straight was therein and thereby an artist. (Applause).[18]

Fra's criticism of the terms 'home', 'professional' and 'amateur' and his emphasis on women's dress all have a bearing on the values expressed in his and Jessie's 'Serbian' inventions. One reason for him raising the problem of professional versus amateur was that many prizes in Kirkcaldy were divided between such categories, the vast majority being designated 'amateur'. That most 'amateurs' were also women would have rankled with the egalitarian ethics he subscribed to and whose cause he persistently fought for. While suggesting a challenge to concepts underpinning the exhibition, his concern with 'home' (and disregard of 'industries'), as well as his condemnation of contemporary 'art education', actually reveals his sympathy with the principles of the Home Arts and Industries Association, the craft revival society with which Kirkcaldy, by title at least, was affiliating itself. For the HAIA organisation, founded in Shropshire in 1884 and run mainly by women, was concerned with sustaining rural (and subsequently urban) communities through local training in transferable skills as well as developing handicrafts threatened by the spread of urbanisation and mechanisation. By providing technical courses and organising exhibitions it afforded makers skills and agency so that they might on the one hand democratise their own artefacts and spaces and on the other contribute to the community and its economy.[19]

If Kirkcaldy was a somewhat late adherent to the HAIA cause, it was also an independent and rather idiosyncratic one, in that any sign of attachment to the London-based HAIA was not publicly acknowledged, and besides conventional 'handicrafts', it not only included the 'fine arts', but also photography, kinetic models and cookery. Such range would have appealed to Fra. In his duty as judge of 'fine arts' he was asked to rank first according to the classes of professional, amateur and children under fifteen, and second as to whether a work was 'original' or a 'copy'. Although no physical evidence of winning entries appears to have survived, we should note that in terms of 'professional original' he awarded first prize in oil painting to Jennie Davidson, an artist who ran a studio in Edinburgh and regularly exhibited at the Royal Scottish Academy, and first prize in painting on ceramics to James Sharp, an employee of Fife Pottery, in nearby Gallatown, for his rose-decorated tea service. In terms of printmaking, Fra's winners included Dr David Watson Geddie of Aberdeen for an etching of the city's Mitchell Tower, and a Miss Fraser of Dunfermline for a crystoleum entitled *Sunshine*. Unsurprisingly, given the conventions of gendered handicrafts, no men's names are among the numerous winners of needlework prizes, women winning everything in all classes, from embroidered bedspreads to bedroom slippers, work bags, appliquéd blouses and smocked dresses. In subsequent years, irrespective of Fra's call for integration, little changed at the Kirkcaldy exhibitions in terms of how categories and the genders of prizewinners aligned; instead, new sections for apprentices and artisans were added. That said, a Newbery influence remained, since for the 1904 exhibition, Fra's mantle as judge for fine arts and needlework was assumed by John Duncan and Jessie's Glasgow School assistant Ann Macbeth. Was it coincidence that Jessie's cousin, some-time collaborator and former fellow student at the Glasgow School of Art, Edith Rowat, of Paisley, won first prizes for an appliqué bedspread and cushion?[20] The Newbery legacy was to continue through community and family ... or, we could say, networks of correspondences ...

By the Clyde

Macbeth, with a Serbian twist

Much has been made of Jessie's impact on the teaching and practice of needlecraft while she was at the Glasgow School of Art. She is also acknowledged as mentor and inspiration to Ann Macbeth, who, after being Jessie's assistant in the embroidery department from 1901, ran the department for more than a decade following Jessie's retiral in 1908. Macbeth, who never married, was more prolific than Jessie, boldly developed her predecessor's visual language (particularly in terms of figuration and scale), taught other crafts (metalwork, bookbinding, ceramic decoration), exhibited and lectured widely, and published several needlecraft (and other) textbooks between 1911 and 1929. Both Jessie and Macbeth were supporters of the Women's Social and Political Union, the Pankhursts' organisation that campaigned for women's suffrage in the years before the First World War. Macbeth's activism surpassed that of Jessie, being expressed in quilt and banner design/ making, and demonstration, these even leading to a term of imprisonment in 1912.[21] Her artistic being was also profoundly marked by her deeply held Christian belief and Protestant work ethic.

Testament to Macbeth's skill and furtherance of art was first paid by Fra, not only through his appointment of her to the staff of Glasgow School of Art, but also through the tribute to her artistry that he published in *The Studio* in 1902 (see appendix 2 and chapter 7). In his homage Fra emphasised that her departure from convention was an act of both labour and creativity:

> *She is content simply to be a worker, doing practical and useful work, and finding for it a place in the market and by it a subsistence for her self … when at length she turned her attention to traditional ornament, she found herself in a position to ignore it, and to start where the mediaeval ornamentists did – namely, at and with Nature … being a creative artist, instead of a follower of tradition, … gave her a distinct advantage … Ornament … must be a personal belonging … Miss Macbeth … set herself steadfastly from the very first to execute work which should enter into daily life and have an interest because it was a part of our everyday surroundings. And in this endeavour she is much helped by her own very practical outlook on things. Thus, how dress and personal adornment could be simplified and at the same time beautified, early made a strong appeal to her. How stuffs, plain, yet of sound quality and of good colour, could be beautified by the addition of embroidery or other aids to decoration, led her to essay the art of appliqué and to endeavour to mosaic upon a ground an ornamental treatment in another colour, which should enhance the dress as a possession, without adding much to the original cost … with Miss Macbeth the setting of one piece of coloured cloth upon another, and the putting of a border of sewn thread or silk around it, gave the added piece all the appearance and value of a precious metal or of a jewel set among its surroundings. Further, these spots of colour, thus superimposed, are connected, and the design made into a whole, by spots and lines of colour or by ornament, chiefly floral, characteristically conventionalised from Nature.*

Making connections, as part of a whole, allied to the expression of personal belonging and adornment, are then the stuff of Macbeth's art. Fra denotes Macbeth a worker, yet there is just about no physical labour in her embroidered subjects: rather there are languid, playful or charitable maidens, holy angels, stylised flowers and colour-linear patterns, the apparent ephemerality of which is assuaged by an all-encompassing quiet order of symmetry, grace and harmony. Hence, for example, her treatment of the charitable Elizabeth of Hungary, the patron saint of lace-makers, who she represents as a beautiful, modest young woman caught in a soft hieratic stance as she reveals the miraculous roses cradled in her upheld dress within the oval cocoon of her purple cloak. Different versions of Macbeth's 'St Elizabeth' exist, either designed and sewn by Macbeth or designed by her and made by a friend and/or student (as in that by Elizabeth Wood [married name Jackson], c.1911 [fig. 3.5]), which suggests that she used it as an exercise for those working at the highest level in her embroidery class.[22]

As far as Macbeth pertains to our particular Balkan fabrication enquiry, it is her teaching manuals that contain most correlative matter. If she had broached a central European subject with St Elizabeth, and given the medieval Hungarian a modern Glaswegian twist, her teaching manuals indicate comprehension, as well as adaptation, of techniques, styles, trends and materials from near and far alike. In *Educational Needlecraft* (1911), which she co-authored with teacher Margaret Swanson, she advocated an age-related (from six years through adolescence and beyond) approach to needlework. Through this the craft comprises both an element of formative training and a field for stirring the imagination via a combination of experiment and a quest for 'the graciousness of Art, by which we approach the utilitarian'.[23] In lessons for those over fourteen entitled 'Beginnings of Pattern' and 'Designing with Straight Lines', Macbeth and Swanson enunciate principles of textile design that, despite their use of the term 'barbaric', may be associated with the Balkan handicraft that concerns us. Furthermore they illustrate these with images of student work and diagrams of corner designs that consist of patterns based on simple combinations of perpendicular and diagonal lines that accord with the Yugoslavian embroidery appreciated by the Newberys [fig. 3.4 a–b]. This being the case their text and images are worth iteration here (pp. 112–13). In essence then, Macbeth and Swanson are laying down

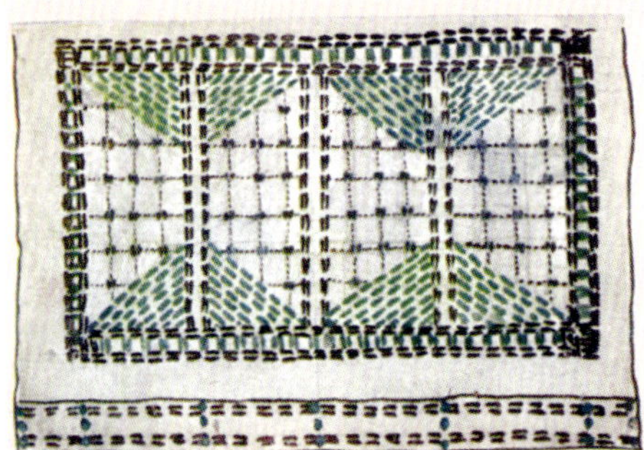 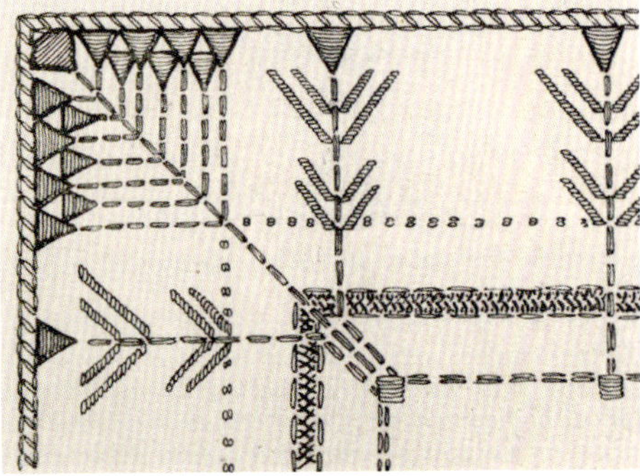

3.4 a–b | Two examples of student work; from Margaret Swanson and Ann Macbeth, *Educational Needlecraft* (London: Longmans, Green & Co., 1911), diagrams 169, 171, pp. 100–101

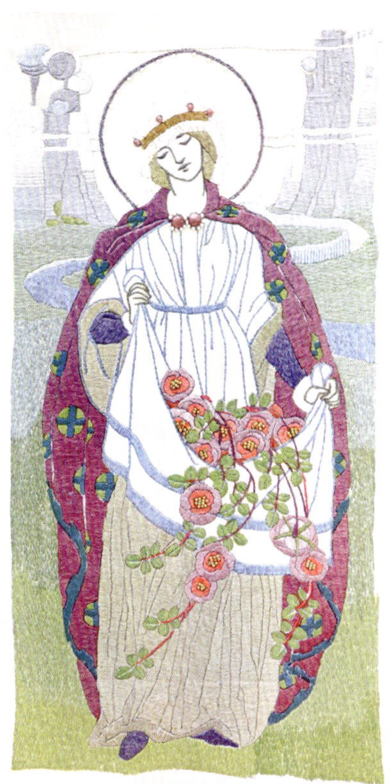

3.5 | Ann Macbeth, 'St Elizabeth of Hungary', 1910 (design by Macbeth, sewing by Elizabeth Wood [married name Jackson]); from *The Studio Yearbook of Decorative Art* (London: The Studio, 1912), p. 99

a practical theory for embroidery which, while possessing applicability to Balkan design, provides an alternative to what they considered the stultifying British system of education. In so doing they are in the vanguard of modern applied art pedagogy, anticipating, for instance, the principles of Soviet Constructivist design of the 1920s. They even stress art as a component of construction and good design being structural. Their rejection of the pictorial in favour of the abstract is given both an aesthetic- and material-based rationale that is contended as a pragmatic and life-enhancing counter to the common preferences for ostentation, abundance, non-utility and the solely machine-made. In this they are following the Newberys' lead.

Macbeth's understanding of the value of handicraft is underscored by a visual and literary erudition that contains within it comprehension of a great breadth of world traditions. Even a cursory survey of her publications uncovers such range, examples including 'very beautiful' Hungarian rug stitchery,[24] 'the finest' Persian, Turkish and Indian pile weaving and knotting,[25] the 'great deal of beautiful and most minute [needleweaving] work done in Armenia',[26] 'the most beautiful variation of coiled cane weaves' that for her is Nigerian stitching,[27] 'distinctive and very beautiful' Pima Indian cane coil weaving,[28] Russian crash decoration,[29] and the attributes of Serbian cord.[30] Given our subject, it is worth pausing on the inclusion of the last in her *Embroidered and Laced Leather Work*. Published in 1924, when she was in semi-retirement, her mention of Serbian fabric anticipates Fra and Jessie's first visit to Yugoslavia by two years. Within two of the forty-five examples that comprise the illustrated techniques of the book, Macbeth first visually describes the technique of making Serbian cord and then shows its potential application – as straps to a leather bag [fig. 3.6 a–b]. Admitting that her diagram 'will show the method of working better than the description' her only literary allusion to its merits mentions it being 'a very pretty crochet cord [that] can be made on the fingers [and] which is more elastic than the twisted cord'.[31]

*

... any recurrent stitches, or groups of stitches, in orderly arrangement resolves itself into Pattern, and the making of such pattern in the construction of seams and of hems on garments or household gear is one of the most primitive developments of artistic decoration in civilization – in fact, it is frequently the first, and almost the only, civilized trait among certain barbaric peoples. Now design in its broadest sense may be either decorative or it may confine itself to bare utility with no hint of beauty about it. Design is, in fact, any work that is not accidental, but in the sense in which it is generally used as 'Applied Design', it signified an intentional combination of utility with more or less of ornament, and is specially used in connection with what are called 'Applied Arts'. Design should in its elements be applied, first of all, to adorn and strengthen the construction of those things we work at. In architecture, in making of furniture, in the construction of everything we use in our houses, the value of the work is increased tenfold if this quality of Beauty be combined with its form.

There seems no reason why, if it do not combat with the utility of the work, we should not make ornament of our hems and seams far more than we do. Surely we have no reason to be ashamed of them! And if this structural design were insisted upon, there would be less need for the application of trimmings such as lace and complicated braiding which, unless it be of the most expensive, is unprofitable to wear, and now that we have learned the general application of stitchery we may make use of the sewing machine for long seams, and expand our hearts and our handiwork in adding ornament and beauty to such parts of our garments as may be most enhanced by them.

In making ornament of embroidery for garments or for useful household articles, it is important to avoid any too pictorial or naturalistic representation of floral or other forms.

If pictures are designed it is essentially not on our clothing... On our garments and on most textile fabrics we want Pattern – not Pictures, and a pattern is built up in an entirely different fashion from a picture.... We can make good pattern out of any single shape, but in its beginnings it is best to keep to more or less geometrical forms, and to apply our ingenuity to seeing how many different things we can make of them... The work of the hand in construction and invention demands all our reasoning powers: the eye must balance, proportion, and measure with accuracy; the mind must consider the strength of the material to resist tension, and wear and tear, the suitability of the work for its ultimate use. Harmony of colour, beauty of form, poetry of symbolism, even these can all be contained in the simplest design worked with a needle and thread, so that many branches of study, mathematics in particular, are represented in the design a girl may make in her clothing or other stitchery, if she be permitted to exercise her powers rightly upon its invention.

Border patterns are the best suited for the designer as the preliminary exercises in planning embroidered decoration, and at first all such decoration should be made with a ruler on straight lines only, vertical or horizontal... The student must above all bear in mind the method of stitchery she wishes to adopt, and plan her design that it may be well suited for this… the student should give herself plenty of practice in these straight-line designs, as herein lies the fundamental plan for making any good pattern on woven texture. Too many diagonal lines are not advisable, they give a restless effect, and are difficult to work on the cross of the material. The best design is that which abides by and insists upon the limitations imposed by the difficulties in working the material.

from Margaret Swanson and Ann Macbeth, *Educational Needlecraft* (London: Longmans, Green & Co., 1911), pp. 97–100.

*

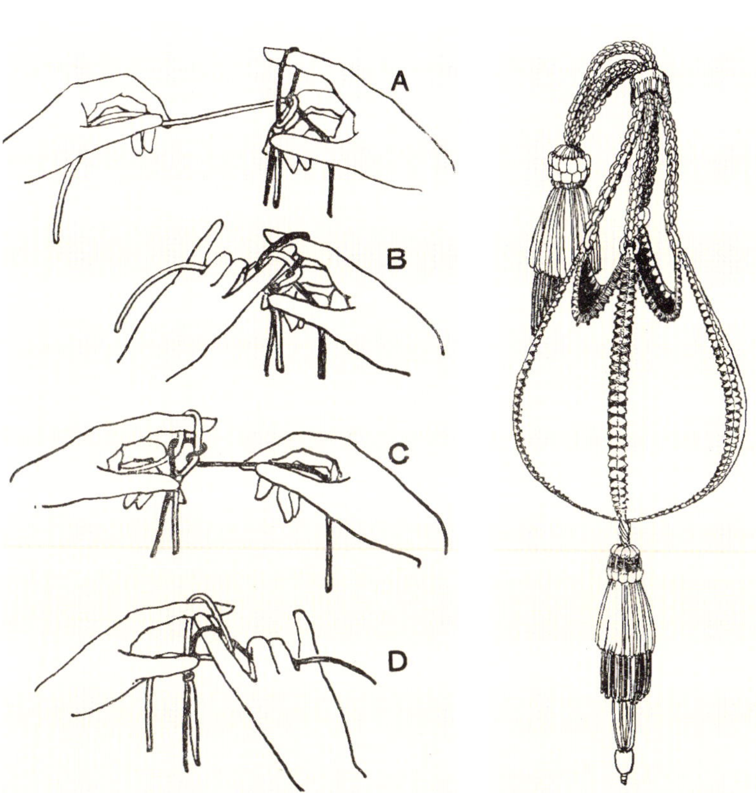

3.6 a–b | Serbian cord [left] and leather bag [right]; from Ann Macbeth, *Embroidered and Laced Leather Work* (London: Methuen & Co., 1924), pp. 38–39

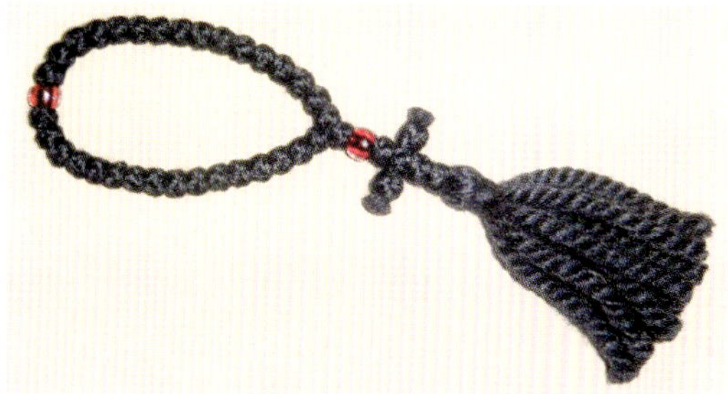

3.6 c | Serbian Prayer Rope (*brojanica*), thirty-three knots, wool

The fact that Macbeth turns the Serbian cord into an element of a practical, modern and stylish personal article is telling of her ways of invention from tradition. She even proposes complementing it with 'handmade tassels', plus 'a soft sliding ring, made by wrapping several strands of silk round the cords when gathered together, and buttonholing over the wrapping' so as to 'give a pretty finish and close the opening of the bag'.[32] In so doing she is adapting the craft of the traditional Serbian Orthodox prayer rope (*brojanica*) to secular use [fig. 3.6c]. She makes no hint of this, or of the religious symbolism of the knots and tassels, though behind her art is always her Christian conviction, as revealed through the final sentence of her introduction to *Embroidered and Laced Leather Work*, with its quote of work 'law' from Ecclesiastes (9:10): 'In this, more perhaps than in most handicrafts, holds good the law, "whatsoever thy hand findeth to do, do it with thy might" …'[33] This supplements her contention, in other texts, that creativity is God-given, that craftwork is 'of the Kingdom of Heaven' and that

this power to create … is, in fact, one of the most vital sides of religion in us, and perhaps the most important to us. It brings us into direct kinship with the Great Creator of all things … This Holy Spirit

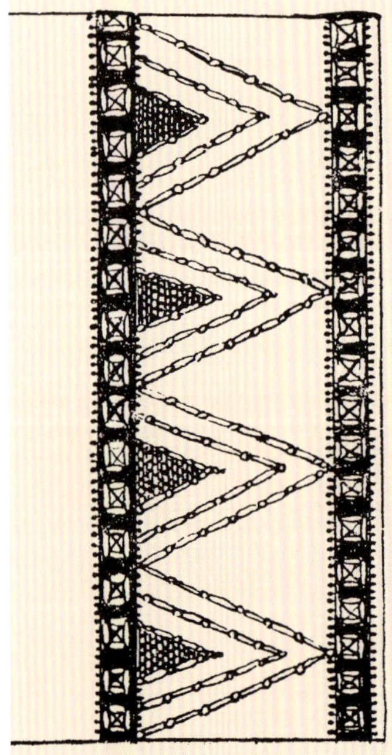

3.7 | Ann Macbeth, 'Runner decoration'; from Ann Macbeth and May Spence, *School and Fireside Crafts* (London: Methuen & Co., 1920), p. 70

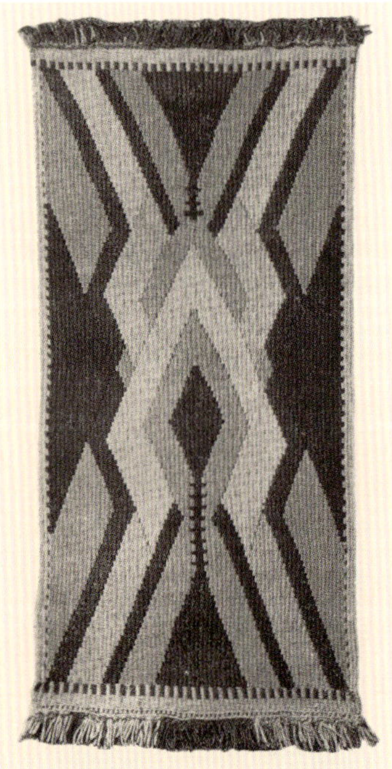

3.8 | Ann Macbeth, 'The Ullswater Rug', wool; from Ann Macbeth, *The Country Woman's Rug Book* (Leicester: Dryad Press, 1929), p. 57

Across her publications Macbeth complements careful and succinct written explanation of technique with drawn or photographic illustration. The work reproduced can be hers or that of students or colleagues (individual attribution is only occasionally given). What becomes clear is that in the 1920s the textile design she promotes is mainly based on geometrical patterns, the lines, colours (where indicated) and placement

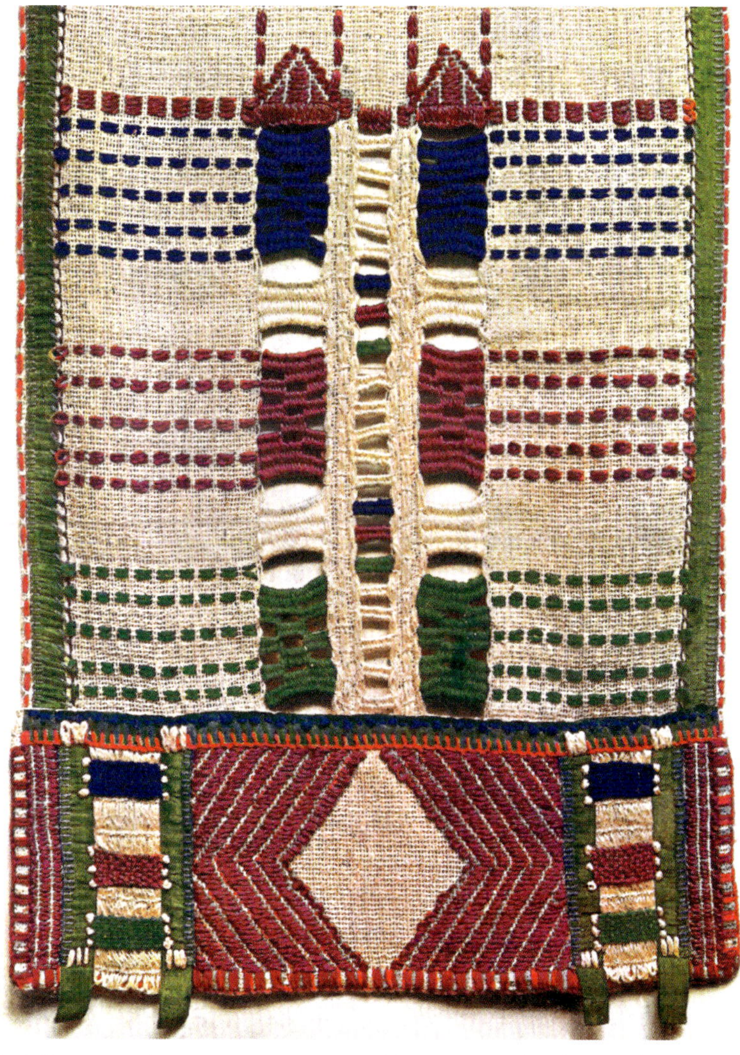

3.9 | Bureau scarf, cream cotton canvas, needleweaving wool and cotton decoration, silk binding; from Anne Knox Arthur, *An Embroidery Book* (London: A.& C. Black, 1920), plate v, opp. p. 64

of which correspond with a great deal of Balkan peasant embroidery. Hence the considered prominence of repeated rhomboids, triangles, rectangles, circles and the occasional stylised floral motif. Our selection from her images shows a preference for these as applied, not to dress, but to household articles: a runner, woollen rug, bureau scarf and linen curtain.[35] Such emboldened abstract expression, with its association (conscious or 'God-given') with folk design of multiple cultures, is a much-neglected quality of mature Macbeth [figs 3.7–3.10]. Yet it should be taken as a significant high point in her work, a beacon of her instinct for, or alertness to, creative correspondence.

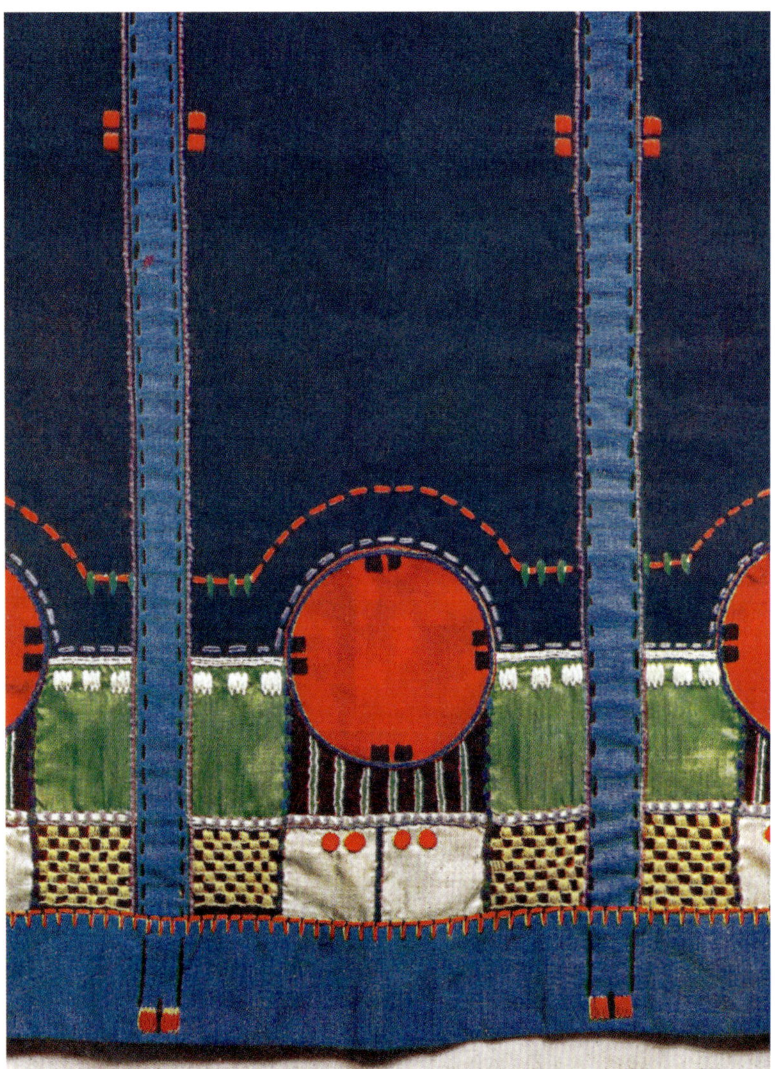

3.10 | Portière, black linen, silk, cloth, linen appliqué; from Anne Knox Arthur, *An Embroidery Book*, (London: A.& C. Black, 1920), plate IV, opp. p. 49

Dewar, with a Romanian turn

Following Jessie's influence on Macbeth, as well as their mutual advocacy of women's rights, skills development and the beautiful coordination of material, space and pattern, it fell to two other women members of staff at Glasgow School of Art to further advance Clydeside Balkan fabrications. The first to do so was De Courcy Lewthwaite Dewar, who studied metalwork and graphic design at the School in the 1890s before being appointed (by Fra) instructor of enamelwork around the turn of the century. She was employed by the School for almost four decades. Having, in the 1920s, developed a 'geometric and boldly coloured Czechoslovakian folk-art influenced style',[36] in the 1930s Dewar visited Yugoslavia and Romania. She gave illustrated lectures on her observations and experiences at Harkness House, a centre for local unemployed men and women in Bellshill, fifteen kilometres east of Glasgow. Her sister Katherine was warden of the centre, she acting as her assistant. While precise details of the first talk remain scanty, we know that it derived from a trip made in August 1932 by both sisters, and that it was given shortly after they returned and involved 'sketching out the characteristics of the natives under discussion, and their relationship to the other states in Europe'.[37] More is known, as indicated below, about the Dewar sisters' next Balkan sojourn, which took place the following summer, when they reached Romania via Hungary and Serbia. A second visit to Romania occurred in August 1936. The journeys comprised fieldtrips that principally blended geography, sociology and biology and which were organised by the Le Play Society. This was a new 'regional studies' group founded by polymath and, as we have seen, early Newbery associate Patrick Geddes.[38] Dewar's main role seems to have evolved into that of fieldwork artist and data gatherer, her drawings accompanying photographs, plans and maps as visual evidence to support the written text and tables.

If pattern and its interrelations were at the heart of both Jessie's and Macbeth's work, then in a distinct way the same can be said of the objective of the Le Play Society. In his foreword to the society's report of its Yugoslav trip, geographer and politician Halford Mackinder noted the transdisciplinary aim of the group's fieldwork as being 'to detect identical pattern in a variety of phenomena', to 'wait for the pattern to emerge from the facts and not seek to put it into them', and thereby to avoid 'partizanship of outlook'.[39] This derived from Geddes' formulation of Le Play's regional survey concept as social study of the organically interlinked units of 'Place, Work and Folk'.[40] In visualising this, the artist of the society's logo contextualises Dewar's own Le Play fabrications [fig. 3.12]. The image represents the simplified figures of a man and woman in generic costume standing (man holding a spade and woman pointing) in cultivated and wild nature either side of a tree. Above them, emerging from wavy lines that mark the golden ratio of the composition, is a building which is a composite of modern factory, silo and historicist institution or residence. Underpinned by 'PLACE WORK FOLK', with arrows pointing in two directions between the words, the logo summarises Geddes' principles of community study. S.H. Beaver has pointed out that Geddes himself designed a diagrammatic device in which Geography (place), Economics (work) and Anthropology (folk) were shown as the basis upon which sociological enquiry should be constructed.[41]

The visual characteristics of the Le Play Society logo used on publications by them that featured Dewar's artwork helps us to both place and read the language of that artwork. In terms of 'Yugoslavia' there is just one Dewar image: an edited version of her pencil drawing of a 'corn-and-tool shed' at Gradišnik farm, high up in Slovenia's Alpine Solčavsko region [fig. 3.13]. Being located some fifty kilometres north of Ljubljana, the farm, while then being in Yugoslavia, is just north of our Balkan peninsula line (see below, chapter five). Still, the vast majority of the region's peoples are Slav and the area, for all its mountainous isolation, marks a meeting point of Alpine, eastern and Mediterranean Europe. Geographers Dudley Stamp and Arthur Davies led the Le Play Society fieldwork on the Yugoslav trip, much of the local arrangements being made by Fanny Copeland.[42] Stamp noted that the area was chosen because 'it is still possible to study the life of the inhabitants, who are untouched by the sophistication which results from contact with tourists of all nations'.[43] He also recorded that the region was divided into two parishes, that of Solčava and Sv. Duh [Holy Spirit], the latter, in which Gradišnik was located, comprising, at 1,250 metres above sea level, the highest 'village' community in Slovenia. His survey

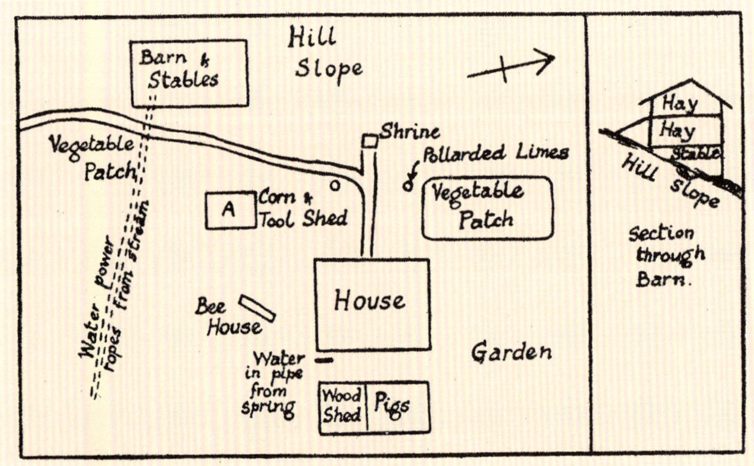

3.11 | Gradišnik farm plan; from L. Dudley Stamp (ed.), *Slovene Studies* (London: Le Play Society, 1933), p. 32

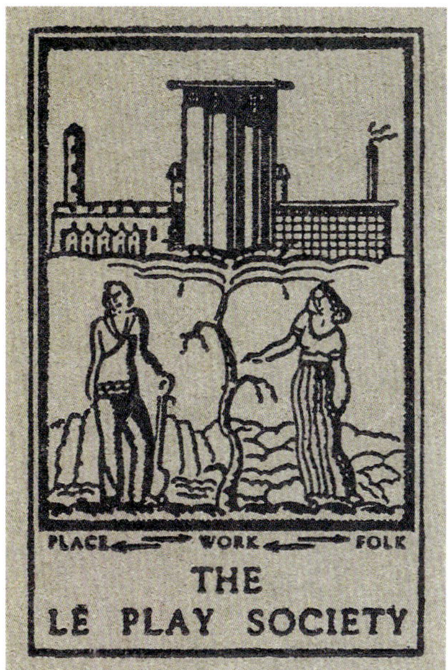

3.12 | Le Play Society logo, *c.* 1932;
from H.J. Fleure and R.A. Pelham (eds),
Roumania: East Carpathian Studies (London:
Le Play Society, 1936), cover

considers the nature of the few subsistence farms in the Matkov valley, the first of which was Gradišnik. The Slovene identity of the owner's family, their occupation with forestry, and a mix of pastoral and arable farming is mentioned. The details are accompanied by a plan of the farm [fig. 3.11], photographs of its highland situation and family shrine, and Dewar's drawing of its corn-and-tool shed. The picturesque timber architecture of the latter, with its cantilevered gables, verandahs and the repetitions of its stylised hooks and openwork (simple floral and bulbous motifs) correlate with the Romanian vernacular designs Dewar was subsequently to represent in other Le Play Society publications. With the pitch of its roof jutting up through the diagonal of the hilly, tree-lined horizon, its compact, relatively complicated yet well-proportioned form presents itself as a fragile object of human craft set against the grandeur of peaks, forests and farmland that surround it. That it has survived, while the rural economy it epitomised has withered, could be seen as testament to Dewar's eye [fig. 3.14].[44] In fact, what she has captured is a *kozolec*, originally a hayrack-barn, that was used for drying and storing grain. The distinctive architecture and widespread appearance of the *kozolec* across Slovenia has led to its becoming a primary national symbol.[45]

The Gradišnik *kozolec* image, together with its role in the Le Play Society Slovenian regional study, acts as an introduction to Dewar's, and fellow society members', Romanian fabrications in the reports they classed as Eastern and South Carpathian Studies. Again these are correlated with published observation of pattern and correspondence, starting with a fabrication metaphor:

> *Running through all the various studies, and linking them together, is a thread which each of the workers recognises as of the essence of the pattern. That thread is the special interest of the geographer in all that he sees, his capacity for tracking the constant inter-relation between Man and Nature.*[46]

This fragment of Baron Meston's foreword to *Roumania* contains words regarding the geographic thread and pattern of the Le Play Society's work that complement the publication's full-page frontispiece by Dewar

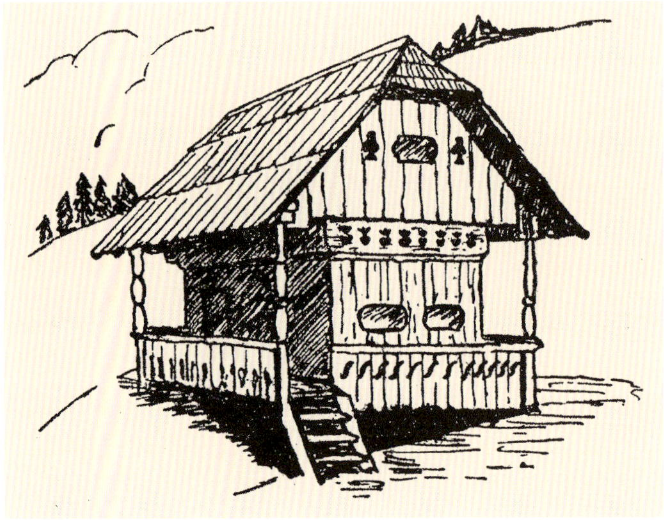

3.13 | De Courcy Lewthwaite Dewar, 'Corn-and-tool shed, Gradišnik farm'; from L. Dudley Stamp (ed.), *Slovene Studies* (London: Le Play Society, 1933), p. 33

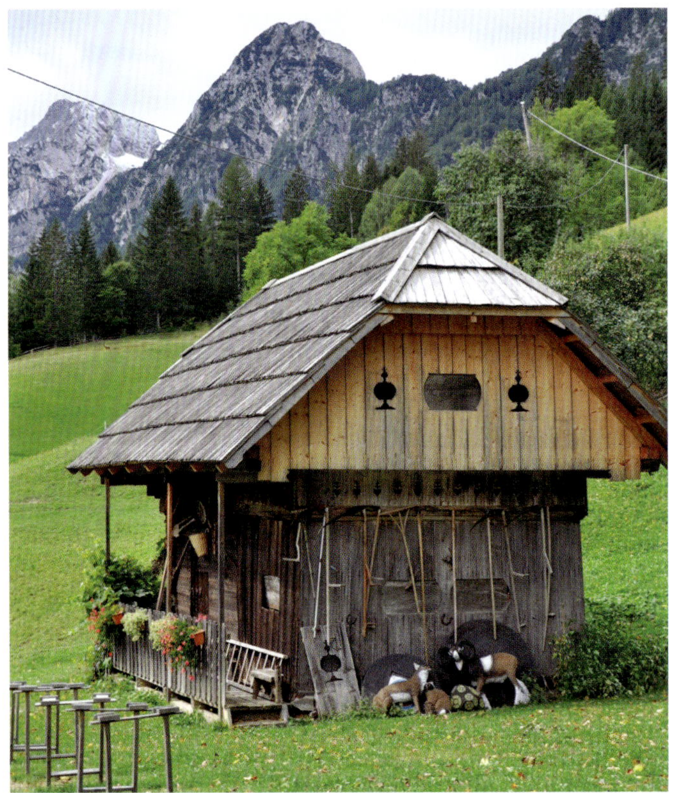

3.14 | Corn-and-tool shed, Gradišnik farm, 2016
TURISTIČNA KMETIJA GRADIŠNIK

[fig. 3.15]. What does she depict? A Romanian peasant woman in embroidered folk dress winding yarn from distaff to spindle. But more than that, she is contained within vertical borders that are comprised of repeated geometric motifs, with rhomboids, zigzags, circles and crosses dominating. So with this black-and-white print Dewar transmutes Fra's *Serbian Women* into a paper icon of Romanian type. Now, however, this is based on close *genres de vie* study in the field and as an integral part of a group survey committed to the examination of individual and community response to 'the stimulus of a particular environment'.[47] Hence Dewar's image introduces a swathe of documentation

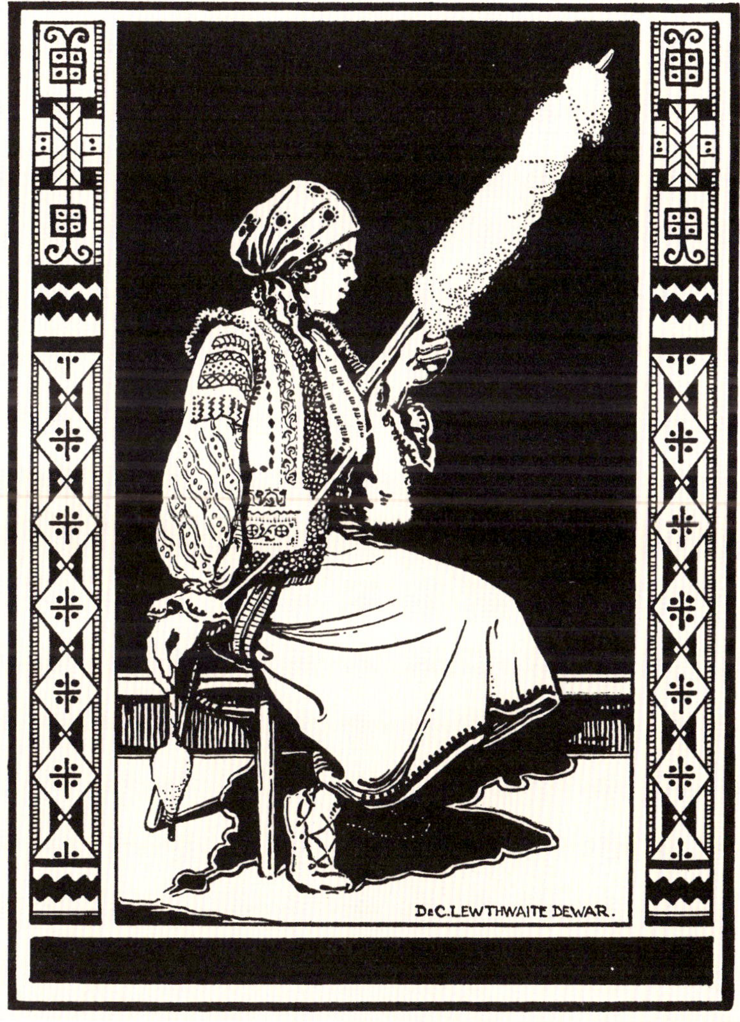

3.15 | De Courcy Lewthwaite Dewar, 'Romanian peasant woman'; from H.J. Fleure and R.A. Pelham (eds), *Roumania: East Carpathian Studies* (London: Le Play Society, 1936), frontispiece

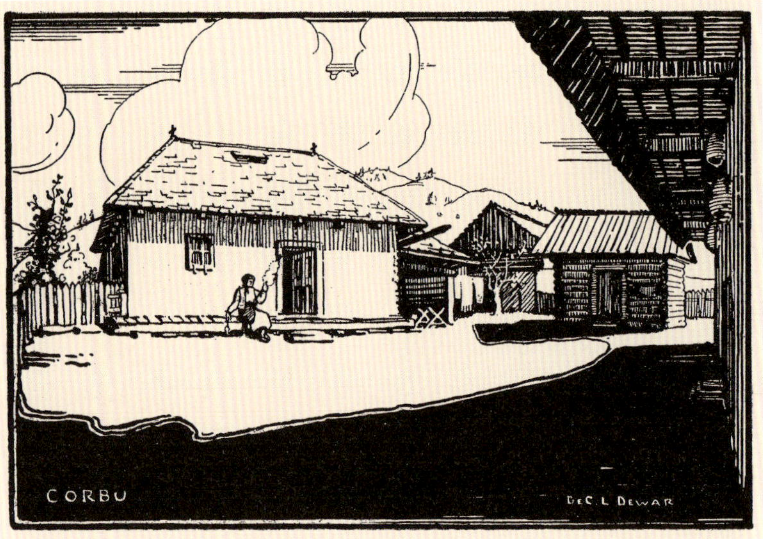

3.16 | De Courcy Lewthwaite Dewar, 'Corbu farmstead'; from H.J. Fleure and R.A. Pelham (eds), *Roumania: East Carpathian Studies* (London: Le Play Society, 1936), p. 43

and interpretation of central Romania, with particular attention being paid to the east Carpathian (Transylvanian) mountain village of Corbu. So while the pose, dress, low seat, sunlight, shadows and abstract setting might echo that of and around the leftside figure in *Serbian Women*, this distaff side derives from a settlement six hundred kilometres northeast of Belgrade (and 2,500 kilometres southeast from Corfe Castle). Furthermore, she is accompanied by a set of images and text that add specificity.

Of these images, first there is her half-page graphic print depicting a Corbu peasant farmstead, the caption of which instructs the reader to compare it with the reproduced farmstead plan [figs 3.16, 3.17]. Through such means we can determine that Dewar's viewpoint is from close to the dairy and cart shed looking across the yard of the steading to one of its two cottages, beyond which, moving clockwise, is the weaving shed, stable and oven. Dewar has chosen to sit under a shade-providing cantilevered gable so that she can focus on the sunlit cottage on whose verandah, between open door and window, sits a woman winding yarn from distaff to spindle. Now a small but key component within a larger domestic setting, the woman of the frontispiece (which we may take her to be) loses the pattern detail of her costume. Furthermore we are given a glimpse beyond the enclosure to the hilly landscape, cleared of its forest, of its environment.

Dewar's images and the plan are designed to cohere with text, photographs and maps. As such they are chosen to make 'clear … the principal features' of 'a group of typical Roumanian farmsteads', that

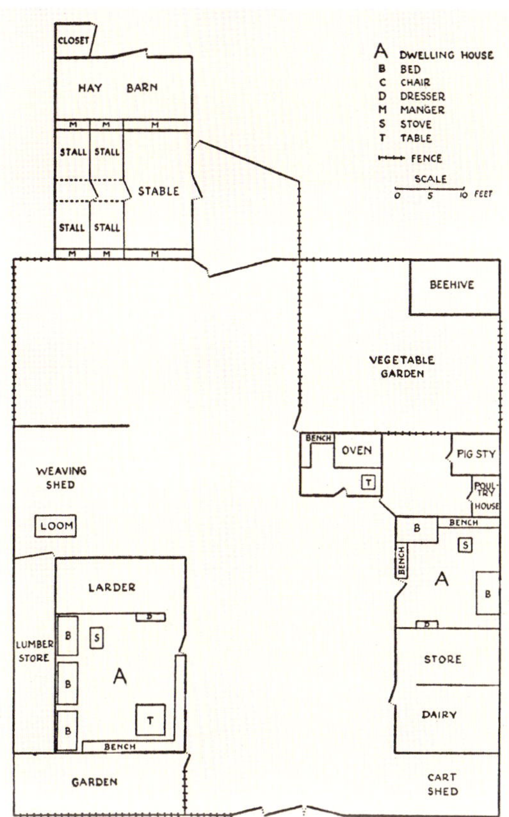

3.17 | Corbu: plan of peasant farmstead; from H.J. Fleure and R.A. Pelham (eds), *Roumania: East Carpathian Studies* (London: Le Play Society, 1936), p. 67

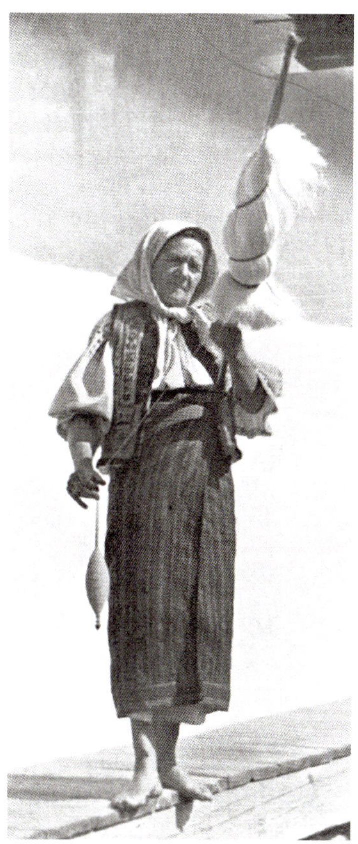

3.18 | Henry J. Howard, 'Romanian peasant woman'; from H.J. Fleure and R.A. Pelham (eds), *Roumania: East Carpathian Studies* (London: Le Play Society, 1936), opp. p. 49

is, with two dwelling houses 'usually built of roughly-squared, less frequently of sawn, timber' which are either plastered over or 'caulked with clay before a colour-wash is applied …'[48] The text goes on to note that the roofs are usually of shingles and are not pierced by chimneys because the cooking is done in an outhouse. More is made of the physical location in the Bistricioara valley, the 'dispersed' village type, the population (Romanian majority; Szekler, Gypsy and Jewish minorities), farming, 'other occupations' and 'future'. Numerous statistics are added. The significance of textile work is pronounced, and with a gender twist. Thus:

Household effects are kept down to a minimum, but upon their manufacture an enormous amount of time and skill is lavished, especially in the case of textiles. The skilfully-woven designs on the tapestries and pillows … are an illustration of such effort …

The outstanding feature of the Carpathian villages is the remarkably high standard of peasant craftsmanship. The degree of artistic expression revealed in their clothing is particularly striking, and although best seen on festive occasions it is scarcely less noticeable in their ordinary working garb. Wool, flax and hemp are the traditional fibres used, but imported cotton yarn is beginning to displace linen for some of the lighter summer garments. Most of the dyestuffs are obtained from local plants, for example, red from the leaves of the wild crab apple, yellow from the osier, black from the alder or birch and fawn from the walnut, but imported dyes are beginning to be employed. The mordant used is salt, but colours other than black fix themselves in wool without salt treatment.

Spinning with a distaff is the normal occupation of the women in their leisure time during the summer, very little knitting being done at all. The other processes of combing, weaving and dyeing are also undertaken by the women, as is the embroidering of dresses and household linen, but the embroidering of the sheepskin waistcoats which are worn by both sexes is done by one or two men who specialise in this craft …

'Dot', or Marriage Portion. A girl of moderate means brings to her home on marriage: seven to nine pillows, blankets and sheets; at least fifteen towels; four or five carpets or rugs, to adorn the walls; personal clothes dependent on her skill. She will try to have special clothes for the great festivals such as Easter, Christmas, etc.; Sheep, cows, and her share of the heritage from her father. It is said that a girl begins to make her 'dot' at the age of 6 years … few adults remain unmarried.[49]

Given such social and artistic importance it is unsurprising to find that Dewar's images also have close counterparts in the survey photographs. Four of particular relevance are by the naturalist Henry J. Howard, with three of these, of textile production, likely to be depictions of the same Corbu farmstead. Their captions are worth citing. First, that of the photograph of a solitary woman with distaff and spindle, reads: 'Spinning with a distaff – an occupation symbolical of the traditional life of the Roumanian peasantry in the hill country.' [fig. 3.18]. So 'symbolical' is this woman that she appears to be posed in front of the same Corbu farmstead as Dewar's. Barefoot, she stands on the planks of the wooden platform under the cottage eaves. The windowless wall behind her is plastered (apparently white), with its log construction visible at its corner. Beyond this is a sliver of darkened space that coincides with that of the weaving shed shown at the end of the house in Dewar's picture and the plan. In bright sunlight the woman stands facing the camera at a similar viewing angle to that of Dewar's, yet now from a closer position. While the woman wears embroidered waistcoat and chemise, plus headscarf and overskirt, she is older than the figure in Dewar's frontispiece. Given the younger subjects of the two other Howard photographs this suggests that she is the matriarch of the household. For those images depict a younger woman, with features and dress more akin to those of Dewar's women [fig. 3.19 a–b]. Here, however, the seated woman, while wearing an identical overskirt to that of Howard's older subject, seemingly does not need to wear a waistcoat as she combs wool through the iron spikes of her wooden implement and weaves on her home-made loom in her open, sunlit, shed. And she also does not need to hold distaff and spindle. For this is done by the child to her left. The child, like their younger sibling and mother, copies their grandmother in looking directly at the camera lens, their look wary. Only when sitting at the loom does the woman offer a half-smile, as if relaxing into her objectification by the alien camera-wielder. Who is she? Who are her children? What was their fate? And what was the fate of

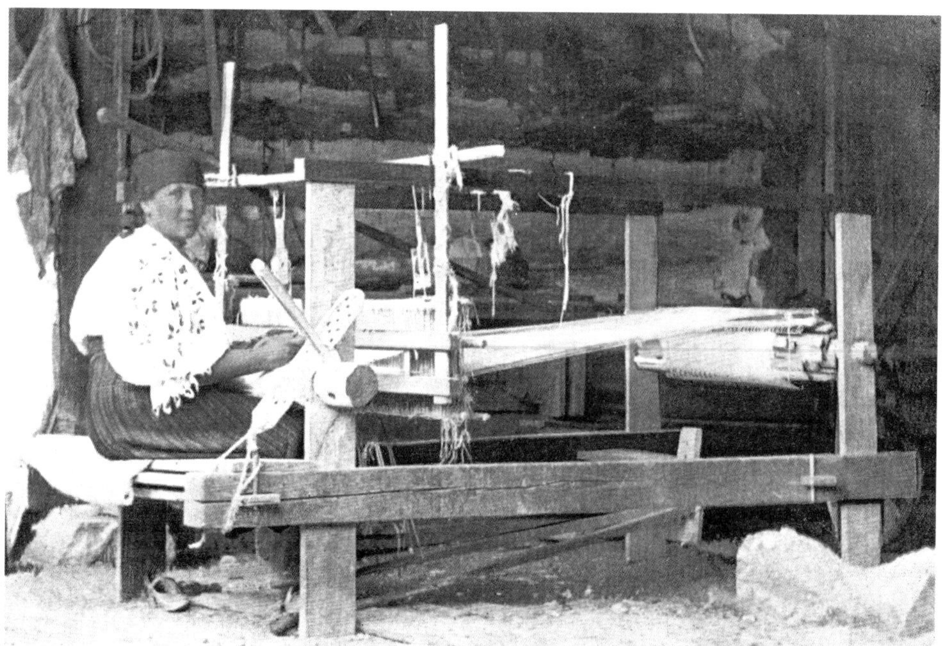

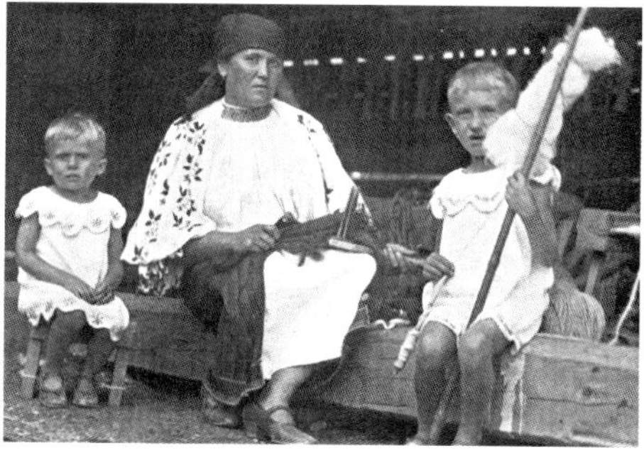

3.19 a–b | Henry J. Howard, 'Corbu farmstead fabric production'; from H.J. Fleure and R.A. Pelham (eds), *Roumania: East Carpathian Studies* (London: Le Play Society, 1936), opp. p. 73

the objects, instruments and homes of their craft? Surely it should not be too difficult to find out. And thereby go beyond the typecasting of Howard, Dewar, the survey authors and indeed that of the Newberys' Balkan fabrications.

The fourth Howard photograph that correlates with Dewar's and Fra's is the first of only two granted a full page in the report [fig. 3.20]. Now, however, we are taken out of Corbu to Borsec, a small town and spa with a Hungarian majority, about seventeen kilometres west. The report sees Borsec as the nearest marketplace for Corbu's surplus products. Hence the image is a close-up of a young Romanian peasant couple in national costume posing on a wooden bench at Borsec fair. Its caption notes 'the man is wearing trousers of thick, home-woven material and home-made shoes, whilst the woman is wearing modern button boots. The coats are of sheepskin embroidered with coloured wool.'[50] While their waistcoats and the woman's overskirt are very similar to those of the Corbu peasant women we have seen, the former also have rich embroidered floral and geometric motifs that accord with those reproduced as the penultimate plate of the report [fig. 3.21]. In this we are presented with front and back views of waistcoats for a woman and man. As such they represent Romanian (and with that Corbu) male needlework, the sight of an example of which caused a stir during Dewar's talk in Bellshill about her travel impressions:

> *Miss Dewar showed various handicrafts – the waistcoat of sheepskin embroidered by their men taking the fancy of the audience most. In Roumania the men are really able to appreciate intelligently the women's embroidery, since, like our Prince of Wales, they do it themselves. Some pottery and a young spruce tree whose bark was carved with a penknife in intricate patterns, and batiked and painted Easter eggs completed the crafts. Hungarian embroidery by comparison was more eastern in feeling, even to the use of mirrors in it and was more gorgeous and unrestrained.*[51]

Dewar's acquisition of the waistcoat, and drawing her audience's attention to Romanian male embroidery – with its suggestion of diversity and alternatives to stereotypical gendering of activity – was carefully considered. Her own practice and teaching of metalwork broke with British gender conventions, as did her active involvement in, and designs for, the women's suffrage movement. Furthermore, having early on been something of a medievalist in her enamelled metalware and jewellery, through her post-First World War travels in Europe, not least the Balkans, she acquired an appreciation of how modern styles could comport effectively with tradition. Fabric design played a key role in her understanding. Thus in Romania, after becoming one of the first international visitors to what was arguably the region's most significant

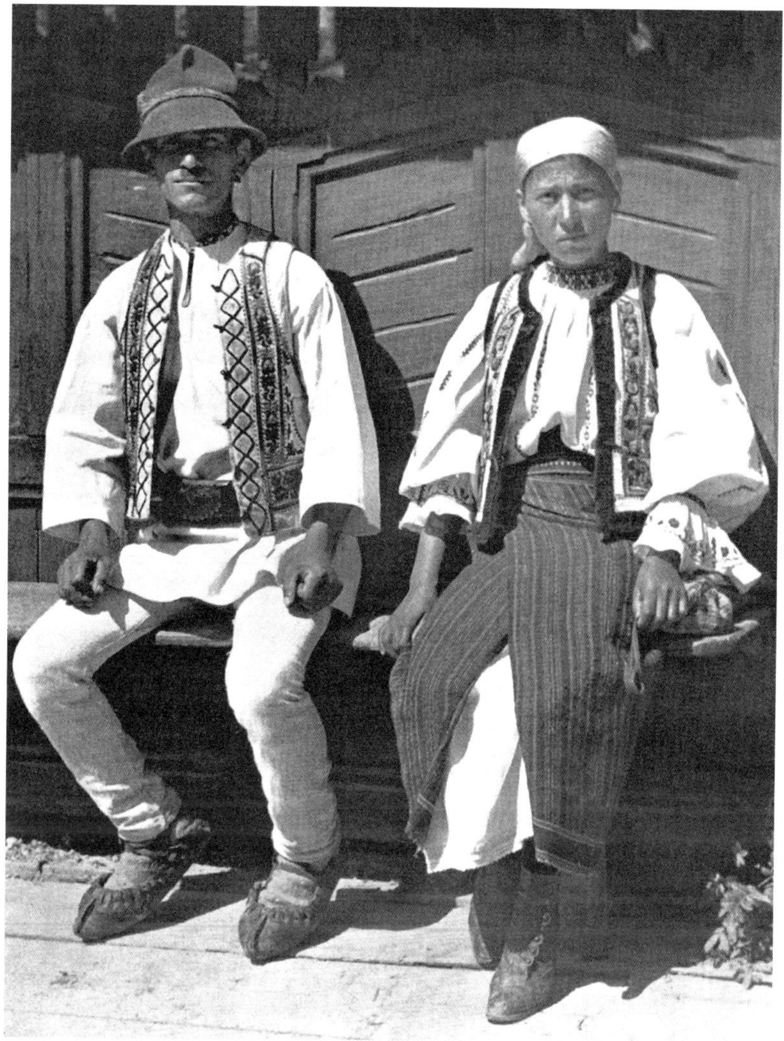

3.20 | Henry J. Howard, 'Two Romanian peasants at Borsec fair'; from H.J. Fleure and R.A. Pelham (eds), *Roumania: East Carpathian Studies* (London: Le Play Society, 1936), opp. p. 13

large-scale modernist building – the new Gaz Electra Company Rest House at Snagov, some forty kilometres north of Bucharest – she noted (for her Bellshill listeners) significant strengths of its unified visual and material language:

> *... built, in cubist style, for the employees of the municipal hydro-electric works to spend a holiday. Every room had a special colour scheme, worked out on the walls, carpets, curtains, chairs and bed-spreads. The roof was flat and suitable for sun bathing and the house overlooked the lovely lake.*[52]

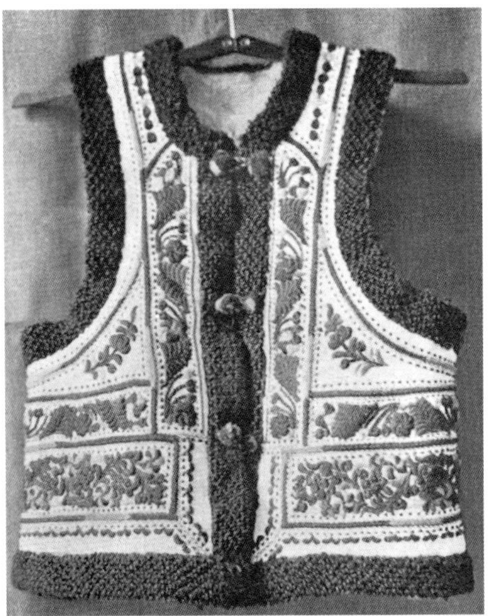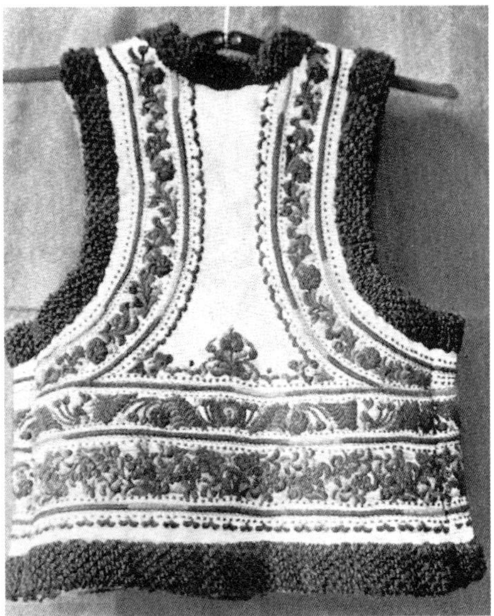

3.21 a–d | Romanian peasant woman's [above] and man's waistcoats [below]; from H.J. Fleure and R.A. Pelham (eds), *Roumania: East Carpathian Studies* (London: Le Play Society, 1936), opp. p. 76

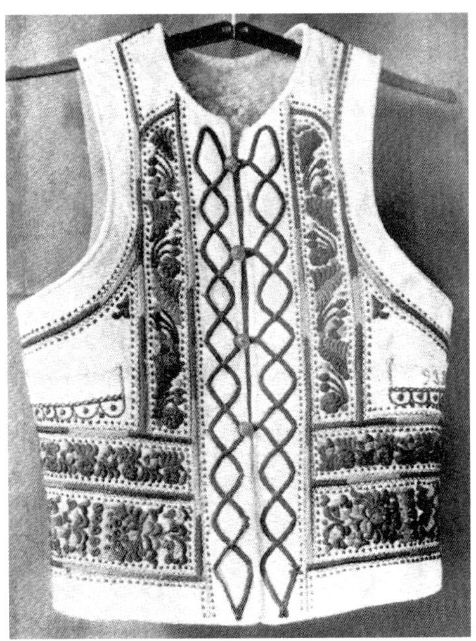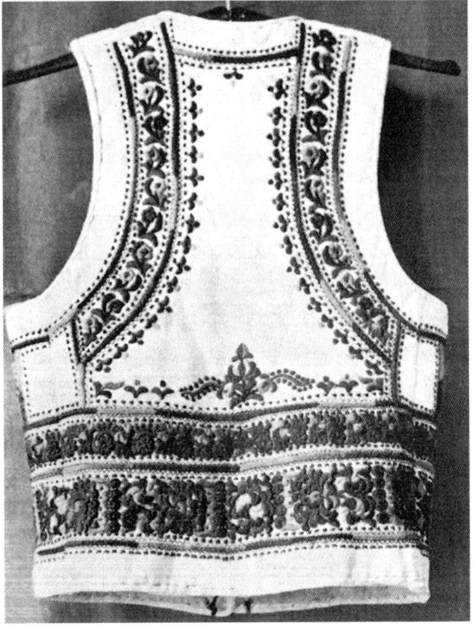

Dewar's concern here for the whole (that is, the coordination of textiles, furniture, colour, shape and environment, as well as her intimation of forms of relaxation made possible and enhanced by the combination of functionalism and aesthetics), espoused in the early 1900s, actually goes beyond that of one particular analysis of the building written in the late twentieth century, which concentrates exclusively on its architectural structure.[53] As such, and with her conveyance of uplifting interior and exterior, she provides an important, mostly Newberyan Glasgow School of Art-inspired, appreciation of artistic integration with life. This was particularly important for the Harkness House audience. Opened in October 1931, the centre was organised by the British Association of Residential Settlements and funded by the American philanthropist Edward Harkness through his Pilgrim Trust. During the five years of its existence it acted as an adult crafts, education and social institute in one of Lanarkshire's, if not Scotland's, most deprived areas, where the local weaving, mining and steel industries were then in rapid decline and unemployment at record levels. Operating out of a converted bank, pub and steelworks canteen, it also provided scholarships for foreign travel and education, published a journal, curated exhibitions of members' work and organised numerous educational and social excursions, the former particularly to Glasgow School of Art and Glasgow University. Upon its opening Katherine Dewar had stated that learning, exploring and experimenting in numerous fields of art lay at the core of the centre's mission. Needlework, inspired by Jessie's and Macbeth's teaching and practice, had a prominent place in this core (despite Jessie's contribution going unacknowledged):

> *The 'reform in needlework' was the invention or idea of a student at the Glasgow School of Art, Miss Ann McBeth [sic], and was taken up by the Glasgow School of Art so extensively that its practice has spread all over the country. A pupil of Miss McBeth in this new artistic fashion in sewing work, Miss A. Knox Arthur, is to take the needlework class at Harkness House, so it will be assured that the very first-hand knowledge of the new cult and practice will be available to all who have the good sense to attend.*[54]

Though Harkness House organised joint classes in some arts, there was greater choice for women, with needlework being solely the distaff-side domain. Hence, presumably, the interest in it as a male practice. An exhibition of Anne Arthur's needlework was on display at the centre at the time of its opening. Then, recognising how Bellshill had been enhanced by the arrival of eastern Europeans during the coal mining boom years (in fact it was known locally as 'Little Lithuania'), 'Miss Dewar complimented the Poles and Lithuanians on their beautiful handicraft and gave a warm invitation to that part of the community to participate in the movement now being formed.'[55] Evidently the Dewar sisters were alert to a range of the qualities of eastern European folk art and how these may be incorporated into contemporary Scottish work. It was not by chance that they headed to the Balkans in the first two summers after Harkness House opened and that thereafter Baltic met Balkan fabrications in Bellshill.

Such openness to cultural variety, and to how learning of some of its ways may offer opportunity for development, informed the remaining artistic contributions that Dewar made to Le Play Society publications. None of these feature the textile work that we have hitherto considered. Hence, her final image for the East Carpathian survey was

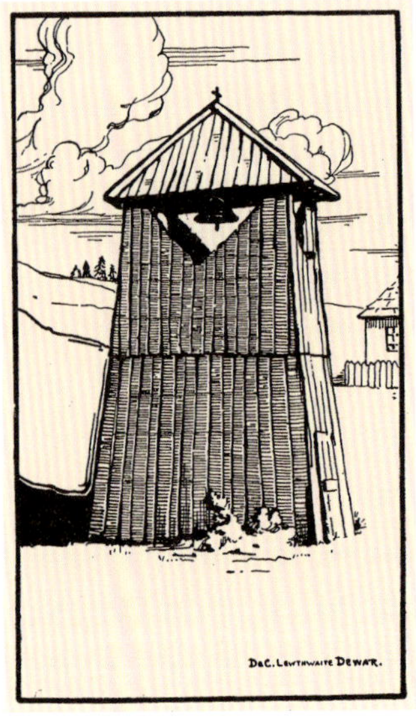

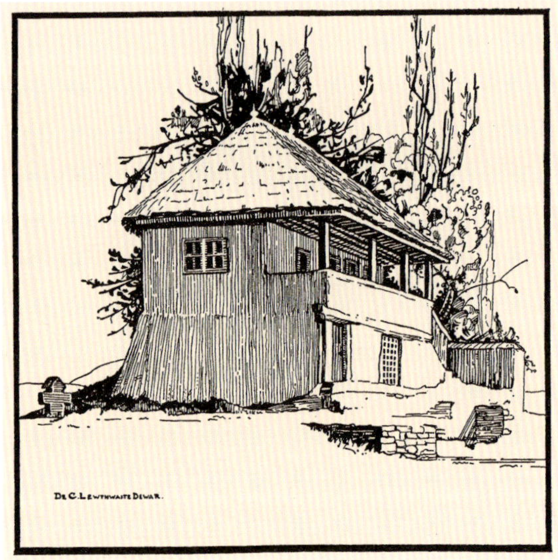

Clockwise from above

3.22 | De Courcy Lewthwaite Dewar, 'Borsec bell tower'; from H.J. Fleure and R.A. Pelham (eds), *Roumania: East Carpathian Studies* (London: Le Play Society, 1936), opp. p. 35

3.23 | De Courcy Lewthwaite Dewar, 'Potters' house'; from H.J. Fleure and E. Estyn Evans (eds), *Roumania II: South Carpathian Studies* (London; Le Play Society, 1939), p. 31

3.24 | De Courcy Lewthwaite Dewar, 'Potters' Church of the Assumption of the Virgin, Curtea de Argeș'; from H.J. Fleure and E. Estyn Evans (eds), *Roumania II: South Carpathian Studies* (London; Le Play Society, 1939), p. 24

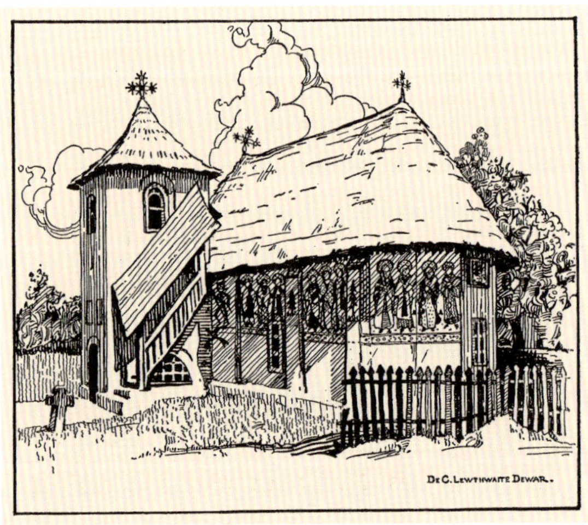

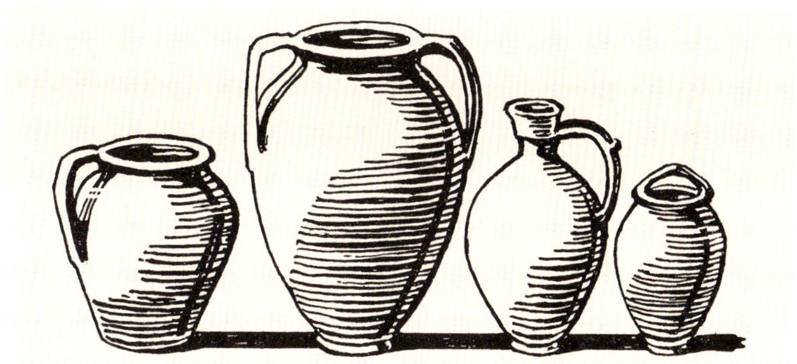

3.25 | De Courcy Lewthwaite Dewar, 'Pottery'; from H.J. Fleure and E. Estyn Evans (eds), *Roumania II: South Carpathian Studies* (London; Le Play Society, 1939), p. 26

of a wooden bell tower in Borsec, while her drawings for the South Carpathian report were of 'The cream-washed and painted church of St. Mary at Curtea de Argeș', 'A small house in Curtea de Argeș of similar type to Mayor's house' and four examples of local pottery: jars captioned 'Brown clay. White & green slip' [figs 3.22–3.25].[56] Focusing on the ancient town that was once the capital of Wallachia, this second survey highlights a society quite distinct from that of Corbu to the north. Now it is the craft of pottery that comes to the fore in text and image, emphasising its prominent place in the local economy. Thus we know that Dewar's painted church is close to the homes of 'numerous craftsmen, especially potters',[57] and that her house is almost certainly that of a potter, with photographs, plans and descriptions of it included nearby. Irrespective of this prominence for pottery, fabric making and textile art comes a close second and is subject to numerous photographs (many again by Howard), not least of the richly embroidered local dress, the floral motifs of which often have a vibrancy lacking in the Corbu designs.

By illustrating the Le Play Society publications and bringing at least some of their findings to Bellshill, Dewar's Balkan fabrications are a unique, but integrated, artistic expression of what Beaver discerned as a key achievement and legacy of the society's fieldwork, beyond its import into the philosophy and curricula of geography: 'the fostering of international good-will through the contact of scientists and ordinary people across the barriers of political boundaries, race and language.'[58]

Mann, with a Balkan slant

It remains to be discovered how much more evidence of Balkan craft influence there is in Dewar's little-known late work. What is certain is that an awareness of Balkan peasant art surfaces in designs by her younger contemporary, Kathleen Mann. As Jessie's, Macbeth's and

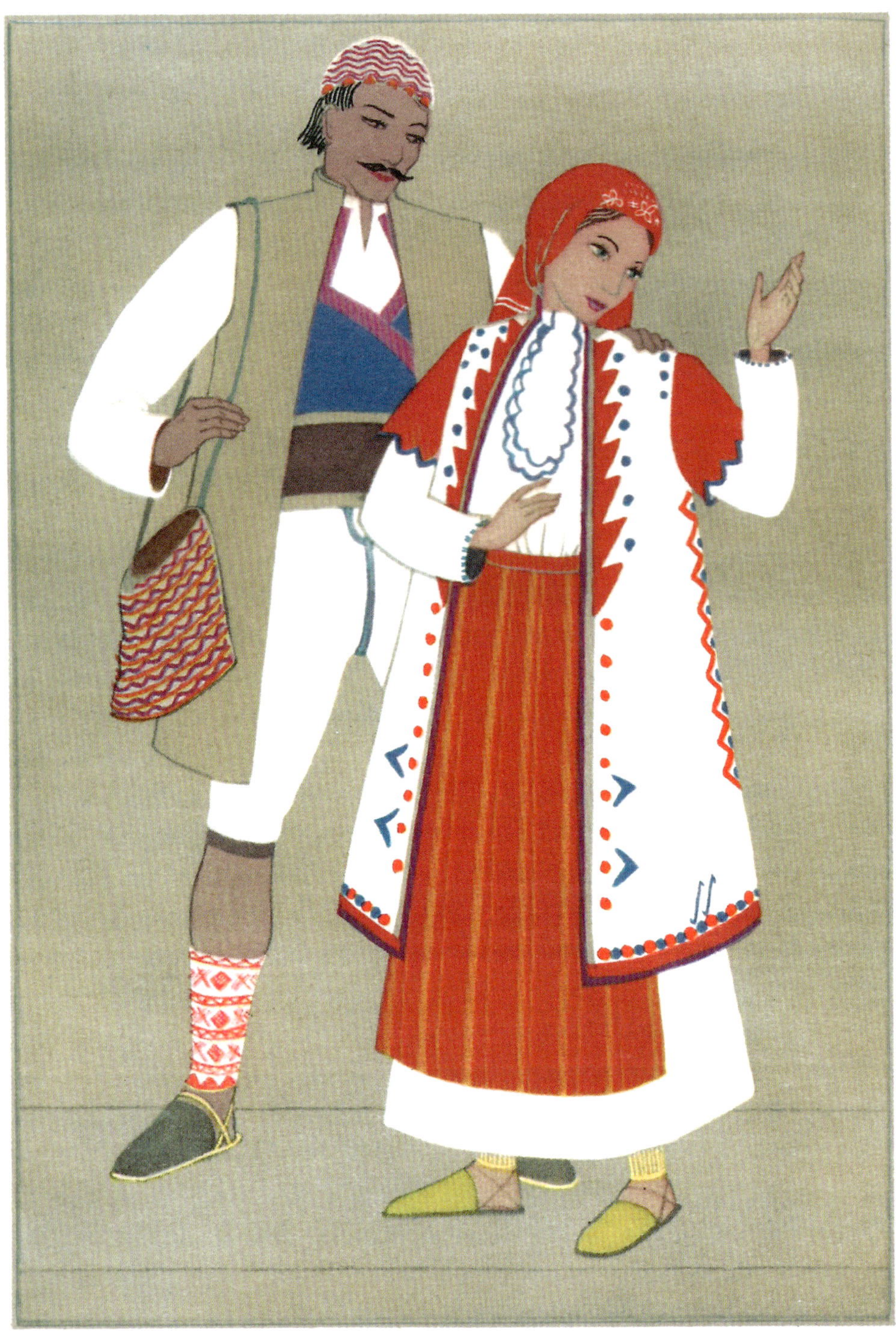

3.26 | Kathleen Mann, 'Yugoslavia'; from Kathleen Mann, *Peasant Costume in Europe*, Book 2 (London: A.&C. Black, 1936), opp. p. 90

Arthur's successor in advancing new approaches to embroidery at the Glasgow School of Art, following her appointment in 1931 she promoted greater spontaneity, large-scale, and creative use of machine embroidery.[59] An active participant in the Modern Embroideries Society's exhibitions and the Needlework Development Scheme, for the latter she was enlisted, along with other staff from Scotland's art colleges, to travel to Europe to collect examples of contemporary and peasant embroidery that could then be distributed to schools and further education institutions as teaching aids.[60] She was dispatched to France and Italy for this purpose in 1934. Simultaneously Mann was engaged in the preparation of textile art books, designed as aids to practice, that featured her interpretation of embroidery designs from across the continent, including the Balkans, for example *Peasant Costume in Europe* (1931 and 1936), *Embroidery Design and Stitches* (1937), *Appliqué Design and Method* (1937) and *Design from Peasant Art* (1939). She placed two colour plates and sixteen line drawings of Balkan dress in the second volume of *Peasant Costume*. If her sources were samples brought back to Scotland by her colleagues on the Needlework Development Scheme, she provides no reference to this (or any other source). Nevertheless, she enacts a Balkan performance that sees Croatian, Bulgarian, Serbian, Macedonian, Montenegrin, Bosnian and Albanian design simplified and stereotyped 'in order that the shape of the garments and the designs imposed upon them may be the more easily read', the ultimate aim being 'to present in a convenient form typical examples of peasant costume … useful to the artist and designer'.[61]

Mann's Balkan costumes in *Peasant Costume* feature fifteen female and five male figures.[62] They all stand, most facing the viewer. The majority pose and gesture dramatically. Hands are peacefully open, except on two occasions where they are modestly clasped. Eyes, with a few notable exceptions, are averted. There is no sign of engagement in labour other than two men carrying small articles strung over a shoulder. Hence, the only evidence of distaffs, spindles, needles, and so on is in the schematic representation of dress. Through this an association with the artistic images of Jessie's postcard collection is manifest. Frequently, but not always, Mann identifies the Balkan nations whose costumes she illustrates. She commences with a colour plate of Croatian dress (captioned 'Yugoslavia') [fig. 3.26], its serious couple in coordinated pose and gesture. Here, the woman wears an embroidered white outer garment, red-striped apron, white dress and red headscarf, somewhat akin to the clothing of Fra's *Serbian Woman*. In the book, however, the image is paired with the second Balkan colour plate, representing 'Bulgaria' [fig. 3.27]. Again we are given a couple, now more obviously posed as dancers and with ample red and green embroidery on the woman's pinafore dress that combines geometrical pattern with floral motifs.[63]

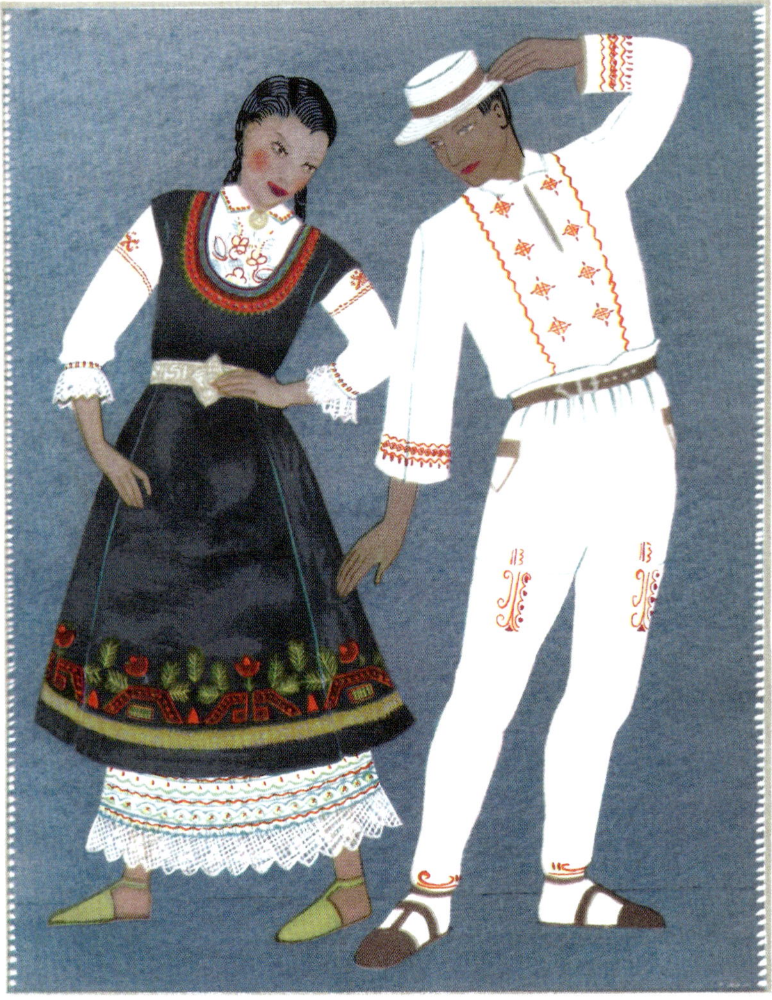

3.27 | Kathleen Mann, 'Bulgaria'; from Kathleen Mann, *Peasant Costume in Europe*, Book 2 (London: A. & C. Black, 1936), opp. p. 100

The one *Peasant Costume* image that Mann labels as Serbian shows a girl standing awkwardly with bent arms and index fingers pointing in different directions [fig. 3.28a]. She describes her intricately decorated outfit and then expands to Serbian folk design generalisations:

A Serbian costume of great beauty … the costume is full of interest, from the shallow fez-shaped hat, trimmed with heart-shaped metal discs, beautifully embroidered skirt, bodice, and apron. The chief colours used in the designs of the Serbian peasants are yellows, reds, and blues. Woven and embroidered designs often have yellow-green or cream grounds. Zigzags, diamonds, and squares are commonly used as motives.[64]

If the image and description partially correlate with and partially belie Fra and Jessie's 'Serbian' costumes this only reinforces the idea of their and the wider British Balkan fabrication that is our concern. Furthermore Mann's Serbian dress contains no colour and few of the motifs she mentions, it rather being dominated by floral patterns and straight lines. However, her 'Serbia' image is preceded by a drawing she labels 'Belt from Macedonia', comprised of rich rhomboid and zigzag patterns [fig. 3.28c]. In addition, her final drawing is of a costume she identifies as 'Macedonia'; this shows similarities, not least through the rows and columns of busy zigzags covering the apron and hems, with the designs in the Newberys' collected and painted works [fig. 3.28b]. She complements the drawings with a simplistic note on Macedonian ways, which over-imagines the extent of the needlework:

> *the people of Western Macedonia, who now live in Yugoslavia, are of a lively and entertaining character and skilled in many handicrafts. Heavy coloured fringe is an outstanding note of their costume. Scarcely*

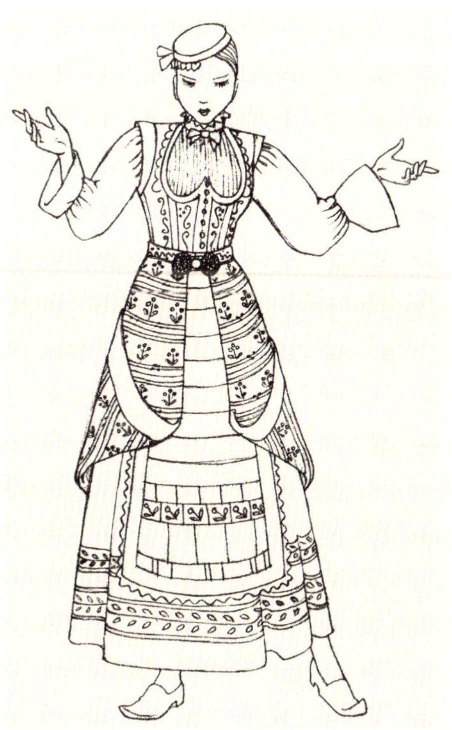

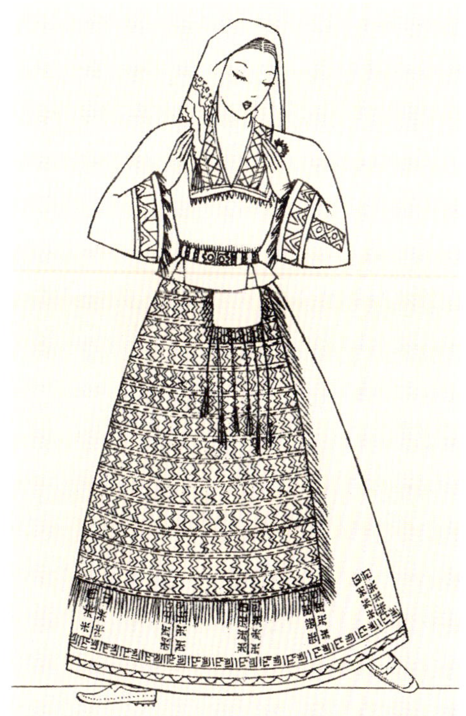

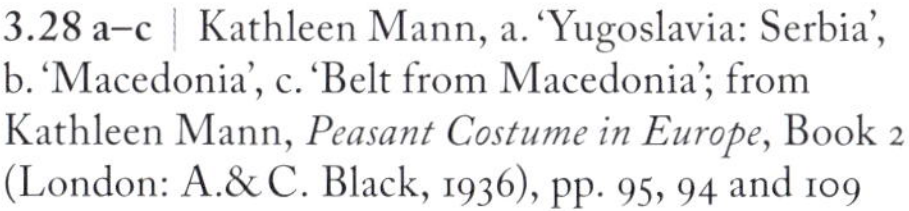

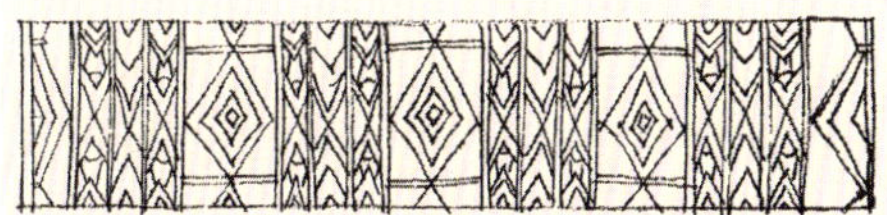

3.28 a–c | Kathleen Mann, a. 'Yugoslavia: Serbia', b. 'Macedonia', c. 'Belt from Macedonia'; from Kathleen Mann, *Peasant Costume in Europe*, Book 2 (London: A.&C. Black, 1936), pp. 95, 94 and 109

Of Mann's other books it is *Design from Peasant Art* that contains numerous Yugoslavian and Romanian motifs and designs derived from them. It has eight colour plates of her own textile art, which she complements with descriptions of technique, composition, colour, subject and hints of sources. The last comprise: Hungarian, Yugoslavian, Swedish, German, Romanian, Swiss and Russian, with one not having a particular source. Each plate is a distinct essay in needlework, the variety being intended to show ways in which interpretation of peasant craft can fuel modern art:

> ... *peasant work must be approached for inspiration in design, with the mind of an artist who seeks refreshment by studying these works and will use their good qualities, adding to them that something which the individual alone can give.*[66]

The colour plates complement an array of drawings on more than seventy pages. These move from sketches of folk motifs – originating in a great range of crafts from many parts of Europe – through to her own designs, which utilise those peasant forms in an original manner, some

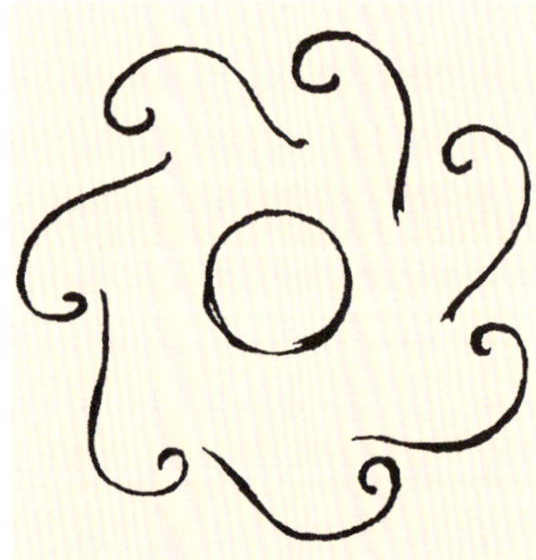

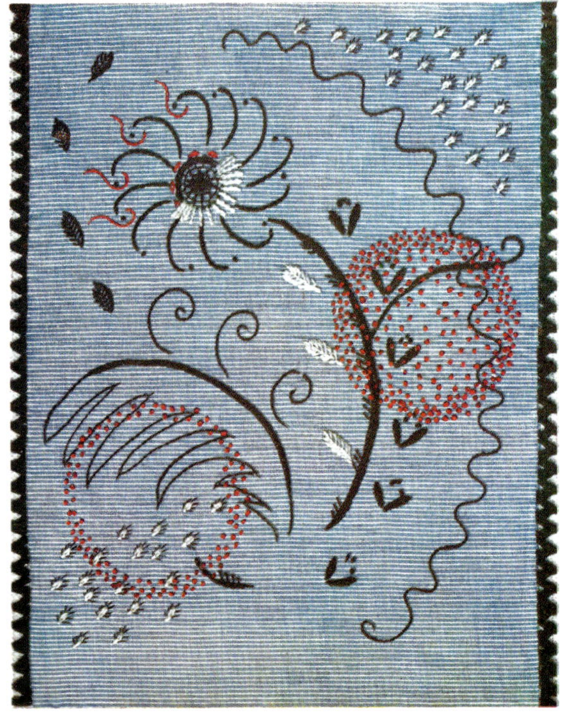

3.29 a–b | Kathleen Mann, 'Yugoslavia', flower sketch [above], and 'Floral Motive on Blue and White Material', embroidered shirting fabric, cotton, filoselle and mallard floss [right]; from Kathleen Mann, *Design from Peasant Art* (London: A.&C. Black, 1939), p. 31 and opp. p. 18

being adapted for expression in a particular medium, such as linocuts, wood engraving, leatherwork and china- and glass-ware. Through this compilation she gives a broad, syncretic setting to her Balkan observations and experiments, thereby attempting to open up new avenues for design, free from adherence to rules, conventions or divisive national motivations. As such hers is a liberal, pacific alternative to the aggressive exploitations of peasant visual languages that were simultaneously being promoted by schism-inducing fascist regimes across the continent in the run-up to the Second World War.

The two Balkan-inspired colour designs shown serve as cogent examples of Mann's ways of creative extrapolation. She introduces the first – 'Floral Motive on Blue and White Material' [fig. 3.29b] – thus: 'The floral motive around which this design plays is from Yugoslavia.'[67] No further details are given apropos the source although several pages later (p. 31) a line drawing captioned 'Yugoslavia' [fig. 3.29a] represents a highly simplified whorl, the separate petals of which move in hooked rotation akin to the flower in Mann's floral motive. In her description of the first image she emphasises spontaneity, though she also stresses how choices are made in terms of stitches, knots, thread and colour. The composition is balanced by an interplay between its circular and curved forms, giving the work a sense of organic, rhythmical movement. In this there is also a touch of Jessie's and Macbeth's love of abstracted floral-linear motifs, yet with a new, seemingly freer, vitality. Adding another Balkan slant, she notes that both the black and the white leaf shapes are created in Romanian stitch, that is their longer stitches are centrally tied by a shorter, slanted stitch.

While the red, white and black 'Floral Motive' was stitched on the blue and white horizontal lines of a tightly woven shirting fabric, Mann uses a looser hexagonal net as the basis for her second Balkan work [fig. 3.30]. The marked difference between the two is intimated by her description, this giving more detail as to the inspiration: 'The idea for this panel came from a Rumanian icon painted on glass.'[68] Her visual reference to this is her sketch from a Transylvanian icon of the Mother of Sorrows [fig. 3.31]. In fact she appropriated this from a black-and-white photograph of the icon reproduced in Oprescu's *Peasant Art of Roumania* [fig. 3.32].[69] The Romanian peasant vogue for such craft began around the turn of the eighteenth century, being introduced from Austria, Bohemia and Bavaria, though the treatment of figures and composition shows Byzantine influence. The subject of the sorrowful Mary with crucified Christ was popular among Transylvanian glass icon painters, several examples being found today in Romanian museums. Mann's borrowing is clear but so is her departure from the icon. In her transference to textile she not only simplifies but alters. Christ, angels and buildings vanish. White curved lines appear, like pulses crossing the composition, the effect of which, as Mann notes, is both

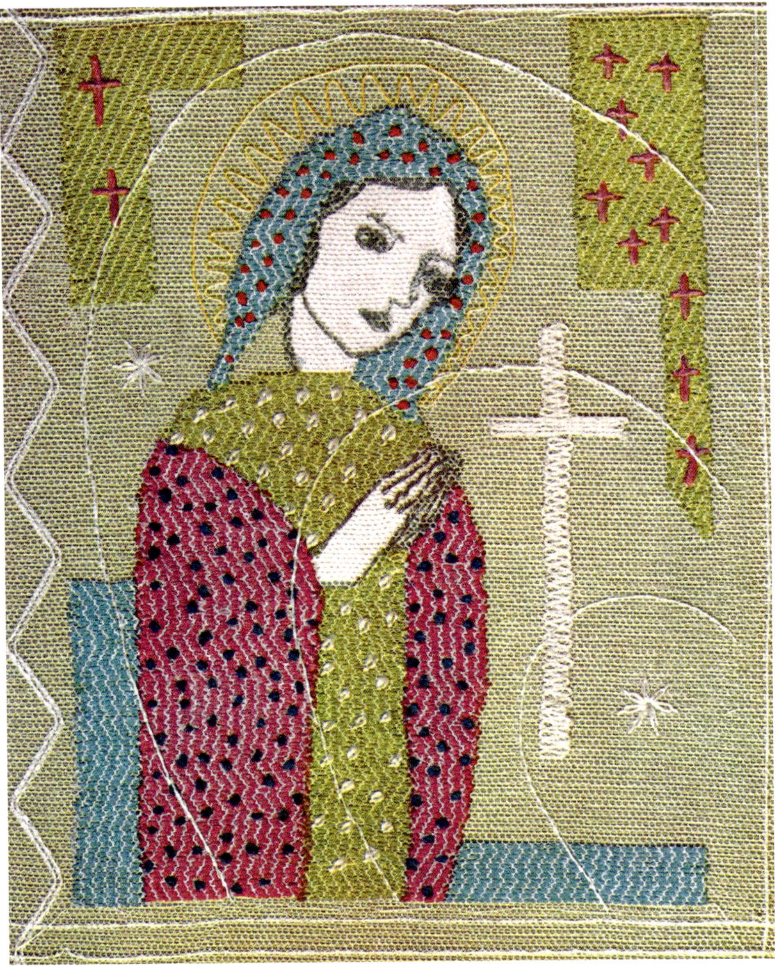

3.30 | Kathleen Mann, 'Virgin Mary', coloured thread on net fabric; from Kathleen Mann, *Design from Peasant Art* (London: A.&C. Black, 1939), opp. p. 54

to hold the materials together and to add white, 'so that the mass of the white face and hands should not seem too sudden'. They lead the eye to the cross, the Virgin and then beyond to the background of small crosses and zigzag border. So while detail is lost it is also added. Hence too the addition of relief through the thicker threads of the zigzag and cross, and the breaking up of the masses of the Virgin's robe and head-dress by interplays of diverse stitches and knots (using dull and shiny thread).

Ten years on, her Virgin is Mann's answer to Fra's Macedonian-ish *Annunciation*. She stated that her colours, while 'not dull … have a certain sombreness which is in keeping with the subject'.[70] Her attraction to Romanian religious art is enunciated in the introduction to *Design from Peasant Art*, along with how it offers an alternative side to peasant

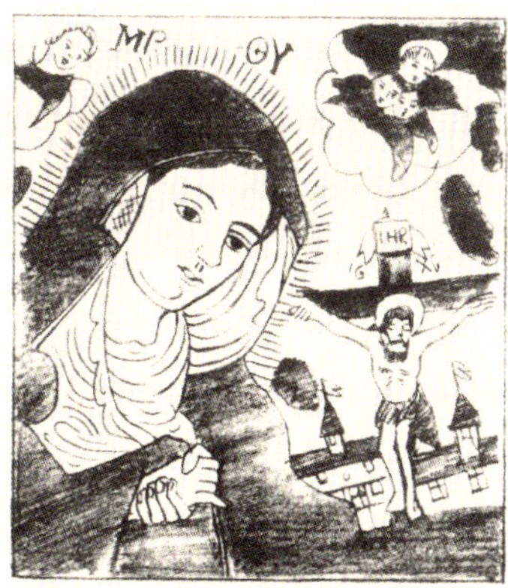

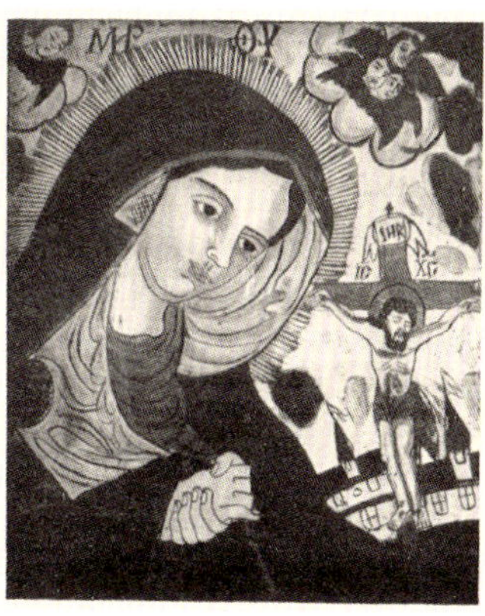

3.31 | Kathleen Mann, sketch of Transylvanian 'Mother of Sorrows' icon on glass; from Kathleen Mann, *Design from Peasant Art* (London: A.& C. Black, 1939), opp. p. 23

3.32 | Unknown artist, 'Mother of Sorrows', pre-1929, icon on glass, Nicula, Transylvania; from George Oprescu, *Peasant Art in Roumania* (London: The Studio Ltd., 1929), p. 8

art. Thus she differentiates between that which is 'beautiful either because of its gayness, richness or fanciful qualities' and 'more serious work in the icons', including her sketched Romanian ones, 'which have a quaint, primitive dignity'.[71] She subsequently revels in the polychromy of Romanian wooden grave crosses and wayside calvaries, as well as the assemblage craft of the stars of Bethlehem carried by Romanian boys at Christmas.[72] Mann reproduces her sketch of what she calls a 'painted wooden wayside cross' replete with primitive Madonna and Child (p. 39), plus her own design 'inspired by a Rumanian wayside cross', which is essentially a linear study of a girl's head, full-face and in headscarf (p. 70) [fig. 3.33]. She claims that this 'Virgin's head … is

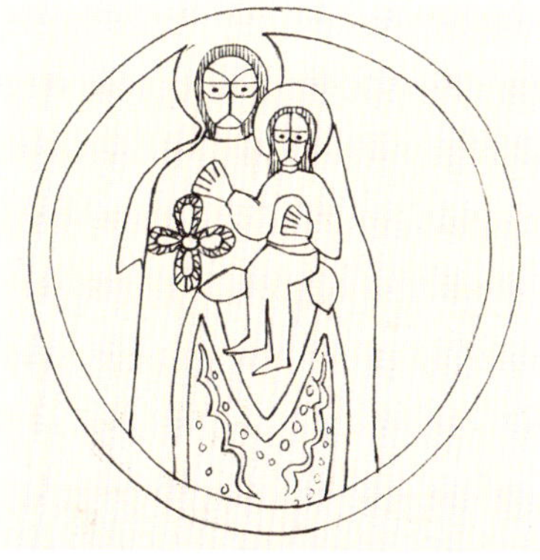

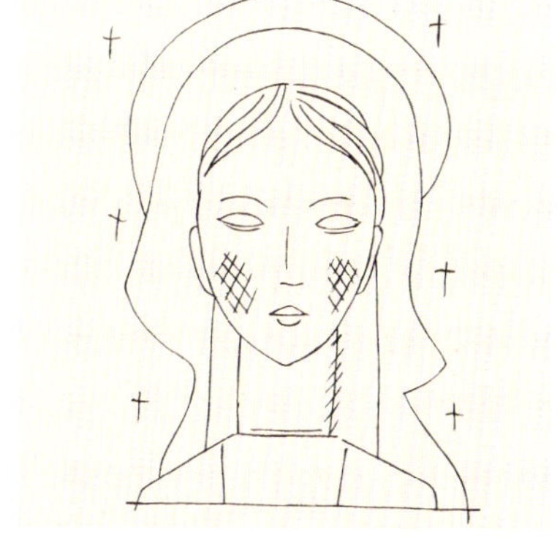

3.33 a–b | Kathleen Mann, 'Romanian wooden wayside cross', sketch [left], and 'Virgin', design sketch [right], from Kathleen Mann, *Design from Peasant Art* (London: A.& C. Black, 1939), pp. 39, 70

designed with a feeling for long perpendicular shapes to gain a serene and dignified effect.'[73]

In recognising the creative use to which Balkan peasant art could be put by contemporary artists Mann also offered numerous other simple drawings, many of which feature stylised bird, animal, floral and geometric motifs. Thus she shows a bird pattern border of a Romanian carpet, an embroidered Romanian deer and horse, and a Romanian bird and flowers from painted chinaware, plus an embroidered man's hat and a whole range of floral patterns from Yugoslavia. She finds bird motifs favoured in peasant design and argues for their frequently exhibiting 'a delightful stretch of fancy'.[74] With this in mind she presents two of her own designs from 'Yugoslav' birds, without mentioning medium or individual nation [fig. 3.34 a–b]. Instead she makes formal observations, noting that the first is within a circle whose border changes at seemingly arbitrary intervals (from radiating lines to zigzags). That this is a vivacious feature of 'many peasant works' adds to its potential value for the contemporary artist. Likewise, with the bird of the second design she comments on stylistic traits as a priority, this time indicating how she departs from her source:

> *the method of breaking the outline with short radiating lines was present in the original, but the disposition of the design is very different. In the Yugoslav example the bird formed part of a very intricate floral design.*[75]

These two little black-and-white sketches, for all their seeming modesty and playfulness, beg to be realised in colour and/or as textile,

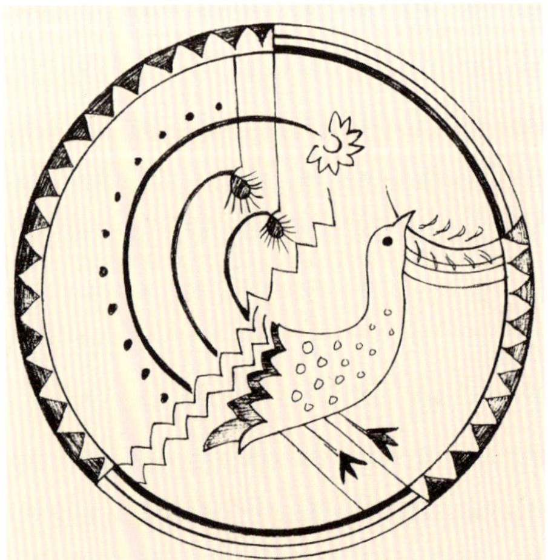
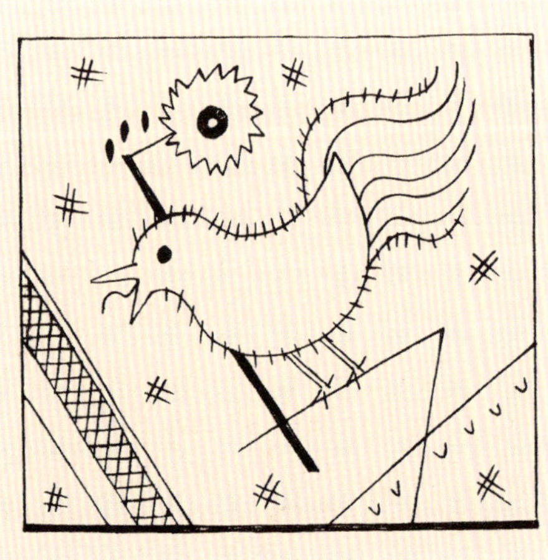

3.34 a–b | Kathleen Mann, designs sketches from Yugoslav bird motives; from Kathleen Mann, *Design from Peasant Art* (London: A.&C. Black, 1939), pp. 69, 77

ceramic or carved work. Yet, with their accompaniment to her realised Yugoslavian- and Romanian-inspired needlecraft, Mann completed her published Balkan fabrications and in so doing iterated an artistic journey constructed upon the inventive, synthetic trajectory of the Newberys.

Through the family

Fra and Jessie's adherence to the principle of good design for quality and fair living is apparent through Fra's Scottish east-coast work and it shares much in common with Arts-and-Crafts movement doctrines developed in Britain and overseas from the late nineteenth century. That it also impacted on their followers in Glasgow, not least three women artists who, coincidentally or otherwise, ventured into distinct forms of Balkan fabrication in the 1920s and 1930s, is significant. Most importantly, it is the couple's acculturative consideration of: 1. past, present and future; 2. local convention and adaptation; 3. the benefits brought through coordinated making and training of hand, eye and mind, that determines the character of their work and influence. Such consideration distinguishes *Serbian Women*, its transfer to Dundee, and Fra's and Jessie's teaching and evaluating on the banks of the Tay, Forth and Clyde.

But besides such handing over and down of their mutual, ultimately Balkan-tinged, all-encompassing aesthetics, is that which they passed on to their offspring in terms of objects brought back from southern Europe. Surviving examples of the various ceramics, jewellery and garments in the family collections are hard to definitively identify with a particular community or region, yet they are united in being fine functional objects, skilfully handmade and richly decorated. Examples include jugs and dishes with rich overglaze painting of simple linear, floral and bird motifs (the latter possibly Transylvanian) [fig. 3.35]. Also intricate gilded/silver and semi-precious stone brooches (Balkan so-called *tepeluk*-style headdress ornaments), earrings, bracelets and clasps (some of the latter possibly Bosnian) [fig. 3.36]. There is a strong possibility that at least one or two of the dishes are the bowls Jessie mentioned buying in Sofia, while the jug with small blue and green curvilinear motifs could have been acquired by her in Niš in 1926 since its style is that of ceramics produced in the Serbian region east of the Great Morava River.

Some of the jewellery might just have been included in the children's, grandchildren's and great-grandchildren's dressing-up boxes that Fra's and Jessie's great-granddaughters recall. Certainly the textiles were. That many got very well used, decayed and lost is inevitable. What survives, besides those already mentioned as appearing in

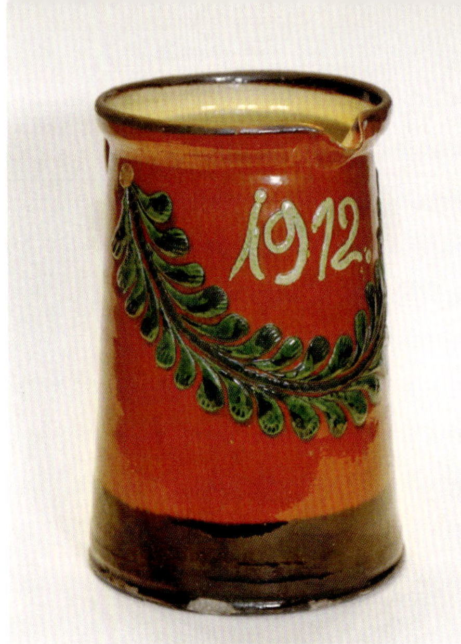

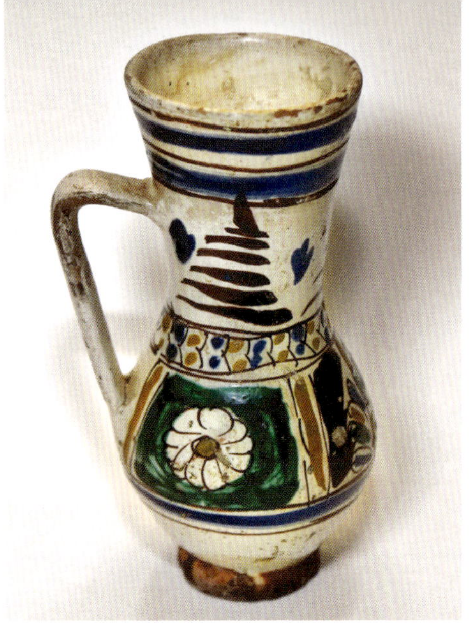

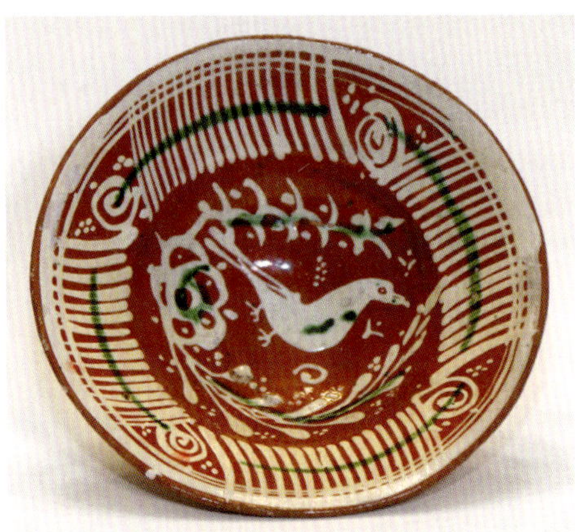

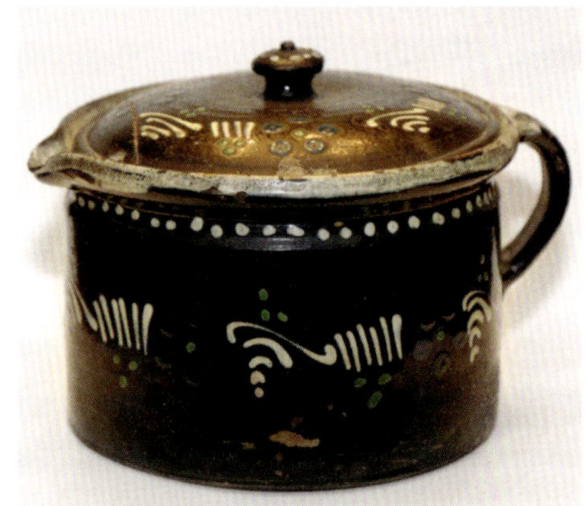

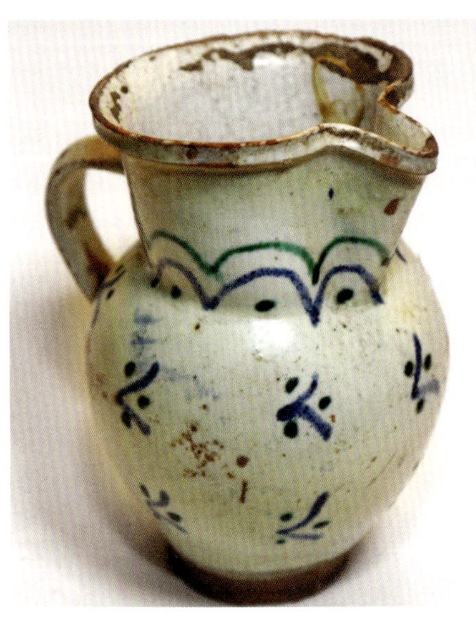

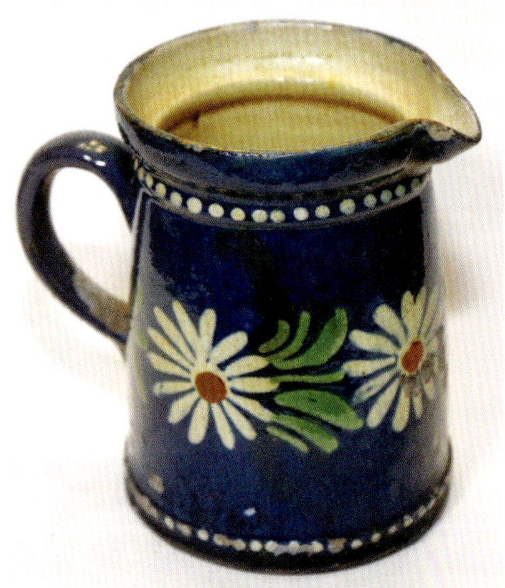

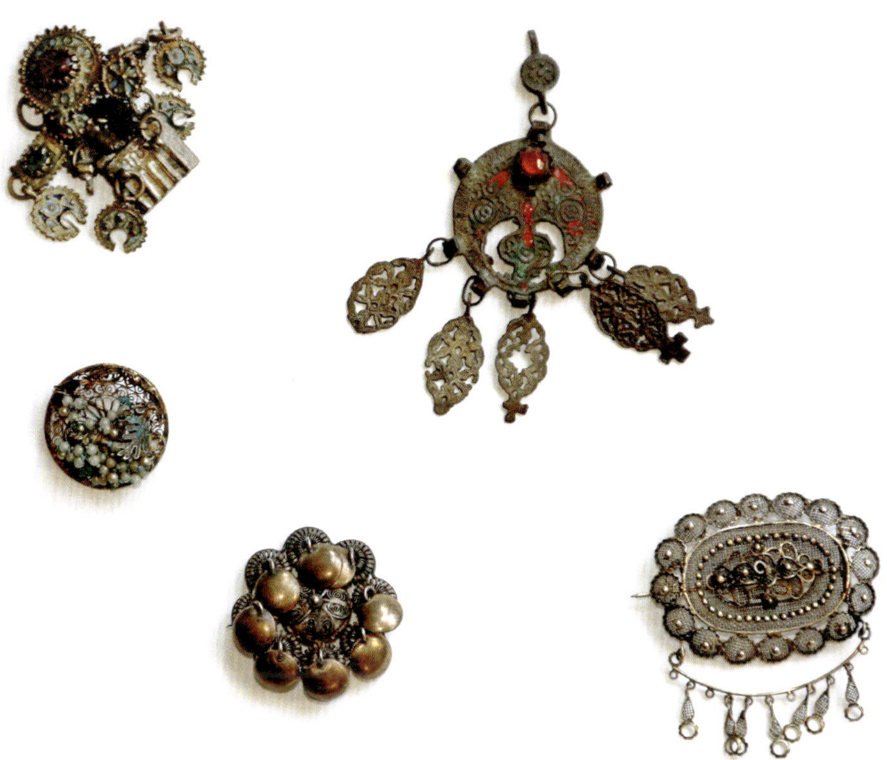

3.36 | Jewellery, *c.* 1920s, various metals, gems; collected by Jessie Newbery
PRIVATE COLLECTION

Serbian Women and *Serbian Musician*, include another richly embroidered waistcoat, this time of sheepskin lined with black wool and embroidered with bright, vaguely floral and abstract designs that suggest Romanian, Hungarian or Croatian origins [fig. 3.37]. There is also a woman's headscarf whose ends are embroidered with multiple bands of woollen zigzags, in keeping with those worn by the Catholic Mirdita (Albanian) womenfolk of Prizren, southern Kosovo [fig. 3.39].[76] Another shawl, this time embroidered with pink stylised trees, could be Transylvanian [fig. 3.38]. Among the other articles handed down are two distinctive linen bags, both decorated by bands of embroidered, predominately red, geometric motifs [e.g. fig. 3.40]. There are also two more aprons, one being embroidered with a swathe of bright blossoms that could possibly be Hungarian or Croatian [fig. 3.41].

That Jessie added her own touches to the fabrics, including, to the apron, a braid sewn under its fringe, indicates that these were not just

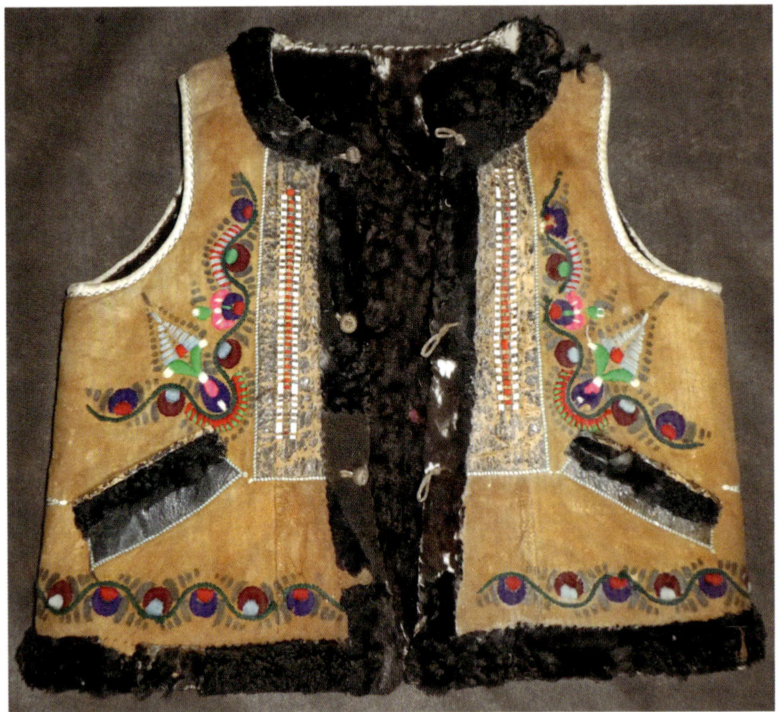

3.37 | Waistcoat (Romanian, Hungarian or Croatian?), *c.* 1920s, sheepskin, wool; collected by Jessie Newbery

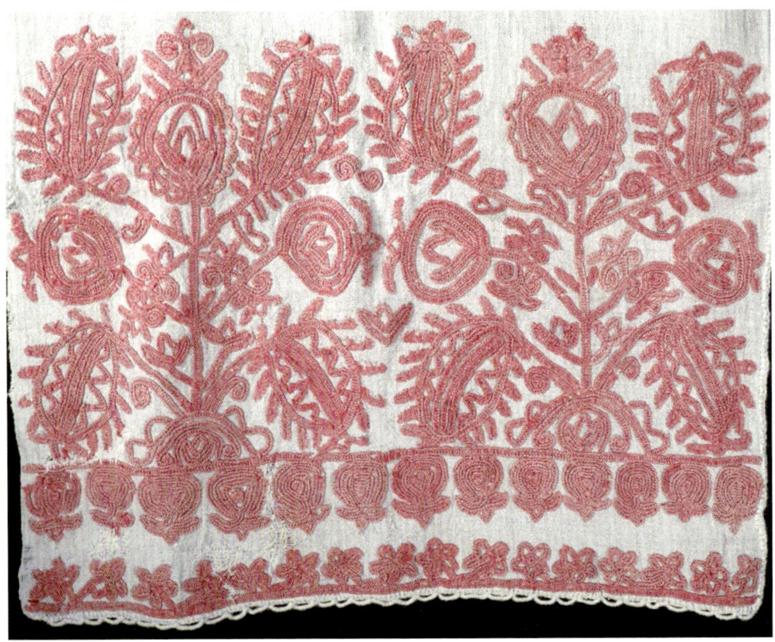

3.38 | Shawl (Transylvanian?), *c.* 1920s, linen, wool; collected by Jessie Newbery

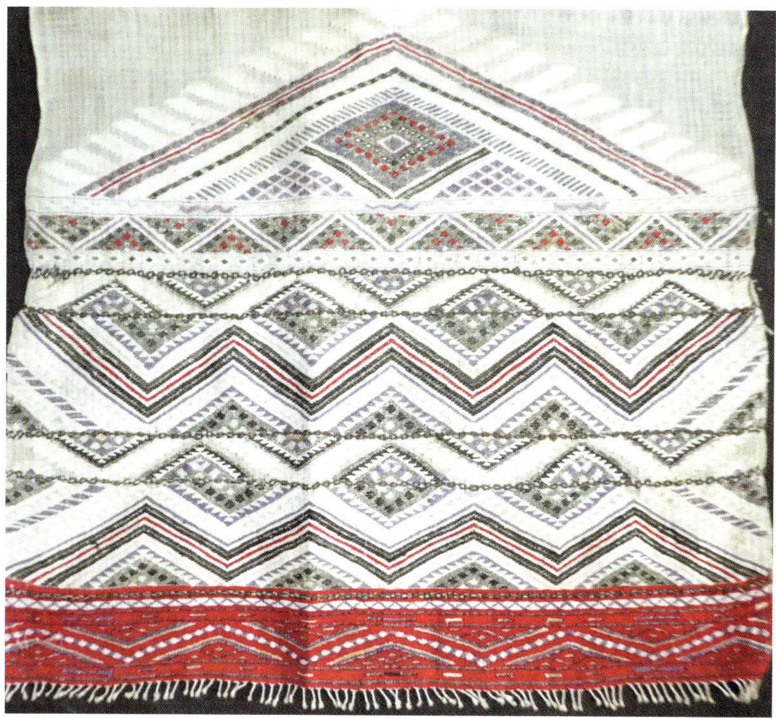

3.39 | Headscarf (Kosovo?), *c.* 1920s, wool; collected by Jessie Newbery

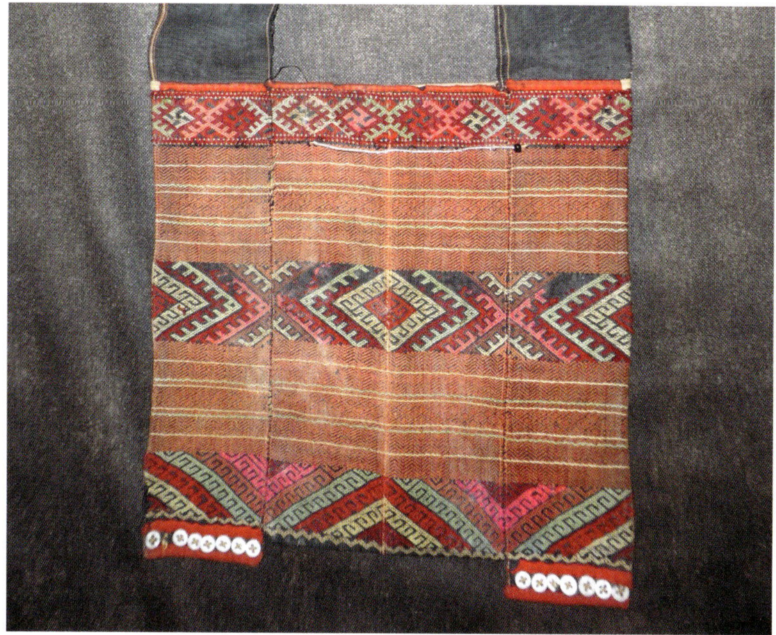

3.40 | Bag (Serbian?), *c.* 1920s, linen, wool; collected by Jessie Newbery

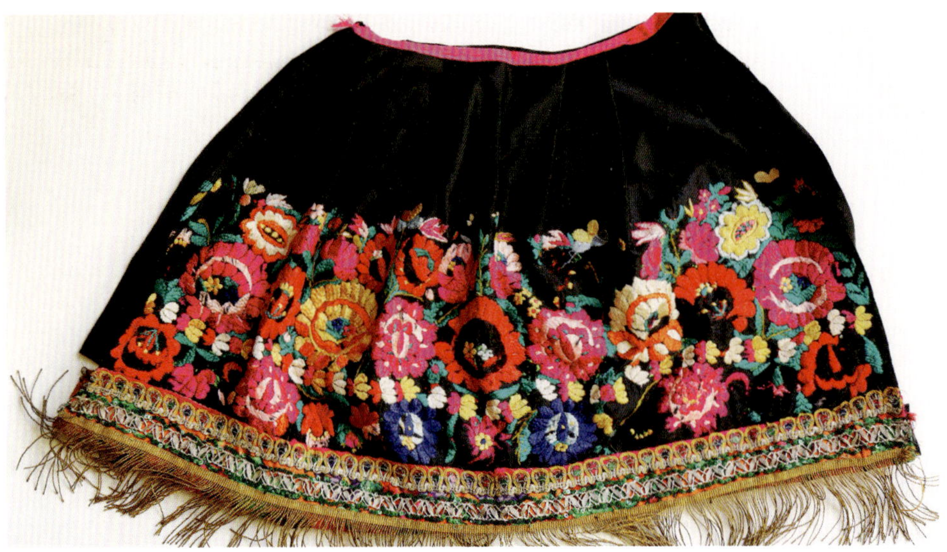

3.41 | Apron (Croatian or Hungarian?), *c.*1920s, embroidered silks on black satin; collected by Jessie Newbery

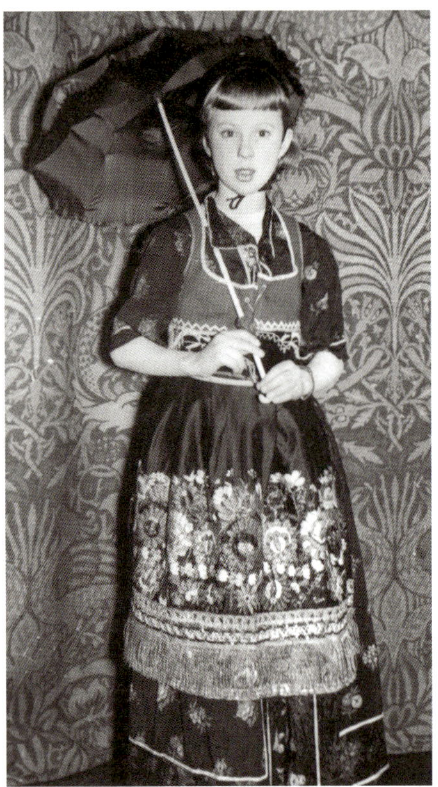

3.42 | Nicole Roberts wearing 'Vojvodinan' bodice and Croatian/Hungarian apron, *c.*1954

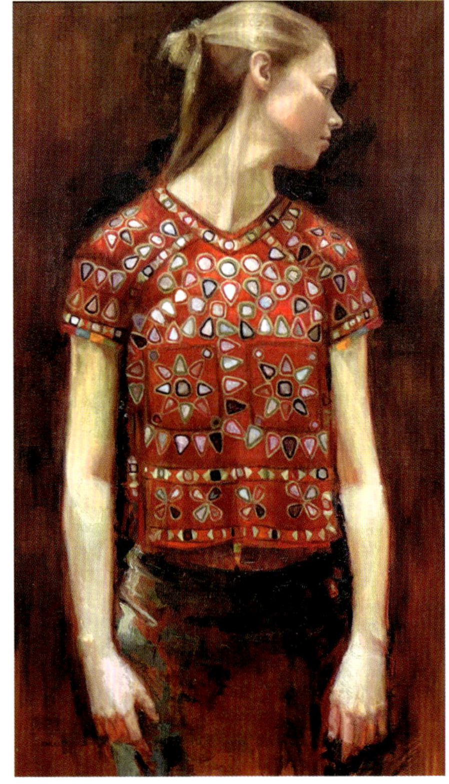

3.43 | **Denise Findlay** | *Mirrors*
2006, oil on linen, 107 x 61 cm

collected as souvenirs but also utilitarian objects whose appearance and function were open to adaptation. A photograph of a great-grand-daughter, Nicole Roberts, wearing the apron and a Balkan, possibly Vojvodinan, bodice indicates its use into the 1950s [fig. 3.42].[77] Further-more, in the late 1990s–2010s, a great-great-granddaughter, Denise Findlay, herself a figurative artist based in Glasgow and trained at the School of Art, painted a series of portraits in oil, including *Mirrors* (2006) [fig. 3.43], in which her models, sometimes fellow descendants of Fra and Jessie, wear ornamented collars and tops derived and re-interpreted from Jessie's collection.[78] Irrespective of any Balkan origins or references through such incarnations and images we glimpse Jessie's abiding, familial, network of correspondences.

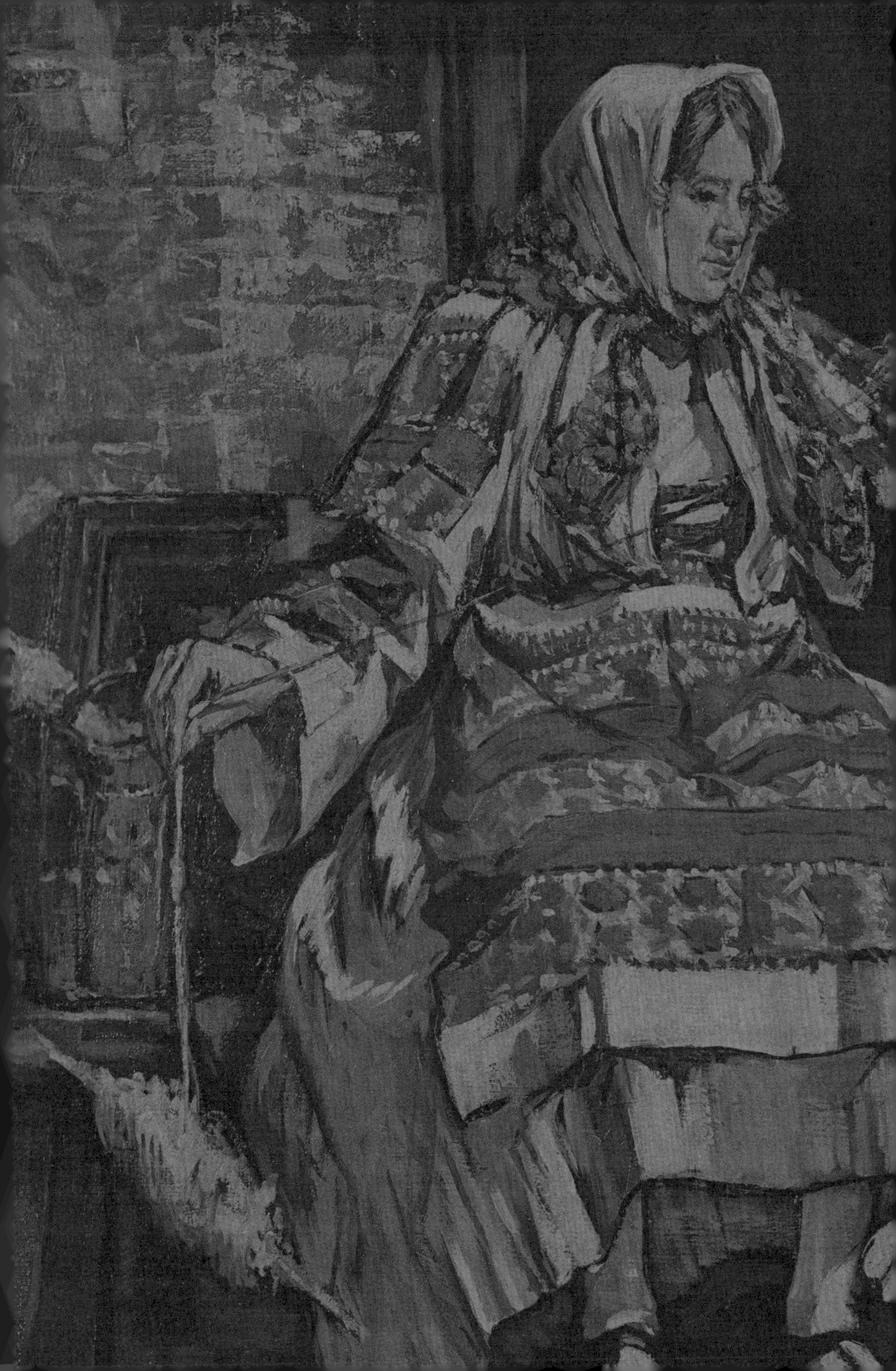

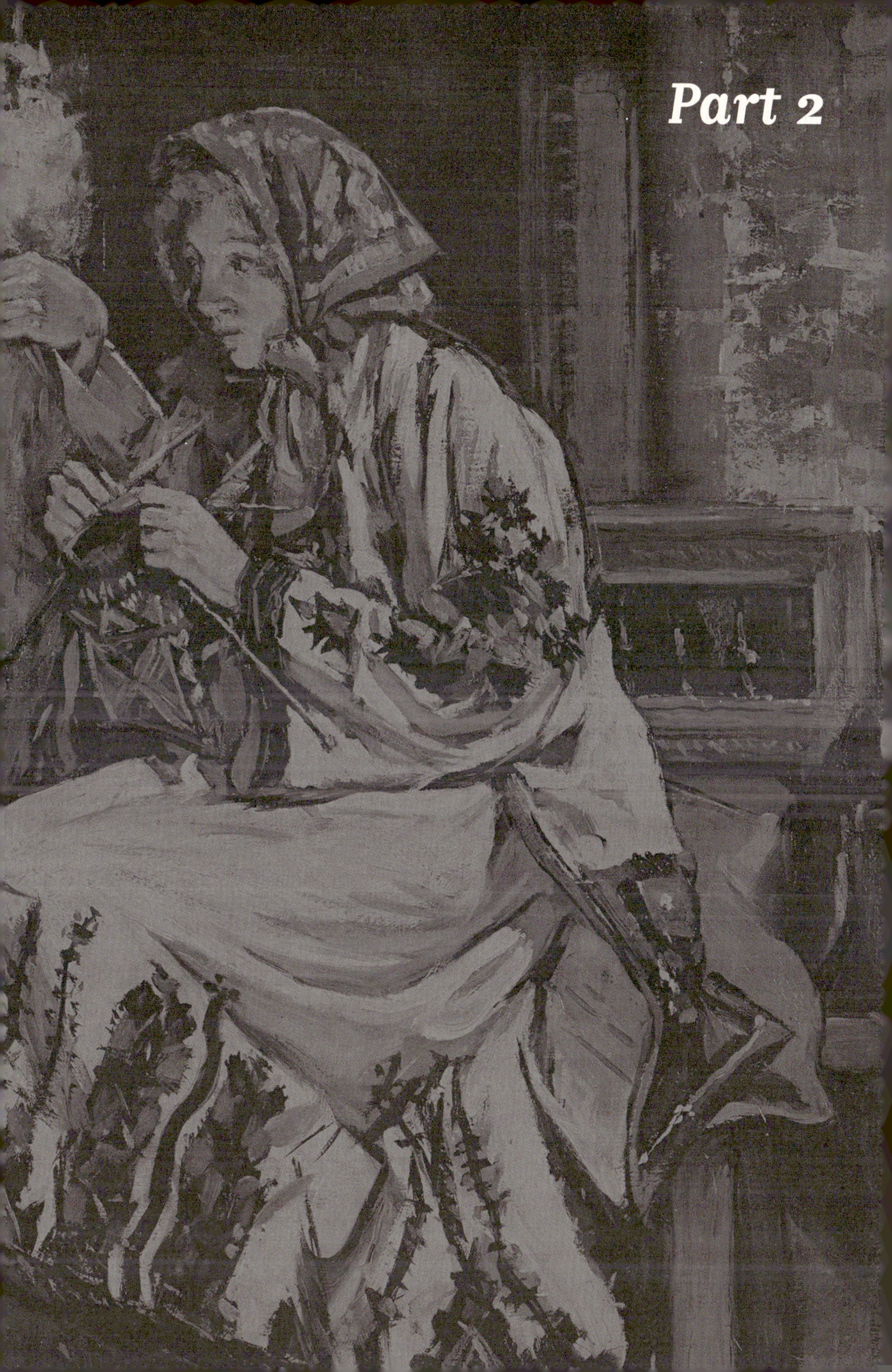
Part 2

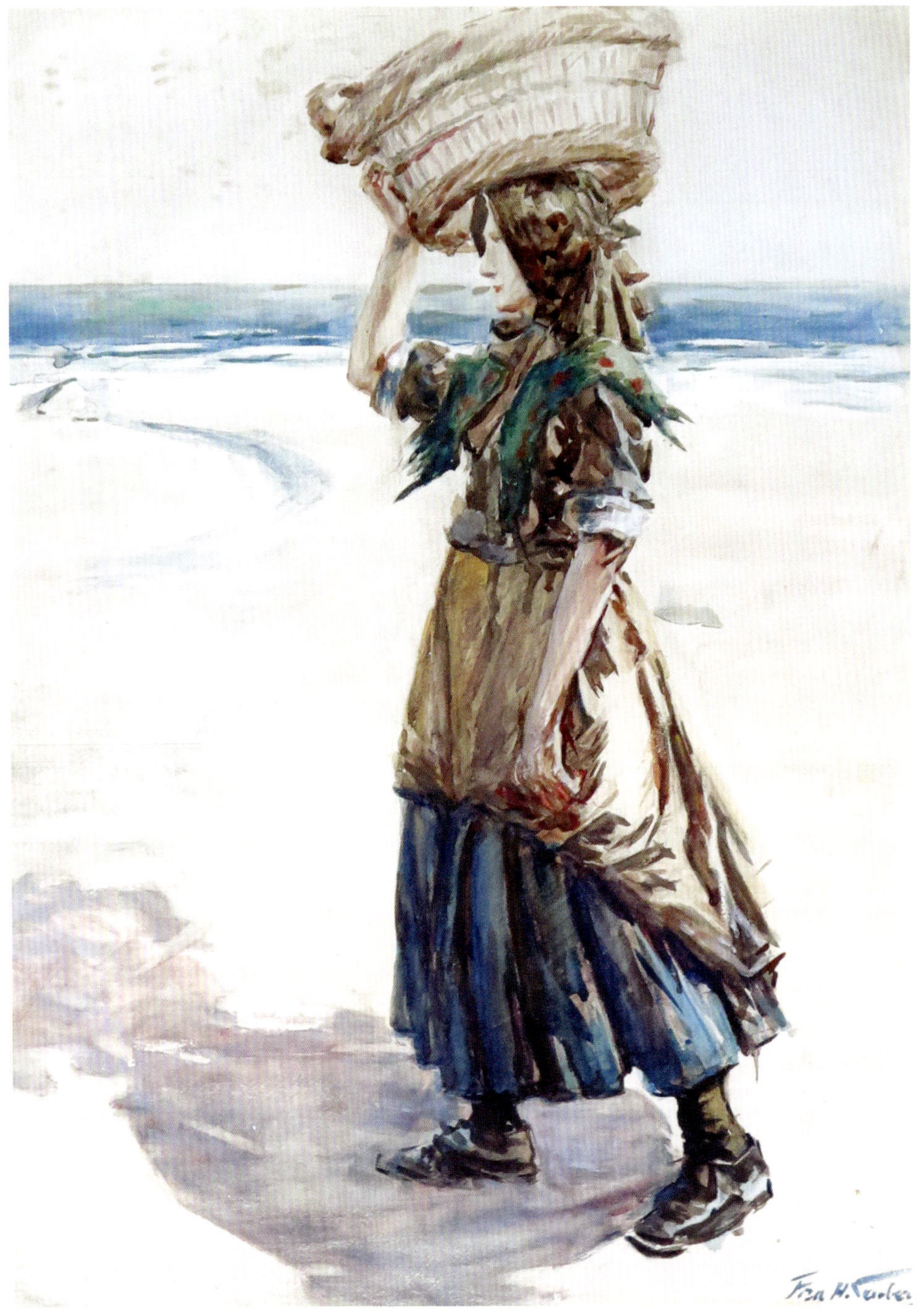

4.1 | Fra Newbery | *The Nimbus of Toil* | 1897, watercolour on board, 73.5 x 52 cm

4 CROSS-STITCHING
BALKAN CULTURE
AS INTERCULTURE

Filipino and lace traces

Three interrelated questions remain: 1. Where did Fra and Jessie's love for Balkan ornament and folk craft come from?; 2. How representative of Balkan culture was that which they saw, collected and interpreted?; 3. How does their acquaintance with the Balkans fit into the interwar context of the wider British, as well as other states', awareness of Balkan identity, history and potential?

In discussing the Newberys' Dorset years George Rawson observed the following:

> *In autumn … the couple would set out on their annual month–long excursion to the continent: to Italy, Spain or the Balkans. These trips with their complex itineraries were well planned and made good use of the railway timetables. Their favourite destination was Yugoslavia which they probably discovered in 1926 when they also visited Sofia in Bulgaria and Constantinople. They were particularly impressed by the still existing traditional culture: the peasant clothes, which Jessie described in detail in her letters and which they bought and brought back with them; the pottery; the jewellery; and the churches.*[1]

Such acknowledgment is useful, introducing as it does their Yugoslav fascination. We, however, need to go further. For 'suddenly', in their last years as creative artists, both Fra and Jessie adopted and adapted 'Serbian' articles, designs and subjects. Hence, in addition to being 'impressed' they set about creating works invigorated with new qualities of hybridity. In fact, as this essay hopefully shows, the Newberys' 'Balkan' folk turn was embedded in, and the ultimate fruition of, their mutually held philosophy of culture as interculture.

One key that runs across the threads of their 'Balkan' fabrications is agriculture, and with that stewardship of land and sea. After all, *Serbian Musician* represents a shepherd and *Serbian Women* the process and making of textiles derived from the products of farming (be they wool or flax). Lives and livelihoods dependent on cultivation or collection of nature's resources feature regularly throughout Fra's oeuvre. A cursory glance at titles of the pictures he exhibits over his career exemplifies this, for example: *The White Farm* and *Fishing* (1892); *The Nimbus of Toil* (1897); *Warden of the Marshes* (1899); *The Shepherd's Star* and *Net Mender* (1908); *The Bo'sun* (1909); *The Fen Reeve* (1915); *Tales of the Sea* (1916); *Cornfield* (1917); *The Reaper* (1918); *Dorset* (1923); *A Fisherwife* (1927).[2] Two versions of *The Nimbus of Toil* are known, both anticipating Borelli's 'Peasant Woman from Northern Dalmatia' painting-postcard (1928/29), discussed in chapter one [fig. 4.1].[3] All three works offer dignity and humanity through the poise of their solitary, purposeful and upright labouring women, who in Fra's case, instead of a platter of fruit, bear large wicker baskets on their heads and are frozen in their vertically cropped, sunlit, path. Standing on an empty beach in front of the sea, the suggestion is that Fra's working women are fisherwives aware of the place in which they find themselves.

The Newberys' subsequent move to Balkan-inspired creativity chimed with this concern for the nobility of work with the fruits of nature, not least because, as Jack Dunman was to show, in the 1920s almost eighty per cent of the Yugoslav population worked in agriculture, the vast majority of these being independent peasant smallholders.[4] That Dorset-born Dunman was to spend his life campaigning against the social ills wrought by twentieth-century undervaluation of that most essential of industries, agriculture, and himself made a tour of Yugoslavia in order to be able to cross-evaluate Croatian methods, coincides with the folk-based direction of the Newberys' interculturalism. The fact that the majority in Britain were starting to lose sight of food, clothes and concomitant craft production due to mechanisation, urbanisation and economic crisis sparked their mutual concerns. The crux was a fundamental problem that needed exposing both politically and artistically: despite the necessity of food and clothes, what was taking place in the United Kingdom was a rapid loss of employment and skills in agriculture, this in turn engendering wholesale loss of interest in how and where 'stuff is produced'.[5] As early as 1902, Fra, in calling for an end to the undervaluation of embroidery, had pointed to the primacy of agriculture's and needlework's mutual issues:

And the needle bears with it a dignity of labour that, if it be not greater than the plough, is yet one that puts it into the same category of absolute necessities. For man, if he cannot live without the plough, can equally as little do without the labour of the needle.[6]

Given the above, one way of comprehending the Newberys' evolution to 'Serbian' material is by returning to their last years in Glasgow, and in particular some hitherto overlooked public expressions of Fra's. In 1916, one-and-a-half decades before Fra's *Serbian Women* was described as 'picturesque and congenial', his two entries at the Royal Scottish Academy annual exhibition were deemed 'a gem' and 'forcible, but rather coarsely painted' respectively.[7] The former was a small portrait of *John Allonby*, a blacksmith who was depicted working at his forge in the North Pennine village of Warcop, where the Newberys had spent their summer in 1915. That the latter was denoted 'forcible' and 'coarse' may well stand in Fra's favour, especially if we recall that it was created at the height of the First World War, just at the moment when Meštrovic's contemporary sculpture was being criticised by conservative voices for being 'wilful, inchoate'.[8] Both of Fra's works have disappeared and hence we have to suspend judgement on their style and merits. What we can say, however, is that the second painting was groundbreaking in its subject matter, its title being *A Philippine*. A painting with the same title was shown by Fra at the Royal Scottish Academy's autumn exhibition in 1918, while in 1919 he displayed *A Filippino* in Newcastle and in 1920 *A Filipino* in Bristol. The lack of evidence concerning this work (or these works) is frustrating, not least given the southeast Asian archipelago being in a state of wartime limbo with regard to the indigenous population's fight for independence from American occupation. Even so, Fra's painting of a Filipino potentially makes it one of the first of such a subject by a British artist. Besides this, the work marks a departure for Fra that will only reappear, and hence also culminate, in his and Jessie's *Serbian* compositions. For otherwise throughout his four decade exhibiting career his paintings were almost exclusively of British subjects: in the main, when not being portraits of family or acquaintances, they were drawn from rural folk-life across the land, be that in, for example, Fife, Dumfriesshire, Yorkshire, Suffolk, Devon or Cornwall. Despite the dominance of these island peoples and terrains in his oeuvre Fra's conception of art was never restricted by national boundaries; hence his move to Filipino and Balkan themes should be regarded as at one with a 'catholic and eclectic approach to style which mirrored his broad artistic culture'.[9] So while betraying a debt to Whistler and English Aestheticism, he was also something of a follower of the Hague School of realists, the French naturalists and a great range of so-called Old Masters, as well as being ever the student of art as a whole.

Furthermore, also in 1916, he expressed his concern for peasant craft in a way that more directly anticipates his and Jessie's subsequent turn to Balkan folk culture. For in October, in a lecture entitled 'The Economic Status of British Lace-Makers and the Desirability of Original Design in Modern Workmanship', he bemoaned the craft's lack of economic viability and its treatment as 'auxiliary employment' for women, whatever their class. Criticising the notion that a female lace-maker's earnings 'were regarded as supplementary to her husband's wages', he offered ideas for the craft's economic and artistic development (including via assistance from the needlecraft and embroidery section of the Glasgow School of Art). His comments on the art of making lace and its quality were equally telling, since for him 'lacemaking was on the whole a peasant industry … in design and artistic treatment the peasant-made lace was equal to anything done by more aristocratic workers'.[10]

In and between letter lines: Mind like a dynamo, desires like a chameleon's skin

We commenced our enquiry with excerpts from Jessie's letters to her daughters and a study of her and Fra's postcards. In order to more fully understand their Balkan sympathies it is worth dwelling briefly on the text of some of their surviving letters from their European travels, particularly to their daughters, since these capture when, what and how they are experiencing the cultures they encounter. From these we glean much with regard to their keen concern for cornucopian land, sea and manual craft (including that of food). These are supplemented by an alternative form of correspondence – that is, a letter by Fra to the editor of *The Observer* newspaper, which, likewise, reveals alternative forms of encounter and legacy. As such we come to see how they transformed notions of educational 'Grand Tour' into 'Beyond the Classical Tour'. To an extent this is in keeping with their times, which brought a move to railway-based tourism and a certain waning in the perception of classical (Greek and Roman) antiquity as 'the' pinnacle of civilisation. That said, they remained very alert to the sublime attributes of classical art and architecture. Taken as a whole, it becomes noticeable that Jessie (the chief epistle writer) pays close attention to all kinds of encountered local peculiarities, be they cultural, culinary, equine or botanical. In this, no doubt, she is mindful of her correspondents' own interests as much as conveying her own. As Fra notes her 'mind [is] like a dynamo and desires like a chameleon's skin' (appendix 1, 1926: 3).[11]

The correspondence network moves chronologically and geographically as follows: 1924 (March) Sicily and southern Italy; 1925 (autumn) southern France; 1926 (autumn) central Europe, Balkans and western Turkey; 1928 (autumn) Spain, including the Basque country; 1929 (Yugoslavia, particularly Croatia); 1930 (autumn) Tuscany. Evidently there are gaps and questions with regard to itinerary (Jessie mentions, for example, an earlier trip to Spain (1924:2). Nevertheless we find continual emphasis on the following: countryside, hill towns, wild flowers, horse types, peasant life and dress, colour, art and architecture – this being the case whether it is, for example, Calabria or Dalmatia. Furthermore, in the main, they are drawn to the southern littorals of Europe, their difference from the majority of contemporary tourists being not just what they saw and sought out in these, but that they also explored extensively away from them. It is worth adding that, in their detailed and intimate letters to their daughters in particular, they make observations about each other's tastes, foibles and skills.

What then is picked out that may be related to the Serbian fabrications they made upon their return from the Balkans in 1926? First, the treasures of Sicily (1924:2) are manifold, extending from Palermo's Byzantine mosaics, its 'very beautiful port … very oriental', to Taormina's handicrafts (pottery, needlework), Syracuse's Greek theatre, fields 'blue with purple anemones … & wild jonquils', and Palermo's 'Beef olives on Rizzotta'. Jessie spends most time (1924:3) describing the old hill town of Enna ('Castello Giovanna/Giovanni' as she calls it), and in so doing combines her abiding passion for textile craft with observations on built tradition:

> *3500 ft high a little hill town – very primitive – with interesting Italo-Norman architecture of the 15th century. The peasants – men – all wear black hooded 'cloaks' – & top boots or cotton rags rotted round their legs & undressed hide mocassins [sic]. The women wear black shawls – these clothes make the foregrounds so much in keeping.*

In her next letter (1924:4), from Naples, Jessie expresses her admiration for the ancient Greek city of Paestum, which she has clearly visited years earlier, though she writes more about the 'picturesque but very poor peasants – on donkeys' than on the classical remains. She also praises Calabria as 'really untouched Italy', with 'fishing boats of gay colours & fishermen … peasants … dressed in mediaeval clothes – black red & white – & the oxen were so beautiful – white but not too white – with dark rims round their eyes'. In addition, while bemoaning the decadence of Naples painting, she distinguishes impressions of copies and originals in reporting on the sculptures and bronzes in the Neapolitan Archaeological Museum:

> *very beautiful – although in a way familiar as casts of them are not uncommon in England. But the casts have not the wonderful colour of the originals – the patina is emerald & ultramarine crusting the darker bronze.*

In terms of their actual Yugoslavia-related correspondence, beyond that which we have already discussed above, details from their letters of

1926 are most telling. Indeed these are ultimately the most significant documents presently known in terms of revealing the Newberys' Balkan acquaintance and approach. It becomes clear that their final destination was actually Istanbul ('Constantinople') and that their route southeast included stops at Zürich, Innsbruck, Vienna and Budapest (1926:1). Thereafter they had spare days to fill crossing the Balkans before a later-than-expected, rescheduled, arrival in the Turkish capital. Hence their stays at Belgrade, Niš and Sofia are longer than anticipated. Jessie's first Serbian letter is to her daughter Elsie and was written in Niš, the 'queer little borderland town between the West & the East' (1926:2). The halfway point between Budapest and Istanbul, Niš then had a population of around 30,000 (Serb majority, mainly Roma, Bulgarian and Jewish minorities). In early times it had been Roman, Byzantine (birthplace of Emperor Constantine), Bulgar and Serb, while from the late-fourteenth to the mid-nineteenth century, despite changing hands briefly on several occasions, it had been governed by the Ottomans. The Newberys' stay coincided with Niš having returned to Serbian control for the second time in recent history, first in 1878 and then in 1918 following its liberation from First World War Central Powers' occupation. Hence its being, in 1926 at least, 'such an untourist ridden place that there are no postcards of it to buy'.

As with Sicily, Jessie's eyes dart from architecture to peasant dress and sustenance. With regard to the first, she picks out equally: 'One little white Mahomedan mosque', 'one Greek Church Cathedral (new but simple, & traditional)' and 'houses & shops only one story high – & red tiled'. In so doing she points first to the Islam-aga Hadrović mosque. The only one of nineteen mosques to survive as a place of Muslim worship, this, having been built in 1870, was also the last of the Ottomans' mosques. A simple white cube with pantiled roof and minaret, the mosque is in the centre of Niš, close to the Newberys' hotel (the then newly completed 'Palas') on what was in those days King Aleksandar Square and is now King Milan Square. The 'Greek' Cathedral of the Descent of the Holy Spirit was likewise nearby and relatively modern, having been built between 1856 and 1872. A basilica with five domes, curvilinear gables and arcades on three sides, the large Orthodox cathedral, for all that it was 'simple, & traditional', comprised an eclectic mix of styles, its architect Andreja Damjanov turning it into a Balkan Romanticist fusion of Byzantine and Baroque.

The allure of dress and fabrics never left Jessie, hence she spells out at some length her sightings, particularly in or near Niš's remnants of its Ottoman bazaar. Popularly known as 'Coppersmiths' Alley' (subsequently Kopitareva), this was a street of around one hundred metres' length containing small shops and kiosks of potters, metalworkers and weavers. Her notice therefore was attracted by: 'plenty of pottery'; plus, as cited in our introduction, 'fascinating orangy/brown sheepskin coats with the fur inside - & apliqued with thinner black leather & bright green pink yellow blue red shewing through punch holes in the black ... prototypes – very primitive – of our Lilley & Skinner sandal ... peasants not so thrilling some of them in Turkish trousers – just women'.[12] That she, and/or Elsie to whom she was writing, should have been wearing/knowledgeable of Lilley & Skinner sandals may not sound surprising given that Lilley & Skinner were one of the largest retailers of footwear in Britain at the time. However, women (as men) in Britain had only recently begun to wear sandals and they were a sign of emancipation. Their simplicity of design and convenience of wear, together with their combination of ancient and modern tradition, would, of course, have appealed to Jessie. That they convey a certain humility and informality (or organic closeness to the earth), unlike more conventional leather shoes, could also have been a factor for her. While we lack knowledge of her particular examples, her discerning of a relationship between Niš and Lilley & Skinner sandals is indicative of the design-oriented thinking she spelt out in her 'creed'. Furthermore, we also know that she brought back from Serbia pairs of *opanci*, the moccasin-type sandals seen in Fra's 'Serbian' paintings.

To the descriptions of Niš handicrafts Jessie added mention of 'beautiful yokes of oxen in very primitive carts' and '2-horse fiacres' (a type of carriage) as well as, for food's sake, 'grapes – beauties' and details of a hitherto untried delicacy she had tasted in Belgrade: '"Jaoort" [yoghurt] a kind of curdled milk – made in pots that just hold a portion for each person – eaten with sugar – delicious'. That in 1926 Niš lacked postcards for her to buy should not prevent us from using two slightly earlier ones in order to visually complement her observations. While one shows the oxen, carts and craft booths she wrote of [fig. 4.2], the other, originally published in 1895, includes drawn and hand-tinted views of the cathedral, the square where Fra and Jessie stayed, and, at bottom left, within a frame topped by fancy Baroque volutes, a group of three women representing 'national costume from the Niš area' [fig. 4.3]. Dare we suggest these three as primitive prototypes for Fra's *Serbian Women*? After all, note the unison of embroidered aprons, hints of *opanci* and sense of community confirmed by the light hand-on-shoulders touch between them. On the other hand that touch is of idle hands, plus the women are viewed full frontally, appear in an ornate interior with ceramics rather than distaff and spindle, and, with only the central figure seated, the triangle they form points downwards: in short they are posed as if for a formal portrait by the card's photographer, Petar Aranđelović. Fra's creativity took him in different directions.

Jessie's second Serbian letter (1926:3) was written to daughter Mary about a month later than the first and sent from Belgrade. With much catching up to do she covers considerable ground. Food, wild flowers (along with trees and shrubs) and architecture again feature, with more

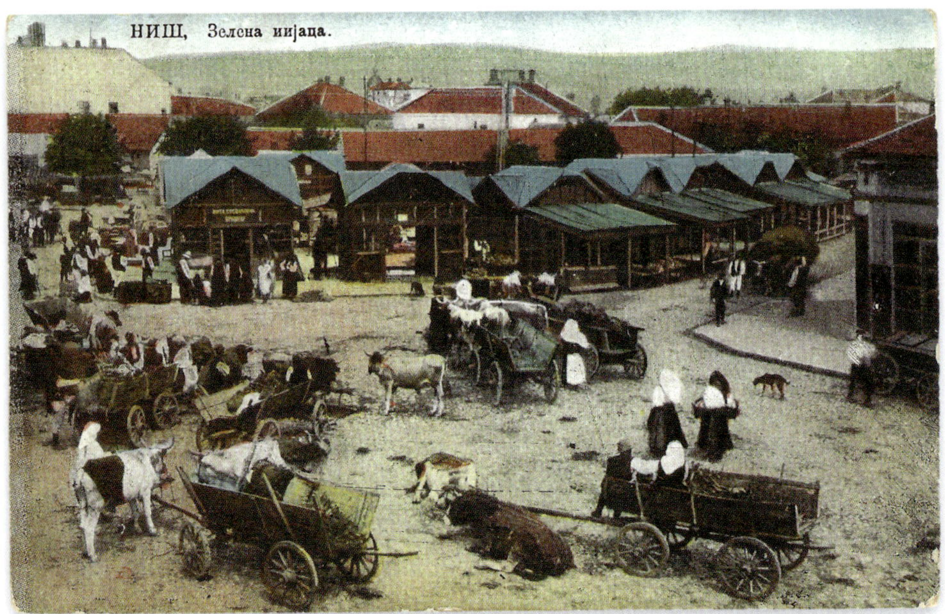

4.2 | Niš market scene, postcard, (Ljuba Mladenović, *c.* 1920s)

on yoghurt and its recipes, as well as 'branching pine woods', 'Cistus & heath' and the observation that 'the small 2 story Belgrade houses that remain are very attractive'. With the last she is pointing towards *konaks*, nineteenth-century villas which interpreted, and modernised, Turkish traditions with their cantilevered gables, pantiled roofs, centralised design, and open-plan, multi-functional *divanhanas* (divan spaces). The most widely recognised of these are two built close to historic centres of Belgrade by Prince Miloš Obrenović for his family around 1830, that is, the Prince Miloš and Princess Ljubica *konaks*.

In the Introduction we discussed this second letter's drawings of Bulgarian braid that Jessie acquired in Sofia and of the coat with gold diaper and scarf that she bought in Niš on their return there after Istanbul. That Niš also provided her with a jug of 'black pottery with gold encrustations', seemingly as a present for Mary, is indicative of how the material culture of the 'queer little borderland town' offered her particular creative mind food for thought (and hence translation into designs for the Corfe pageant and, no doubt, more). Significantly she makes a connection between the 'lovely coat … with its camel hair coloured & stiff' and 'Rodier'. In so doing she once again reveals her awareness of trends in contemporary western European fashion, this time with regard to recent experiments by the Parisian House of Rodier. In 1926 Rodier was well known in Britain as a leading designer and maker of Art Deco-style dress, hence Jessie's link is not extraordinary,

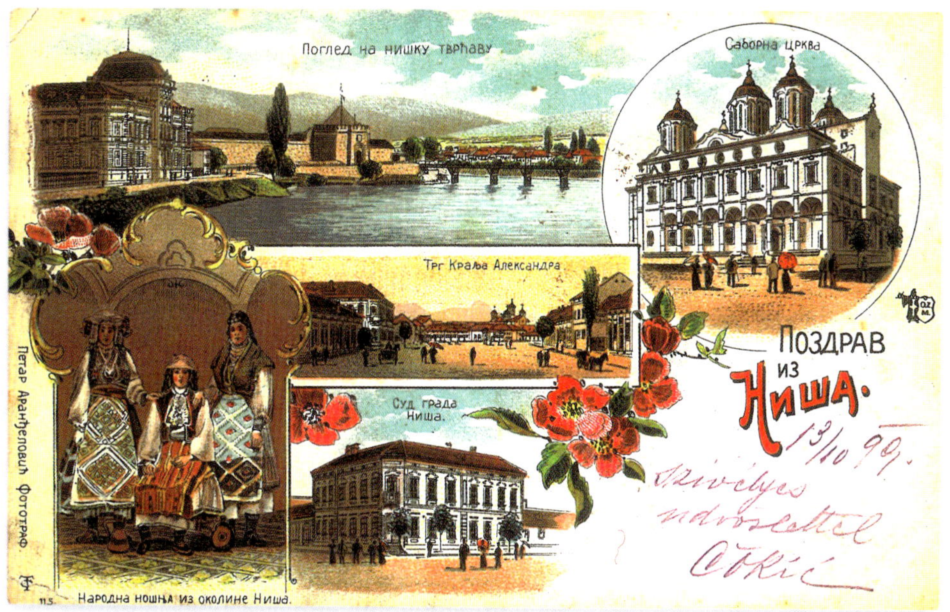

4.3 | 'Greetings from Niš', postcard featuring 'National Costume from the Niš Vicinity' [bottom left] (Petar Aranđelović, Niš, *c.* 1895)

especially given that Rodier produced striking patterns and simple, stylish fabrics, often in cashmere. But in doing so she is showing how attuned she is to fashion that innovates through tradition: after all Rodier had shown, not least at the Paris 1925 Exposition, but also through its wide advertising and selling, how it could edit, adapt and interpret motifs from the decorative arts of French colonial territories, be they those in Indo-China or equatorial Africa. Was she not to do something of the same, but lacking the colonialist baggage, with her Serbian turn?

Elsewhere in the second letter Jessie mentions other handicrafts and purchases. In terms of Belgrade, in a reference that reinforces the Serbian capital's 'eastern' aspect, she highlights 'Chelims' (kilims) as 'handmade carpets' that are 'very interesting' (see Pirot kilims below). She notes the '2 articles of apparel' which she has bought and will reveal back in Corfe – these presumably, as mentioned previously, also acting as costumes or inspiration for costumes in the pageant and Fra's 'Serbian' paintings. Further acquisitions are 'some bowls' from Sofia, and, from Istanbul, an 'old Persian lamp – blue or green with black decoration', which had broken in transit. The latter was complemented by Fra's purchase of a Quran 'with 2 vellum pages of illumination – which he is very proud of'. Jessie's singling out of the material and artwork is predictable, given her and Fra's perspectives, especially since the inclusion of vellum is indicative of tradition- and animal-based making whose handicraft had been losing out to, and threatened by, mechanised paper-making since the mid-nineteenth century. Further-more, despite Fra knowing four languages, neither he nor Jessie would have been able to read the Arabic text (assuming that was his example's language) – hence, of course, they were drawn to the holy book's visual and material aspect. This accords with their also not knowing the vocabulary, syntax or history of Balkan costume, ceramics or metal-ware. Their reading and comprehension might therefore be regarded as superficial, insufficient or incorrect … and in many ways it was. Yet it grasped (or grasped at) the language of the material combined with the means for, as well as results of, artistic facture. In essence, they avoided much tourist-style dilettantism through being driven by beliefs and practices expounded in Jessie's creed, for example 'material, space, and consequent use discover their own exigencies', 'I delight in correspon-dence' (see appendix 2: 1).

The Quran acquisition also says much for Fra's non-denominational approach to religion (albeit that he and Jessie attended the Episcopa-lian Church of St Bride's while they lived in Glasgow). Linked to this is its coincidence with ideas he expounded regarding 'The Holiness of Beauty', the title of a lecture he gave in Lanarkshire to the Uddingston Literary Society in the autumn of 1903. In that lecture he had explored the art-religion interface 'from the earliest times to the present day', in-cluding 'the uses to which art and love of the beautiful were put in the early Jewish Church' and art's application as 'adornment of the Pagan Church', as well as its 'elevating influence – whether in architecture, sculpture or painting … in the history of the early Christian Church'. The surviving report does not mention whether he extended his survey to Islamic or other non-Christian forms of religious art, though it did stress that his emphasis was on 'the intimate relations which had all through the ages existed between art and religion – between holiness and beauty'.[13] Thus, his Istanbul purchase of an illuminated Quran, of which he was 'very proud', fits with his being moved by the spirit of aesthetic design irrespective of individual doctrine of belief. As seen in the subsequent synthetism of his Swanage *Annunciation*, his, like Jessie's, was a transcendental artistic worldview.

Fra and Jessie's pursuit of a holistic creative spirit led them, in Istan-bul, to a fount of Byzantine art: the Chora Church of the Holy Saviour (then, as throughout the Ottoman era and before a seventy-five-year hi-atus as a museum, the Kariye Mosque). That this church-mosque-mu-seum is located to the south of the Golden Horn, close to the southern entry of the Bosporous Strait makes it, for us, a symbolic marker of the furthest reach of the Newberys' Balkan perambulations and fab-rications. As such the Newberys' visit to this *Gesamtkunstwerk* of mo-saic and fresco art contains a further, distinct, outcome: an exhibition in London, at Fra's *alma mater* the Victoria and Albert Museum. Fra wrote of his crucial intervention, which led to the exhibition opening in summer 1928, in a letter published on 29 July in *The Observer* (see appendix 1). He commenced it thus: 'As the artist responsible for the copies of the mosaics and frescoes of the Kahrie Djami being brought to London, and for their acceptance for exhibition by the Victoria and Albert Museum'. Thereafter he disputed contentions made in the previous *Observer* issue (22 July) by critic Paul Konody about the state of the former church, the datings of its artworks and the selections for display. In so doing he revealed that 'we', that is Jessie and he, had met up with the Russian-Ukrainian artist Dmitri Ismailovitch there, 'congratulated him on his very successful studies' and 'found that the frescoes were suffering from water percolation … [though] the Turkish Government had the matter in hand, and were executing repairs'.

Fra's *Observer* letter details that (apparently without Jessie since he changes to first person singular) he then visited Ismailovitch's studio, across the Golden Horn in Pera (now Beyoğlu). He notes that 'to the best of my recollection, [I] saw copies of practically every group and single figure mosaic of the Kahrie Mosque'. Upon his and Jessie's return to Dorset Fra had persuaded Martin Hardie, Keeper of Engraving, Illustration, Design and Painting at the Victoria and Albert, to exhibit Ismailovitch's images.[14] As Jessie had mentioned her and Fra spending 'a day on the sea of Marmora with Colonel & Mrs Woods' in her Belgrade letter it could be possible to assume that Fra was able to pull some strings with the British Embassy in Turkey, since Colonel Harold Woods was the highly influential commercial secretary there, reporting directly to the Department of Overseas Trade.[15] One problem, however, is that Ismailovitch had departed Istanbul in 1927 and then in the summer of that year exhibited at the Brooklyn Museum, New York, 'a large group of [his] drawings and paintings which accurately reproduce the frescoes and mosaics in the 14th century Church of St Saviour (Kahrie Djami), Stamboul'.[16] At least thirty of these works were shown, over the course of the next year, in Boston and Rio de Janeiro, Ismailovitch having settled permanently in Brazil in 1928. And it was from Brazil that Ismailovitch sent his artwork, as indicated in the catalogue of the London exhibition by the Victoria and Albert Museum's director, Eric Maclagan.[17] Nevertheless, we have Fra's published word that he was 'responsible' for Ismailovitch's work 'being brought' to Britain and for their 'acceptance for exhibition' by Maclagan. Furthermore, the exhibition catalogue was created by Muriel Clayton, one of Hardie's assistants in the museum's Department of Engraving, Illustration and Design.

While Fra's role in initiating the exhibition goes unacknowledged by Maclagan, Clayton and Konody, the latter two provide important clues as to the nature of the display and its significance. In so doing they hint at what attracted the Newberys to both the church's artwork and its visual interpretation by Ismailovitch. Konody noted:

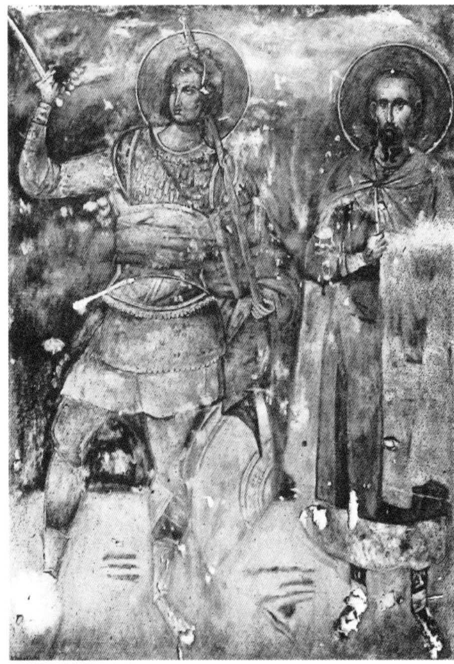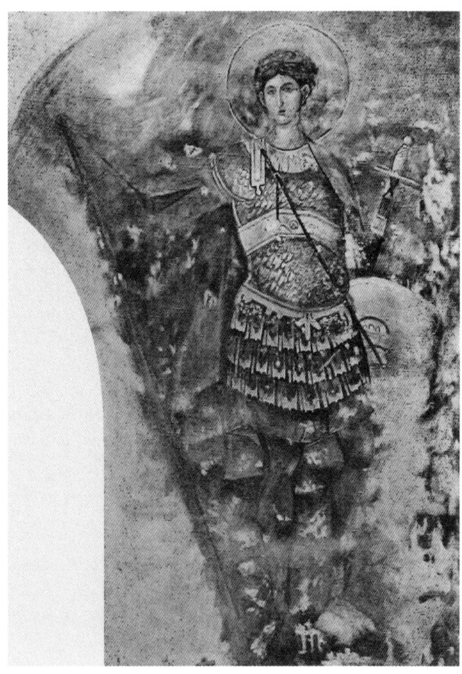

4.4 a–b | Dmitri Ismailovitch, painted copies of Ss Procopius and Sabbas Stratelates [left] and St Demetrius [right], frescoes, Kahrie Djami, mid-1920s; from Muriel Clayton, *Mosaics and Frescoes in the Kahrié-Djami Constantinople Copied by Dmitri Ismailovitch* (London: Victoria and Albert Museum, 1928), n.p.

Mr Ismailovitch has shown unusual dexterity, especially in his painting of the mosaic borders which are shown framed with their corresponding figures. The effects, too, of age and damage are as perfectly rendered as paint will allow. The forty-four various drawings and paintings involved seven years of careful study and work. The building itself is illustrated by several oil, tempera, and water-colour sketches, and the exhibition even includes a mosaic-worker's palette of thirty-six colours, made up from fragments which had fallen from the walls.[18]

Clayton's catalogue complements Konody's and Fra's epistolic observations with black-and-white reproductions of four Ismailovitch copies: two apiece of mosaics and frescoes. The latter are captioned Ss Demetrius and Lupus, and St Theodore Stratelates, although restoration and subsequent scholarship has identified them as Ss Procopius and Sabbas Stratelates, and St Demetrius, respectively [fig. 4.4]. They form part of the scheme of martyr saints painted along the southern wall (lower zone) of the pareclesion, this being the chapel on the south side of the church. According to Paul Underwood they complete, with three others (Ss George, Theodore Tiro and Mercurius), a characteristic Byzantine iconographic group of 'commanders, or generals, of the army of

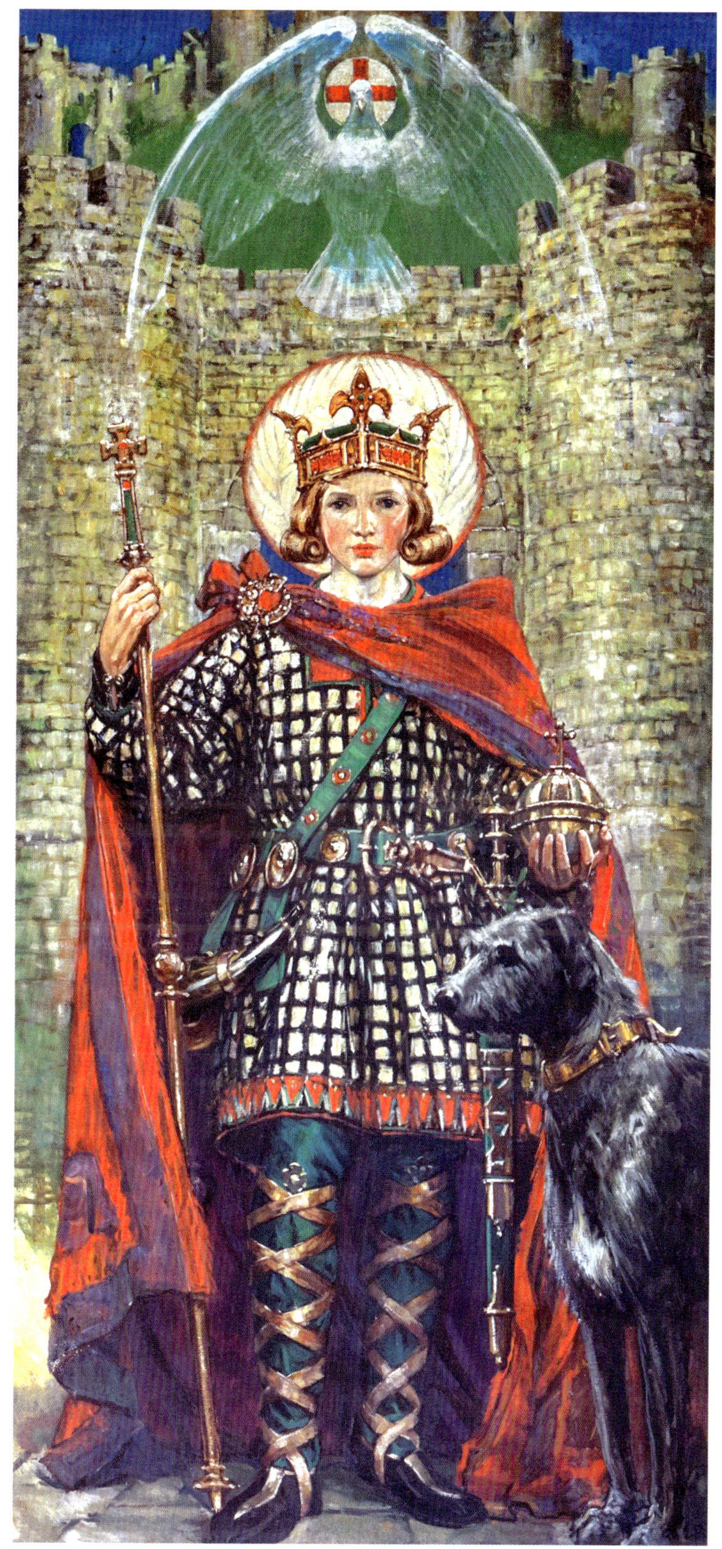

4.5 | Fra Newbery
St Edward of Wessex: King and Martyr,
A.D. 979 | 1926, altar-
piece, central panel,
Church of the Holy
Spirit and St Edward,
Swanage, oil on canvas,
c. 300 x 140 cm

military saints'.[19] As such, and with their stylised full-length frontality, both the originals and Ismailovitch's copies of the military saints can be seen as counterparts to Fra's painting of Edward the Martyr King and Saint of Wessex for the altarpiece of the Swanage church and the Corfe Castle village sign [figs 4.5, 2.14]. It was no coincidence that these were created either side of his visit to Constantinople.

Despite the formal and iconographic relationship between the Chora Church wall paintings and Fra's St Edward images, in his *Observer* letter Fra revealed he felt the frescoes to be 'of little account in comparison with the wonderful mosaics'. Clayton's catalogue reproduced Ismailovitch's interpretation of two principal examples of the latter: Christ Pantocrator, the first image to confront the church visitor, it being over the outer narthex's entrance to the inner narthex; and an image of Theodore Metochites offering the church to Christ, which filled the lunette over the next door within, that is the inner narthex's main entrance to the nave [figs 4.6, 4.7]. This is not the place to visually deconstruct these key dedicatory and devotional panels, or to dwell on the differences between the restored mosaics and Ismailovitch's copies.[20] Suffice it to note that the image of Theodore Metochites, the Grand Logothete of Byzantium, presents him as the patron of the church whose rebuilding and decoration he had sponsored in the early fourteenth century. Metochites' patronage resulted in the finest mosaic masterpiece of the Palaeologian era. His image as donor, offering a model of the church to an enthroned Christ, replete as it is with his remarkable *skiadion* hat and *kabbadion* caftan, distinguish him as Emperor Andronikos II's most senior official. It also accords with Fra's

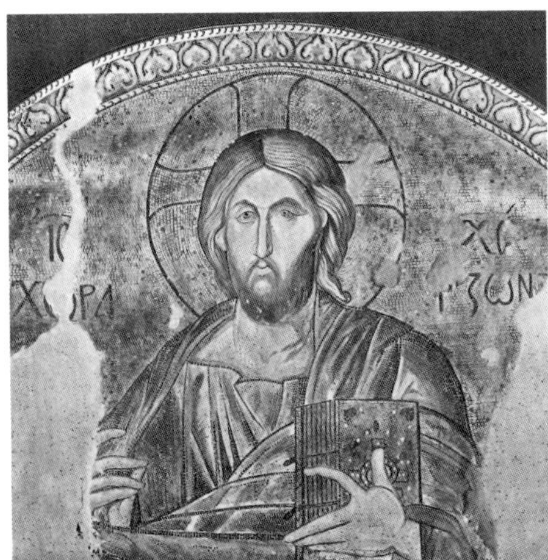
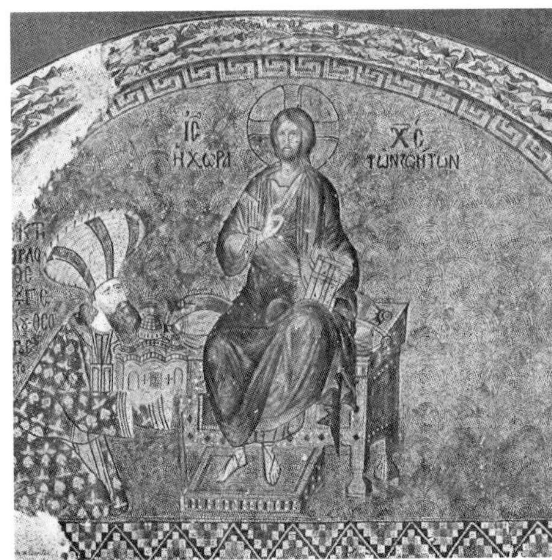

4.6 a–b | Dmitri Ismailovitch, painted copies of Christ Pantocrator [left] and Theodore Metochites [right] offering the Church to Christ, mosaic panels, Kahrié Djami, 1925; from Muriel Clayton, *Mosaics and Frescoes in the Kahrié-Djami Constantinople Copied by Dmitri Ismailovitch* (London: Victoria and Albert Museum, 1928), n.p.

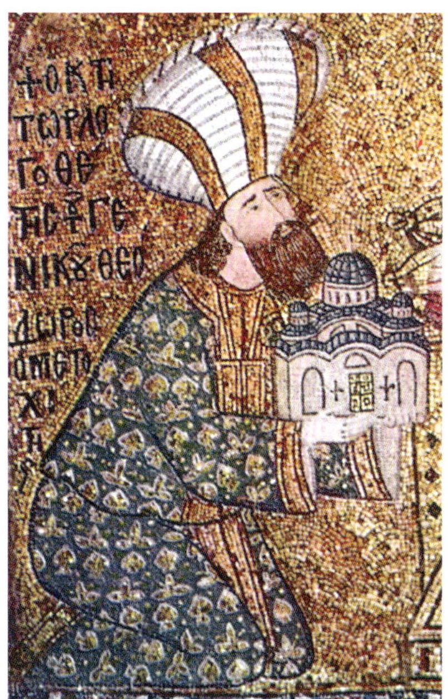

4.7 | Unknown artist, 'Theodore Metochites offering the Church to Christ' [detail], mosaic panel, Kahrie Djami, early 14th century

concern for donor portraiture as already discussed. But more significantly, the richly patterned, bold shapes and strong colours of Metochites' garb convey a refined sense of fabric and love of costumery that would have greatly appealed to the Newberys' love of textile art.

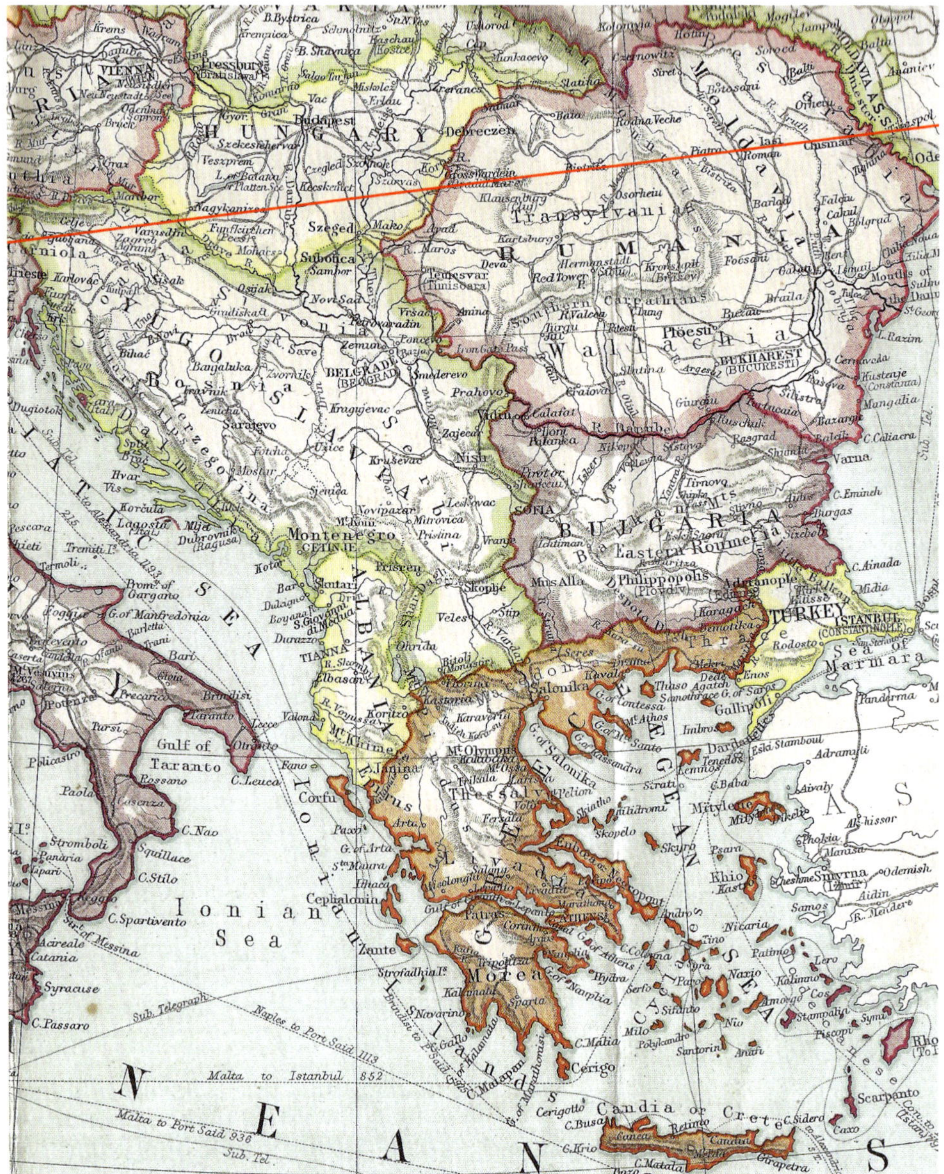

5.1 | Map of Balkan peninsula (1930 political boundaries); from *Europe* (London: Philips' Authentic Imperial Maps, *c.*1930)

5 STITCH-UPS
ALTERNATIVE BALKAN EYES

Scene-setting

Given the inventiveness of the Newberys' creative reaction to their Balkan experience and at the same time, as we have shown, how that reaction fits with aesthetic concerns they had nurtured over more than four decades, one may be tempted to view such a 'Serbian' turn as an isolated phenomenon brought about by a chance visit to a region largely shunned by British artists. Yet it belongs to a political and artistic context in which the Balkans region was emerging as a fount for significant supra-Balkanic attention, appropriation, modification and interpretation. The fact that the First World War had been started by Austrian Habsburg policies in the Balkans, and that Britain and France were allied in opposition to the Central Powers, concentrated minds, not least artistic ones, in both western realms. Furthermore, the Allied victory, combined with the dissolution of Germanic and Turkish imperialist regimes, brought about a new wave of investigation into, and 'support' of, Balkan cultures. As mentioned above this coincided with desires to reinforce the grip of their fledgling monarchies so that, strengthened, they acted in British and French colonial and economic interests. The opening up of tourism, via enhanced transportation and accommodation services, inevitably also played an important part. That the region – especially its largest part east of mostly Catholic Slovenia and Croatia – was mainly Slav, Orthodox Christian and Muslim, and hence 'other' to most (especially establishment) British and French conceptions of self, proved to be a minor concern. In fact, such qualities helped reinforce the exoticising, stereotyping fantasies of the Western entertainment media (from literary fiction to pictorial 'journalism', theatre and film). As far as the powers and individuals producing such send-ups were concerned, the Balkans were simultaneously ripe for bringing 'into the fold' and, to an acceptably small or under-recognised extent, ripe for contributing to change within that superior 'fold'.

This is not the place for a survey of the politicised British paradigms of the Balkans. Indeed many enquiries have already been undertaken which usefully frame and appraise these in various ways.[1] It should, however, be noted, as such enquiries have vividly shown, that the historical British illusion of 'Balkan' has commonly been pernicious, puerile, prejudicial and patronising.[2] That it could also be positive or neutrally ambiguous is by no means unknown but is more seldom the case. That it may be a form of superiority-complex-induced, orientalist 'othering' is more likely. Those responsible for this mainstream view are unlikely to have been aware that their disparagement could be an expression of unintended compliment, since the 'barbaric' cultures they were belittling and separating themselves from (while imposing upon them) comprised forms of mature, traditional civilisations far less likely to wreak planetary havoc than those champions of 'Western' supremacy and omniscience making the judgements and interventions. Suffice it to say that here we follow the lead of Vesna Goldsworthy, whose concern has been to deal 'neither with the "Balkans as a metaphor" nor with the "real" Balkans, but with the process which connects them, the negotiation which leads from reality to the creation of a metaphor'.[3] Hybridisation of cultural expression is a frequent result. Hence we also contextualise the Newberys' work with reference to Serbian trends in art and living (not least with regard the peasantry) as well as work conceived for an international audience by those of mixed or Serbian origin.

The complicated, ambiguous, contested appellation and definition of 'Balkan' still needs some qualification. For our purposes, the only factor deciding the use and meaning of the term is physically geographical. As such it relates to a peninsula (and nearby islands) whose territory ends near the cities of Odessa (east) and Trieste (west) [fig. 5.1]. The imagined straight line between these smudged points presently runs through seven states. Beneath it there are at least eight more current states. While the states are irrelevant for our enquiry and the land-based 'boundary' line is thankfully both artificial and culturally permeable, such a conception allows us to envisage a Balkan topography and thereby a sense of place for an elaborate and mutable medley of nature, people, customs and art. The medley experienced and interpreted by the Newberys may only have been a fragment of a larger one but it was a life-affirming fragment. As such it conforms with the notion that all existence and enquiry is fragmental. However inconvenient, it may be helpful to remember that 'Europe' is not an entity but a fragment and one in which, as Jessie, we may seek out 'inevitable relation of part to part' (appendix 2: 1).

Given the foregoing, my frequent use of the terms 'Europe' or 'south-eastern Europe', as well as 'western', is equally as problematic as 'Balkan', if not more so. This despite their currency. After all there is even less chance of drawing an imaginary dividing line across the landmass of Eurasia than there is between the northeastern and northwestern points of the 'Balkan' peninsula. If we must conceive a 'thing' or 'unit' called Europe, as it seems we must and persistently do, then we should not forget that the lands, creatures and art it contains are all peripheral in the wider scheme of things. Such observation is of course far from new, but there is a tendency to neglect it. Europe does not exist except in human mind and political structure: breaking up into islands it is the westernmost tip of the Earth's largest continent of which, in most generous calculations, it comprises less than one-fifth of the total surface. Britain, and indeed Dorset, Scotland, Glasgow and Paisley, are the periphery of the periphery. Considering human society remains far from the postcolonial stage that many have signalled as having already arrived, the British Isles' peoples may be best served, while constructing their lives, communities and identities, and while transcending their shores open-mindedly, by recollection of their actual geographical place. Then those resident on the islands may have the right to conclude that 'Balkan' is a civilised southeastern corner and 'Britain' is a civilised northwestern archipelago. Fra and Jessie's life-affirming Serbian turn comes in the wake of some 1,200,000 Serbians (or around twenty-five per cent of the Serbian population) being killed in the First World War and before a further million-plus Yugoslavs were killed in the Second World War. These losses far outstrip the horrific numbers of deaths of citizens of the United Kingdom, Serbia's wartime ally.

By a limited contextualisation of the Newberys' Serbian fabrications we can come to some comprehension of how they relate to the larger fragments from which both of them drew nourishment. Therefore we should see, that, for all their flights of fancy, they were tapping into a vein of serious artistic intent, and revealing, as well as developing in unexpected ways, the richness of that vein. We have already introduced the British treatment accorded to Meštrović. It might be compared with that of Charles Rennie Mackintosh, Fra's prodigy and his and Jessie's close friend in Glasgow, in that the art-powers-that-be seemed for many years only to have room for one such 'genius' from outside their capital cliques, and even then often subjected the artist (frequently irrespective of strengths or weaknesses) to considerable unfair adverse criticism. Perceived outsider or peripheral status is a Janus-faced attribute, capable of bestowing advantage and disadvantage. Furthermore, knock-on effects of outsider-genius identification can be such that while members of Meštrović's and Mackintosh's circles may be mentioned and appraised, such profiling was, and remains, prone to being highly selective and ephemeral. Artistic limelight is intrinsically fickle.

Similarly, with regard to France and Modernist design, it was Le Corbusier and his 1911 sojourn to southeast Europe that, exceptionally, was allowed to be seen as a catalyst for 'European Modernism'. This because it was deemed so remarkably pioneering in terms of his 'discovery' of white-cube vernacular architecture with verandahs and enclosed courtyards. There is no doubt that the Swiss architect Charles-Édouard Jeanneret, as Corbusier was then known, developed a sincere and profound interest in Balkan design, and with that Balkan peasant ceramics (even though he was quick to denigrate its peoples and places). Furthermore, that he melded ideas and forms derived from these into his groundbreaking version of a synthetic yet pure and rational International Style that had far-reaching effects is without question. His 'Five Points of Architecture' are heavily indebted to southeast European building, spatial organisation and surface treatment. Of course, for many, myself included, there is great beauty in what he achieved. Yet his interest and radical break with European historicist styles should be seen as equivalent to the Newberys'. For, like them, his new art was founded on appropriation of and reinvention through 'alternative' tradition. That Fra and Jessie's Balkanism culminated in a florid, decorative mélange in which history and figure were overt while Le Corbusier's produced plain, often undifferentiated and non-colour, surfaces, only goes to show the wealth of the well from which they drew. If each side offers forms of sublime synthetic art, then appreciation of their sources in their own right and in terms of their correspondences should never go amiss.[4]

It is no coincidence that Le Corbusier's modern architecture also owes a debt to the formal language developed by Mackintosh in Glasgow, and taken, often through Fra's intervention, to Europe via exhibitions, around the turn of the twentieth century. Given the reams of papers and seemingly endless stream of exhibitions and other forms of public testament that have been dedicated to Le Corbusier's Balkan epiphany it would seem fair to ask for alternative ways of incorporating his achievements into the journey of modern artistry. Could we (by which I mean anyone) not consider, for example, that there is room aplenty for a Balkan (or Balkan-settled) designer, architect, builder or maker, or, say, group of 'craftists', particularly without them being émigrés to the 'great centres', to be seen as worthy of more than passing interest, let alone influential? Studies are being made (see below) and awareness of groups' and individual contributions are growing, but more interest would be welcome and widely beneficial. Multi-polar and multi-focal conceptions of artistic value offer rich rewards.

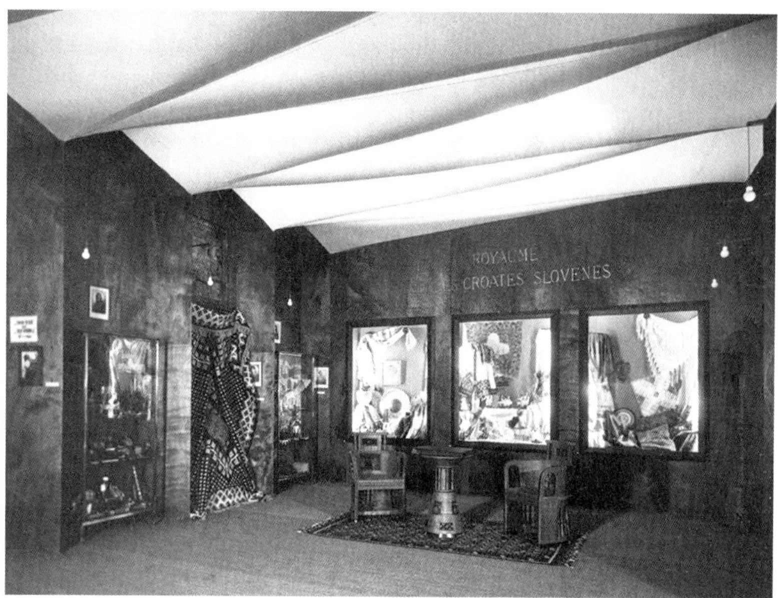

5.2 | Kingdom of Serbs, Croats and Slovenes section, Grand Palais, Paris Exposition
Internationale des Arts Décoratifs et Industriels Modernes, 1925; from album of
photographs of Yugoslav sections

Paris 1925

The above homily over, our concern here is primarily with British artistic eyes on the Balkans and what those eyes produce in terms of local
output and development. We might conceive of the Newberys' vision as
filtered through lenses provided by their background. Certainly their
initial exposure to anything 'Balkan' is likely to have been through the
pages of English-language published sources rather than direct contact. Even so we have already surmised that they may also have seen
Yugoslavian art via Meštrović's exhibitions in Britain. Furthermore,
since we have suggested that they probably attended the 1925 Paris Exposition Internationale, it remains a distinct possibility that they would
have visited the various 'Kingdom of Serbs, Croats and Slovenes' sections. If they did, they would have encountered work that anticipates
their own in distinct ways. And even if they did not, the event, the first
of its kind for Yugoslav applied art, was a showcase of trends that reveals the currency of the Newberys' Balkan-inspired pieces, occurring
as it did just over a year earlier than the first of these. The Yugoslav
state invested in the following: the 'national' pavilion of the Kingdom,
a sales pavilion, and architecture, applied art, theatre and education
sections [figs 5.2–5.6]. The main national pavilion was located close to
the Grand Palais, where three sections were located. The sales pavilion

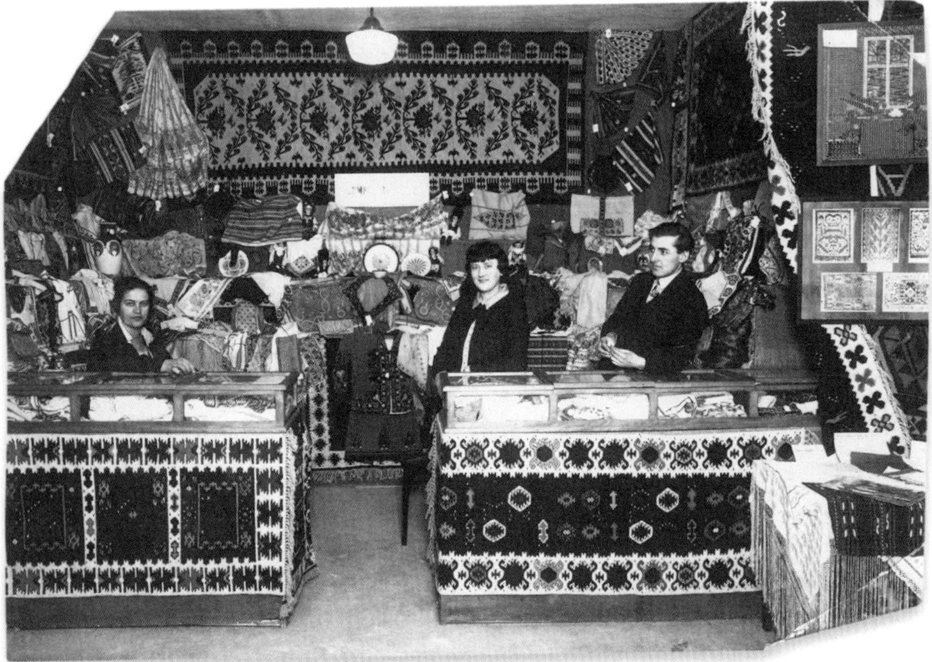

5.3 | Interior, Kingdom of Serbs, Croats and Slovenes sales pavilion, Paris Exposition Internationale des Arts Décoratifs et Industriels Modernes, 1925

and architecture display were across the River Seine on the Esplanade des Invalides. Thus the new Yugoslav state joined the French design-cum-trade-and-colonial jamboree, being one of around twenty invited foreign states, its pavilion located in the same row as the Italian, Soviet and Spanish.

In both the national pavilion and the Grand Palais, Yugoslav art was predominantly exhibited in large display cases. What these vitrines showed, in keeping with the fabric-dominated window displays and products of the sales pavilion, was that a great deal of modern work was by women and that textile art led the way. A few black-and-white photographic reproductions, exhibit lists and descriptions survive, the most useful being in the catalogue of the Yugoslavian section.[5] The catalogue text (appendix 4), written by France's leading Balkan-specialising art historian, the Byzantinist Gabriel Millet, is highly illuminating with regard to historical and contemporary Yugoslav art and politics. Of prime significance for us is how he sees distinctive trad-itions being assimilated into the country's new art and what they result in:

Popular ornament is still alive … Threatened by industrial products, as everywhere, it needs support. Attached to their past, the Yugoslavs have made a good effort to preserve peasants' taste and sense of decor-

ative art. Such a task has befallen the state and its schools, their works being exhibited … in the Grand Palais, e.g. the Schools of Arts and Crafts (Obrtna škola) *and the women's vocational schools* (Ženska stručna škola) *… as well as its workshops … it has also called for private initiative, with women establishing groups in the big cities: in Belgrade, the Circle of Serbian Sisters* (Kolo srpskih sestara); *in Zagreb and other Croatian cities, the Association for Conservation and Dissemination of Croatian folk arts and crafts* (Udruga za očuvanje i promicanje Hrvatske pučke umjetnosti i obrta). *In Ljubljana, such motivations have been brought together in an official institution, the State Central Institute of Women's Domestic Crafts* (Državni osrednji zavod za ženski domaci obrt).

Each of the great historical regions has its tradition and it is these that the big cities' schools and, particularly, associations strive to preserve and spread. Thus, the Belgrade Circle has embroidered sleeves for the farmers of Kosovo and Peć. The Zagreb Association has patterns with which the Sisak peasant women adorn their scarves in muslin designed for luxury coats, and Ljubljana lace is designed in the same spirit. Thus there is a clear difference between Croatian or Slovenian products and those from the Balkans, even from Dalmatia. The first recall seedlings of flowers from Persian carpets of Kerman, others reproduce geometric patterns or floral motifs in broken lines bequeathed by Byzantium or the Orient. Zagreb therefore opposes Belgrade: shapes and colours mark the characters that a different past has imprinted on men's souls.

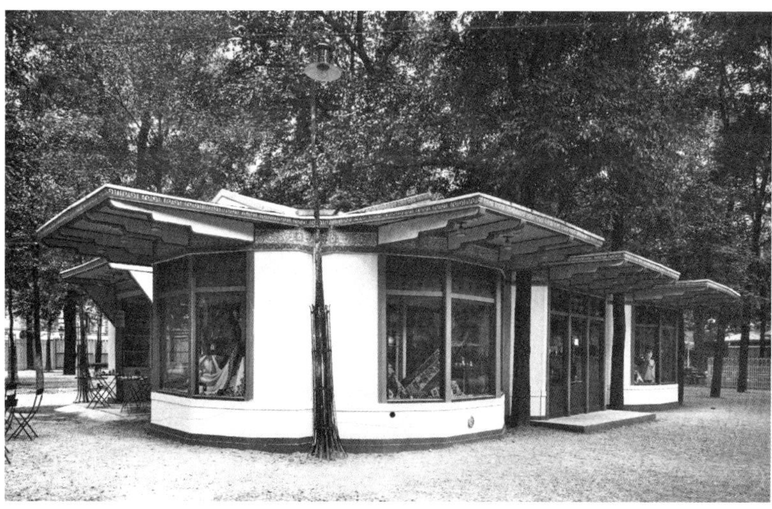

5.4 | Exterior, Kingdom of Serbs, Croats and Slovenes sales pavilion, Paris Exposition Internationale des Arts Décoratifs et Industriels Modernes, 1925; from album of photographs of Yugoslav sections

Croatian women have given a great deal, in almost all the vitrines, and our eyes quickly get used to recognising their manner. They work on a white background and almost entirely cover the surface they propose to decorate. Their design is very simplified. Flowers and branches of Persian carpets lose their precise contours and only give an assemblage of round, curved or sinuous, wide and heavy shapes. Colours are also simple. The overall result is a rich and full effect. Usually one colour dominates, with a few different tones that make it vibrate. Thus two cushions (Pavilion, nos 240 and 248), of the same design, one in golden yellow, with a little green-grey and old pink, the other in pale purple, with indigo blue, emerald green and light yellow; or even a crêpe de chine shawl (no. 238), where a few touches of pale green, golden yellow or indigo blue soften the radiance of dark vermilion. The masterpiece of the genre is a superb white dress which has its own vitrine on the first floor of the pavilion (no. 216). In this serried embroidery, we lose ourselves counting nuances of the dominant blue tone: pale blue, several grey blues, slate blue, indigo blue. A little gold and red add to the effect, which is incomparable …

Now we come to Belgrade. The preference is for broken lines. We also find beautiful red nuances, but with vigorous greens in clear opposition (Pavillon, no. 276). It gets even better: another dress of great style (no. 275), singularly severe, black on white. The contrast is striking. And it is not a product of chance, a lucky find. It is the expression of deep thought …[6]

It has to be assumed that Millet was hired to provide such text because it was considered that he could best display French erudition in Balkan matters and with this lend international authority to the salient qualities of the Yugoslav work. His appraisal is valuable, in that, for all its skirting of certain issues and developments, he clearly distinguishes visual and material peculiarities from different parts of Yugoslavia. Furthermore, we can relate his description of rich Croatian embroidery techniques and motifs to surviving photographs: the first of Vitrine One in the national pavilion, the second showing part of Vitrine Six in the Grand Palais.[7] That of Vitrine One shows, on either side of a range of mainly Croatian art, an evening coat by the Women's Professional School in Zagreb and a tablecloth by the Zagreb Women's Association, both in white fabric embroidered with modern polychromatic interpretations of traditional geometrical motifs [fig. 5.5a]. That of Vitrine Six appears more cropped, but it still shows an assemblage of needlecraft, including parts of an embroidered jacket, cloths and dress, from the Women's Associations of Zagreb and Petrinja and the Split Vocational School [fig. 5.6]. The Newberys' collection of Croatian postcards contains costume images redolent of both Millet's observations and the embroidery in the images. In fact three of the artists of

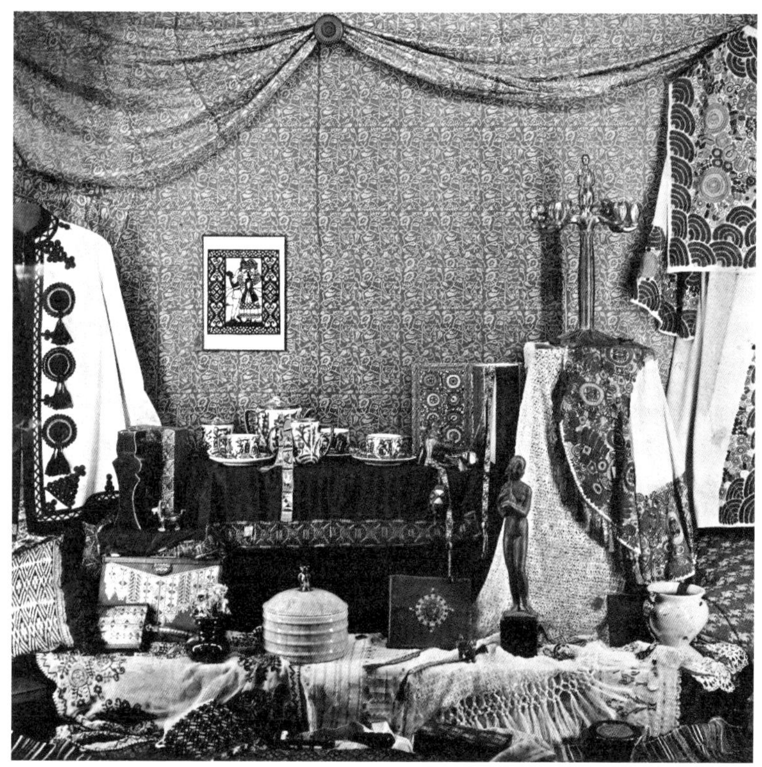

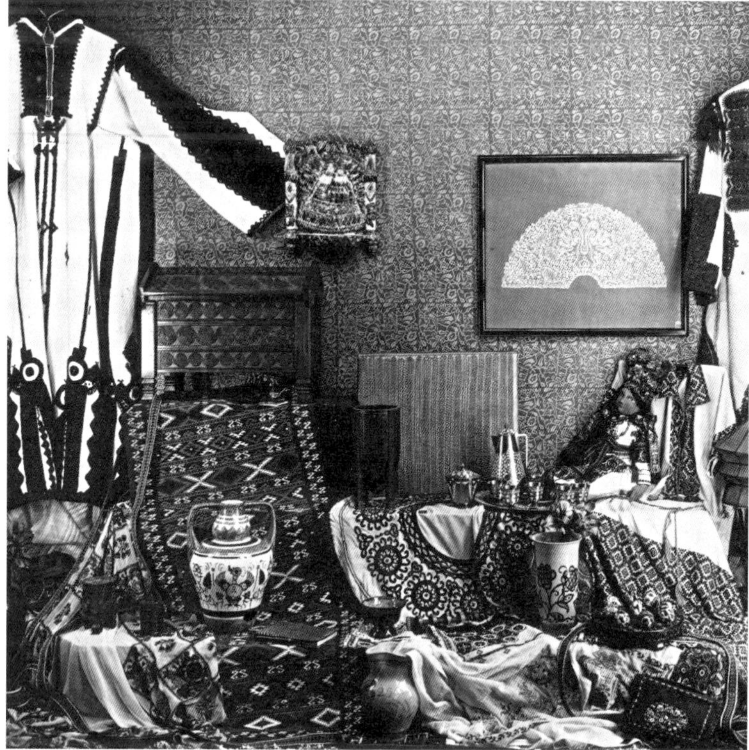

5.5 a–b
Vitrine One
[top] and Vitrine
Seventeen [right],
national pavilion;
from album of
photographs of
Yugoslav sections

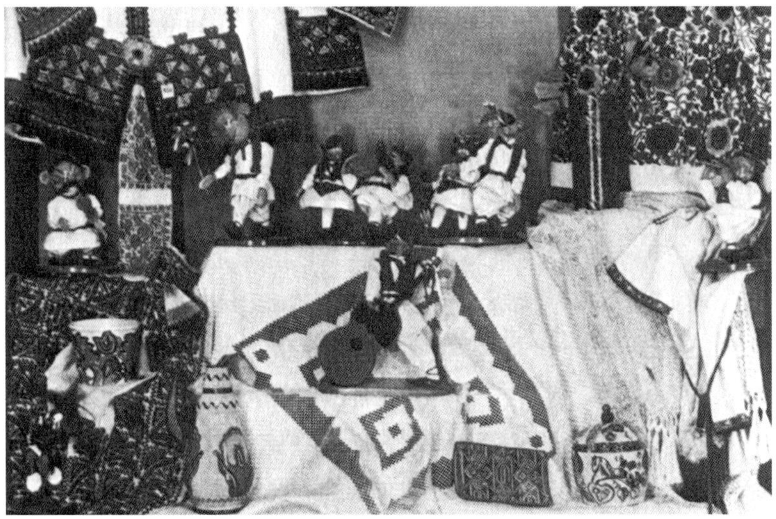

5.6 | Vitrine Six, Kingdom of Serbs, Croats and Slovenes Section, Grand Palais;
from *Encyclopédie Internationale des Arts Décoratifs et Industriels Modernes au XXème Siècle*
(Paris: Exposition Internationale des Arts Décoratifs et Industriels Modernes, 1925),
vol. 6, plate LXXII

these (Sertić, Vanka and Kirin) participated in the Yugoslav section,
their work betraying a closer attachment to folk convention than that
of a raft of their more modernising contemporaries, such as Zagreb
designer Neli Geiger or her France-based Serbian counterpart Dušan
Janković. Besides this, Millet's summary of Belgrade designs – at the
end of the quote above – fits with a photograph of another display case
(Vitrine Seventeen in the national pavilion), this having two tunics
partially visible hanging either side of the image (by the Circle of Serbian Sisters, Belgrade), which are almost certainly the two he picks out
for their bold linear and coloristic design [fig. 5.5b]. His consideration
of these as beautiful and profound, combined with their appearance
being suggestive of a stylish, modernised, strong and simplified version
of the Newberys' Macedonian costumes, reinforces our sense of 1920s
place of the latter.

Millet did not dwell long on the decoration of the Yugoslav pavilion, yet there too a relationship with the Newberys' work was to be
found. Completed by a team of Croatian artists (and one Montenegrin),
the entrance hall and staircase included stained glass windows and a
painted frieze in which peasant life was represented through close-up
stylised figuration. Elongated vertically, the ten side-window panels
(plus an eleventh rear-window) imparted a spiritual quality through
their imagery of angelic folk musicians, farming couples and individuals [fig. 5.7]. These surrounded centralised small, open-air, groups, on
the one hand three separate panels of women workers (with gathered
crops, flowers and grape-bearing infant), and on the other a panel

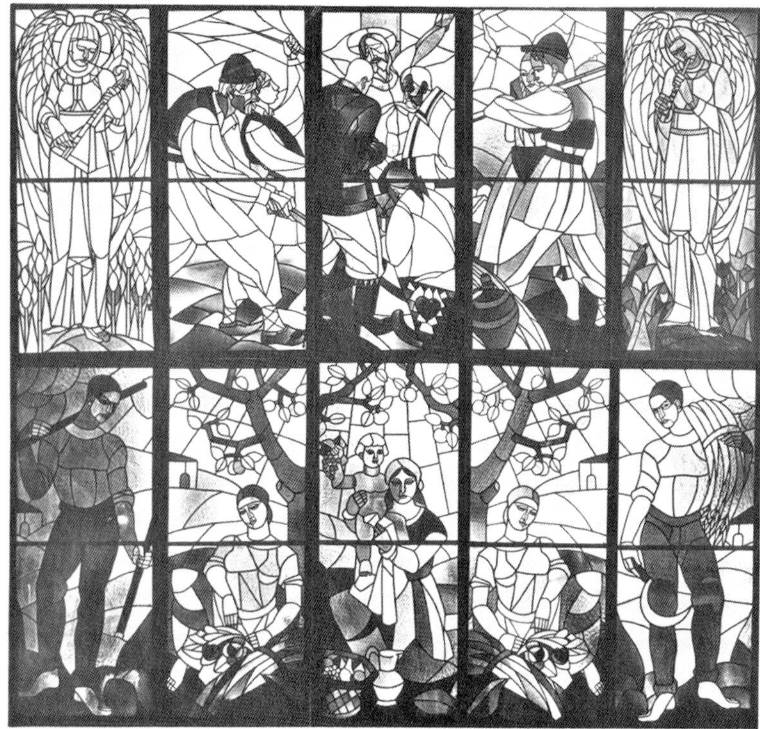

5.7 | Stained glass panels (designs by Milo Milunović, Marijan Trepše, Maksimilijan Vanka, Zlatko Šulentić, Jozo Kljaković; executed by Ivan Marinković atelier, Zagreb), Kingdom of Serbs, Croats and Slovenes national pavilion, Paris Exposition Internationale des Arts Décoratifs et Industriels Modernes, 1925; from album of photographs of Yugoslav sections

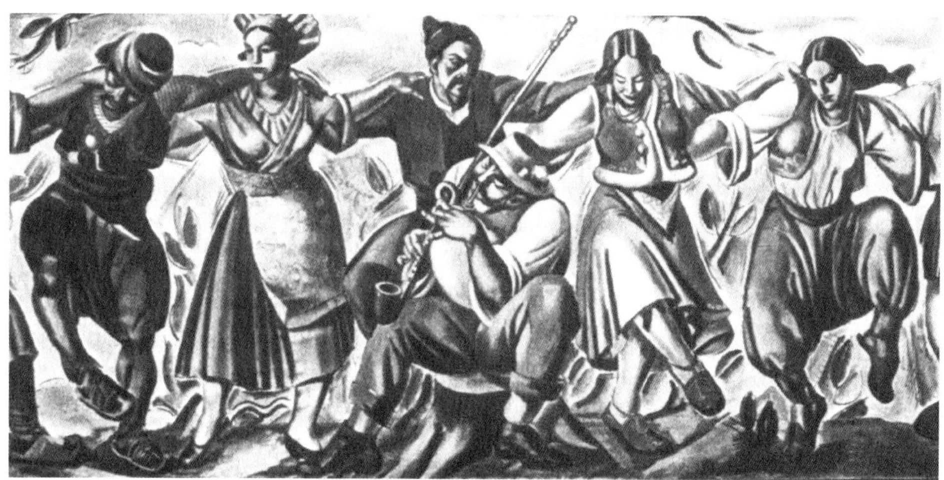

5.8 | Vladimir Becić, *Kolo*, staircase mural, Kingdom of Serbs, Croats and Slovenes national pavilion; from *Encyclopédie Internationale des Arts Décoratifs et Industriels Modernes au XXème Siècle* (Paris: Exposition Internationale des Arts Décoratifs et Industriels Modernes, 1925), vol. 2, plate XCVI

depicting three older folk in their best attire before a crucifix. The work of five Zagreb-based artists, including Vanka and the Montenegrin Milo Milunović, the simplicity of the panels and their flattened delineated forms denies Fra's painterly substance while still turning the surface-filling folk into allegories of Balkan Christian identity. The staircase murals by another Zagreb painter, Vladimir Becić, were similarly focused on national types, though now the more robust, dynamic and vividly coloured figures were enjoined in a forward-facing, shoulder- and waist-holding, circle dance (*kolo*), their *opanci*-wearing feet lifting from the ground [figs 5.8, 5.9]. The liveliness of the painting has an almost caricatural vigour absent from Fra's quieter, more meditative and relatively sedentary English faux-Balkan folk. Irrespective of inflection, both Becić and Fra articulate lyrical, synthetic visualisations concerned with the furtherance of Balkan peasant traditions via a coming together of peoples. Their play with identity has much in common.

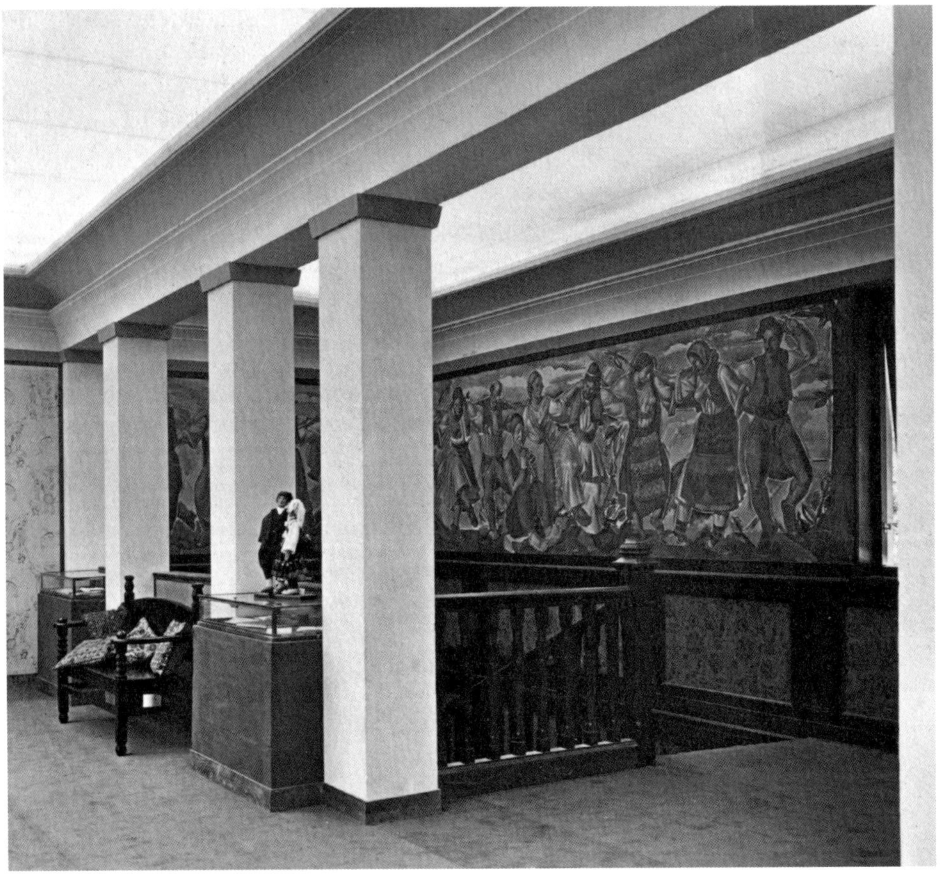

5.9 | Vladimir Becić, *Kolo*, staircase mural, Kingdom of Serbs, Croats and Slovenes national pavilion; from album of photographs of Yugoslav sections

How modern? How Serbian? How Macedonian? How British? How Balkan?

The Serbian modernist turn

Evidently the Newberys' Balkan turn of the late 1920s, for all its novelty and idiosyncracy, is not an isolated occurrence. That it evolves from their previous work, and at the same time contributes to a contemporary momentum being imparted to Yugoslav art, is apparent. Yet two aspects call for further consideration in order to gain a more complete sense of its historical place. First, how does it conform to notions and outputs that may be termed Balkan avant-garde, that is 'modernist'? And second, how does it lie within the ambit of other British artistic and literary takes on Balkan material culture of the interwar period?

As 'Balkan' eyes have been motivated to turn 'West' with new urgency in recent years, so a wave of English-language studies dedicated to unfurling modernising tendencies in the arts of southeast Europe has been set in train. Because the Newberys painted and wrote of 'Serbian' folk, how Serbian art developed in the 1920s and 1930s, and how it has been positioned, is most relevant to our study. Three books stand out, the first two with titles that peripheralise apropos modern trends in Europe: Ljiljana Blagojević's *Modernism in Serbia: The Elusive Margins of Belgrade Architecture 1919–1941*, Jelena Bogdanović et al.'s *On the Very Edge: Modernism in the Arts and Architecture of Interwar Serbia (1918–1941)* and Nikola Ivanović's *Identity(ies): Representations of Women in Serbian Painting (1918–1941)*.[8] While such publications have left a lacuna (for the Anglophone world) in terms of the great majority of artists and organisations from the region who/which did not modernise their material language so radically, the texts nevertheless reveal something of the extent and direction of so-called 'avant-garde' impulses. Blagojević focuses on Belgrade, with the functionalist, mainly institutional, architecture of Nikola Dobrović, Dragiša Brašovan and Milan Zloković distinguished, not only from the capital's cheap, cramped and ramshackle new dwellings for its 100,000-plus new residents, but also from the little-mentioned war-devastated and still tradition-bound provincial centres and villages from which they had arrived.[9]

On the Very Edge offers a broader view, taking in as it does a greater range of architecture, painting and applied art, including that which more obviously blends Balkan historical conventions and, say, contemporary European rationalism. It also emphasises the highly significant input of women as modernisers, be they makers, designers (including architects) or writers (or a combination of these). Still, there is little sign of equivalence with Fra and Jessie's work, the exceptions being the more ethnographic paintings by artists of the same generation as

them but created in the late nineteenth century, such as Uroš Predić's
Industrious Little Hands (1887) [fig. 5.11] and Paja Jovanović's *Preparation
of the Bride* (1888) [fig. 5.10]. Here we need only consider the former,
which, as Lilien F. Robinson points out, offers:

> *a remarkable insight into a young girl's domestic world, its lessons
> and adult expectations. The little girl is undertaking what was tradi-
> tionally the first knitting project, a pair of socks. Predić's presentation
> is honest, direct, and exacting yet subtly didactic. The intensity of her
> concentration and the dexterity with which she accomplishes her task
> are evident. Rather than contrived, she is real and her task specific.
> As a result, we understand the implicit message of societal respect for
> and value of her youthful industry.*[10]

While being 'real', Predić's girl is also iconic. She is seen half-figure
and frontal, her dark silhouette set against an abstract, yellowish backdrop. The paleness of her industrious hands and face stands out from
the rich reds, browns and dark blues of her elaborately embroidered
large collar and chequer-pattern of her dress. And yet she is no peasant
girl, as the prominent gold bracelet on her left wrist reminds us. That
both Predić and Jovanović had trained at the Viennese Academy, and

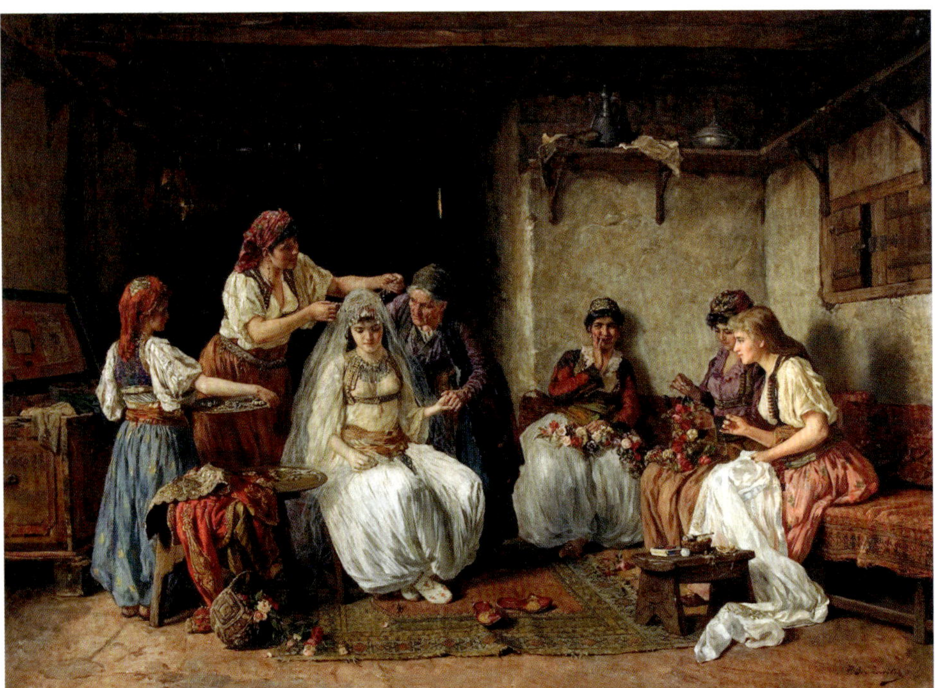

5.10 | Paja Jovanović | *Preparation of the Bride* | 1888, oil on canvas, 96.5 x 135 cm

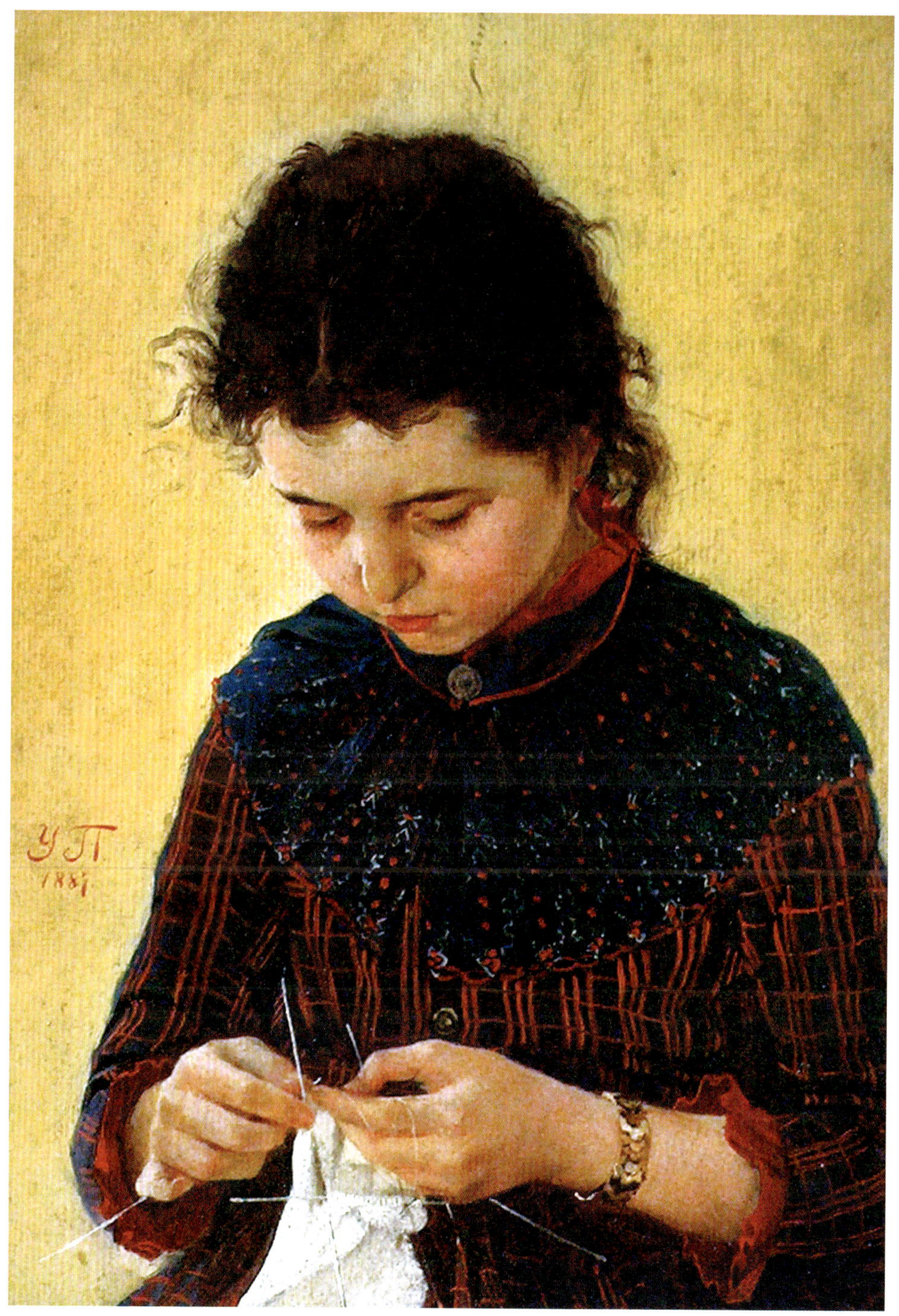

5.11 | Uroš Predić | *Industrious Little Hands* | 1887, oil on wood, 27 x 15.5 cm

NATIONAL MUSEUM IN BELGRADE

Jovanović had subsequently gained commissions from London galleries for paintings of Balkan life, helps to explain their turn to representation of folk traditions. In essence, their eyes and hands were thus hybridised by an awareness of more Western metropolitan-based desires for images of their little-known homeland, be it 'other', 'oriental' or simply a fragment of a larger whole.

On the Very Edge harkens to 'progressive' art and literature groups of 1920s Belgrade, that is, Zenit and Oblik.[11] In a curious twist, the Newberys' Serbian turn can be seen to relate more to the anarchic first than the more conservative modernist second. For Zenit, the brainchild of radical writer-artist brothers Ljubomir Micić and Branko Ve Poljanski, advocated contemporary art and society being led by a modern 'barbarogenius' creativity that would counter the Europeanisation of the Balkans with the Balkanisation of Europe. In their mutually related ways Fra and Jessie engaged in such a process, this irrespective of their artwork being stylistically and materially different from the Zenitists' preferences for movements from Neo-Primitivism/Expressionism to Futurism/Dada/Constructivism. While being pro-Serbian and internationalist, Zenit's anti-establishment stance was certainly more provocative than the Newberys' (though we should not forget Fra's condemnation of the path of typical British art schooling and his attempts to overturn artistic hierarchies). As a small, 'fringe', group with big aspirations (for social transformation), Zenit was active for five years from 1921, its public appearances being via its journal, evening events and, subsequently, gallery. The Newberys' autumnal 1926 Serbian sojourn occurred between the dissolution (by state intervention) of Zenit and the appearance of Oblik, a group that was more of an umbrella-style exhibiting society for the new generation of artists. Led by painter Branko Popović, Oblik's art remained more conventional than that of Zenit, both in terms of medium (painting, graphic art and sculpture being prioritised) and with regard to its treatment of painterly or plastic figure and space. In the main its artists were attracted to different strands of Post-Impressionism and Neo-Classicism, through which they explored nature and body without recourse to stereotypical images of Yugoslavian national costume. On the contrary, for all the colourism and formal experimentation of Oblik members' work, their Balkan folk tended to be fashionable, cosmopolitan types, their objects more likely to be signalling city refinement than peasant earthiness.

It has been left to Ivanović in *Identity(ies)* to focus on the representation and place of women in Serbian art of the interwar period. In so doing he has challenged the modernism narratives of the other books. By conceiving and examining a range of four identities (national, gender, sexual and self) he has been able to reveal variety in style, place, body and personhood considerably beyond that of his English-language predecessors. He uses the language of fabrication to suggest that modern Serbian visual identity was a heterogenous complex of interwoven/interlaced and diverse 'painterly poetics and ideologies'.[12] The pluralism he sees is brought out not only by numerous examples of painted, drawn and photographed challenges to a heteronormative axis but also by the representation of dress as a playing field for civic and ethnic encounter. Thus he considers the guising articulations of costume, be that as constructions of ethno-history, power, class or gender. So, while he examines distinct 'mother-of-the-nation' images of Queen Marija, he also brings out the self-queering paintings (and spaces) of, for instance, Zora Petrović and the self-exoticising/cross-dressing photographs of Milena Barilli. In the process he utilises salient examples from the world of Belgrade theatre, and in particular the imagery of professional actresses, be that in stage roles or as their more private selves. This, as well as his study of female nudes, leads him to reference redefinitions of assumed gender positions and activities as expressed in contemporary illustrated Serbian magazines and women's initiatives. Thereby, he claims:

> ... *women* [*were*] *the initiators of numerous new phenomena in Yugoslav inter-war culture. Women in Serbia climbed onto* [*the*] *social stage in the second half of the nineteenth century and the arrival of the new century was marked by the foundation of* Kolo srpskih sestara (The Circle of Serbian Sisters) *in 1903, as initiated by Nadežda Petrović.* [*The*] *inter-war period brought a series of women's and feminist associations and youth sections such as The Society for Enlightening the Woman and Protect*[*ing*] *Her Rights, Belgrade Society, Small Female Entente, Women's Party or Popular Women's Union of Serbs, Croats and Slovenes.*[13]

For all his mention of Serbian women's political groups, as well as a number of individual women who broke the mould through forms of 'auto-voyeurism' in their painted self-portraits, Ivanović mostly steers clear of analysis of the roles played by women in art societies, exhibitions and criticism. He also principally restricts his enquiry to painting (with some cross-referencing of photography and graphic art) and does not reference contemporary Balkan fabrications by non-Serbs or textile (or other applied) artists. Thus his fabrications of Serbian inter-war identity, while crossing over with ours, have a different trajectory and content. One work he does illustrate that we can use, to make the point of our fabricating similarities and differences, is Beta Vukanović's *Woman Spinning* (*c.*1920–25) [fig. 5.12]. While he includes this in his study of 'ethno-civic modernism'[14] and he mentions Vukanović as Serbia's first female caricaturist, he provides no visual analysis of her peasant woman with distaff and spindle, seated, in national dress, before a

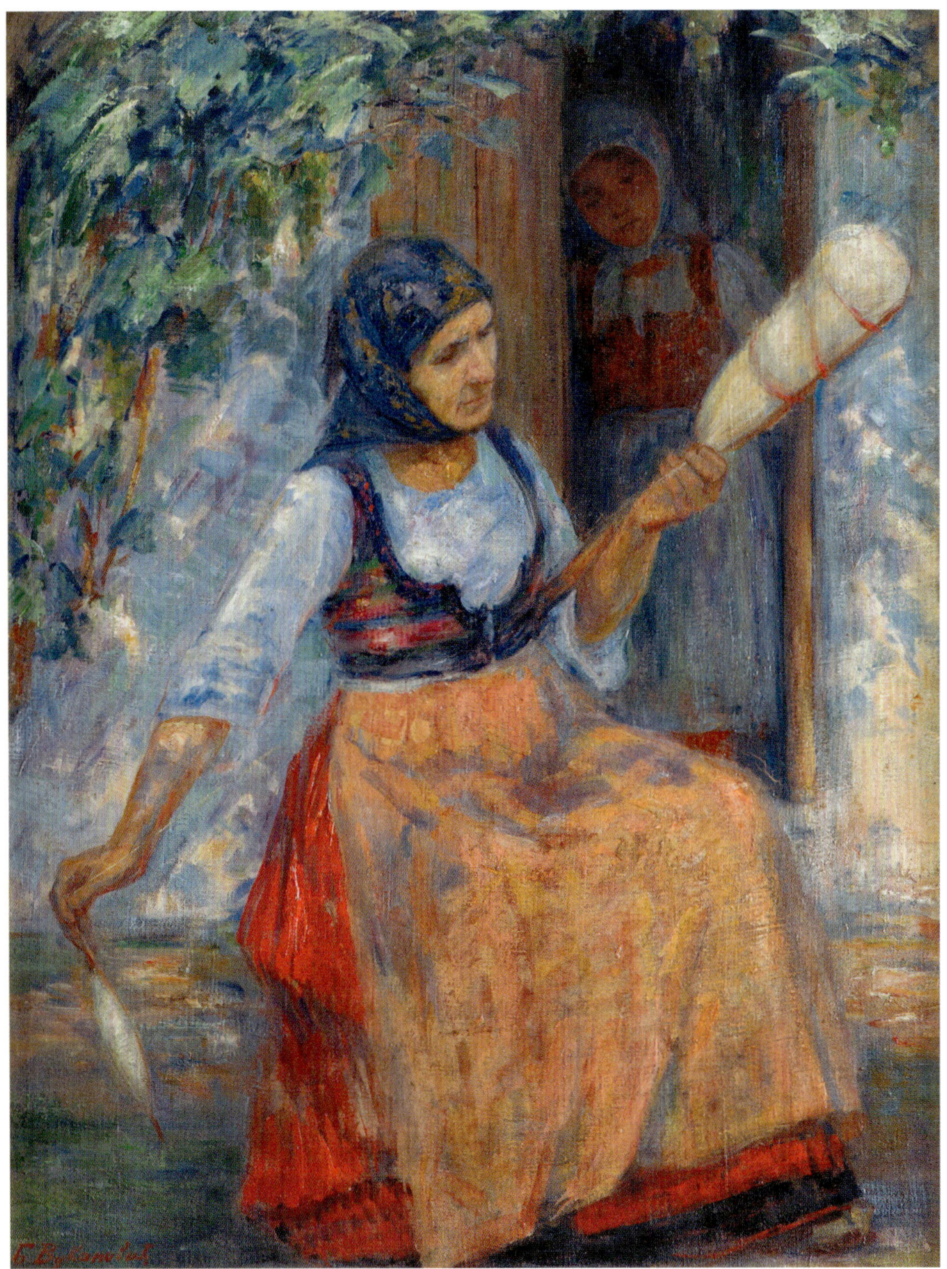

5.12 | Beta Vukanović | *Woman Spinning* | *c.*1920–25, oil on canvas, 87 x 65 cm

cottage door. It is therefore left to us to compare this with works such as Fra's *Serbian Women*, including as it does a girl, also in folk costume, gazing out over the threshold of the door, towards us, her reality and future. *Woman Spinning* needs no specific national or personal identification. So while she and her younger companion are presumably based on individuals seen by Vukanović, she represents certain cultural and gender awareness. It is not the concern of Ivanović that Vukanović was German (born Babette Bachmayer) and settled in Belgrade in 1898 after her marriage to Serb painter Rista Vukanović; that she taught women art students at the art school she and her husband took over in 1900; and became a founding member of the Lada art society in 1904 and of the Association of Fine Artists in Belgrade in 1919; or that she was an advocate of plein-air painting, Impressionist light and transience.[15] But such cultural and ethnic hybridity, as well as her constructions of Serbian womanhood, fit the terms and nature of our enquiry very well.

Closer Serbian artists and alternative Serbian womanhood

As it turns out, despite Ivanović's valuable intervention we still need to move beyond the 1920s Serbian art groups favoured by recent Western publishers to find parallels with the Newberys' propositions of 'Serbian' identity. At the same time, in her introduction to *On the Very Edge*, Bogdanović suggests the reasons for such a contradiction: the vestiges and prevalence of art histories constructed according to Western-centric paradigms and how the propagation of these inhibits pluralist argument by assumption and the imposition of simplistic power-relation models of centre and periphery. Hence, what is actually required is an even more nuanced 'understanding of the complexities of modernity and modernism within their semantic and geo-historical frameworks' than the valiant attempt at such that she and her co-authors supply.[16] For our case, this means expanding any concept of 'modernism', from that of a purist orthodoxy based on formal abstraction and anti-historicism to an adulterated, liberal idea of Zeitgeist capable of including forms of artistic expression that translate from, and experiment with, traditional values. We might call this (and the Newberys' work) intermodernism. As Bogdanović implies, being modern should certainly not always have to mean being in opposition to tradition. That being so, there is scope for another early-twentieth-century artistic Serbia where overlap with the Newberys' creations is more in evidence. This means looking beyond the groups and individuals who have hitherto been given preferential treatment due to association with that considered 'mainstream' modern (which might better be identified as art history's 'corporate' branding of modern). Thereby our horizons may include an array of largely neglected artworks, artists and associations, the last featuring the Southern Slav Lada Society (founded in 1904 and still active), Cvijeta Zuzorić Association (1922–41) and the Zograf Society (1927–40).

That artists could, and many did, move between groups, styles, subjects and creeds only reinforces the transitory, symbiotic nature of identification. My concern here is not to detail the interests at play in the evolving Serbian art scene but to pick out particular relationships with the Newberys' fabrications of Serbianness. So, although all three of these less acknowledged groups blended national and international, new and old, and the first two enjoyed a longevity and influence well beyond the others of their era, suffice it for us to acknowledge a visual lexicon akin to that of Fra and Jessie from just three painters, two female, one male, who challenge the old modernist 'canon': Nadežda Petrović, Miloš Golubović and Danica Jovanović. To these we add a small selection of 'hybrid' artworkers and art commentators who further elucidate the Newberys' Serbianism.

Of the three painters, it was Petrović who pioneered a new way for Serbian art and Serbian women that, like the Newberys' dedication to art-life reformulation, amounted to unstinting campaigns for creativity. As Lidija Merenik has pointed out, Petrović's own image is anything but restricted to that of straightforward purveyor of folk tradition: photographs show her in multiple guises, from urbane fashion to artist's garb, nurse's uniform [fig. 5.13a] and a modern version of embroidered 'ethno' dress [fig. 5.13b].[17] As such she is drawn into Jessie's fold of textile-reform artist. That she herself surpasses Fra's painted faux-encapsulation of Serbian tradition-bearing womanhood was further reinforced by the creative and intellectual energy she expended on advancing art in her homeland, whether as expressionist painter,

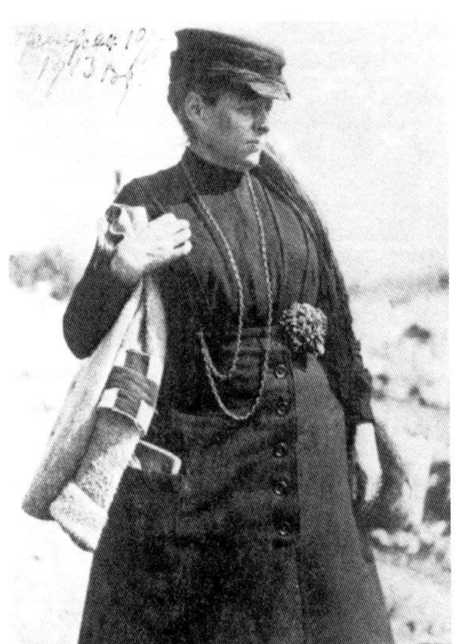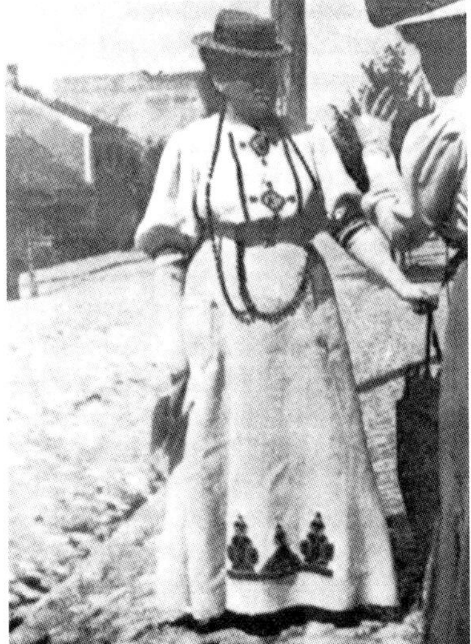

5.13 a–b | Nadežda Petrović in nurse's uniform, Prizren, 10 April 1913 [left], and in modern folk dress, 1908 [right]

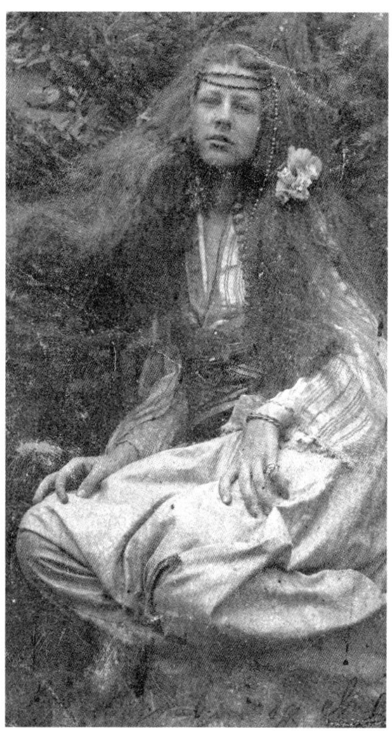

5.14 | Nadežda Petrović, 'Anđa Petrović', *c.*1907–8

photographer, art teacher, organiser of art and welfare societies or critic. Her own photographs go beyond revealing accomplishment in conveying Serbian mood and moment, be that peaceful family reflections or records of her time as a nurse on the front line during the Balkan Wars of 1912–13.[18] Hence they also capture, for example, her Parisian studio (1910–11) and her middle-class sisters, including Anđa, who posed for her as a young, confident daydreamer in folk costume, as if a Pre-Raphaelite muse [fig. 5.14]. For all her creative and intellectual versatility, her most favoured turn was to peasant subjects, and she imbued her painted fieldworkers, villagers, girls and musicians with a painterly vigour gained through thick strokes and impasto. Her *Two Peasant Women* and *Shepherd Playing a Pipe* indicate mostly closely her relationship to Fra's imagery, the rustic musician of the latter standing before two women in national costume, haystacks and cropped village architecture, the abstracted treatment of which is typical Petrović [figs 5.15, 5.16]. A friend of Meštrović, she was also his equivalent as a forceful painter of Balkan drive and deliverance.

The remaining two painters were less diverse and strident than Petrović, yet their imagery parallels Fra's in that they too sought occasional recourse to the representation of ethnographic type. One of the most renowned of early-twentieth-century Serbian painters, Golubović's career was established on the basis of what Petrović and Vukanović had achieved in terms of art organisation and pedagogy in Belgrade.[19] Having moved through Symbolist and war phases he became particularly notable as a 1920s portrait and landscape artist. His images of Serbian women ranged from salon-style 'high'-society ladies to that of a restrained, classically posed girl entering womanhood and showing her refinement and learning through her genteel features, book and the fine lace borders on her dress [fig. 5.18]. But he also turned to country folk and around 1930 painted *Spinster*, a picture of a young woman or girl seated in the shade by a picket fence pulling yarn from distaff to spindle [fig. 5.17]. That she is alone and gazes directly at the viewer accords with Fra's *A Serbian Woman* although her dark dress, light headscarf and setting in a hilly rural Balkan landscape counter his Dorset artificiality.

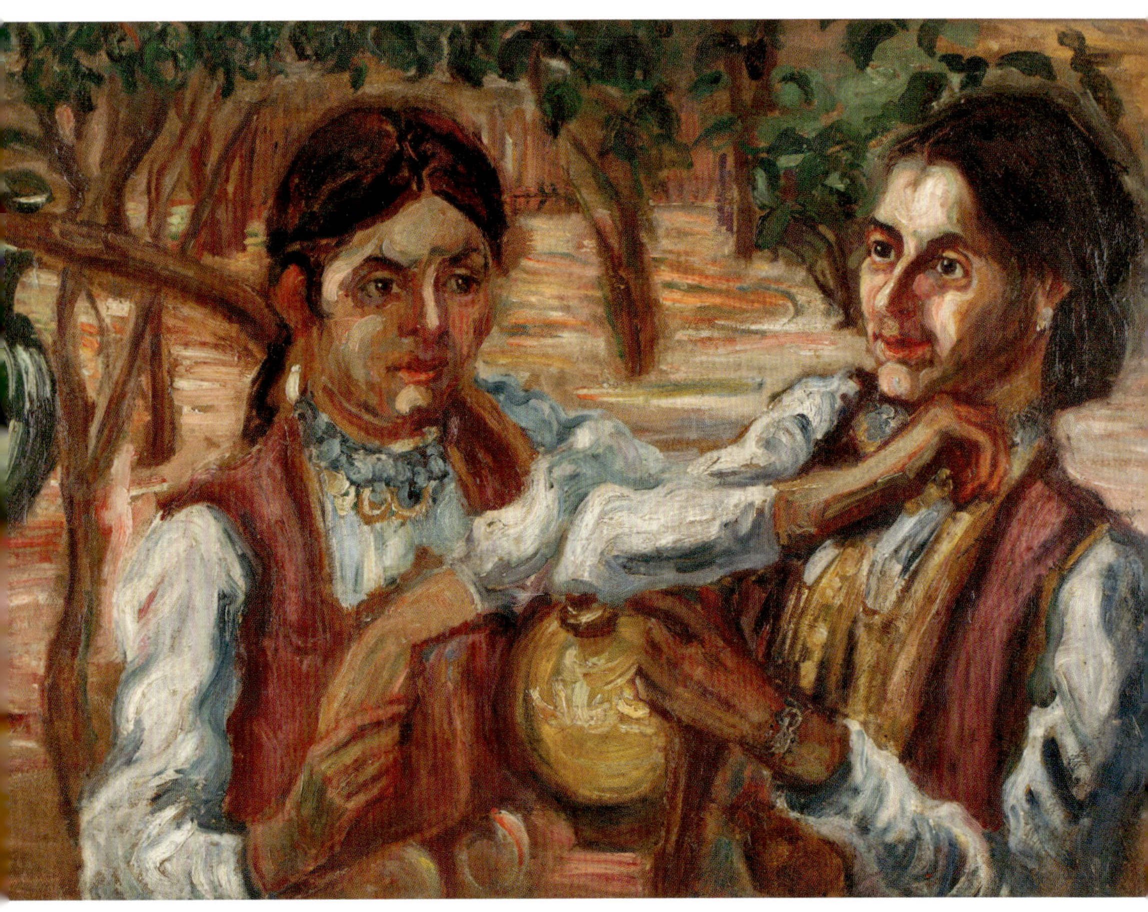

5.15 | Nadežda Petrović | *Two Peasant Women* | 1905, oil on card, 66 x 96 cm

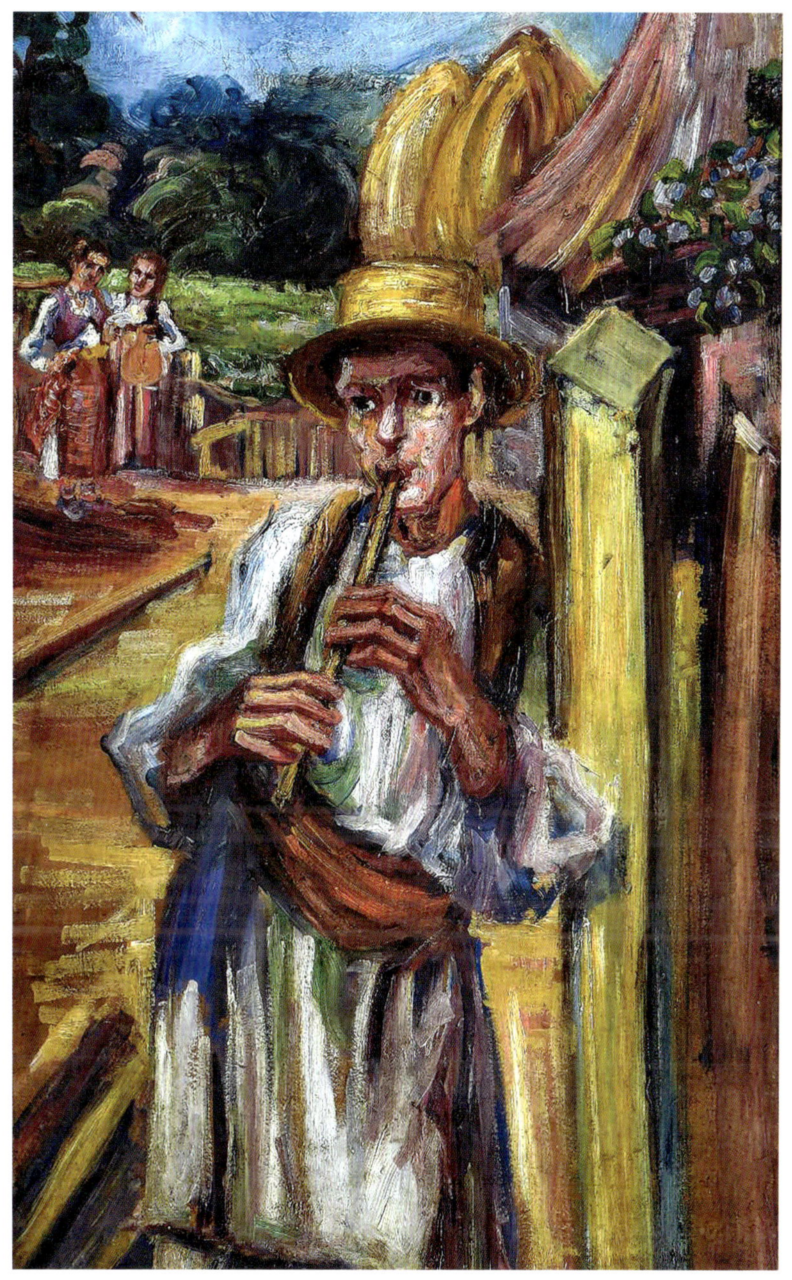

5.16 | Nadežda Petrović | *Shepherd Playing a Pipe* | 1906, oil on card, 78 x 49 cm

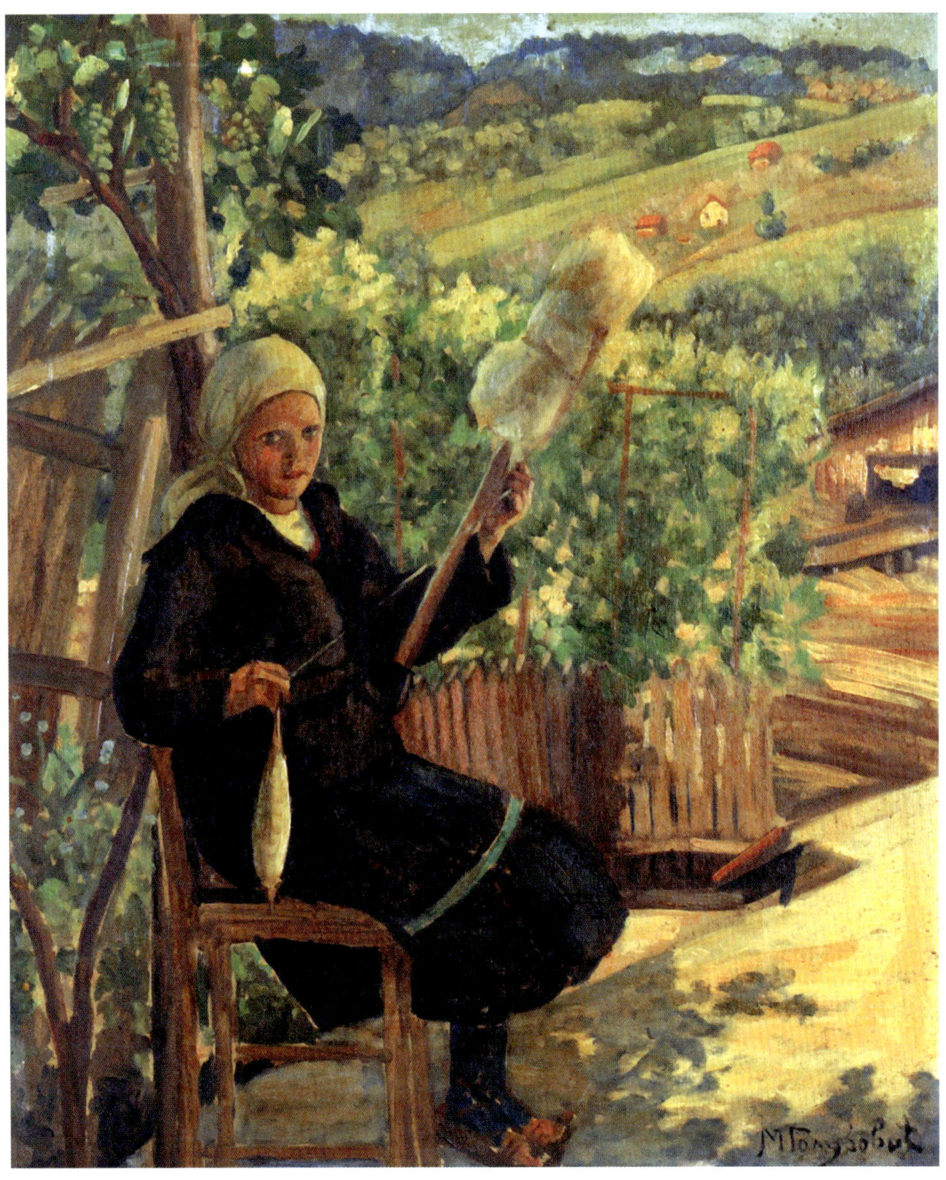

5.17 | Miloš Golubović | *Spinster* | *c.*1930, 55 x 47 cm, oil on board

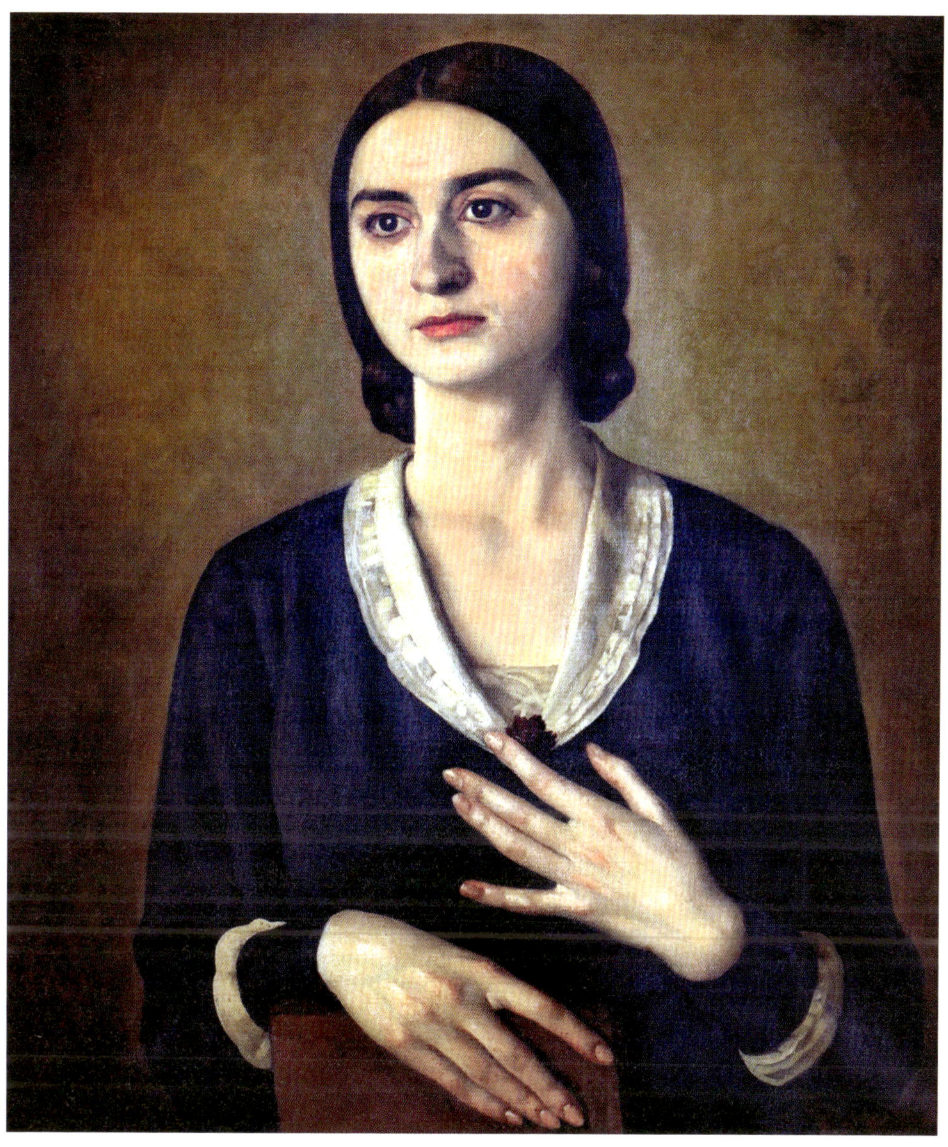

5.18 | **Miloš Golubović** | *Girl* | *c.*1925, oil on canvas, 68 x 58 cm
PRIVATE COLLECTION, COURTESY OF MADL' ART AUCTION HOUSE, BELGRADE

Danica Jovanović began her full-time art studies at Vukanović's School of Painting and Drawing in Belgrade in 1907, her two years there preparing her for entry into the Damenakademie in Munich.[20] In the summer holidays (1910–13) she made journeys home to Serbia from Bavaria. During the trips she made numerous oil-on-cardboard sketches of country life, many representing peasant women (and occasionally men) in folk dress [figs 5.19–5.21]. The lack of finish and detail, together with settings on earth tracks between fields and distant cottages, suggest quick work from life, as if in preparation for some more 'complete' studio follow-up. In the quality of abstract swiftness she comes closest to Fra's *Waiting*, while her lack of definition contrasts with the opposite approach used by him in his other Serbian imaginings. Furthermore, unlike Fra's fabricated fabric-makers Jovanović's women are multi-taskers: they have agricultural work to undertake, while also being spinsters, as evidenced by their carrying of distaffs, multi-coloured aprons, bags and baskets. Though similarly anonymous and ethnographic types, these solitary Serbian women, from various parts of the country, have no time to gaze at viewers, or even for

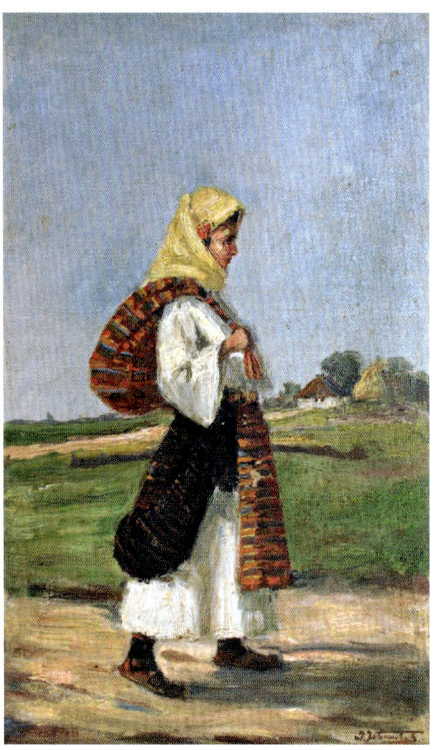

5.19 | Danica Jovanović | *Peasant Woman with Woven Bag* | *c.*1913, oil on canvas on cardboard, 44 x 27 cm

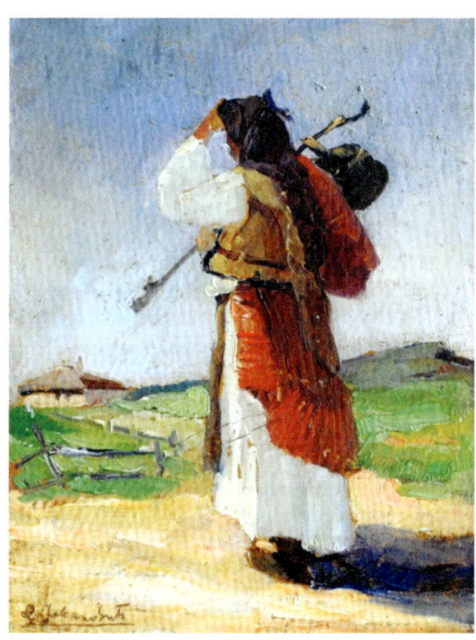

5.20 | Danica Jovanović | *Peasant Woman* | *c.*1913, oil on canvas on cardboard, *c.* 22 x 20 cm

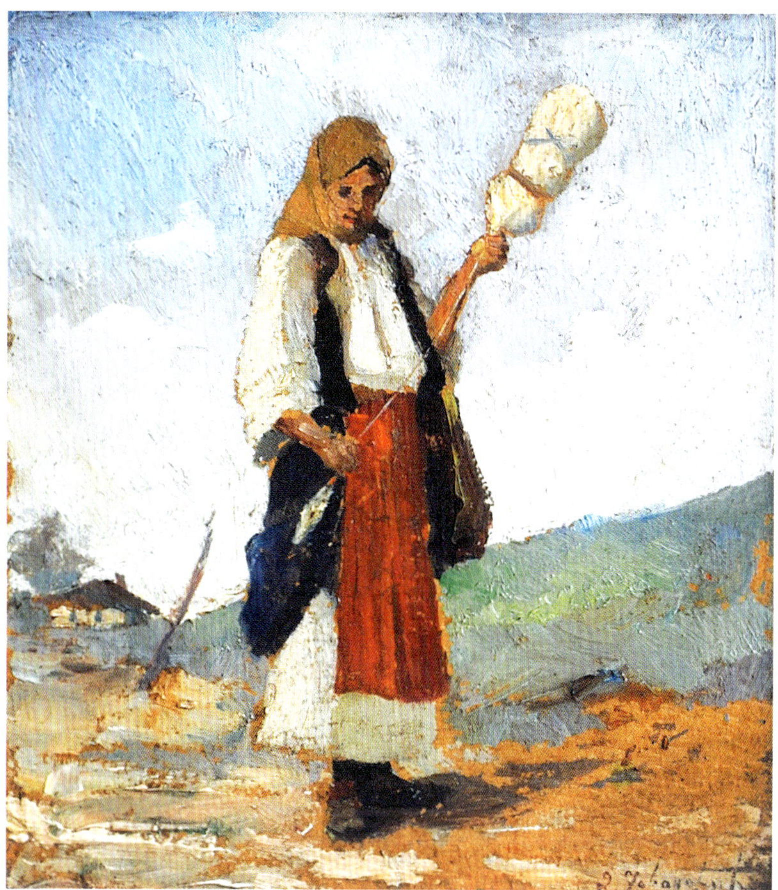

5.21 | Danica Jovanović | *Peasant Woman with Distaff* | *c.* 1913, oil on canvas on cardboard, 22.5 x 20 cm

conversation, instead being turned to look at their way or craft. They also mark the climax of Jovanović's art and life. After graduating from the Damenakademie, she returned to her home village of Beška in the Vojvodina region of northern Serbia in 1914 with plans to work on embroidery subjects and practice with women in the more impoverished rural south (particularly northern Macedonia). Instead, on 12 September that year, in the nearby Petrovaradin Fortress, at the age of twenty-eight, she was shot by an Austrian firing squad, along with other villagers, during the first Habsburg campaign in Serbia of the First World War. How little could Fra and Jessie have known of Serbian women's sacrifice a decade before their arrival, and, with Jovanović alongside Petrović, the losses that this inflicted on art.

The Macedonian stitch-up

Associating the Newberys' Balkan work with conflict and death would seem counter-intuitive, and yet, in many respects, it is an account of struggle for national recognition and liberation. Since it incorporates Croatian and Macedonian symbols under a Serbian banner, it is the painting and craft of assimilation. At the same time Fra's harmonised imagery of faux-rural Serbian folk can also be taken as his, quite likely unwitting, sense of the close blood-ties of the Slav peoples whose distinct costumes he melds together. As such he is a unionist representing the side that came out strongest in the establishment of the post-war Yugoslavia that he and Jessie visited. But we also know from his British work that he is simultaneously a regionalist, keen to bring out, if still with artistic licence, differences of place, culture and history within a greater integral whole. As such he did not label a Devon shepherd or a Renfrewshire embroiderer English or British. So does he have double standards for 'home' and 'abroad'? Probably. But the matter is also one of embedded life experience versus passing acquaintance, as well as his determination for the right of creativity not to be hidebound.

Fra and Jessie's collection and representation of Macedonian costumes as works of art indicative of peaceful bearers of tradition and belief belie the pain behind their survival. Macedonian territory had remained under Ottoman control until the end of the Balkan Wars of 1912–13, this despite its Slav peoples having fought on the victorious side in the Russo-Turkish War of 1877–78. That the gains of the eastern Orthodox nations of the region were partially wiped out by the political reorganisation (largely by Germanic-led, including British, outsiders) of the Treaty of Berlin that followed did not dent the ambitions for independence of the Macedonians (the majority of whom identified as Bulgarian) or their Bulgarian neighbours. One result was a prolonged internecine struggle, with Macedonians first seeking autonomy within the Ottoman empire, then being pulled towards a fledgling Bulgarian state, and then, in the wake of the First World War, being incorporated into Yugoslavia and becoming southern Serbia (or what Serbians also called 'Old Serbia'). Macedonia's own ethnic groups were drawn in different directions, be they Bulgarians, Serbs, Greeks, Albanians, Romanians, Jews or Romani. That journey was far from peaceful, violence erupting with particular intensity after the failed 1903 Ilinden-Preobrazhenie Uprising by Macedonian separatists spurred by Bulgaria. Its suppression and reprisals by the Ottoman Turks brought thousands of Macedonian casualties and devastation to hundreds of rural communities.

The Macedonian struggle was made manifest in a painting shown at the second Southern Slav Lada exhibition, held in Sofia in 1906. One of three works contributed by Bulgarian Valcho Antonov, when exhibited, was entitled *Macedonian Woman* [*Македонка*] [fig. 5.22]. Antonov's

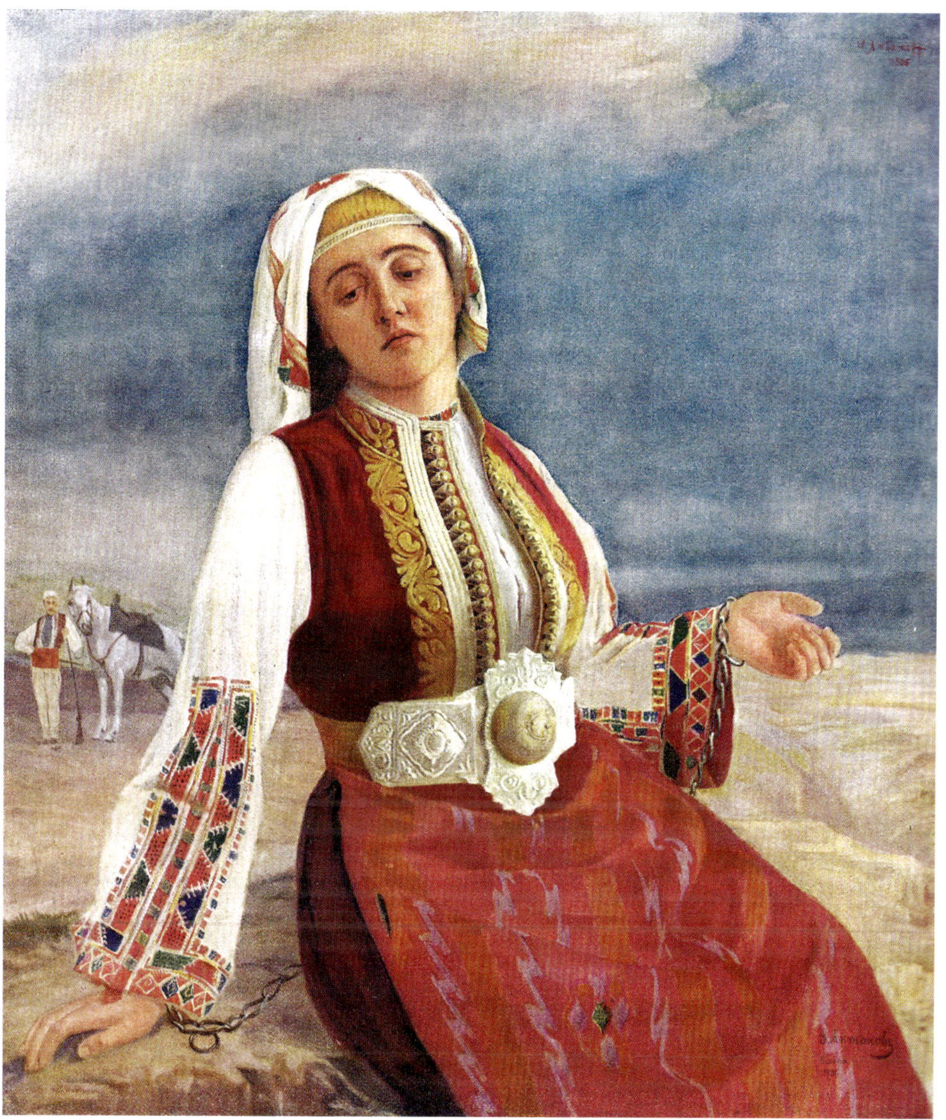

5.22 | **Valcho Antonov** | *Macedonian Woman/A Macedonian Slave* | 1905
from V. Antonoff, *Bulgarien vom Beginn seines Staatlichen Bestandes bis auf unsere Tage (679–1917)*
(Berlin: Georg Stilke, 1917), plate 39

representation of Macedonian womanhood showed marked similarities, and, simultaneously, starkly alternative allegorical meaning, to Fra's canvases. In the first place we are presented with a close-up image of a seated young woman in embroidered national dress, her white cloth chemise bearing bold, abstract geometricised sleeve motifs akin, but clearly not identical, to those of the younger figure in *Serbian Women* and the Virgin in the Swanage *Annunciation*. The spirituality of the latter is further recalled by her white headscarf, downcast eyes and the diagonal positioning of her hands. Yet rather than annunciation this is lamentation, a Macedonian Pietà, the cross of the woman's body suggesting a nation crucified but with a dignity which implies readiness to rise again. So instead of Fra's blemish-free faces we are presented with a countenance whose serenity contains hints of dark shadows around the eyes and a frown on the brow. An embodiment of stoic suffering, in lieu of hands working distaff, spindle and yarn in front of her body, here we see wrists linked by a chain behind her back and empty hands held in gestures of self-support and humility.

The background to Antonov's symbolic figure features, on the left, a man with rifle and horse turned, as guard, towards the woman and the viewer; to the right an extensive barren Macedonian landscape is shown. Storm clouds gather above. Thus *Macedonian Woman* is an icon of national and religious identity. That she also wears a large and richly decorated metal buckle (*pafti*) around her waist (hiding her girdle) not only pays tribute to a further Macedonian craft, but also suggests she is a bride. Isolated from her groom and people she grieves for their lack of liberty more than her own. The message then is that, in the face of adversity, faith in traditional Macedonian culture, custom and church will overcome. Yet the painting also works at another level: since it is by a Bulgarian artist whose learning and career was sponsored by the Bulgarian court, and whose audience was both Bulgarian and international, it is also a statement of Bulgarian desire for Macedonia.[21] In fact, Antonov's woman is a Bulgarian Macedonian; while speaking for 'all' Bulgarians she is also an embodiment of the post-1878 'rump' Principality of Bulgaria, representing its quest for freedom from Ottoman suzerainty and regional expansion. For this Bulgaria, her 'Macedonian' appellation meant a Bulgarian from Macedonia.

After Bulgaria's (German) Prince Ferdinand declared independence from the Ottomans in 1908 and then himself tsar, *Macedonian Woman* became the property of the Royal Bulgarian Ministry of Culture. In 1917 it was to make a reappearance, but this time in a book published by Antonov, in German, in Berlin and with a new title: *A Macedonian Slave* [*Eine mazedonische Sklavin*]. Reproduced full-page and in colour it was the very last of the volume's thirty-nine images. It became the volume's climax at a moment when Bulgaria – fighting on the Central Powers' side (and hence against Serbia) – had laid claim to Macedonia ('Vardar Macedonia'); and so the painting seems to reiterate the struggle for 'rightful' dominion. Now, however, it is also accompanied by Antonov's text, which relates its allegory to the fate of a particular Macedonian woman:

The eyes of the liberated Bulgarians were on Macedonia, where their brothers, with whom they had shared the same fate for five centuries, still bore the heavy burden of slavery [*see fig. 5.21*, A Macedonian

Slave]. The will, which clearly emerged from the real and desperate sighs of the sufferers of the Vardar, as well as from the Struma and Mesta [river regions], penetrated over the Rila Mountains and aroused loud echoes in the hearts of their brothers.*

**A Macedonian Slave. In 1902 Arsana Kuzmanova, a young Macedonian woman from Trebisht, Dibër district (Macedonia) was captured by an Albanian gang and taken to Albania. At the time of the Macedonian rebellion of 1903 she was freed by a band of Macedonians led by her bridegroom and taken back to Macedonia. Now she lives in Sofia as a happy wife and mother of two children.*[22]

So, painted in 1905, *Macedonian Woman*, aka *A Macedonian Slave*, is a 'portrait' of Arsana Kuzmanova, a Bulgarian from the area where western Macedonia joins Albania. Her village of Trebisht was a community in which Bulgarian Pomaks (Muslims) formed the vast majority and Bulgarian Christians a tiny minority (around 2.7%, or some seventy people from just over 2,500). Lacking the veil that was part of the national costume for Pomak women, Antonov's *Macedonian Slave* appears to purse her mouth – ready perhaps for the collective sigh that Antonov perceives and which unites the eastern Orthodox Bulgarian peoples. With her variation of embroidery designs, colours and belt, she is also to be distinguished from Fra and Jessie's Macedonians, Trebisht being approximately two hundred kilometres southwest of their Upper Vardar places of making. In sum she signifies the western reach of the Bulgarian territorial gaze. Another reproduction of a painting by Antonov that appears in the same book as *A Macedonian Slave* – entitled *Bulgarian Woman from West Macedonia* (1899) – shows a further variation on ethnic Macedonian dress and offers much for comparison [fig. 5.23].

Through costume, composition and appellation Antonov and the Newberys make manifest the torrid early-twentieth-century tug-of-war for control of Macedonia between the two dominant south Slav sides (and their respective, politically unreliable, international supporter-manipulators). Such a tussle also belies a photograph reproduced in Antonov's tome that portrays Tsar Ferdinand's daughters, Princesses Eudoxia and Nadezhda [fig. 5.24]. Placed immediately after separate images of their two ('spear-side') brothers in ceremonial military uniform within stately interiors, the princesses are depicted outside, close to nature, in Bulgarian national costume, and 'spinning' yarn from distaffs to spindles. Dressing up the Roman Catholic Italo-German girls as Bulgarians for official photographs started from an early age and was continued by the princesses into adulthood. With the spinning props looking theatrical and the gazes of the girls directed forward, towards and past the viewer, the teenagers recall the studio-posing figure of Fra's *A Serbian Woman* rather than those of his *Serbian Women*.

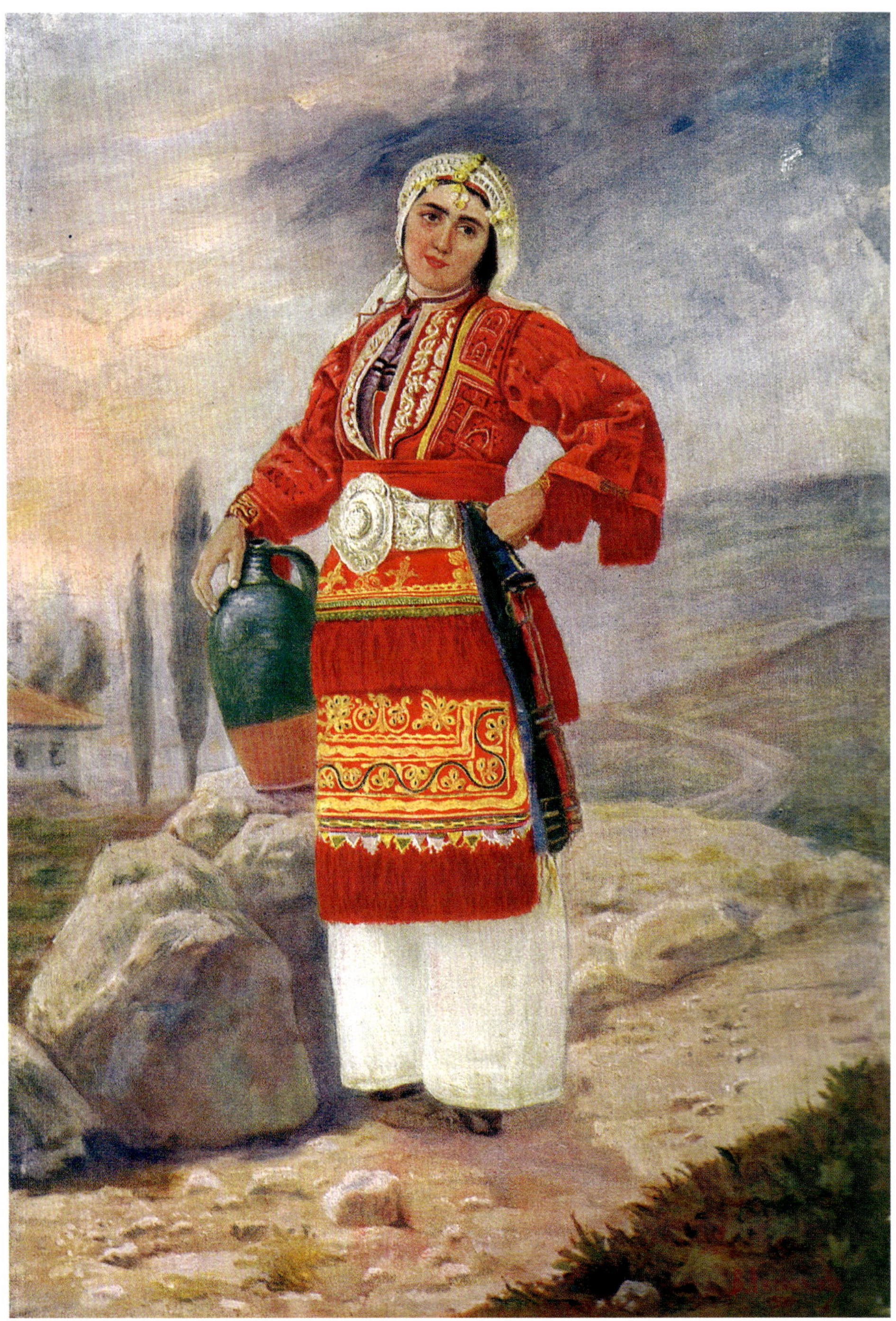

5.23 | Valcho Antonov | *Bulgarian Woman from West Macedonia* | 1899
from V. Antonoff, *Bulgarien vom Beginn seines Staatlichen Bestandes bis auf unsere Tage (679–1917)*
(Berlin: Georg Stilke, 1917), plate 38

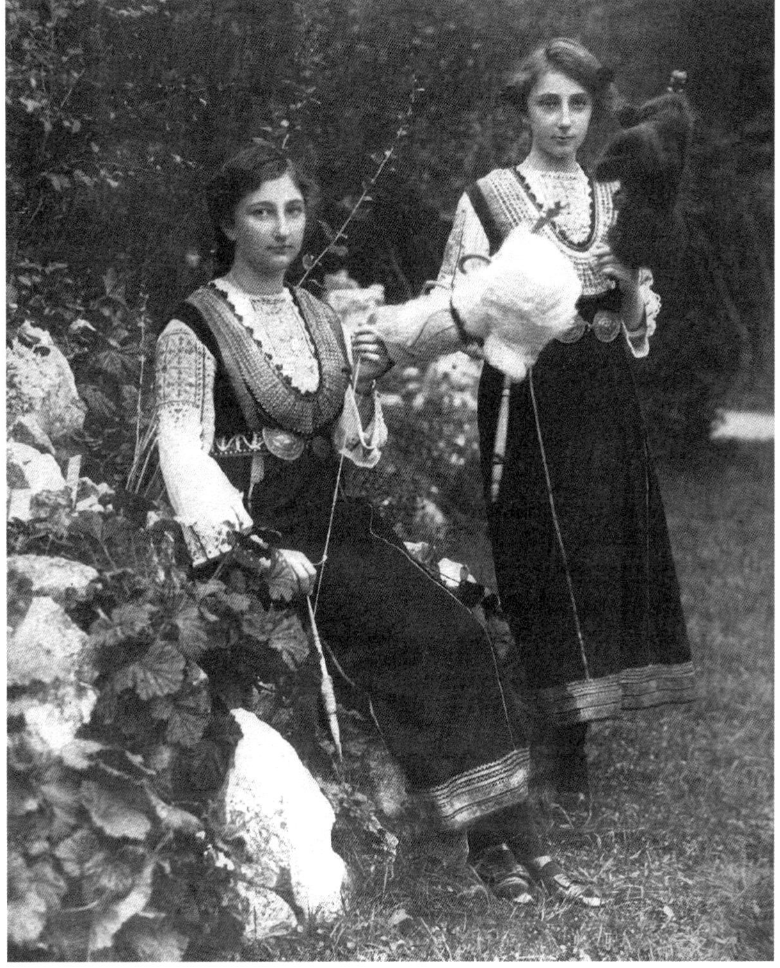

5.24 | Princesses Eudoxia and Nadezhda of Bulgaria, *c.* 1914; from V. Antonoff,
Bulgarien vom Beginn seines Staatlichen Bestandes bis auf unsere Tage (679–1917)
(Berlin: Georg Stilke, 1917), plate 28

Their disconnect with fabric-making craft and labour is also latently
expressed through their lack of aprons as well as in the neglible amount
of yarn on their spindles, as opposed to the mass of wool on the distaffs
they clasp with their left armpits. Despite the deceits of such national and gender performativity, Eudoxia, more than Nadezhda, closely
identified with the Bulgarian people. In fact her 'turning native' exposed the paternal deception behind the early national dress photographs, for when romance and marriage with a Bulgarian officer were
in the offing in the 1920s, her father, exiled in Coburg, intervened to
ensure curtailment. As a result she never married, though she continued to immerse herself in Bulgarian culture until she was forced into
German exile at the end of the Second World War.[23]

Hybridisation fabrication

Within twelve months of *Macedonian Woman* being shown in Sofia, works by the Southern Slav Lada group, along with numerous other officially approved paintings, sculptures, handicrafts and actual peasants from Yugoslavia and Bulgaria, were on display in the hugely ambitious Balkan States exhibition at Earl's Court, London (summer 1907). Befitting Antonov's visual lament, Macedonia did not feature as a state due to the fact that it was still nominally Ottoman. It was, however, present in the collection of national costumes brought from the Belgrade Ethnographic Museum, which included mannequins, mostly female, dressed in Macedonian garb. There was also a small display of Macedonian embroidery and other handicrafts mounted alongside Albanian, Herzogovinan, Bosnian and Dalmatian stands in a 'general exhibitors' section of one of the halls. Could Fra and Jessie have seen the show? Certainly they would have heard about it as the publicity, including postcards, reviews and illustrated catalogues, was huge. That the exhibition represented a degree of detente between Britain and Serbia, after years of frosty relations due to British support for other nations' Balkan interests (not to mention its own), augured well for subsequent allegiances during and between the ensuing world wars.

The burgeoning (if prone to faltering) Britain-Serbia relationship was further signalled in 1907 when three sisters, Mara, Lena and Natalia Jovićić, walked into the fashionable Art Nouveau-style photographic atelier of Milan Jovanović in central Belgrade and had their portraits taken in 'Serbian national costume'.[24] [fig. 5.20]. In their early twenties, the sisters were grouped perched on the edges of ornate curule-style seats, their vivid silhouettes standing out against an artificial, pale backdrop representing a fragment of a park scene, replete with staircase, stone railing, neo-classical vase, slender trees and verdant bushes. Staring directly at the camera lens, their hands are idle and the long sweep of Mara's white dress hides any sign of folk footwear. Dressed in contrasting richly embroidered garments, abundant jewellery and hair ornaments, the sisters strike poses of polite society decorum. According to Draginja Maskareli they wear, in all probability:

> *different combinations of costume elements taken from the urban and folk dress of Kosovo and Metohija … We see large thread-covered buttons, with corals on top, on Lena's (centre) and Natalia's (right) dress … Mara (left) is wearing a* džube, *a typical long coat, usually sleeveless and of a specific cut … Lena is wearing a* jelek *waistcoat and apron. I think, but am not quite sure, that Natalia wears a* mintan *jacket with long sleeves and over it a* džube *with open sleeves or an* anterija *upper dress. All the sisters also wear shirts with traditional embroidered decoration … the headgear has some costume elements but could be modern constructions.*[25]

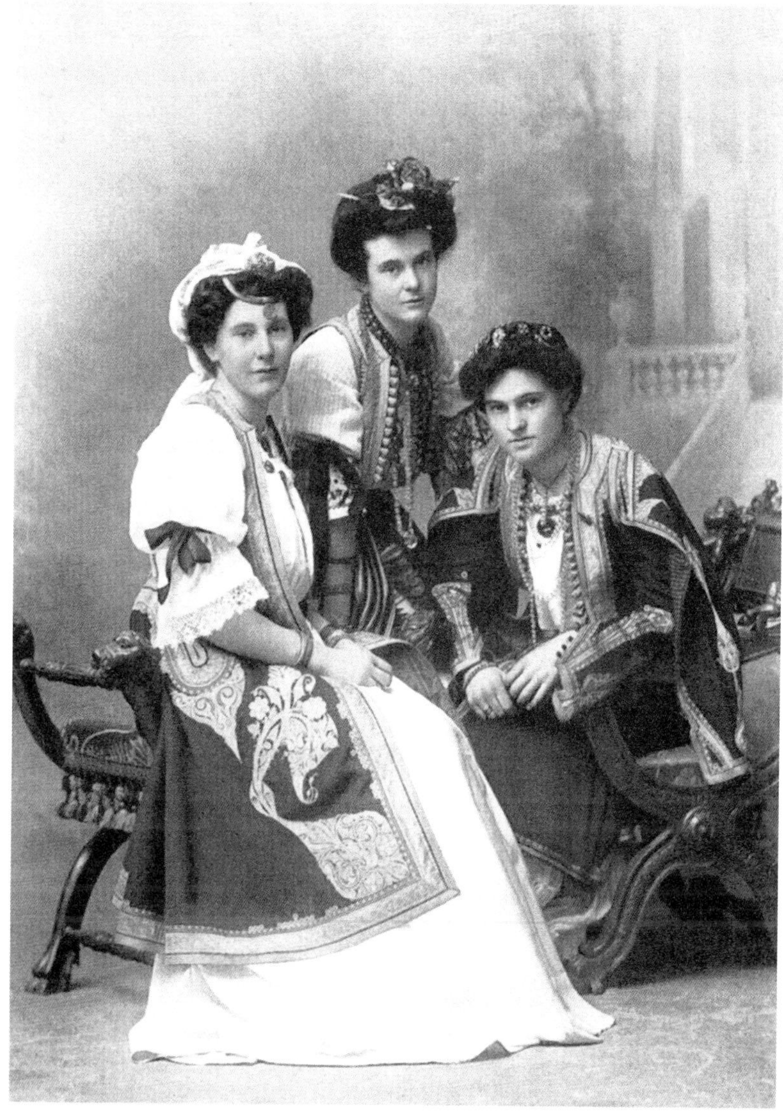

5.25 | Milan Jovanović, 'Mara, Lena and Natalia Jovićić', 1907; from Lena A. Yovitchitch, *The Biography of a Serbian Diplomat*, London: Epworth Press, 1939, opp. p. 257

Natalia, at twenty-four, two years older than her twin sisters, is adorned by silk and/or velvet upper garments, the passementerie work of their metal-thread embroidered trimming indicative of exquisite Serbian handicraft. The women are viewed frontally, relatively close-up and are composed into an ascending triangle. How near and yet how far, then, from Fra's working *Serbian Women*. Engaged in their handicraft and each other the latter's placement on a vernacular bench contrasts with Jovićićs' momentary, photographic faux-association with the trappings of European power. No distaff, spindle or needles, nor quite such a low viewpoint, for these young women.[26] Still, in Jovanović's portrait of Lena by herself, her intricately patterned *jelek* and front apron with geometric linear motifs evidently have some similarities to the garb of Fra's left-side woman [fig. 5.26].

The Jovićićs represent a small minority of Serbian women (up to thirteen per cent) who were educated city dwellers belonging to a rising middle class. Fra imagines the remaining vast majority of the agriculture-based society. And yet both and neither visual codifications are early-twentieth-century Serbian women. For, as with Fra, the Jovićićs are not all that they may seem. Only Natalia was born in Belgrade. The twins Mara and Lena were born in London. Their mother, Alice Mary Rutherford, was Scottish, the daughter of an Edinburgh

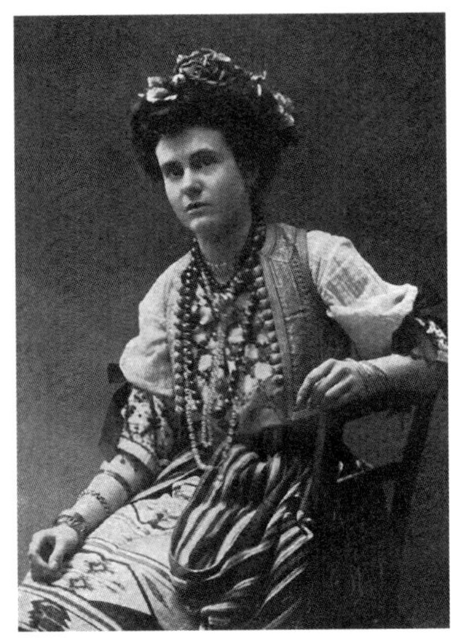

5.26 | Milan Jovanović, 'Lena Jovićić', 1907; from Lena A. Yovitchitch, *Pages from Here and There in Serbia* (Belgrade: S.B. Cvijanovich, 1926), frontispiece

bootmaker. It was their father, Aleksandar Jovićić, son of a Belgrade priest, who was a Serb. All three sisters lived much of their mature adulthood in Edinburgh. Peripatetic in their youth, with long spells in Belgrade, Germany and Switzerland due to their father's posts and then war, they were educated by Scottish governesses, as well as their mother and grandmother. Natalia studied painting in France. Mara was an able skier and mountain climber. Both were skilled seamstresses. Lena trained as a singer in Geneva and became a writer.[27] Clearly, then, the label of 'Serbian Women' is even more elastic and subject to alternative forms of hybridisation than that which we have hitherto suggested or encountered.

Lena Jovićić published her first English-language book on Serbia in 1926, the year of the Newberys' visit.[28] Transliterating her surname from Cyrillic she became Yovitchitch. Jovanović's photographic portrait of her appeared as the frontispiece. Her name was absent, the caption reading 'Peasant national costume'. In fact across her writing there is little overt acknowledgement of self or personal identity, the frontispiece's visual fabrication being most telling, not least because within her subsequent pages she reveals the significance of peasant dress, and her relish of it. This then, in essence, takes us back to Fra and Jessie's sense of Serbian identity. Furthermore, in her next book, *Yugoslavia*, published just before the Newberys' 1929 trip to Dalmatia and Croatia, she expands her study to the dress of Serbia's near neighbours (for relevant citations and their context, see appendix 5).[29] Both texts feature illustrations which support such a concern, the first with photographs of peasants and old architecture by Yovitchitch and a Miss B.E. Brown, the second with reproductions of watercolours, including four by Alfreda Marcovitch showing scenic sides of Yugoslav regional capitals. Of these, Brown's image of a Kosovan shepherd and Marcovitch's interpretation of the market on Jelačićev Square in Zagreb may be taken as prime examples of peasants and dress that accord with the Newberys' fabrications, while providing more authentic settings replete with sheep and stalls [figs 5.27, 5.28].[30]

Yovitchitch's written texts conflate a love for the 'picturesque' peasant and appreciation of the urban modern. She differentiates those places where the two 'rub shoulders' from those where 'it is quite the exception to see western clothes', noting that in the latter 'distaff and spindle accompany the women wherever they go'. She then launches into a description of their labour and 'gorgeous' costumes that are 'rich both in colouring and design, supplying subjects for "pictures" in legion enough to rejoice the heart of any artist'. With her claim that Serbian peasant embroidery's 'workmanship ... beauty ... and designs ... prove [it] ... a fine art' being provided alongside her review of a pioneering exhibition of contemporary Yugoslavian art, she brings herself firmly into the Newberys' aesthetic orbit, while refuting Fra's ostensibly restrictive take on Serbian womanhood.

In fact, Yovitchitch highlighted the first exhibition of the recently founded Cvijeta Zuzorić Association, without even mentioning that this was a group run by women. That this group was responsible for sponsoring more Yugoslavian artistic change and presence than either of the western-proclaimed Zenit or Oblik societies is significant. Indeed, in its raising of funds for Serbia's first purpose-designed exhibition

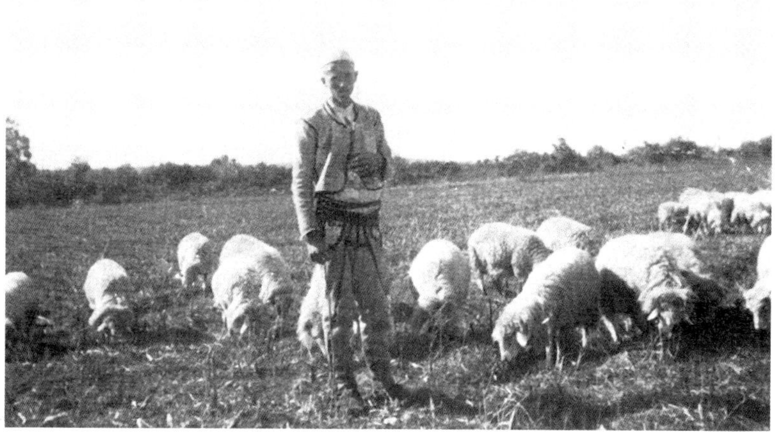

5.27 | B.E. Brown, 'Kosovan shepherd', pre-1926; from Lena A. Yovitchitch, *Pages from Here and There in Serbia* (Belgrade: S.B. Cvijanovich, 1926), opp. p. 136

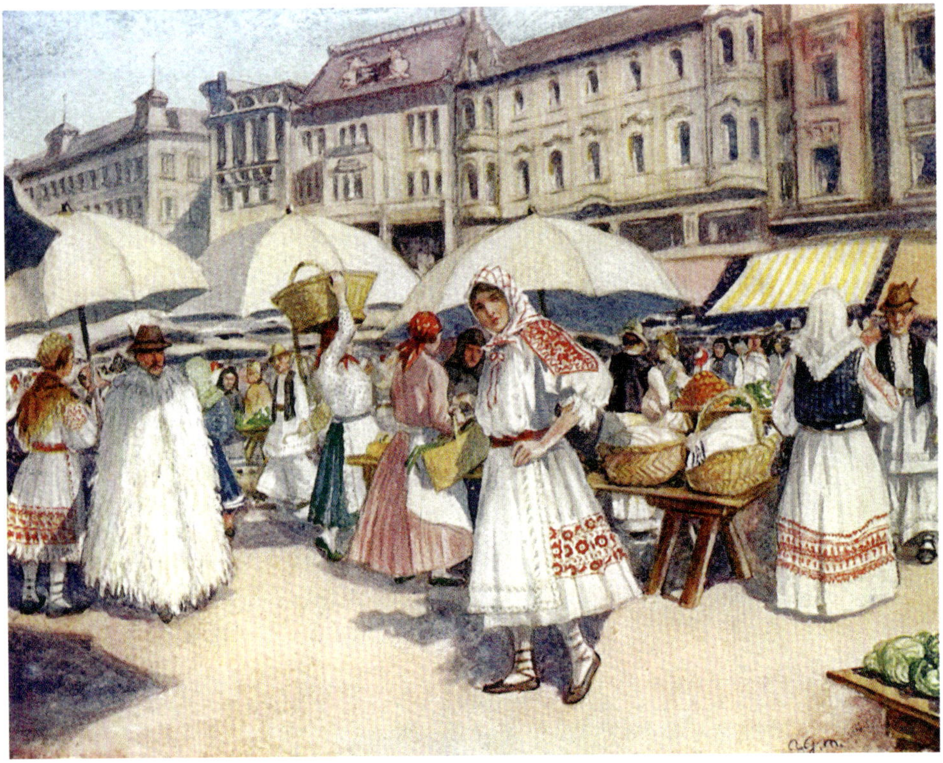

5.28 | Alfreda Marcovitch, 'Jelačićev Square market, Zagreb', pre-1928;
from Lena A. Yovitchitch, *Yugoslavia* (London: A.&C. Black, 1928), opp. p. 10

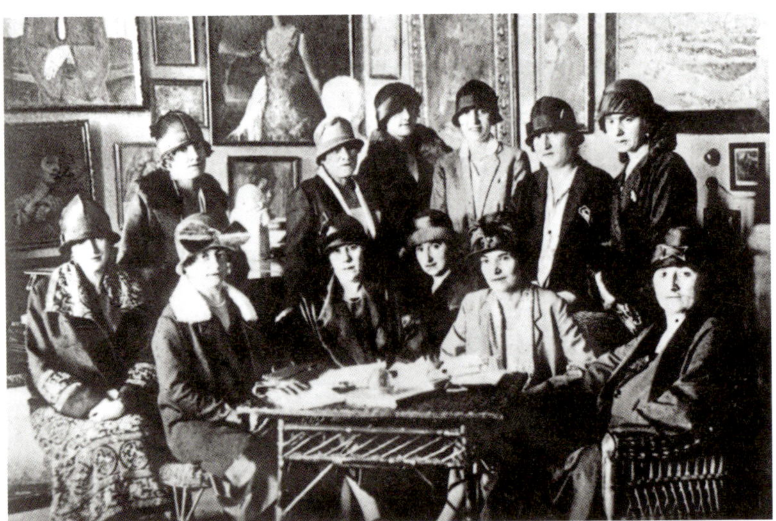

5.29 | Cvijeta Zuzorić Association, members, *c.* 1925

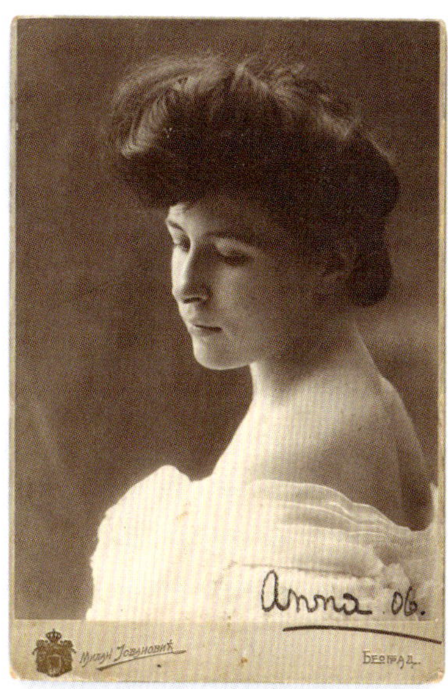

5.30 | Milan Jovanović,
'Ana Marinković', *c.*1906

building, from 1928 the group also provided a permanent Belgrade venue for Oblik, Lada and other modern arts associations to display their work.[31] Its first president was Ana Marinković, a painter who had initially studied art under Petrović. Besides exhibitions the group also organised literary events and concerts. Supported from its 1922 outset by the director of the Art Division of the Ministry of Education, Branislav Nušić, the group was named after Flora Zuzzeri (Cvijeta Zuzorić), a sixteenth-century poet and hostess of an art-literary salon in Ragusa (Dubrovnik). Photographs of the group's committee members from the mid-1920s and of Marinković from around 1906 (by Jovanović) raise further questions about Fra's stereotyping of the Serbian female [figs 5.29, 5.30]. For in these, the dress of the women, along with the fragments of paintings with women as subjects visible on the walls behind those in the group portrait, show them as dedicated followers of contemporary European fashion and principally non-peasant. Of course they are also identifiable individuals, not just visual tropes. And as Yovitchitch's review indicates, from their first exhibition the Zuzorić Association promoted artists irrespective of gender and style. The group also organised exhibitions of international art.

On 29 September 1926, the very day Jessie wrote to her daughter Elsie from Niš, the Zuzorić Association opened its 'Exhibition of Contemporary Parisian Masters'. Held in the halls of the Academy of Science in Belgrade, the display included work by Pablo Picasso, Robert Delaunay, Sonia Delaunay, André Lhote, Henry de Waroquier, Léopold Survage, Marc Chagall, Ossip Zadkine and Tsuguharu Foujita. Further research is required to identify individual pieces, though reviews in the Belgrade weekly *Ilustrovani List* and newspaper *Politika* reproduced a lithograph of a townscape by Foujita, *Les Rugbymen* and a portrait of a woman by Lhote [fig. 5.32], a female nude by Zadkine [fig. 5.31], one of Robert Delaunay's *Eiffel Tower* paintings and a Cubist drawing of two (seemingly) women by Picasso [fig. 5.33].[32] *Politika* also noted that Sonia Delaunay, apparently the only woman participant, 'brought a lot of beautiful decorative works'.[33] We may speculate whether Fra and Jessie saw the show, yet even if they did not their Serbian turn bears consideration in relation to its known exhibits. In particular, *Serbian Women* can be regarded as a response to the Picasso, not least since the monochrome latter appears to objectify women rather differently:

for example the vertical format and multiple viewpoints show fragments of a seated and a standing figure, their bodies reduced to compilations of a few facetted planes, broken geometric forms, curved and straight lines.[34] Lacking obvious clothes, the standing figure has loose hair and a dark wedge cleaving one of her two part-faces. She appears to hold a flat oblong object, this in turn cleaving the headless seated one, who has parts of smaller rectangles beside her. Such elements are counterparts to the apron and woollen 'sock' of Fra's *Serbian Women*. If Picasso's figures are artists, then their art is more likely painting than textile art. In any case there is correspondence between the works.

A month after the opening of the Parisian Masters show, on 27 October 1926, this time just when Jessie was writing to daughter Mary from Belgrade telling of her purchases of folk costumes and pottery, the Zuzorić Association opened the first one-person exhibition of Croatian artist Sonja Kovačić (Tajčević). It was held in the House of the Circle of Serbian Sisters, a women's charity. Again *Politika* reviewed the show, indicating, through its text and reproductions of Kovačić's intermodernist *Portrait of a Girl* and *Girl's Head* [figs 5.34, 5.35], how far removed this younger painter was from lingering stereotypes of Balkan peasant womanhood.[35] Compare these idle, flesh- and hair-exposing females with Fra's spindle- and needle-wielding, costume-covered women: alternative fabrications of the distaff side.

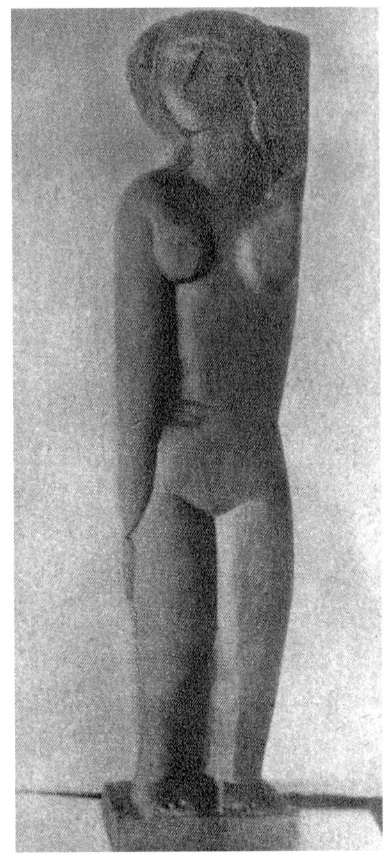

5.31 | Ossip Zadkine, *Woman*, n.d.; from 'Изложба савремених париских сликара', *Илустрован Лист*, no. 41, 10 October 1926, p. 31.

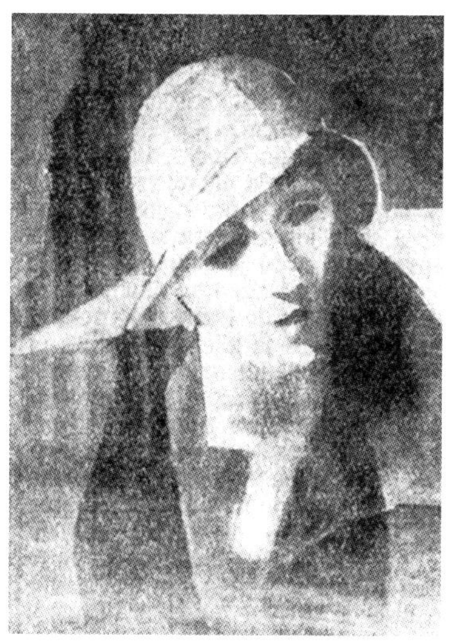

5.32 | André Lhote, *Portrait of a Woman*, pre-1926; from, 'Изложба савремених париских мајстора', *Политика*, 29 September 1926, p. 5

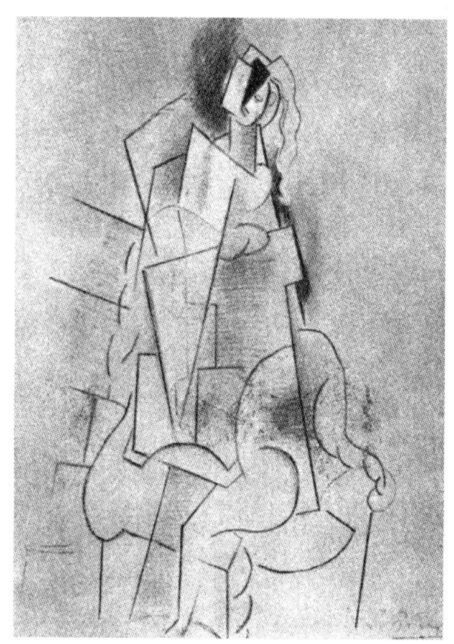

5.33 | Pablo Picasso, drawing, n.d.; from 'Изложба савремених париских сликара', *Илустрован Лист*, no. 41, 10 October 1926, p. 31.

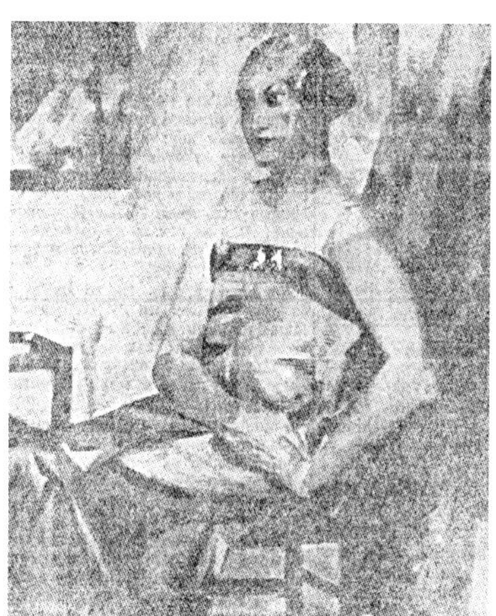

5.34 | Sonja Kovačić (Tajčević), *Portrait of a Girl*, *c.* 1926; from 'Изложба слика r-ђе Соње Ковачић', *Политика*, 27 October 1926, p. 5

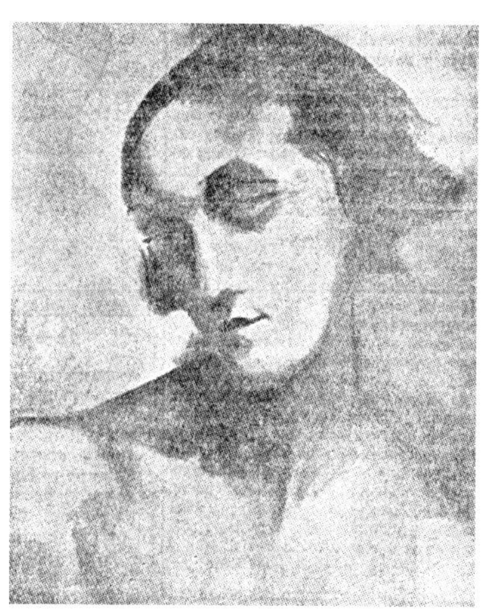

5.35 | Sonja Kovačić (Tajčević), *Girl's Head*, *c.* 1926; from 'Изложба слика r-ђе Соње Ковачић', *Политика*, 27 October 1926, p. 5

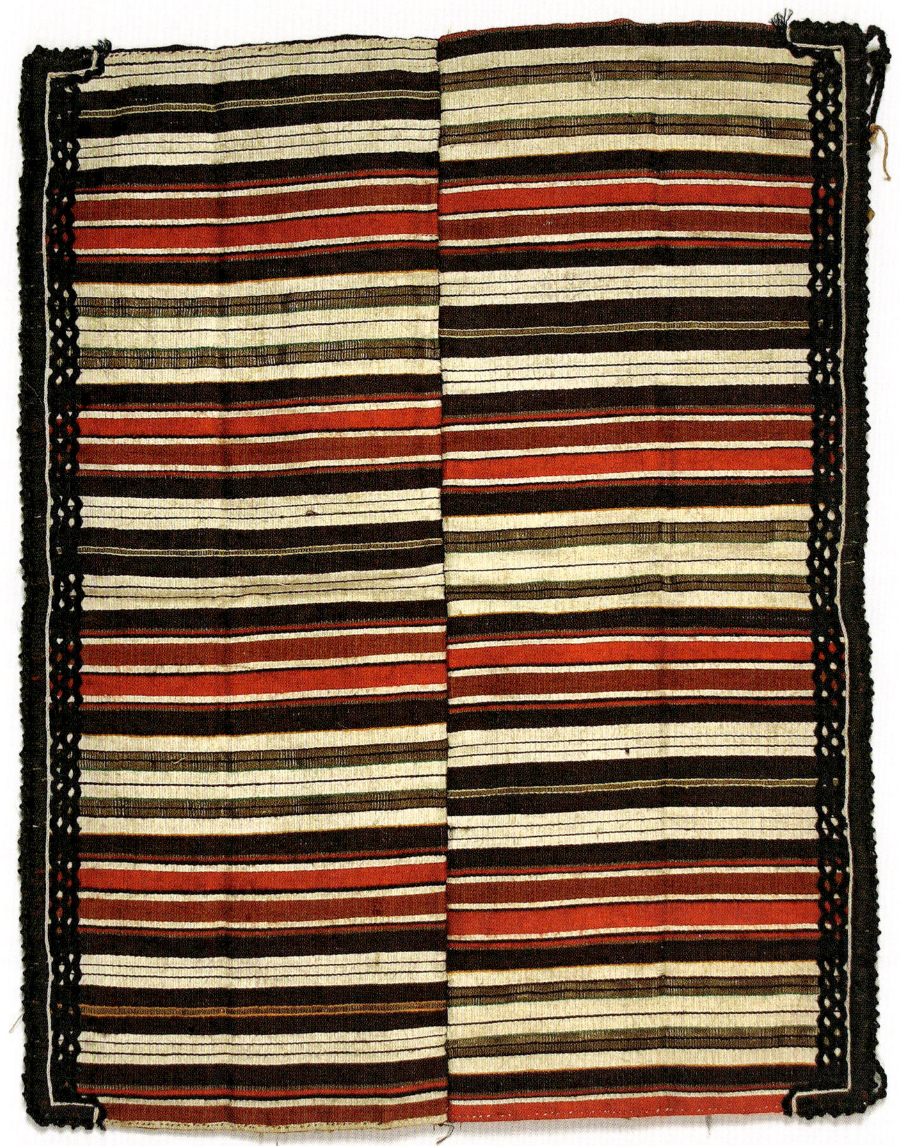

6.1 | Textile cover, *c.* late 1920s

WRAPPING ANEW THE AGE-LONG HIDDEN SPARK
BALKAN ARTS MATTER

Fractals of art and life

Fra and Jessie's Serbian twists and turns, for all the apparent Janus-faced originality and typecasting they contain, tap into a moment in modern history when British continentalism, however uninfluential and marginalised it was, developed an empathetic and philanthropic attitude to Europe's wartorn and rivalry-ridden southeast.[1] A crucial factor within this was a new understanding (which particularly arose during and after the First World War) that a positive present and future could be created by learning lessons from those whose societies and artwork had been adulterated very little by the prevailing modernities of many European cities, towns and villages.

Thus the Newberys and their ilk (not least the Le Play Society fieldworkers) are not simply looking back to look forward but to the side, to where back was also front. In so doing they formed a small set of enlightened British Balkan advocates who communicated a learning, through craft, that we can propose as being based on a 'fractal' conception of personhood and collective. For us this means their work, in its making, materiality, appearance and possible figuration, like themselves, is construed as an individual 'whole' body that is at once composed of smaller bodies (these also internally complete) and a unit of a larger body (community). Since this is a paradigm of relations of precipitates they join in this community with other creative proponents of Balkan identity, from within the region and without. The effect is one of distributed mind where the Balkanist 'clan' is composed of many relations, itself becoming a 'person'. The multiple artworks or literature of this clan is a phenomenon of 'doing', or efficacious agency; every piece is also a form or instantiation of person, characterised by an element of protension that anticipates future works and another of retention that derives from earlier ones. Each piece fuses internal mental process and external transaction (through material entity). Our job here is to make some sense of these relations through a combination of context construction and unit analysis. Whether this diminishes the likelihood of fraught and contentious 'side-taking' may be doubted but it can also be considered an ambition.[2]

Fractal I: 'Dikitsa'

Perhaps unsurprisingly it is mainly women who express creative British Balkan advocacy akin to the Newberys, examples from different spheres being Annie 'Dikitsa' Dickinson, Jean Milne, Ethel Mairet and Rebecca West.[3] While the first three await thorough exploration in terms of their Balkanist fractal bodies and relations, West's art-body of *Black Lamb and Grey Falcon: A Journey through Yugoslavia* (1941) has been thoroughly dissected by others for its creative propositioning of Balkan identity. For all four, acquaintance with Balkan peasant crafts, particularly embroidery, proved critical for the ensuing development of their own art. Of the four it was Dickinson, originally a painter, who, having been involved in the Cotswold arts and crafts movement prior to the First World War, most fully immersed herself in Yugoslavia, settling there for some two decades after the war. Born in 1864, the same year as Jessie, she founded craft schools for orphans, collected Bosnian textiles, designed furniture, fittings and clothes (often blending Bosnian motifs, local materials and simple Cotswold arts and crafts styles), and organised exhibitions of furniture and embroidery in Belgrade and London. In 1928, in an interview for a Serbian women's magazine, *Woman and the World*, 'Dikitsa' (as she became known) claimed that 'as an adherent to theosophy, it is my belief that I must have been a Serb in a former life'.[4] Furthermore, as early as October 1918 she was in Dundee, at the City Chambers, 'appealing for sewing materials for the women of Serbia'.[5]

Dickinson's Serbian reincarnation began in 1915, when together with her sister Frances and brother-in-law James Berry, she helped run the Red Cross hospital at Vrnjačka Banja in central Serbia. Held prisoner there when Habsburg forces seized control in November 1915, despite privations, the following Christmas she, her sister and other members of the unit assumed fancy dress and put on a performance of 'Pepeljuga', the Serbian variant of Cinderella. Pepeljuga's fate and her ill-treatment by her stepmother centre around her spinning while watching over grazing cattle. Her original loss of spindle is followed by life-threatening punishments involving the enforced spinning of bags of hemp of increasing size. She only completes these with the aid of her

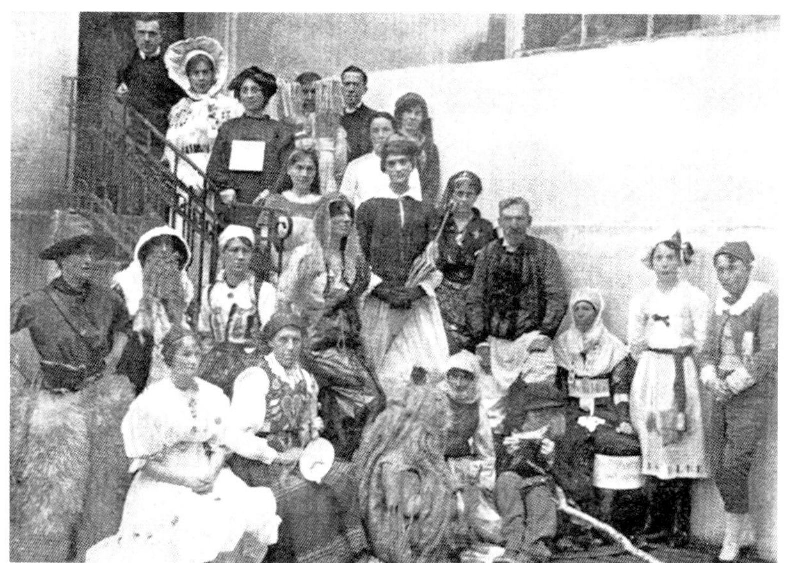

6.2 | Fancy dress party, Vrnjačka Banja Red Cross Hospital, January 1916; from James Berry, F. May Dickinson Berry et al., *The Story of a Red Cross Unit in Serbia* (London: J.&A. Churchill, 1916), opp. p. 256

mother reincarnated as a cow, after which, despite being incarcerated at home with impossible-to-complete domestic tasks, she is able, three times and with the help of two doves, to get to church (and back) in the finest embroidered dress sourced from a chest that magically appears on her mother's grave. She eventually marries the prince who found the slipper she lost on her dash home the third time. A photograph of the members of the Red Cross unit, most of them British women, shows them dressed up in their 'fancy' costume [fig. 6.2]. While there is a cow girl, Santa Claus, a gypsy woman, a Pierrot-style figure, an elegant dame with umbrella and a Little Bo-Peep lookalike, at least four women appear in peasant dress and religious attire. Positioned closest to the camera these include the centrally seated Annie Dickinson, replete with a *gusle*, a traditional Balkan stringed musical instrument (or *gusle*-style distaff), 'Pepeljuga' with hemp and spindles, and, seated third to the right, her sister, whose garb appears a form of nun's habit and coif. Frances reported:

> *much ingenuity was displayed in the manufacture of costumes from a very limited choice of materials … We dramatised the story of Pepelyouga, the Serbian Cinderella, culled from Petrovitch's* Hero Tales and Legends of the Serbians, *and wove into the drama allusions to other Serbian myths and national heroes. With the help of costumes and spindles borrowed or bought from peasants, and with Pirot carpets on the walls, the setting was made as typically Serbian*

Was this then the start of the British Serbian performance turn that
saw a certain climax with Fra and Jessie's Corfe Castle pageant a
decade later? Of the many tales reproduced in Petrovitch's 1914 English-language retelling it was Pepeljuga alone which brought forth the
stereotype of the young spinning peasant woman as a cornerstone of
Serbian identity. And yet it was Pepeljuga that appealed to the British
medical contingent, its choice and her ability with the spindle serving
to highlight both contemporary British loss of handicraft skill and the
romantic cultural perceptions that remained. It fell to Annie Dickinson, like the Newberys, to challenge such loss and exoticism, through
practice, display and promotion.

If Dickinson's quasi-Serbian transmogrification began in 1915, a decade and a half later it was in elastic full swing and being recognised.
Contemporary photographs of 'Dikitsa's' handicrafts-school exhibition
in Belgrade in 1931 show modern functional wooden furniture accompanied by cloth embroidered with folk motifs, the latter hung from
walls and placed on a bed and reclining chair. In one photograph, sets
of compact, functionalist dining furniture are complemented by uphol-

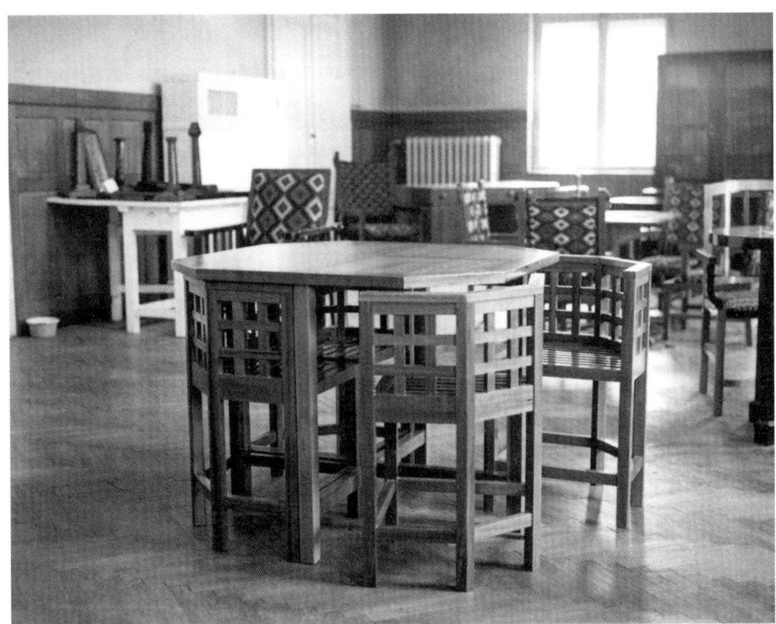

6.3 | Annie Dickinson's Handicrafts School exhibition, Belgrade, November 1931

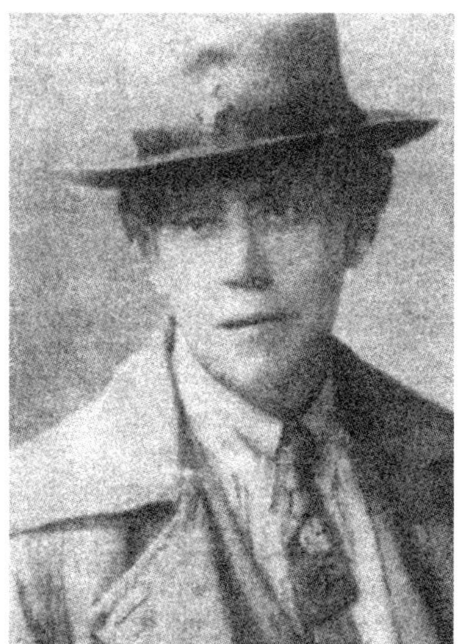

6.4 | Annie Dickinson, pre-1928; from
Жена и свет [*Woman and the World*],
no. 1, 1928, p. 14

stered armchairs with bold repetitive rhomboidal patterns which appear to be modern interpretations of Pirot (or similar) kilim designs [fig. 6.3].[7] As a reincarnated Serbian woman Dickinson took hybridisation fabrication to a new level, as reinforced by her anonymous obituary writer, who considered her to be: 'A woman with strongly marked features and slightly masculine appearance … of eminently practical and entirely unsentimental enthusiasm'.[8] Her photographic portrait in *Woman and the World* shows her immaculately dressed in collared shirt, tie, waistcoat, jacket and pork pie-style hat [fig. 6.4]. A badge, probably indicating her membership of the Serbian Red Cross, is attached to her hat, while her tie is held in place by a clip whose metal badge appears to represent a seated woman with distaff and spindle. Given that her masculinised appearance is completed by short hair, exposed ears and expressionless forward gaze, this small clip would seem to be the only semblance of stereotypical Serbian womanhood that she bears. No doubt it also signals the cause of Serbian peasantry to which she dedicated her mature years.

Fractal II: Mairet

In 1930, in Travnik, Bosnia, where she had a woodworking school, 'Dikitsa' was visited by Ethel Mairet. There, she 'admired Annie Dickinson's fine collection of tapestry-woven aprons, all handspun with good dyes'.[9] Mairet, like Fra, was from Devon, and, like Jessie, she made a major contribution to the advance of her chosen fabric craft. In some ways she took over where Jessie left off, beginning her weaving and dyeing experiments in 1909 (albeit in the Cotswolds, coincident with Dickinson), the year after Jessie retired from the Glasgow School of Art. And she closely followed the Newberys with two trips to Yugoslavia in 1927 and 1930, shortly after both of theirs. By this time established as a weaver and teacher of textile arts in the artists' community at Ditchling, Sussex, Mairet's journals, sketches, collections and subsequent work pay tribute to what she gained from the Balkans. Her source collection held at the Crafts Study Centre, Farnham, contains a range of Balkan items, from braids, belts, socks, covers and an apron to samples of weaving and embroidery. Some of these are identified with some precision (for example, Macedonian apron, Bosnian men's and women's belts), while others have no indications of source (place or material). The three examples illustrated here have been chosen for their strength of design and variety of object, as well as their range (informative to non-existent) of metadata. They are catalogued as follows: 1. Sock, hand-knitted, pointed toe and heel with tie cord, animal hair and metal threads, black, red, brown and shades of green. Probably Southern Yugoslavia [fig. 6.5]; 2. Woman's belt, Serbia (incomplete), one end fringed, goat's hair and other materials. Local name: *tkanica, pojas*. Made in Kosovo [fig. 6.6]; 3. Item from Ethel Mairet Source Collection [a textile cover] [fig. 6.1]. All three works are marked by strong geometric patterning, their variations of diagonal and straight bands being picked out in vibrant combinations of colour, with red, black and beige dominants. While all are likely to be Balkan, even 'Yugoslavian', how specifically Serbian, Kosovan, Macedonian or otherwise they are remains open to question.

Mairet's Balkan craft collecting, observing and interpreting shows much kinship with Fra and Jessie's. Yet, as with them, and for all the acknowledgement of her artistic achievements, this experience has been little appreciated. Thus far, it has been left to Margot Coatts and Tanya Harrod to highlight its significance and with that Mairet's 'serious purpose of creating living modern textiles'.[10] Mairet herself identified the outstanding quality of Balkan work in *Hand-Weaving To-Day: Traditions and Changes*, a pioneering analysis of the state of weaving (including study of materials and techniques, and their potential for development) across various parts of Europe in the 1930s. Informed by her visits to, and contacts within, the Balkans, the penultimate section of her second chapter is a eulogy to the region's fabric design and making sensibility, as in:

> *The most cultured peasant weaving of Europe is found in Jugoslavia, especially in the intricate and restrained work of the south – in Macedonia … In the remote valleys of these southern countries an aesthetic understanding and a technical quality of weaving has been preserved that has not been reached anywhere else in Europe. There is a restraint and simplicity of design and colour with an understanding of material which is unsurpassed. There is also a comprehension of the aesthetic born of long ages of struggle – the instinctive acceptance and knowledge of beauty as a necessity. In the Macedonian weaving there is a different quality from the ordinary European peasant weaving. It has the qualities of both East and West; the intricate delicate design with incredible technique (entirely un-European) is expressed with great restraint of colour. It is comparable only to the finest weaving of India and the Far East.[11]*

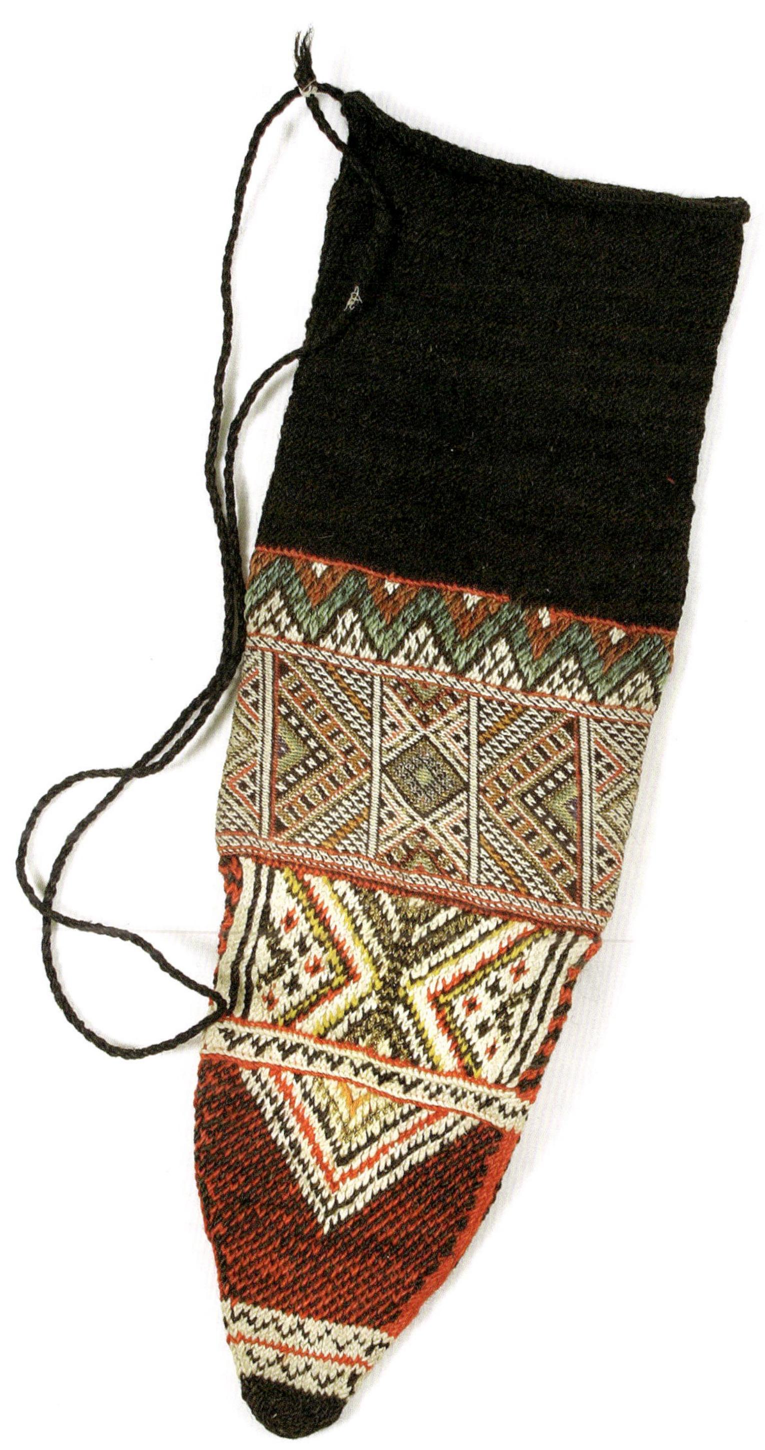

6.5 │ Sock, probably southern Yugoslavian, late 1920s, animal hair and metal threads, 33 x 15 cm

ETHEL MAIRET SOURCE COLLECTION (RECORD 6, 2004.202.5), CRAFTS STUDY CENTRE, FARNHAM;
© ESTATE OF ETHEL MAIRET

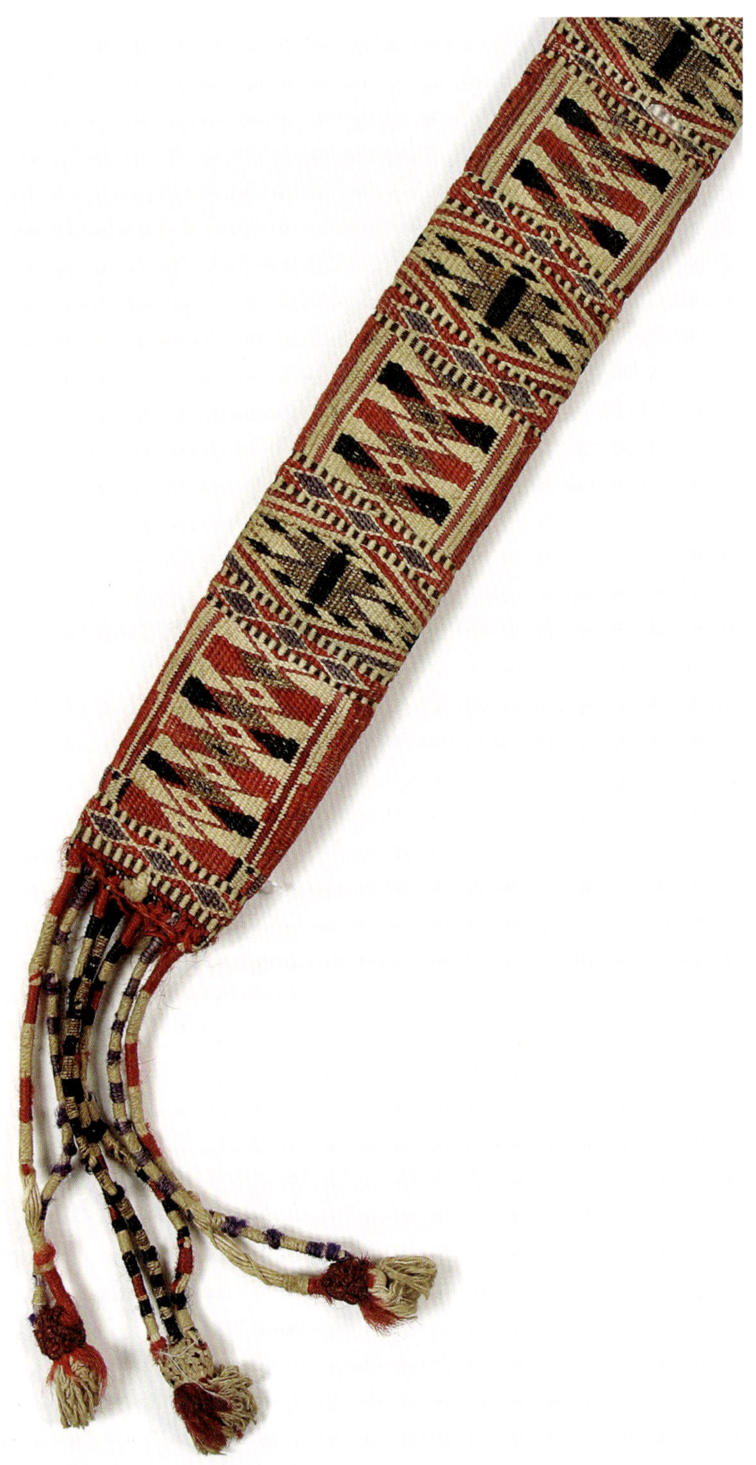

6.6 | Woman's belt, Serbian (made in Kosovo), *c.* late 1920s, goat hair

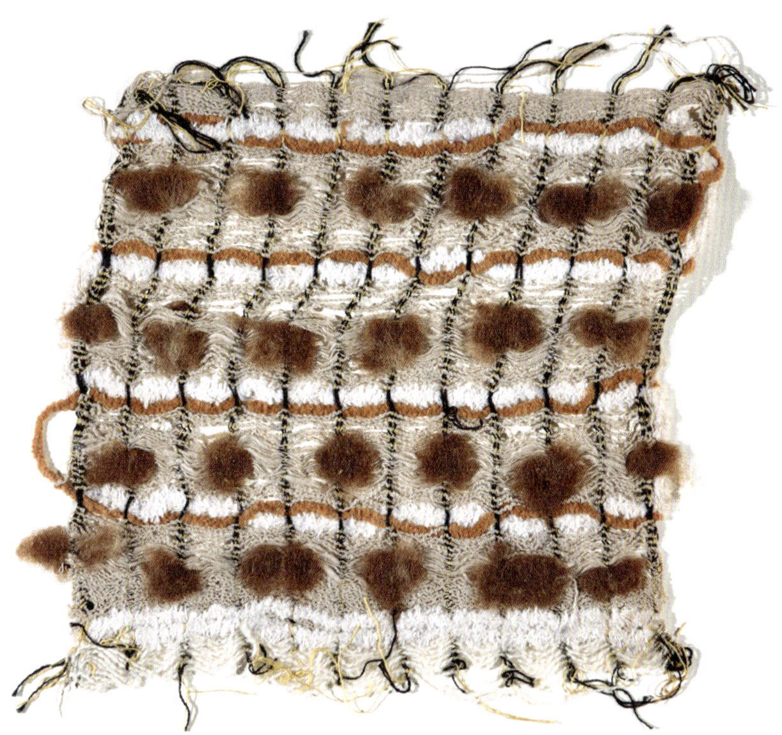

6.7 | Ethel Mairet, 'Sample', early 1930s, woven fabric

Taking her art-body in different directions to those of the Newberys (for example, to investigations of colour and texture through her own plain-weave fabrics), Mairet joins the distributed mind of the Balkanist clan. A glance at the early 1930s Mairet fabric samples in the Crafts Study Centre (Farnham) and V&A collections reveals a love of rough linear patterning far from the Newberys' relish of intricate embroidery motifs; and yet in some of the colour combinations (and contrasts) as well as the play with geometry they connect, and they connect with what attracted her attention in the Balkans [fig. 6.7].[12] A closer study of Mairet's 1930s and subsequent artwork than is possible here should be able to convey more precisely how both her practice and visual language were influenced by what she observed. Still, with that in mind, the following compilation of fragments from the journal of her first Yugoslavian visit conveys a perception of Balkan design principles that is clearly carried over into her aesthetic. It also reveals coincidence with and departure from that of Jessie:

[Split, 11 May] Beautiful peasant woman on Quay with large slab of marble on her back bringing it to the boat, wearing close handspun clothes – hand & fine spun. Blue skirt rather full and gathered. Green

bodice, tight, fine red woollen apron & from her shoulders behind, hung a long dark indigo blue dress almost like a cape but with armholes, getting wide at the bottom all the seams beautifully sewn with red.

[Dubrovnik, 12 May] Several shops with old weaving and embroideries … One specially good shop was L. Kraja … he had some fine things & knew intelligently about them. Macedonian fine embroidery.

[Cavtat, 13 May] Mestrovic's little building for a cemetery. White stone, stepped dome, Bronze figure on the top, wonderful bronze doors with the 4 evangelists … Wonderful great massive door handles.

[To Trebinje, Herzegovina, 14 May] Passed woman spinning with spindle & distaff. She was driving a cow in to Trebinye market. Mohammedan women walking about with black nets just over their faces. Women wear tiny hats … a little bunch of flowers in the middle of the crown & always a handkerchief holding the hat on & tied generally under the chin. Some very fine peasant costumes. Heavy woven patterned carpet apron with fringe at the bottom & half way up the sides. White coat, long wide at the bottom edged with colour. The cloth is woven of hard goat or long haired sheep's wool then put in hot water & beaten hard til it becomes thick & felted. It lasts for ever. Sometimes black, light brown but mostly white … The footgear for men … Very beautiful …. The waistbands that the men wore very interesting – sometimes warp striped … sometimes 8" to 10" wide, bright green, dark blue or red … Bought some wooden pipes … Got a boy to play one which he did beautifully, lots of trills and runs. They use them to play up in the hills when tending cattle.

[Dubrovnik, 16 May] Had a long talk with Lujo Kraja. He had brought to show me a very fine Montenegrin shawl woven in natural black & dark blue intermixed fine wool spinning very long & splendid fringe with a touch of red every now & then. Fringe about 30" long. The Herzegovina shawl is thicker & coarser wool with narrow pattern at the end. Men & women wear them.

[To Mostar, Bosnia, 17 May] Villages extremely poverty stricken & the people looked very poor. No handspun stuffs at all, all wearing cheap factory stuff … Interesting groups of peasants passing all either knitting or spinning … Everywhere women looking after the sheep & goats, spinning or knitting sometimes with white wool, sometimes black. Carved wooden distaff & plain wood spindle. Met a group with ponies laden. All the sacks & covers were brightly coloured stripes, yellow red, white, dark blue. Passed through Stolac, a beautiful little Mohammedan town … Saw a weaving shop. Man making

potato bags. Upright loom, warp very close, back & white, weaving it like a tapestry loom, beating it down with a very heavy batten, wooden with iron teeth. They were making the warp in the same shed. Two men walking up and down spinning the goats wool from a sack tied on to their front …

[Split, 21 May] The people have a strong sense of the beautiful. And very good taste in modern dress. Colour of the boats extremely beautiful.

[Split, 22 May] linen & cotton stuff [from Vis island]. Very good handspun & very much sought after … Beautiful soft woolly rugs at a shop in the market place.[13]

Fractal III: Milne

Mairet, like Dickinson, was to come to appreciation of Yugoslavian fabrics via the work of peasant women in distinct parts of the interwar kingdom, with Macedonia first among these. For our third example of an artist within the category of the British Balkanist distributed mind, Jean Milne, encountering the primary craft of Macedonia was epiphanic, as her closest friends in later life recalled:

In [1920] she went to Jugoslavia to work with Ivan Mestrovic, with whom she formed a life-long friendship. The Macedonian embroideries which she saw in Belgrade drew her attention to textile design, perhaps for the first time, and she became deeply interested in pattern.[14]

The experience was, as Tanya Harrod notes, to turn her into 'a textile artist – a maker of tapestry or discontinuous weft rugs that she did not pre-plan, but made, as she saw it, spontaneously'.[15] In fact both Mairet and Milne had long been drawn to the southern Slav Balkans through early acquaintance with the sculptural vision of Meštrović, not least via his 1915 London exhibition. By that time the Aberdonian Milne was herself an established sculptor and metal worker, with her own Kensington studio and an extensive record of British exhibitions and commissions. She had also recently extended her practice of handicraft to that of masseuse in a military hospital. Furthermore, as a friend of Meštrović, she played an important role in the publication of his 1919 monograph. A note by editor Milan Ćurčin details how she temporarily stored Meštrović's sketch for his bronze, *Vestal Virgin*, in her studio and used it as inspiration to pen the volume's frontispiece verses, 'the voice' of these having a 'purposely chosen … re-echo' in the accompanying drawing by Jozo Kljaković [figs 6.8, 6.9].[16] Thus from Meštrović's splay-legged semi-nude symbolic representation of a lost, contemplative, Czech lover we move through Milne's and then Kljaković's messianic elegies to the southern Slav people:

A nation crucified: a people in exile:
Oppression: terrible tyranny of wrong:
Blank black horizon: starless night so long:
O Most Just God! Sleeps Thy slow justice still? Tarries it yet awhile?

A Sculptor prophet: strange flame from the dark
Gleaming through forms known, yet unknown:
The living tree, the vital bronze, the sentient stone,
The elemental clay wrapping anew the age-long hidden spark.

We stand confounded: our thickened eyeballs dim:
Life's clamour deafly falls on untuned ears:
We see the circling of the eternal spheres:
We hear the immortal Sons of God chant the unending hymn.

In both rhyme and drawing we are presented with Serbian tragedy, this being at once the horrific losses and suffering of the First World War and those inflicted by the Ottomans with, and following, the historic Battle of Kosovo in 1389. Both also recall Serbian epic poetry dedicated to the latter. But Kljaković alone adds an image that could be the 'Maiden of Kosovo', who while mourning the loss of her fiancé, brothers and all other Serbians, stands humbly, in profile, head

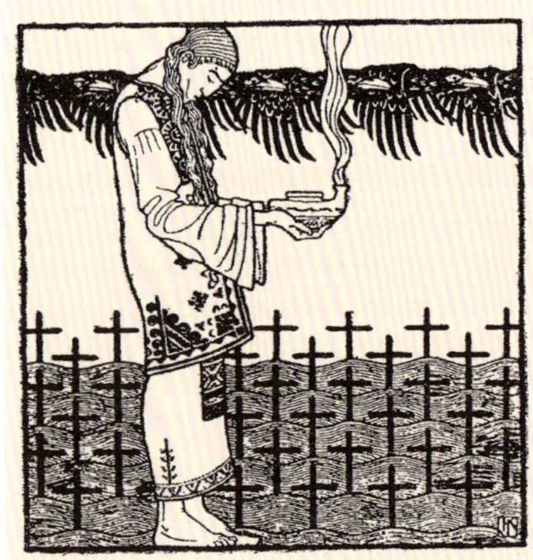

6.8 | Jozo Kljaković, 'Maiden of Kosovo', *c.* 1918; from Milan Ćurčin, *Ivan Meštrović: A Monograph* (London: Williams and Norgate, 1919), p. iv

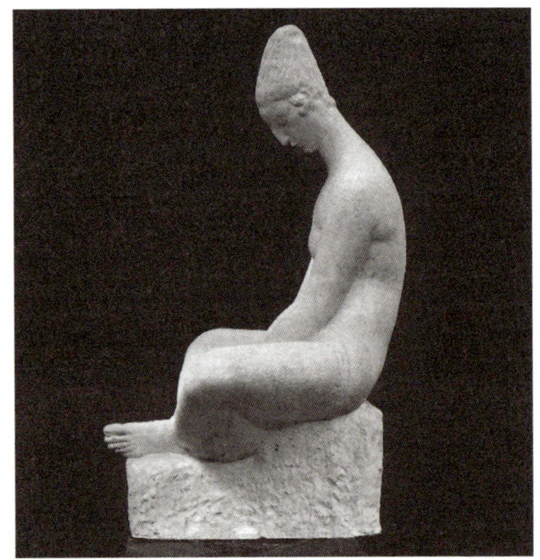

6.9 | Ivan Meštrović, *Vestal Virgin*, 1915, bronze; from Milan Ćurčin, *Ivan Meštrović: A Monograph* (London: Williams and Norgate, 1919), plate XXIX

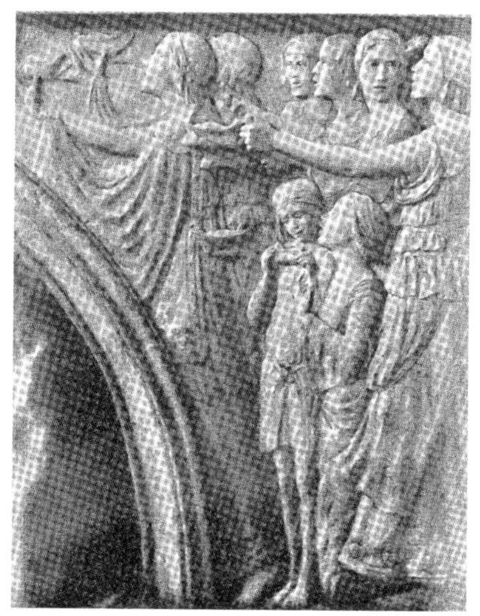

6.10 | Jean Milne, *Wise Virgins,*
*c.*1907–08, relief,: from *The Studio:*
Yearbook of Decorative Art, 1909, p. 58

bowed, among the crosses of their graves and before a line of menacing, sacrifice-inducing, birds of prey (more Austrian imperial eagles than the prophetic grey falcons of Serbian mythology). As an icon of grief, compassion and hope, this barefoot fiancée-widow becomes the Serbian response to Antonov's *Macedonian Slave.* Hence she is also draped in embroidered peasant garb, the geometric motifs and composition of which anticipate those of the Macedonian clothes acquired by Jessie and painted by Fra a few years later.

Ćurčin relates of Milne that being

one of the few women sculptors … [she is also] one of the most ardent admirers of Meštrović. The sincere love and deep understanding on the part of a fellow-sculptor of British nationality speaks perhaps better than anything to the qualities of the Serbian artist.[17]

Such praise for Milne's rare insight into the Yugoslavian torch-bearer is all the more poignant when one considers that her most widely known work was *Wise Virgins* (*c.*1907–08), a spandrel relief panel depicting bridesmaids raising oil-filled lamps (as in the Gospel of Matthew, 25: 1–13), for the arrival of the groom (Christ), and hence entry into the Kingdom of Heaven [fig. 6.10].[18] This representation of preparation for the Day of Judgement invokes a sense of *Vestal Virgin* and 'Maiden of Kosovo'. Is it chance that Kljaković's Serbian maiden similarly offers up a lighted lamp but instead of Milne's upward-gazing women in common medievalist dress, she bends her head in national sorrow? In any case the fractals relate.

Since we know that Milne changed medium after first-hand exposure to Macedonian embroidery in Serbia, there is also Balkan correspondence in her later woven woollen hangings and rugs. Two of her wall-hangings, both seemingly entitled *Integration* and presumably of the 1930–40s, convey her relish of loosely planned pattern [figs 6.11, 6.12].[19] In both, the patterns of woollen colour and line have an elemental quality. With the first, the plum-coloured warp and red, beige, cream, brown, green and pink wefts convey, through their formation into a tufted forest of linked rhombi and triangles, a sense of geometrical play and growth. This is echoed in the second, though here the colder blues and whites join, as rough hexagonals and diagonals, with smaller trapezoids and triangles of brown, maroon, yellow and mauve,

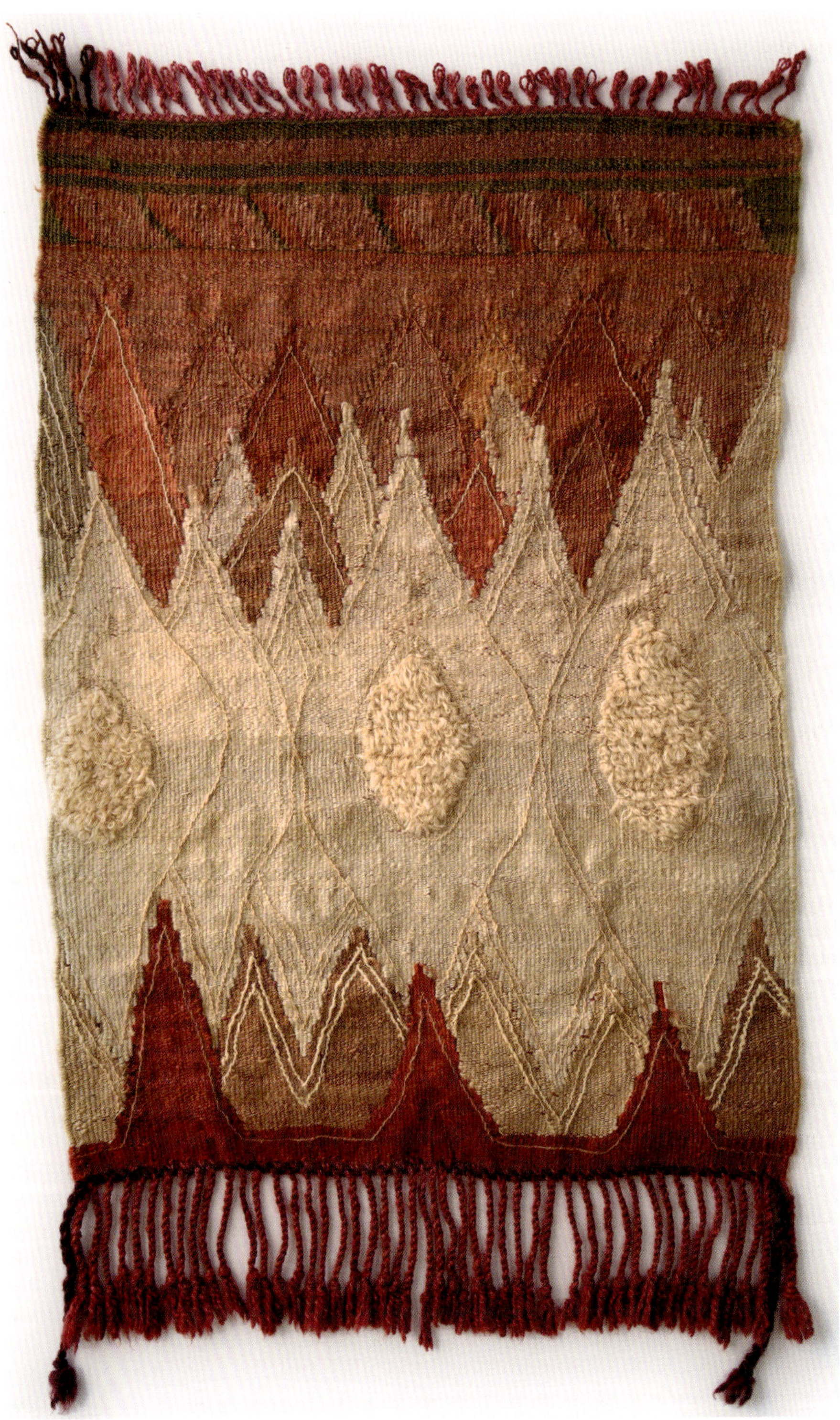

6.11 | **Jean Milne** | *Integration* | 1930s–40s?, wall hanging, wool, 95 x 57 cm
CRAFTS STUDY CENTRE, FARNHAM; © ESTATE OF JEAN MILNE

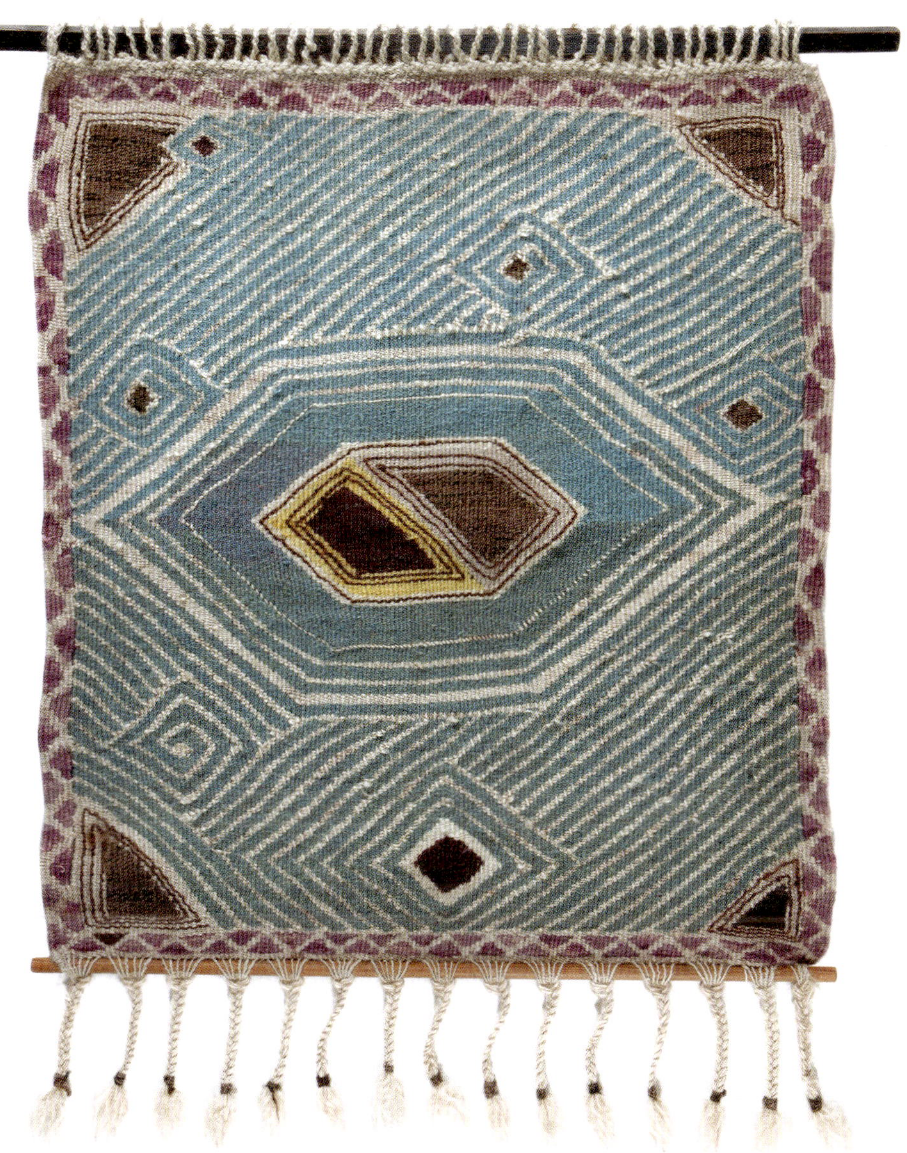

6.12 | Jean Milne | *Integration* | 1930s–40s?, wall hanging, wool, 69 x 49 cm
CRAFTS STUDY CENTRE, FARNHAM; © ESTATE OF JEAN MILNE

to suggest, if anything, rippling water and rocks. Both may develop their form from the patterns of Macedonian textiles, but Milne's creativity did not stop with her Balkan discoveries. As her titles suggest, her motivation was integration, and this led her to incorporate into her work designs and techniques borrowed from her close study of Bushongo woven raffia textiles. Thus, following her Yugoslavian visit, she examined the Congolese palm-fibre fabrics in Paris and Brussels and amassed her own collection, being drawn to them because

> *in these mats she recognized a type of design particularly appropriate for development by the craftsman – which, while maintaining a repeating principle, allows for changes within the repeat and gives scope for the unexpected element so essential to creative work.*[20]

Furthermore, from 1937 she began Shiant rug-making in Scotland, on the Hebridean Isles (the Shiants being a small Hebridean island-group), at the behest of the Highland Home Industries association initiated by her compatriot Millicent, Duchess of Sutherland. Ultimately, from her surviving art and early commentaries, including her own, we can perceive a holistic understanding of art and art education, very much akin to Fra's. Hence, as 'she used her skill with her hands to do, in Gandhi's words, "the duty of citizenship of the world"',[21] so Milne advocated integration of the arts, along with art and life, as key: 'art is not something outside life but a contact that has to be brought to bear on everything we can see and handle'.[22]

Fractal IV: West

Milne's Scottish roots and turn to textiles might align her with Jessie, but her recourse to Balkanist writing also draws her towards Rebecca West. Their literature is vastly different, one work created at the start of the interwar period, the other at its end, with Milne encapsulating her vision of Yugoslavia in twelve brief rhyming lines, West hers in over a thousand dense pages. Such difference should not deceive as to the unison of their Serbian-empathising message. Yet West is, of all our four British Balkanist fractals, the one most closely related to Yovitchitch. For she was half-Scottish through her mother, brought up in Edinburgh, and chose literature as her principal medium of Balkan-inspired expression. Though her writing is far more overtly personalised and politicised (even reaching, according to Seamus O'Malley, British imperialist advocacy of 'aggressive liberal interventionism'),[23] West, like Yovitchitch, still picks out the costume of peasants as a prime creative signifier of Balkan being. Furthermore, in keeping with what has been unfurled so far, it is Macedonian dress more than any other that contains kernel southern Slav personhood. Hence, from an amalgam of citations from her epic travelogue *Black Lamb and Grey Falcon: A Journey through Yugoslavia*, we can see how she notes, in her own fractal way (which simultaneously relates to that of the Newberys and others we have so far considered), the person-artistry involved:

> *I was standing opposite a peasant woman sitting on a window ledge who was the very essence of Macedonia, who was exactly what I had come back to see. She was the age that all Macedonian women seem to become as soon as they cease to be girls: a weather-beaten fifty. There was a dark cloth about her hair and shoulders, and in its folds, and in her noble bones and pain-grooved flesh, she was like many Byzantine Madonnas to be seen in frescoes and mosaics. In her rough hand she mothered her taper, looking down on its flame as if it were a young living thing; and on the sleeve of her russet sheepskin jacket there showed an embroidery of stylized red and black trees which derived recognizably from a pattern designed for elegant Persian women two thousand years before. There was the miracle of Macedonia, made visible before our eyes …*
>
> *It was only our modernity that was shocked …*
>
> *They wear the most dignified and beautiful dresses of any in the Balkans, gowns of coarse linen embroidered with black wool in designs using Christian symbols, which are at once abstract (being entirely unrepresentational) and charged with passionate feeling. Their wide sleeves are thick as carpets with solid black embroideries, stitched in small squares, with often a touch of deep clear blue, which gives the effect of an inner light burning in the heart of darkness. Such garments, worn by grim women … have an effect of splendid storm, of symphonic music, and make no suggestion of facility or charm.*
>
> *The young people were wearing clothes covered with the most beautiful designs being invented in any part of the world today, masterpieces of abstract art, yet the effect was not beauty … it was quite plain that they were suffering …*
>
> *I saw the solemn and magnificent embroideries of the Slav peasant women and knew what degeneration of skill and taste was represented by the bright little flowers and hearts on the Austrian belts that the skiers like to bring back from St. Anton.*
>
> *I find it most natural that the Macedonian peasants should embroider their dresses, that they should dance and sing. For, of course, art gives us hope that history may change its spots and man become honourable. What is art? It is not decoration. It is the re-living of experience … altering its shape … so that its true significance is revealed … Art cannot talk plain sense, it must sometimes speak what sounds at first like nonsense, though it is actually supersense.*[24]

All but fragments of the last citation are avoided by Seamus O'Malley in his penetrating deconstruction of the aporias of West's narrative, with its embedded sense of civilised British superiority over the presumed ignorant, prone to violence, peoples of the Balkans. Thus he exposes her ethnocentrism, 'which ascribes self-consciousness and textual sophistication to Britain or West Europe and withholds it from Yugoslavia', this through her contention that the latter lacks 'adequate historiography … because of its oral and folk nature'.[25] That said, neither he nor West gets near to serious enquiry into the written history of history in the region.

Still, while recognising that she spends most of her time recounting 'violent stories of the Balkan past' O'Malley does admit that she records 'art, language, food, and ritual',[26] and that she uses a metaphor of lost embroidered cloth to convey the difficulty, or even impossibility, of elucidating Balkan history through textual narrative. Furthermore he ascribes her interest in embroidery to the fact that it offered an alternative to literary forms as a way of conveying history. There is, however, a problem, noted by O'Malley, in that West also writes that the women embroiderers 'are of course not fully conscious of the part their embroideries play in the preservation of their ancient culture'.[27] The Newberys, Yovitchitch and the Balkan artists we have discussed made no such suggestion. Yet, to be fair to West, she qualified her assertion of partial historical ignorance by recognising that the embroiderers

are certainly aware that they are about some special business when they sew … that it is an esoteric craft [and] those who are expert in it do not give away their mystery … themes which often reappear in the designs have names and symbolic meanings which are not confided to strangers.[28]

Hence, she pays tribute to Balkan women needleworkers' possession of high levels of both skill and knowledge beyond those of outsiders, in other words their 'supersense'.

Towards a conclusion

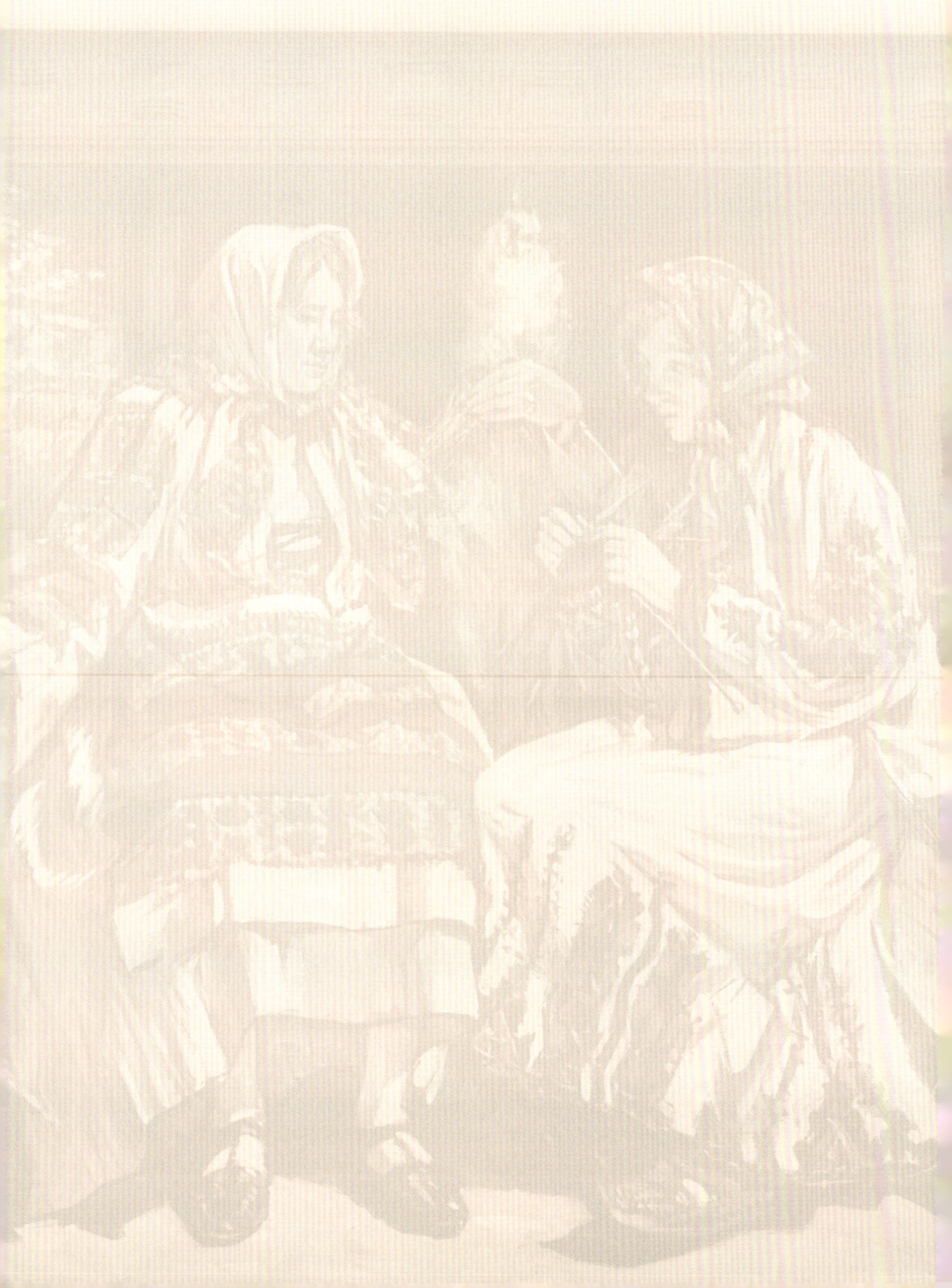

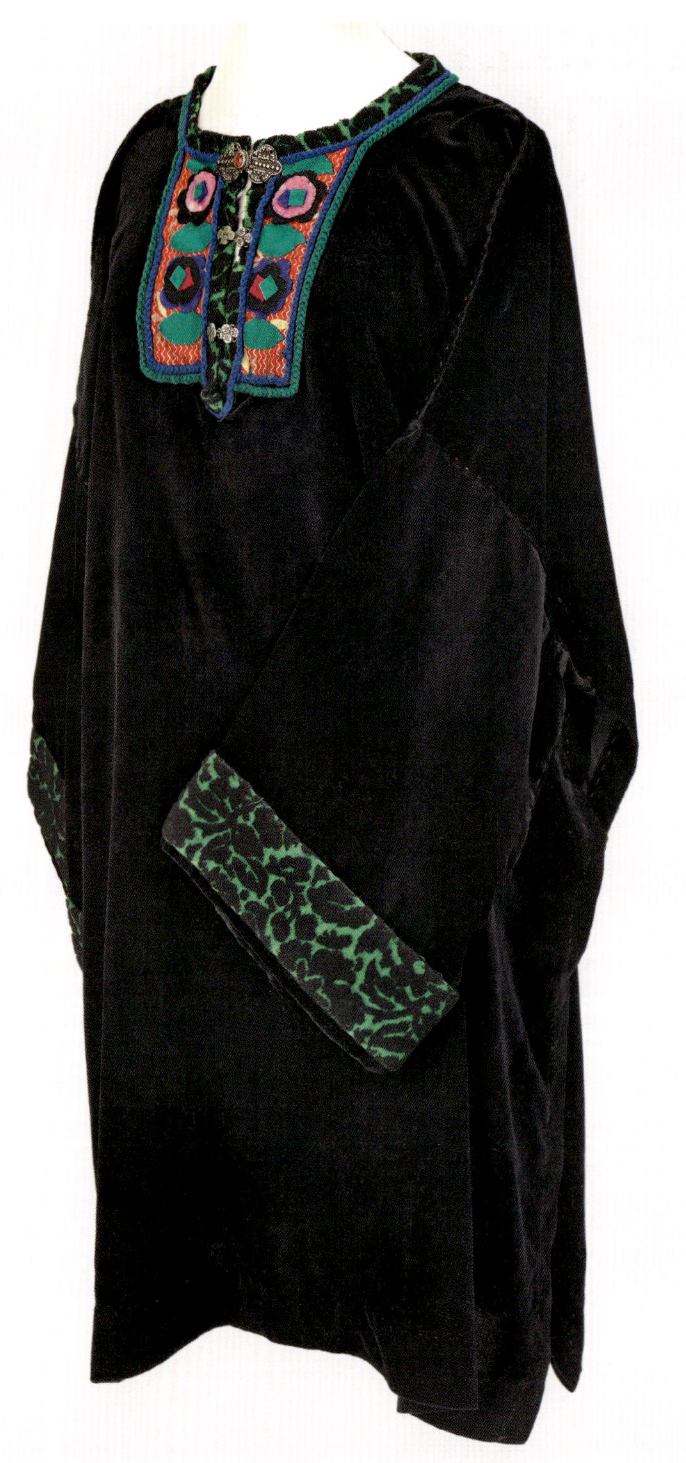

7.1 | Jessie Newbery | *tunic dress*
*c.*1930s, black velvet, wool, felt appliqué, metal clasps

7 A FULLY ACCLIMATISED GROWTH

Winding Up:
'Joy and Woe Are Woven Fine,
a Clothing for the Soul Divine ...'
Jessie's and Fra's Creeds

In concluding his 1897 *Studio* article on Jessie Newbery's art, Gleeson White encapsulated her embroidery work thus:

> ... *the designs of Mrs Newbery, new as they are, are obedient to the laws of symmetry and admirably fitted for their material ... their apparent simplicity is the result of great power; their gay and harmonious colour the evidence of an inborn sense of beauty. Above all they preserve the best traditions of the art, and yet never directly imitate early work; and therefore it is possible to praise them very highly, without once over-stating the case, and still less without regarding them patronisingly as a woman's work. It is pleasant to remember that they chance to be for a craft which has been pre-eminently the province of women from time immemorial; but they may take their place as examples of well-applied art, with no question of sex, and no attempt to evade criticism by a spurious chivalry which is often but a covert form of insult.*[1]

Gleeson White's recognition of Jessie's prowess, together with his determination that they should be considered on their own merits, not as 'women's work', comprised the first serious critical appraisal of her art. That it also accompanied her 'creed', five images of embroidery designs, mention of her creative endeavours in other fields and an assertion that she possessed a style with a 'distinctly personal quality',[2] makes the piece significant, not least for our enquiry into how her art was to evolve in later years and after contact with other cultures.

Jessie was always something of a free spirit when it came to art. She referred to herself as an artist, not an embroiderer. While Gleeson White had alluded to her early bookbinding and metalware designs, besides these and her embroidery work she painted, designed stained glass, taught dress design, mosaic and enamelling, and was 'to the end of her life, a deeply knowledgeable gardener'.[3] Margaret Swain has succinctly encapsulated her textile artistry, with its emphasis on elemental plant life forms, noting that after initially practising coloured woollen crewelwork on linen

> *in the Morris tradition ... she soon began to evolve a characteristic linen appliqué ... This was worked on linen ground, with applied simple stylised flowers and leaves, cut out of coloured linens and held down by satin stitch in silk ... The stems coiled into strong lines, outlining the shape of the article ...*[4]

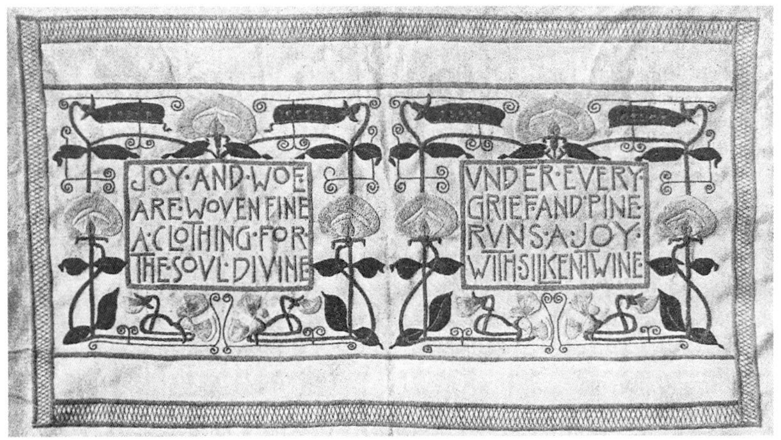

7.2 | Jessie Newbery, 'Joy and Woe Are Woven Fine', embroidered curtain, *c.*1900, from *The Studio*, vol. 23, no. 102, 1901, p. 239

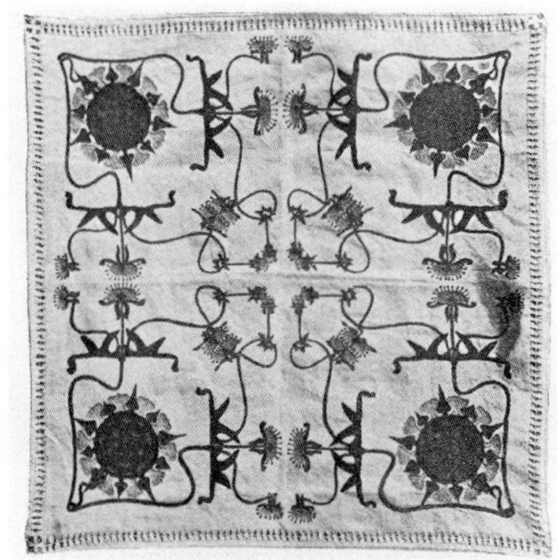

7.3 | Jessie Newbery, embroidered curtain, *c.*1899, from *The Studio*, vol. 19, no. 83, 1900, p. 237

Fiona MacFarlane and Elizabeth Arthur have complemented Swain's observations by giving social credence to Jessie's base-material choices:

> *Mrs Newbery was adamant that embroidery should be a form of art available to all social classes and that it could be worked as effectively on cheap as on expensive materials. Hessian, unbleached calico, linen and flannel were used in classes …*[5]

Although much of her work has not survived due to her making it for use rather than posterity, images show an abiding preference for linear and colour symmetry, her abstract floral motifs given a sense of regular, ordered, growth and burgeoning life through their integrated assemblage of curved tendrils set within grid patterns formed by blossoms, petals, leaves and stems. Every element, from root to tip, is interrelated [fig. 7.3]. The networks of correspondence Jessie created frequently also included beautifully stylised, upper case, written texts, these regularly comprising lyrical fragments of meditations on mortality and *carpe diem* motifs, occasionally with a telling mix of fabrication metaphors. A prime example of the latter, which she made both as an embroidered curtain and cushion cover (*c.*1900), contained William Blake's musings on the warp-and-weft dichotomies of life:

> *Joy & Woe are woven fine*
> *A Clothing for the soul divine*
> *Under every grief & pine*
> *Runs a joy with silken twine*
> Blake, 'Auguries of Innocence', *c.*1803[6]

For this Jessie chose unbleached linen and embroidered it with coloured (blues, greens, pinks, browns, white and yellow) woollen threads, worked in a variety of stitches (stem, satin, long and short) and needle-weaving [fig. 7.2]. Lattices of pea flowers, pea pods and curly tendrils surround central panels with the embroidered inscriptions in distinctive Glasgow Style non-cursive script.

One of Jessie's contributions to the Scottish section of the Prima Esposizione Internazionale d'Arte Decorativa Moderna (Turin, 1902) was a carpet [fig. 7.4]. Unusually figurative for her, she collaborated with the Kilmarnock carpet-makers Alexander Morton & Company to create a work of textile art that anticipated Milne's sculptural *Wise Virgins*. Above her virgins Milne was to include two lines of 'Glasgow Style' superscript, beseeching the young women to action ('There was a cry made: Behold the bridegroom cometh. Go ye out to meet him'), this quote from Matthew 25:6 replacing Jessie's equivalent subscript of 'Gather ye rosebuds while ye may / Old time is still a-flying' – the opening two lines of Robert Herrick's seventeenth-century poem 'To the Virgins, to Make Much of Time'. Jessie's five virgins stand before a row of ('Glasgow') rose perianths (instead of Milne's lamps). Placed at head height, the roses are symmetrically distributed across a stitched trellis, suggesting cultivation. Two women reach out to 'gather' their rosebuds, one looks on, while two others are turned away from the flowers, one of them towards the viewer, hands clasped. Such compilation suggests, besides Herrick, the paradoxical dichotomies of life in Matthew 25's 'Parable of the Ten Virgins' as well as Blake's verse. Significantly for us, Jessie's virgins are also in beautiful embroidered dress, their flowing, comfortable forms containing hems, borders and collars with patterns of simple geometric shapes and lines. Coordinated and yet distinctive, the gowns, along with their accompanying headwear, stress individuality within collective.[7] The five women are at once all humankind and Jessie, with the most active, rose-arranging, figure (the only one without a headcovering and with a long pigtail braid falling from her fair, curly hair) being the closest to a self-portrait.

The personhood of Jessie's artwork was, predictably, also manifested in her own embroidered dress designs. Lacking the literariness we have witnessed in her room furnishings, according to Swain their originality lay in Jessie's own being and becoming:

> *… by temperament and training, Mrs Newbery inclined more and more to an individual style in dress, which revolted from the tightly corseted and hampering styles of her day … She did not consciously*

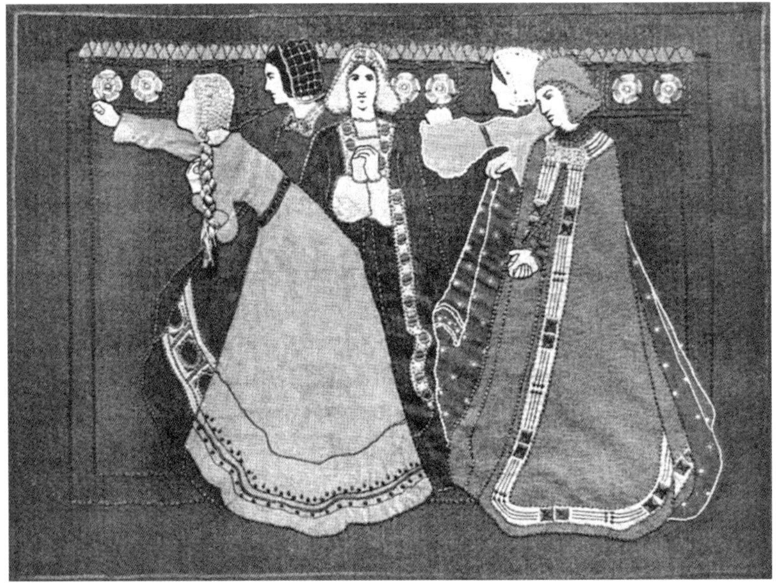

7.4 | Jessie Newbery, 'Gather Ye Rosebuds' carpet, made by Alexander Morton & Co., Kilmarnock, *c.*1901; from *Deutsche Kunst und Dekoration*, vol. 10, 1902, p. 580

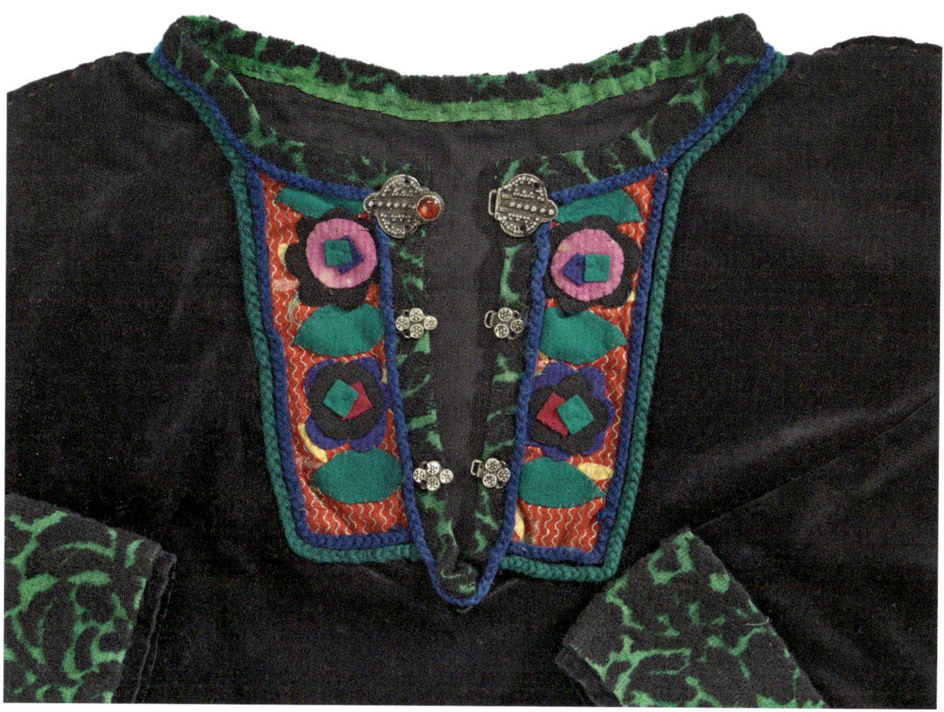

7.5 | **Jessie Newbery** | *tunic dress* [detail]
*c.*1930s, wool, velvet ribbon, ric-rac braid, metal clasps, green glass beads

follow the taste for 'aesthetic dress'; rather, she believed that clothes should be both practical and beautiful. The dresses she made for herself and her daughters were graceful and becoming, with full sleeves and gathered skirts, the yoke, cuffs and belt decorated with embroidery in bright touches of colour, and fastened with woollen tassels to small metal Russian buckles. She aimed for warmth without weight, and had an eye for beautiful materials … As she grew older, she continued to design clothes for herself that were warm and light, wearing loose, straight-cut tunics, joined at the seam with stitchery in a vivid woollen yarn, ornamented at the neck with crochet or felt flowers. They bore no relation to the fashions of the period … but they are very much to the taste of present day art students.[8]

This summation of Jessie's dress sense hints at an evolution affected by her Balkan encounters and collecting. Two tunics, from around 1930–40, that she designed, made and wore herself, show that she was making cuts and adding green ric-rac braid in a way that reinvents what she had gathered from Serbia, Bulgaria and Croatia [figs 7.1/7.5, 7.6]. The ric-rac may well have been the emerald braid she bought in Sofia, about which she wrote (with sketch) in her 1926 letter to her daughter Mary,

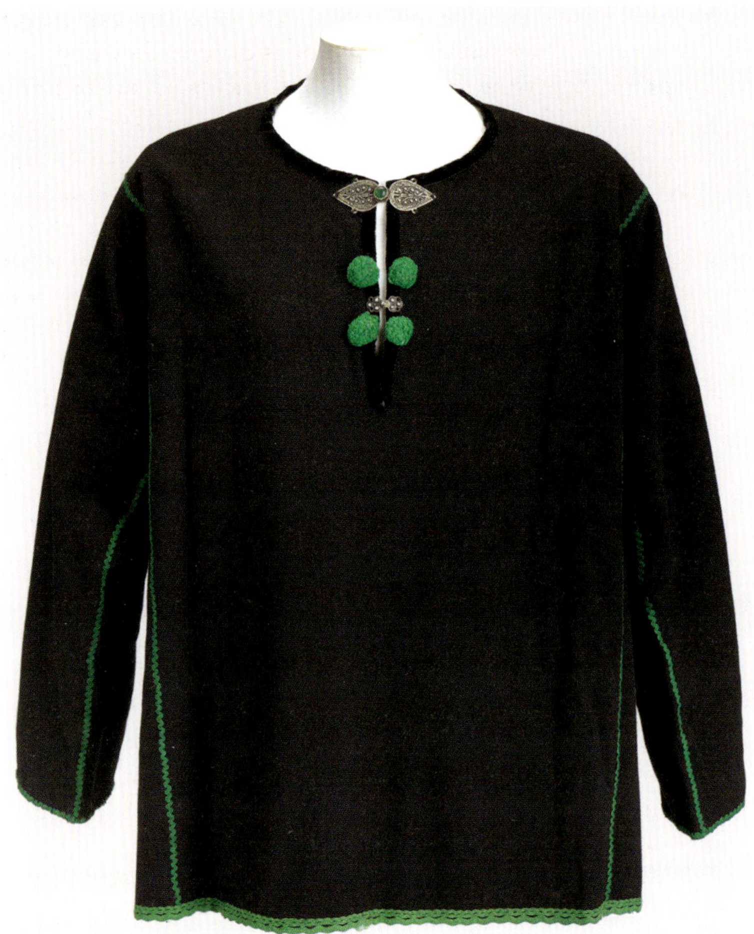

7.6 | Jessie Newbery | *tunic*
*c.*1930s, wool, velvet ribbon, ric-rac braid, metal clasps, green glass beads

asking her if she was pleased (appendix 1). The tunics were inherited by Mary after Jessie's death. Both show a similar rational approach to round neckline, loose fit and rectangular construction that shares a clear design kinship with the Balkan costumes she had recently acquired. In addition, to the shorter tunic, made of fine black wool, Jessie added black velvet ribbon, metal clasps (probably Russian), distinctive green wool pom-pom bobbles and spherical green glass beads around the upper centre-front opening. Eight more green bobbles were added by the ric-ric braid to hold together the open sides beneath the square gussets of the flat-cut, three-quarter-length sleeves. For the longer, loose-cut, more dress-like, black velvet tunic, Jessie added more finely worked Russian metal clasps to the upper centre-front opening, which this time accompany an edging of green wool woven with stylised leaf patterns – also found on the collar and as cuffs to the long-length, loose-cut sleeves. The opening's decoration is completed by long rectangular panels, fringed with blue and green wool braid and featuring very simple black, blue, green, pink and red felt appliqué floral motifs.[9]

Though her post-Glasgow work tends, like Fra's, to be forgotten or downplayed, in 1984 Rozsika Parker, in her groundbreaking book on the content of embroidery, singled out Jessie Newbery as a pioneer, and in particular one who challenged prevailing ideas about the textile craft's significations of womanhood. She based her view on excerpts of Jessie's 'creed' from 1897 (appendix 2):

> *She [Jessie Newbery] speaks the language of desire, not that of duty, says firmly what she likes and what she wants. She believes nothing is common or unclean. She renounces obedience and announces her independence of 'our fathers'. Not only does she reject the self-denying stance of femininity, but she views embroidery in a new light, not as something springing spontaneously from an embroiderer's natural femininity, but as an art with a history which determines but need not limit its practice. Previous theorists had seen embroidery in terms of a past that should be rejected, just as past forms of femininity were rejected as old-fashioned and 'wrong' or conversely rigidly advocated as 'right' in the face of an immoral present. And whereas other theorists wanted work to be 'perfect' in order **to improve the embroiderer**, Jessie Newbery wanted work 'as perfect as maybe' **for the sake of the design** ...*
>
> *Jessie Newbery founded the embroidery department at the Glasgow School of Art, and from being a minor subject in the art school curriculum it soon became the most important 'craft' taught there.*[10]

Parker's insight into Jessie's liberating *raison d'être* for embroidery contains much very valuable truth and yet her selectivity creates imbalance. Nowhere in her text did Jessie mention the feminine. Nowhere did she even mention embroidery: in fact her creed commenced: 'after disclaiming any personal theories of design for embroidery specially'. Furthermore, she did say, and yet Parker omitted:

> *I believe that the greatest thing in the world is for a man to know that he is his own, and that the great end in art is the discovery of the self of the artist. I believe in being the sum of tradition ... I believe in everything being beautiful, pleasant, and, if need be, useful ... I delight in correspondence and the inevitable relation of part to part.*

Thus, for Jessie, as Fra (and, for instance, Milne), the arts, like us, create identity, are one and are part of a bigger 'one', without hierarchy – that is, each one is a fractal.

While Parker might have ignored some of Jessie's primary motivations and values, she still signals key elements of Jessie's avant-gardism; furthermore, she highlights important, seemingly contradictory, issues with regard to embroidery and ideas of femininity that may benefit our comprehension of the Newberys' 'Serbian' turn (starting with Jessie's Macedonian purchases and Fra's *Serbian Women*), together with its network of correspondences. First, she remarks (p. 11) that

> *The manner in which embroidery signifies both self-containment and submission is the key to understanding women's relation to the art. Embroidery has provided a source of pleasure and power for women, while being indissolubly linked to their powerlessness.*

Such apparent aporia is fundamental. For, as Parker is aware, many women who are engaged in the production of fabric, along with the materials and means of its embellishment, form and maintain 'independent social bonds' (p. 15). Yet, as she also makes clear, representation of them at their craft, whether by women or men, also connoted 'conformity to the feminine ideal' (p. 13). Ultimately, the aim for both Parker and us is to show how women needleworkers, and those who visualise them and their art, 'make meanings of their own while overtly living up to the oppressive stereotype' (p. 13). Recalling West, Parker notes that 'embroiderers transform materials to produce sense – whole ranges of meanings' (p. 6), that is, they and their work are far from mindless and in fact possess awareness of being and beauty that conveys experience, and even supersense, beyond the capabilities of the restrictive written or spoken word.

Parker is also correct when she notes that 'embroidery evokes the stereotype of the virgin in opposition to the whore' (p. 2). She uses Dante Gabriel Rossetti's *Girlhood of Mary Virgin* (1848–49, Tate Britain), to illustrate 'The nineteenth-century feminine ideal, represented by Mary embroidering a lily, [which] shows the extent to which embroidery has become associated with the concept of femininity as purity and submissiveness' (after p. 26). This, in turn, invokes Fra's *Annunciation* with its spinning Virgin, lilies, haloes and angels. And yet Fra's Mary is 'Macedonian' or 'Serbian' or 'Yugoslavian' and twentieth-century. That she is also by an English artist may have suited Parker since her history of embroidery and femininity is emphatically British. Herein lie two problems that could be construed as lying at the heart of our enquiry and necessitating it. First, it takes Parker until the introduction of her final chapter for her to admit that her concern has been with British conventions. All the way through her book, and even in its title, the reader is given to understand that what is being conveyed has universality. Such unstated privileging of British perspective assumes a complex of superiority. She even writes 'embroidery summons up both "advanced" civilisation and very early childhood when a primal, unproblematic unity with the mother still existed' (p. 14). So, for all the ambiguities of the female embroiderer trope, no scope is allowed for alternative readings beyond the trajectory of the paradigm upon which she constructs her interpretation. No place is given for the Croatian, Bulgarian, Dalmatian, Macedonian, Serbian troves of textile art, their varied content and multiple meanings. Hence also there is no place even for British correspondences with these. As a result, Parker's virtually unspoken assertion of British paradigm as *the* paradigm has a marked tinge of British liberal imperialist discourse. Her disregard of major embroidery 'parts' means she misses many of the (to quote Jessie) 'inevitable relations' that Jessie and great numbers of others created. Her network of correspondences is elitist.

The second problem with Parker's conceptualisation of feminised embroidery follows on from the first, in that her consideration of process and materiality is limited. Her projection of Jessie as theorist rather than practitioner hints at the issue. Her disregard of the vocabulary, content and meanings of the fragment of a partially misattributed design by Jessie that she illustrates, tells much: in short, nothing of Jessie's visual language is touched upon and even the type of object in her illustration remains unmentioned (according to MacFarlane and Arthur it is a linen mantle border embroidered with coloured crewel wools).[11] Her deprioritising of making and artistry leads to the neglect of makers in cultures where embroidery and the social values placed on it remained high well into the twentieth century (and this, of course, includes societies across the world not covered here). Indeed it is safe to say that the majority of needleworkers were and are parts of alternative networks and hence are neither subject to, nor conform with, the Westernising, modernising, ambit she construes as the norm: Parker's select British and European models comprise a minority. Hence she misses Jessie's crucial isomorphism, her correspondences, not least with those of the Balkans that have been of principal concern to our enquiry. In so doing, for all her astute commentary on the female embroiderer being placed in the 'housewifery' position of dutifully loving provider of domestic comfort for husbands, she also neglects the Balkan (and wider) custom of considering the skill and quantity of a woman's needlecraft as a factor influencing marriage decisions. Without overtly recognising the objectification of women within a subjugating, mainly patriarchal, system, Diane Waller has discussed this in the following terms:

> *Mastery of sewing and embroidery was considered to be one of the most important qualities in a young woman, especially during her pre-marital life. The choice of fiancée often largely depended on the number and artistic qualities of the clothes, embroidered garments and other elements of her dowry. Girls were required to make 'samplers'*

Writing in 2010, Waller uses the past tense for this Balkan practice, whereas in Jessie's time it was still extant. Nevertheless, and for all its signalling of dependence, through it she reveals how personality could be added to the articles created, this according with West's 'supersense' or Jessie's 'discovery of self'.

In contrast to Parker, for Gleeson White Jessie's expression of visual interrelations, her art of fractals, was a high priority. Mindful of the significant role of environment in Jessie's needlecraft, he considered her pieces 'form most pleasant spots of ornament in the larger scheme of decoration of any room where they happen to be placed'.[13] But more than this, it was he who (as cited in our introduction) was mindful of how syncretic they were, blending what he perceived as British conventions and something eastern:

> ... the designs for embroidery, which are singularly attractive, inasmuch as they are not obviously modelled on purely oriental designs, but seem to keep no little of the naïveté of old British work – which may indeed by traced back through continental ancestors to the mystic East, so that it cannot be considered an exotic, but a fully acclimatised growth.[14]

Gleeson White is vague in his allusions to networks of correspondence. He could not have anticipated Jessie's and Fra's incorporation of Balkan design into their work and yet he leaves the door open for it as part of a process of mature growth from wider continental origins.

Of our principal artist couple it was left to Fra to expound on embroidery and how it belonged to the realm of women. In a mode that could be regarded as 'typical Fra', he did so while simultaneously enunciating his most complete theory of art as well as an account of what he regarded as the genius of a woman artist, Ann Macbeth, with whom he and Jessie worked (see introduction, chapter three and appendix two). In a survey attentive to the detail of Fra's record of support for women as teachers and students during his directorship of the Glasgow School of Art, Rawson has pointed out how enlightened, if with some residual male and institutional prejudice, he was for his day.[15] Within this he elucidates the unique place accorded by Fra to women as embroidery artists:

> The only area which Newbery ever singled out as a woman's sphere was embroidery. His point that some women had an exclusively special instinct for the subject, however, may have been made because it never

occurred to him that this instinct might also be possessed by some men who were unlikely to have developed it as it was regarded as an exclusively female preserve … this does not argue that women's abilities or instincts were regarded by Newbery as being in any way inferior. Rather, he seems to have regarded women's work in embroidery as a matter for admiration and as their special contribution to the collective arts of mankind.[16]

Such a position is particularly important for our consideration of Fra's painting of Balkan embroidered costume. For in his choice of subject he was not only relating to parts of southern Europe where this 'exclusively female preserve' persisted but was also allowing its strong and distinctive form to infuse his own art, to vivify and bring a special identity to what turned out to be his swansong. In his appreciation of Ann Macbeth (appendix 2), written in Scotland over a quarter of a century earlier, Fra had lamented the loss of traditional needlework art, and with it qualities of beauty and life enhancement. In so doing he produced a manifesto for art-in-life in which embroidery was to play an essential part. While we have noted his principal association of food and clothes (plough and needle) above, it is worth reiterating here, alongside his perception of poetry in needlework:

> *… the needle bears with it a dignity of labour that, if it not be greater than the plough, is yet one that puts it into the same category of absolute necessities … much of the poetry which comes from the pen is not for a moment to be compared with those harmonies of form and colour which owe their origin to the art of embroidery … much of genius and a great deal of skill was brought to bear upon articles alike of use and for ornament, so that the everyday handlings of life were broidered with beauty and enhanced by art …*[17]

Turning to the past tense suggests that the threat to embroidery concerns its survival and that Fra is engaged not only in drawing attention to that threat but also doing something about it. He understands, like Jessie, that building on and departing from tradition is crucial for art 'to live'. And for this to be ensured artists must know their material, how to handle it, how to experiment and add personhood. Ultimately, with their Balkanist fabrications they 'wrap … anew the age-long hidden spark'[18] that Milne had divined in Meštrović's sculpture and which Fra had urged for as early as 1902:

> *… unless tradition in art be added to, be made to live, and be brought up to date as a living entity, there is a fear that it must die of sheer inanition, and history repeats this lesson. Ornament, to be worthy of the name, must be more than an aggregation of conventional forms*

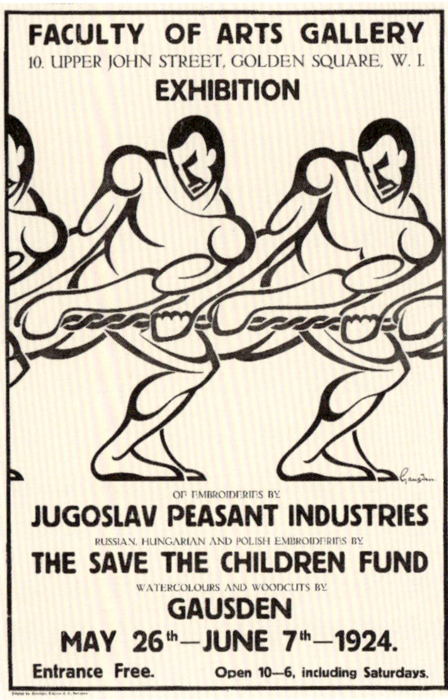

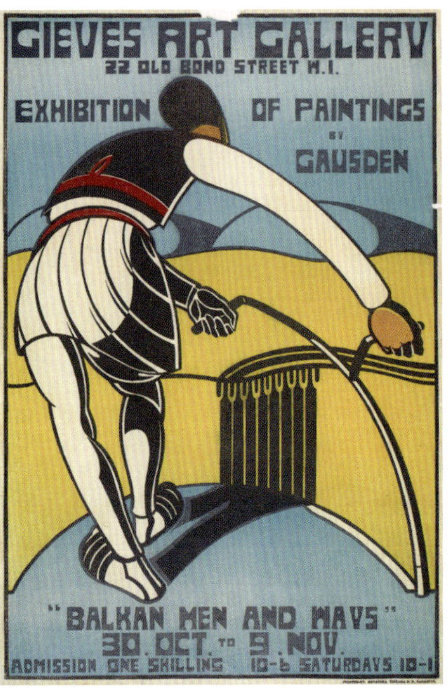

7.7 | Sidney Gausden, 'Faculty of Arts Gallery exhibition', 1924, poster, lithograph
© VICTORIA AND ALBERT MUSEUM, LONDON

7.8 | Sidney Gausden, 'Balkan Men and Ways', 1923, exhibition poster, coloured lithograph
© VICTORIA AND ALBERT MUSEUM, LONDON

to be used on occasion, like recipes taken from a cookery book. It must be a personal belonging, and have a distinct relation not only to the ego of the creator, but also to the period in which it was created. But this presupposes power to transform, talent to adapt, and, above all, genius to create … To be original in any sense of the word is, first, to find out what has been done, and then to learn the further possibilities both of material and of treatment.[19]

As it turned out, the Newberys' 'fully acclimatised growth' and the way in which they added to tradition 'as a living entity', to borrow words from Gleeson White and Fra, through the 1920s was part of a trace of positive British artistic engagement with Balkan art. This trace was constituted not just by those we have considered here, but a small set of others, including the London-based Faculty of Arts Gallery, Sidney Gausden and Bernard Rice.[20] Exhibition posters by Gausden highlight the vein of enchantment with Balkan rustic traditions, not least the vigour, struggles and harmonies of the lives they represent [figs 7.7, 7.8]. Fra and Jessie's own captivation with the Balkans, in particular Serbia, Croatia and Dalmatia, came at a propitious moment in their lives. It was also a moment of relative Balkan calm. Our couple had time and opportunity to join the tourist trails being made to and across the peninsula, helped by their having retired from their institutional employment and their children having grown up, as well as improvements in rail, ferry and accommodation networks. The work, correspondence and collections that their trips spawned reveal holidays and retirement well spent. They found life and art afresh. They were able to capitalise on Fra's knowledge of French, German and Italian, and Jessie having the persuasive, elegant, sensible 'tongue of St John Chrysostom' (appendix 1, 1926: 3). I would argue that their mutual Serbian turn was a high point in their creativity, a new form of coming together that encapsulated, with striking originality, so much that had gone before. As such it expresses Jessie's 'delight in correspondence and the inevitable relation of part to part' in a manner that was hitherto impossible.

The Newberys' Balkanist moment was one of light before the darkness of Fra's post-1930 depression and cessation of painting. It was one of hope. The League of Nations, with Yugoslavia a founding member, seemed, to some at least, to offer prospects for world peace and human rights. Their trips were squeezed between Britain's 1926 General Strike and the Great Depression that commenced in late 1929. The resultant Balkan fabrications captured the moment's widespread optimism. In so doing they provide an antidote not only to recent human-wrought catastrophes but also to the ensuing collapse of world order into multiple forms of barbaric dictatorship and deep state whose bread-and-butter was, and woefully remains, war, mass slaughter and repression on unprecedented scales. Their cry was that people matter, and that art uplifts and unites. More specifically, *Serbian Women* and its associated works are novel creative rejections of divisive intrigues that were engaged in by the political powers and that ravaged the southeastern European peninsula for most of Fra and Jessie's lifetimes – and considerably beyond.

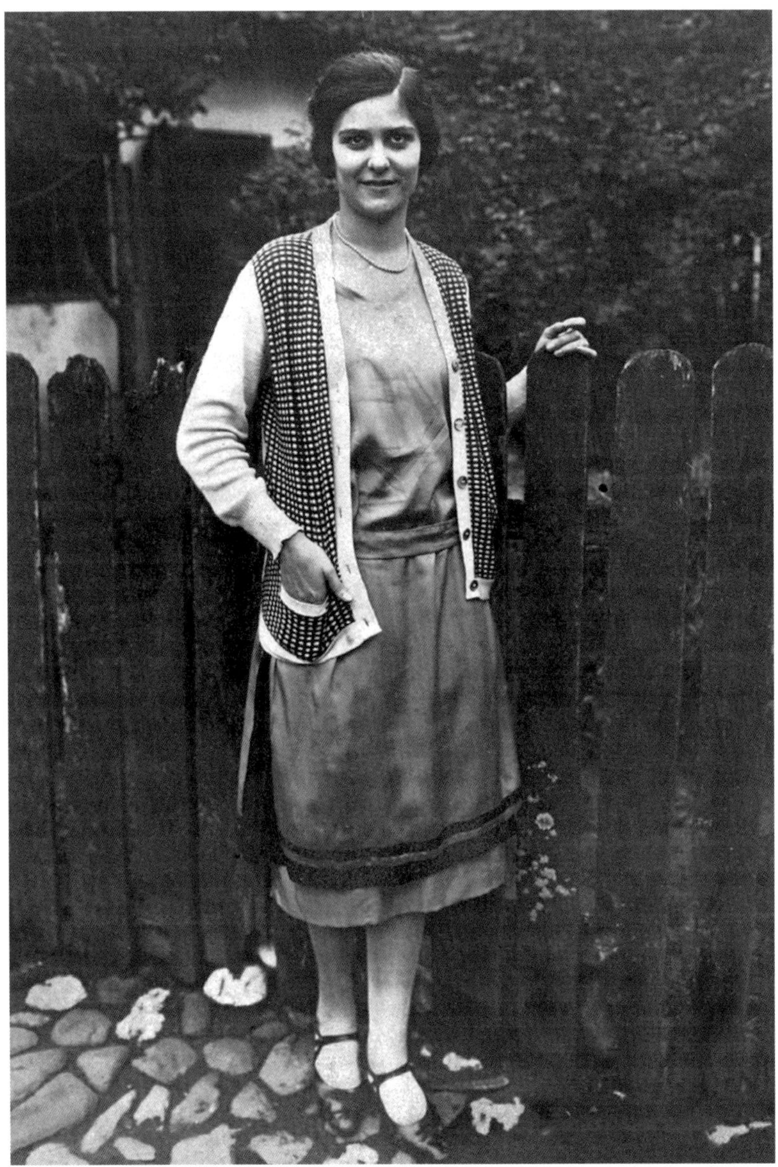

E.1 | Jela, Mira Crouch's mother, Mladenovac, *c.* 1922–25

EPILOGUE
MIRA'S MOTHER

While researching and writing this book on Balkan fabrications I became acquainted with Mira Crouch. Mira sent me scans of two photographs of her mother Jela, the first taken around 1922–25 in Mladenovac [fig. E.1], a small town some fifty kilometres south of Belgrade, the second taken some three or four years later in Belgrade [fig. E.2]. We discussed the images in relation to Fra's *Serbian Women*. Mira observed the following:

> *Traditional dress has been a marker of womanhood, of regional belonging, of homage to tradition and a showcase for skill. But with increasing urbanisation and the emergence of a middle class engaged in trade and administration/education and removed from agrarian existence, pan-European dress and the idea of fashion (i.e. Paris) became dominant in cities. But not quite. For some time hybrid forms prevailed.*

With regard to the first photograph, she then remarked:

> *Note how she is attired. In almost modern, Western style, but the structure of the clothes recalls that of national dress: a long-sleeve shirt tucked into a skirt of mid-calf length which is enhanced by a fancy apron-like overskirt. The costume is finished off with a vest (with pockets!) which is on the verge of decorative. The form/content dialectic of cultural change practically stares you in the face.*

Finally, concerning the second photograph, Mira noted:

> *A companion photo taken in 1927–8 provides a nice and amusing contrast … my mother, emboldened by her marriage to an emancipated*

It struck me that nowhere in all my research
and related exchanges, my own networks of
correspondence, had the move away from
the peasant traditions reinvented by Fra
and Jessie been so evidently or realistically
expressed. Here was a real person, with
whom I felt a tangible, empathetic contact,
capturing the transitions of the times and
place. Flapper culture arrives in Serbia, via
the new middle class, and in a stylish way.
The changes are even conveyed by Jela's
comportment: at first modestly grasping
the old wooden fence and standing, somewhat meekly, before cottage and garden,
and then, seated inside on a leather sofa, smiling more broadly at the
lens, with hair now permed and considerably more flesh revealed.

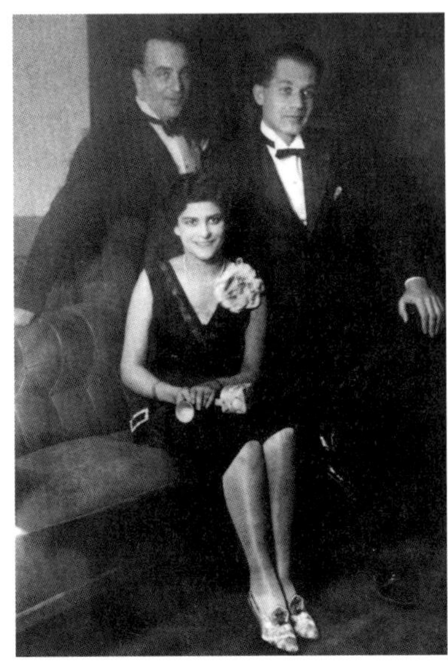

E.2 | Jela, Belgrade, c. 1927–28
PRIVATE COLLECTION

In her illustrated memoir of Belgrade, which focuses on the war
years and the extermination of her father's side of the family, Mira
describes the interaction of Serbian town and country (including the
forced barter of linen, rugs and other fabrics by her Belgrade relatives
in exchange for rural dwellers' essential food supplies). In so doing,
with a linguistic observation that hints at alternative worldviews to
those of the Anglophone world and thereby has relevance for our study
of embroidery and Balkan society, she notes the gendering of nouns in
Serbian. This gendering leads to some nouns that are relevant to our
enquiry being feminine, for instance art, craft and artistry (*umetnost*),
fabric (*tkanina*), distaff (*preslica*) and the example she gives, house (*kuća*),
which is also home. Hence Mira is able to refer to the domestic realm
using the 'she' pronoun.[2] Furthermore, she steers a course through needlework and textile art, from her grandmother's country knitting, to
her urbane aunt's collections and her own creations. As a child, pre-
war, she was invited occasionally into the bedroom of a Hungarian
Jewish aunt 'to see her elegant clothes and beautiful hand-embroidered
bed linen of which she was very proud'. The result was:

*I never got tired of seeing and touching – gently and briefly, as in-
structed – those gorgeous garments and materials. I had a great love
of fabric and a keen interest in working with cloth. Once in a while,
Aunt Vilma gave me bits of silk and wool remnants returned by her*

The hours did not last. Aunt Vilma was murdered, almost certainly at the Mauthausen concentration camp, Upper Austria, in 1942. Like the Newberys' Serbian turn, Mira's relish of material creativity held within it that 'hidden spark' of humanity and social relations so easily trounced by the seemingly insatiable human drive for devastation. Mira is a feminine name, abbreviated from 'Miroslava' and meaning, for southern Slavs, 'in praise of peace'.

Appendices

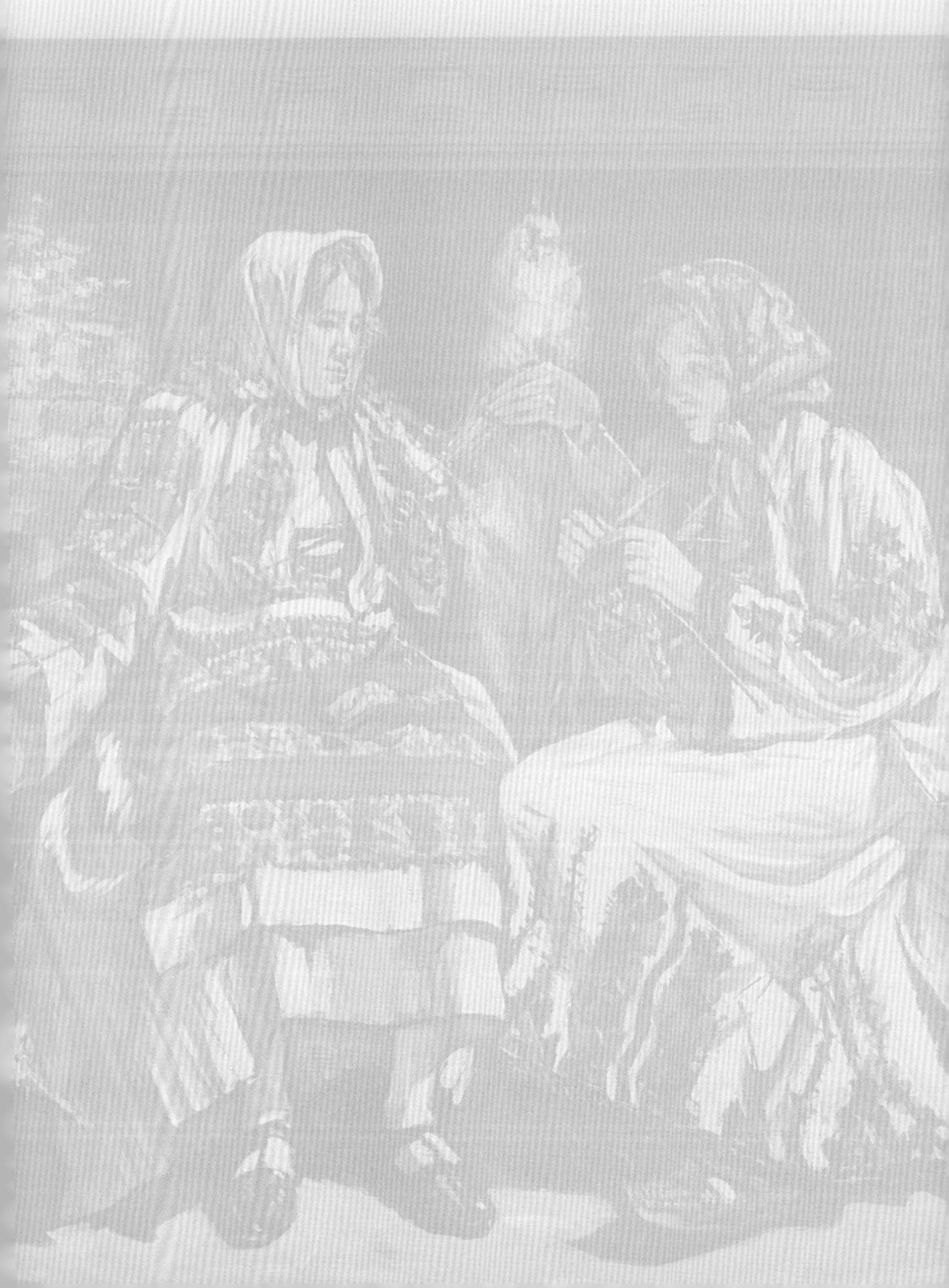

APPENDIX 1
FRA AND JESSIE'S BALKAN-RELATED CORRESPONDENCE

TRIPS TO BALKAN REGIONS

1926

1. Fra

[Undated but *c.* 20 September 1926, no envelope. To Mary or Elsie, one or other of his daughters.]

Buda Pest and a pest it is. A very swelled headed town or city or whatever it is with a second hand quality about it that masks the fact its new. But you know it and know also how proud proud [sic] the folk are in it of it and about it. I took a rest in bed today till 4 o.c (it is now ½ past 5) leaving mummy to do the honns with the American folk who are here.

However we had a good time in Zurich: Innsbruck and Vienna (theatre twice there) and are looking forward to Belgrade Sofia and East of it. We can't get to Constantinople till Sunday week October 3rd! but we shall have plenty to fill in the time especially as we are not intending to come back over most of it. We are looking forward to letters from you when we get to Constantinople.

I see Paisley was dying to get you back. Society there evidently needs your leadership. The new dresses ought to guarantee the soundness of the desire.

Love & kisses
Daddy

2. Jessie

Postmark 30.IX. Niš | Mrs Douglas Lang, Sunnyside, Park Road, Paisley, Renfrewshire, Scotland | Palace Hotel: Nisch: Serbia: 29th Sept. 1926

Darling [daughter Elsie] – here we are after a day in this queer little borderland town between the West & the East. One little white Mahomedan mosque – one Greek Church Cathedral (new but simple, & traditional). long long wide streets with very rough paving – & most of the heavy trafic beautiful yokes of oxen in very primitive carts: very few motors – some 2 horse fiacres – houses & shops only one story high – & red tiled – fascinating

orangy/brown sheepskin coats with the fur inside – & apliqued with thinner black leather & bright green pink yellow blue red shewing through punch holes in the black. Plenty of pottery – too heavy to take home: prototypes – very primitive – of our Lilley & Skinner sandal – a whole street of booths where they are made – peasants not so thrilling some of them in Turkish trousers – just women – I went out this morning to buy a few grapes – beauties – put down 6' – received 4 lbs or more – our chamber maid is a boy with bare feet – & yet neither the hotel nor food is too much below standard. In Belgrade we had 'Jaoort' [yoghurt] a kind of curdled milk – made in pots that just hold a portion for each person – eaten with sugar – delicious. There is a recipe for it in East & West cookery book.

We are to be in Constantinople at least 10 days – from Sunday 2 Oct So perhaps you could send another letter there – Our route home is not settled – nor hotels – but probably we go back by – Adrianople – Salonika – Sarajevo – Catarro [Kotor]: on the Adriatic – Love to my two little boys [grandsons Frederick and Colin Lang] – I hope they are keeping free of colds – we are into hot summer again – & thinnest clothes – Much love to you & all from us both –

Your loving Mother
This is such an untourist ridden place that there are no postcards of it to buy –

Fra
[A note from Fra added to the letter above from Jessie.] German most useful everywhere. French in the Banks etc. not in the hotels. Love Daddy.

3. Jessie

Belgrade. 2–[*c.* 25] Oct 1926

Darling [daughter Mary] – first to make explanations about not giving you addresses to write to – our plans were very unsettled and went on changing.

We meant to go to Salonica – but practically could not get there by train – and sailing there

meant 24 hours at sea – At last – hearing that
all the old part of Salonica – no longer existed
– except 3 very good Byzantine churches with
mosaics – Dad gave it up – I am sure partly
because of me – although I was willing to sail –

Then we meant to go to Sarajevo – but
connections were so bad we gave that up – & so we
are here – which we didn't expect to be but which
I am very pleased about – as with the museum &
the market – & the view of the great plain from on
high – Belgrade lies high – it is a fine place to be in
– & the small 2 story Belgrade houses that remain
are very attractive, the handmade carpets about
here are very interesting – I call them kelims – but
here they are called Chelims – a soft 'ch' – I bought
2 articles of apparel – which you will see when you
and Alick come to Corfe! I would like to buy more
but they are dear even with the exchange in our
favour – by the way – in Sofia – we acquired braid
in emerald – cobalt – yellow & scarlet, & some
bowls – are you pleased

We did not buy much in Constantinople –
Daddy bought a Koran – with 2 vellum pages of
illumination – which he is very proud of – I bought
a little ware old Persian lamp – blue or green with
black decoration – but it was in two when we got
it home – an old break?

Then Nisch – we found was selling that black
pottery with gold encrustations – you had a jug –
which was broken – I got one fairly like it – a lovely
coat – Rodier fabric, camel hair coloured & stiff,
with a little diaper of real gold – hardly tailored.
The scarfe goes through a slot & one end hangs
down behind. Very long – no fur at neck.

In Constantinople we had a day on the sea
of Marmora with Colonel & Mrs Woods &
Lily Wylie (she is staying with them) The day
was windless & warm – & we were happy –
we had tea anchored in a lovely little bay on an
island – then walked over the island – about a
mile through branching pine woods – & Cistus
& heath – (not flowering) & took the steamer
back to Constantinople – this island was not the
island of 'principo' – but one very near Principo
[Principio]. Principo is rather spoiled a garden
city for rich people – for the summer –

Passports have not been exactly a worry – but
the procedure – especially in Turkey is very involved.
To go to Broussa [Bursa] we had each to get 2 new
photographs taken – & a permit for three days
there. To get out of Broussa – another photograph
each & a permit to leave – Broussa is in Turkey
also we had to get a permit to leave Turkey

Coming back through Bulgaria – not stopping
anywhere there – we had to pay a £1 – to get into
Serbia. We ought to have had our passports visa-
ed in Constantinople – & should have paid our
£1 there. We have had our luggage examined at
countless stations – getting in & out of countries
– asked how much Bulgarian money we had – how
much English money we had – was it in currency
notes or credit notes – Daddy has taken it very
quietly – also the various exchanges – he is very
clever at these – His German was a great help till
we arrived in Constantinople – then French was.

My cold – I think – was a slight touch of influenza
– but only kept me in one whole day – but I had
minor troubles – sore throat – internal chill – a
temperature sometimes above 100 – sometimes just
above normal but not ill – just a little off colour –
now I am above it all – & springy again – I lived
on Ja-oort – & biscuits – very good – & rice & milk
always 'on' in the restaurants – as we were in a bed
& breakfast place this was easy.

It seems as if Ja-oort was practicable in an easy
way – by buying 'Lactic Ferment' – directions on
the bottle. But it is most delicate when the milk is
very good & creamy – as in Belgrade – use icing
sugar to eat it with.

Part of this letter was written before we joyfully
received one from Elsie – one from Mary – today
– really great good luck – as after telling Elsie
Belgrade – Belgrade seemed most unlikely. We
leave tomorrow for 2 nights in Zagreb just as a
resting place on our way to Venice for 2 nights –
then Milan – then Basle – but letters would be
welcome in Corfe??

I hope your cold has worked itself away this time.

Yes Prunus Trivola [Prunus Tribola – flowering
cherry-almond] is the lovely Edinburgh one – I
think I almost – or wholly ordered it from Prichard
last spring – 7/6 – Could you spare me your catalogue for a week or so? – about a week after we
go back – we don't go back to Annie – she is getting
married but to 'Elsie' – Mrs Stockley's (who cleans
our drawing room) daughter (who has been 4 years
in service with a very good working mistress in
Dorchester) – but who wishes back to Corfe &
mother & brothers & sisters. My chatter seems to
have run out – Dad is making tea – then we go out
to look over the Danube & the great plain – home
& rather difficult packing – as our empedimenta
grows –

Very hot here – sultry.

Please send this letter to Elsie.

It will be lovely to pick up her letter in Venice –
something to look forward to –

We are so pleased to hear that Alick's mother is
not distressed now. Much love from Mother –

Fra

[Added to the letter above from Jessie.] My two
darlings – Senior and Junior.

When the carter upset his apple cart, silence
reigned, because (as he said) there was no language
created that was capable of expressing his feelings.
Well my fruit barrow is full and although I have
used and had to use four languages (sic) to carry
on this guide and cicerone business, I cannot find
speech sufficiently charged with feeling, wherewith

I could fulfil my feelings. So my dears, cheres; teuers; caras etc I leave it to she with the tongue of St John Chrysostom to hae a crack wi' ye when time and the occasion serve. I have had to handle no less than eight differing and different monetary systems and at the same time travel with a lady with a mind like a dynamo and desires like a chameleon's skin. Love Dad.

1928

1. Fra

'Byzantine Art at South Kensington', letter to the editor, *The Observer*, 29 July 1928, p. 7

Sir. – As the artist responsible for the copies of the mosaics and frescoes of the Kahrie Djami being brought to London, and for their acceptance for exhibition by the Victoria and Albert Museum, through the courtesy of the director, I beg to state that the notice of these works of Mr. D. Ismailovitch in your issue of the 22nd inst. is somewhat mis-leading.

The Kahrie Djami was not burnt down in 1919, and its mosaics have suffered nothing but the passage of time and the effects of the earthquake of 1894. We visited the mosque in 1926, met Mr. Ismailovitch there, congratulated him on his very successful studies, and, on his invitation, I went to his studio in Pera and, to the best of my re-collection, saw copies of practically every group and single figure mosaic of the Kahrie Mosque. That all these excellent studies are not exhibited at South Kensington may arise for reasons of selection and space.

On our return from Constantinople I wrote to Mr. Keeper Martin Hardie, and was glad to receive his consent that these works be exhibited in his department.

We found that the frescoes were suffering from water percolation, but the Turkish Government had the matter in hand, and were executing repairs. The frescoes, however, are of little account in comparison with the wonderful mosaics, and the date of execution of these latter is yet open to establishment. –

I am, Sir, yours obediently,
Fra H. Newbery.

1929

1. Jessie

Miss Mary Spencer Watson. Dunshay, Langton Matravers, Dorset, England | Spalato [Split]. Friday 11th Oct [1929] | (Stamps [3 x 50] of Kingdom of Serbia, Croatia and Slovenia.)

perhaps you would enjoy seeing some of the horses here – spotted black & white like Dalmatian dogs – one little horse on the Quay, piebald – looks all too human with blue eyes and white lashes. We sail tomorrow to Ragusa. Love to your Mother & you. J. Newbery.

2. Fra

Miss Helen Muspratt Artist Photographer, 2 High Street, Swanage, Dorset, England | Dubrovnik (Ragusa) Yugoslavia. Oct. 19 1929 [Cavtat]

This little place contains the Račić monument, one of the greatest of Meštrović, the sculptor's work. We are having a very good time. No rain. Hot sun. Blue skies and a sea in which I had a bathe on Wednesday.

Mrs Newbery sends best regards to you and to Mrs Muspratt
Fra Newbery

TRIPS TO OTHER REGIONS
All Jessie unless otherwise stated

1924 · Italy including Sicily

1

Postmark: Palermo, 20.III.1924 | Mary Spencer Watson, Downshay, Langton Matravers, Dorset, England | 19th March: 1924

Nearly all the carts in Sicily are like this one – & the donkeys wear long tassels at their ears and are very attractive.

My Mary & I carry crusts in our pockets to tempt the donkeys to make friends with us.

We have found so many new wild flowers.
Love to your Mother & you.
From Jessie Newbery

2

Postmark: 20.III.1924, Palermo | Mrs Douglas [daughter Elsie] Lang, Sunny Side, Park Road, Paisley, Renfrewshire, Scotland | Palermo 19th March: 1924.

Darling – I know it is all our fault for not journeying according to plan – but no letter from you or anyone yet! Not even our letters sent on by Mrs Deemer.

Well, I just hope all is well – perhaps on receipt of this – if you sent a letter to Post Restante Florence we might manage to secure it. We shall be, at least, 3 more days in Palermo which Dad especially is much interested in – more pictures & very interesting churches covered in mosaics

– Byzantine – about the same date as St Mark's
in Venice. Mary & I have enjoyed the temples &
Greek theatres immensely – & also the country
walks to them – & then the land round these
antiquities is not cultivated – & so we find [a]
great treasure trove of new wild flowers.

Palermo itself has a very beautiful port – with
wonderful mountains – very oriental & strange
& eerie, all round & a jade green sea.

We meet the Loftus [identity unconfirmed]
everywhere we go – & we have met some quite
interesting Americans – one a young man, with
a travelling scholarship.

We havn't found any pottery since Taormina.
It is quite curious that at T. the smallest place –
were much the best shops for needlework, pottery,
& antiques – dear of course – as it is the haunt
of rich Americans. We just have rooms in this
Albergo – & go out to a Restaurant. We find this
more interesting – & we have better food & and
[sic] it costs less – & more fun.

On the same lines as that dependence of the
Hotel we stayed at in Rome.

We are managing pretty well – the three of
[us] living cheaper than Dad & I alone lived in
Spain. Of course the exchange helps – but that is
not everything. We enjoy the oranges very much
straight off the trees – always with a tuft of green
leaves on them. I hope Alice is quite well again –
& that all the Sunnyside coughs & colds are past
& gone. We have had good weather on the whole
– cold at Girgenti – but warm out of the wind –
in the sun.

We had a very good dish yesterday Beef olives
on Rizzotta. The Olives made of a thin slice of beef
– as thin as ham slices – rolled round pork sausage
meat stewed. The rice cooked in good stock with a
little saffron – not burst – no gravy – stew gravy –
a little over

Much love from us all.

Our Itinerary – Naples Paestum Salerno Amalfi
Rome Florence

3

Postmark: 24.3.24, Girgenti [Agrigento] (but
seemingly written before the letter above) | Mrs
Douglas [daughter Elsie] Lang, Sunny Side, Park
Road, Paisley, Renfrewshire, Scotland | Hotel
Belvidere | Girgenti: Friday Sicily

Darling Elsie.

After a very happy week at Taormina we came
on to Syracuse & spent 2 days there – seeing a
beautiful Greek theatre – in the country – picking
there about a dozen quite strange flowers – all
different from those of Taormina – & walking
round the edge of the island – & threading through
the narrow mediaeval streets.

We travelled 6 hours to Castello Giovanna

[Enna; prior to 1926 known as Castrogiovanni]
3500 ft high a little hill town – very primitive –
with interesting Italo-Norman architecture of the
15th century

The peasants – men – all wear black hooded
'cloaks' – & top boots or cotton rags rotted round
their legs & undressed hide mocassins. The women
wear black shawls – these clothes make the fore-
grounds so much in keeping. But Castello Giovanni
is oh so cold – oh so cold & not a fire in the whole
hotel – the chamber man put copper scaldinis in
our beds with wooden cages over them – but we
had to take them out when we went to bed.

And Syracuse was hot June & Castello Giovanni
was snow cold January. But quite worth freezing
for one night – & so lovely & romantic a birds eye
view of mountain behind mountain – & the back of
Etna & the plains of Etna where Persephone was
gathering flowers. The fields were blue with purple
anemones – & we saw wild jonquils from the
railway – & a child brought us some as a gift – the
very same kind of flowers that Persephone plucked.

We could not stay another night – it was too cold.

Daddy & Mary & I had 2 bedrooms en suite –
& we could not keep people out of them.

I heard a knock at the door – & went to answer
it. A very meek boy – about 18 – said 'may I come in
– I like to speak a little English' – he was a kind of
parasite who floated about the hotel outside & inside.

He tried to attach himself to us next day – but
we objected.

Then the chambermaidman spent most of the
evening with us in our bedroom – Daddy & Mary
quite pleased to air their Italian. And now here we
are – looking down & down over country sloping
to the sea – about 5 miles away – and in the middle
distance are three real Greek temples – that we
hope to visit this afternoon. This morning was grey
so we spent it in the town – & of course met the
Loftus – who were in Syracuse when we were there.
We hobnobbed in a cafe & then went on together
to the Duomo. This hotel is perfect: old, rambling:
very Italian; we have a private terrace to our
bedrooms – about 20 by 30 looking down over an
old campanile – then the country & sea. Food very
good: 3 American architectural students to talk to.
40 Lire a day for everything. 8/ a day – 10 percent
tax on that & 10 percent for service. – & we have to
tip as well – but few to tip.

Much love darling – we hope very much to get
letters in Palermo:

Very sorry we forgot the little birthday boy –
your very loving Mother

4

Postmark: 28.iii.1924 Napoli | Mrs Douglas
[daughter Elsie] Lang, Sunny Side, Park Road,
Paisley, Renfrewshire, Scotland | Naples – Friday
28th March 1924

Darling – Dad & I were Jubilant to get a letter
from you at Cook's the day before yesterday –
& to hear that all was well – about a month ago.
We hope to pick up all the letters waiting for us
at Rome, Florence, Milan, Paris – & then Corfe
Castle! It is strange to think that now our faces are
set homewards – Dad is thinking about the Downs
– He has scored off a Journey waiting to be made
for the last 30 years – & there are no other very
anxiously desired scalps on our journey home.
The weather has been unsettled but we have been
very lucky & we have never been prevented from
expeditions & sightseeing.

Mary will have told you that on the night of
the Amalfi disaster we were in Salerno – & had
planned to be in Amalfi the following day – but
motors were so dear – & it meant motoring there
from Salerno – & motoring over to Sorrento to
catch the train for Naples – that we gave this bit
of our journey up. Paestum was very fine – just
as good & even more so than my impression of it.
Dad was quite thrilled – & he was rather sniffy
about the Girgenti temples.

But what a motor journey we had to get there –
bumpety bumpety bump – lumpety lumpety lump
– over practically unmade country road – you cant
conceive it – I wished myself back in Salerno after
the first five minutes. Mary & I were nearly
bounced out of the carriage. After a while Mary
went in front – & Daddy's weight ballasted the
back of the car better.

But Paestum was well worth it all.

And then there was a festa there – & as we drove
to Paestum we passed trail after trail of picturesque
but very poor peasants – on donkeys – nearly always
2 people on each donkey – & sometimes four – all
riding sideways & with no saddle – but panniers
stuffed with purchases.

Also plenty of donkey carts also well laden.

Some donkeys in Sicily are very small – not
much bigger than Newfoundlands – & the horses
also very small – 7 pretty – not ponies. They draw
very light little carriages seated for 2 – but Daddy
would have to have one for himself.

On the way to Paestum we saw fields of jonquils.

Naples is noisy & dirty. But the sculpture
& Bronzes in the museum are very beautiful –
although in a way familiar as casts of them are not
uncommon in England. But the casts have not the
wonderful colour of the originals – the patina is
emerald & ultramarine crusting the darker bronze.

The paintings are not thrilling – weak – & washy
& decadent – far too much fuss has been made
about them.

I wonder if you will get the Mackenzie's house?
Really it is best to have elbow room when the
children are young – you cannot keep them with
you always.

Remember that we moved into a bigger house
just when you got engaged. Mackenzies house has

lovely situation – just rather far from the town for
walking.

We enjoyed very much the train to Naples
through Calabria –

We started from the hotel at Messina at 4.30 in
the dark – sailed over to San Giovanni (near Reggio)
in the moonlight & early dawn – & then trained
always near the sea & near the mountains past the
lovliest of little beaches – only inhabited sometimes
by fishing boats of gay colours & fishermen – mostly
deserted – & the sea so clear & blue – The villages
were in nooks at a horn of the bays – The peasants
were dressed in mediaeval clothes – black red &
white – & the oxen were so beautiful – white but
not too white – with dark rims round their eyes –
Calabria is really untouched Italy.

Nobody takes the daylight journey because the
train is very slow – & we had several 2nd class
carriages all to ourselves.

The day was perfect – we arrived at Salerno
at 8.30 pm – a long day – but not too tiring. I hope
you have had enough letters Elsie dearest – we have
had rather hard travelling – & often I have been too
tired to write after lunch & after dinner.

Our journey to Rome was a much shorter one –
about 12 days of travelling shorter if you count our
journeys in Sicily.

We have all stood it very well. Dad has been
cross a little – he gets worried at people all trying
to cheat him – 5 times he counted one day –

Write a note to Paris darling

Much love to you & all from your very loving
Mother

We said Goodbye to the Loftus at Palermo

Mr Loftus asked us to dine with them at our
restaurant – & we had a very pleasant evening
together.

1925 · Southern France

Postmark: 22.10.? Le Puy en Velay, Haute-Loire
| Mary Spencer Watson, Duns-Haye Manor,
Langton Matravers, Dorset, England | Rodez
19.11.25

Dear Mary –

We are getting home again.

This is a town high on a hill – we see far away
over a lovely countryside.

Love from J. Newbery

1928 · Madrid, Spain

1

Postmark: 12(?) October 28 Madrid | Mrs [Hilda]
Spencer Watson, Downshay, Langton Matravers,
Dorset – Inglaterra | 'La infanta dona Maria Teresa

de Austria. Velazquez. Museo del Prado. 1192'
(Fototipia Hauser y Menet – Madrid)

No doubt you have seen a reproduction of this –
but the shorthand in producing the shimmer of
grey silver brocade shot with silvery rosy scarlet is
very exciting – we have spent 2 forenoons in the
prado. Love from Jessie Newbery

2

Miss Mary Spencer Watson, Downshay, Langton
Matravers, Dorset – Inglaterra | Wednesday 17th
Oct | 'Arnés pequeno del Principe de Asturias D.
Baltasar Carlos. Hijo de Felipe iv', Real Armeria.
Madrid (Fototipia Hauser y Menet – Madrid)

Even we [sic] saw a dog in armour with a velvet
caparison under the steel – & a bunch of ostrich
plumes on his head. He looked very pround [sic]
& a pet
   Love from Jessie Newbery

1930 · ITALY

Fra

Miss Helen Muspratt, 2 High Street, Swanage,
Dorset, Inghilterra | San Gimignano. Oct 16 1930

Here is the Saint (Gimignano) with his many
towered town on his lap. The quaintest place we
were ever in.
   Regards from both to you & Mrs Muspratt
   Fra Newbery

1931? · Spain?

1

Undated – postmark unclear (1931?) | Fred Lang,
Whiteleigh, Stanely Road, Paisley, Renfrewshire,
Ecozia [sic] [NB different address to those sent to
his mother Elsie in 1924–26; Whiteleigh – large
Arts & Crafts House]

My dear boy Fred
   I wish you & Colin were with us to see all the
strange sights: but you would get very wearied with
all the long days in the train
   Much love from Granny

2. Fra

[Dorset History Centre, Dorchester: D-2566/Acc
9788/box 1] | Mrs Hilda Spencer Watson, Dunshay
Manor, by Langton Matravers, Dorset | Letterhead:
from FRA : H : NEWBERY : | Cavaliere :
Ufficiale : | EASTGATE ; CORFE : CASTLE :
DORSET : | August 5 1931

Gentilissima Madonna.
   I suggest that you send me please a note of
the out-of-pocket expenses, incurred by you in the
transport to and from of the material used by you for
the purposes of the concert. That the performance
was the success we all realised, is due in the greatest
measure to your genius and to that of la vostra figlia
and I am sure I am voicing the feelings of everybody
present that the concert was an unique event, and
one that will long be treasured as a sweet and
pleasant memory.
   il vostro servitore sempre
   Fra. H. Newbery

APPENDIX 2
THE CREEDS OF JESSIE AND FRA

1. JESSIE

J. Gleeson White, 'Some Glasgow Designers and Their Work – III', *The Studio: An Illustrated Magazine of Fine and Applied Art*, vol. 12, no. 55, October 1897, pp. 47–51 | Italicised text is that which was omitted by Rozsika Parker in her *Subversive Stitch*, pp. 184–185

Perhaps in place of trying to interpret Mrs Newbery's artistic creed from her designs it would be more interesting to quote her own words in reply to a request that she would state her ideas on the matter. Therein she says, after disclaiming any personal theories of design for embroidery specially:

"I believe that the greatest thing in the world is for a man to know that he is his own, and that the great end in art is the discovery of the self of the artist.

I believe in being the sum of tradition; that consciously or unconsciously men are all so, but some are more derivative than others.

I believe in education consisting of seeing the best that has been done. Then, having this high standard thus set before us, in doing what we like to do: *that* for our fathers, *this* for us.

I believe that nothing is common or unclean; that the design and decoration of a pepper pot is as important, in its degree, as the conception of a cathedral.

I believe that material, space, and consequent use discover their own exigencies and as such have to be considered well.

I believe in everything being beautiful, pleasant, and, if need be, useful.

To descend to particulars, I like the opposition of straight lines to curved; of horizontal to vertical; of purple to green, of green to blue.

I delight in correspondence and the inevitable relation of part to part.

I specially aim at beautifully shaped spaces and try to make them as important as the patterns.

I try to make the most appearance with least effort, but insist that what work is ventured on is as perfect as may be.

I hope that in the foregoing expression of opinion I have not seemed over egotistic, considering the little sum of work accomplished by me."

Elsewhere in his article Gleeson White makes the following observations about Jessie's work:

… for several years past her work has not been overlooked by those who are alive to modern design. In the last Arts and Crafts [society exhibition] were cushion covers, a mantel border, a book of emblems bound in green morocco gilt, and a quilt shown upon Mr Christie's iron four-post bedstead, all designed by Jessie R. Newbery, who also exhibited a chalice and paten, an altar frontal, and a repoussé alms plate, worked from her designs in the previous exhibition, 1893. Therefore, those who follow closely the history of the applied arts among us will not be unaware of the style of Mrs Newbery's work, not unmindful of its distinctly personal quality. But before that, 'Jessie Rowat', as medallist of South Kensington, was not unknown to those who follow the course of English design somewhat closely. Here we may confine our attention to the designs for embroidery, which are singularly attractive, inasmuch as they are not obviously modelled on purely oriental designs, but seem to keep no little of the naïveté of old British work – which may indeed be traced back through continental ancestors to the mystic East, so that it cannot be considered an exotic, but a fully acclimatised growth…

[Jessie's] creed is one that touches far more important matters than mere needlework, and seems to state not infelicitously the guiding principles of many a designer today…

the Glasgow School… is striving to make beautiful harmonies of colour, and beautiful combinations of line…

the designs of Mrs Newbery… new as they are, are obedient to the laws of symmetry and admirably fitted to their material.

As most of them – the embroideries – were evidently conceived as schemes of colour, they not merely require that important factor to represent them adequately but suffer, and terribly, by translation in black and white. For the artist is not one of those who makes elaborate drawings in monochrome, and adds pigments arbitrarily to them after.

As the schemes themselves show, they are essentially problems in the balance of colour, no less than in the distribution of line. Above all, they suggest needlework, their forms are absolutely

suitable for expression by the needle, they call
for no undue amount of labour, they decorate not
merely the surface to which they are applied, but
also form most pleasant spots of ornament in the
larger scheme of decoration of any room where
they happened to be placed. Their freshness and
novelty when you see them in the actual fabrics
could hardly be overpraised. They speak for
themselves so simply and directly, that the most
sympathetic admirer can do naught but admire.
It is just because they are so good that it is difficult
to catalogue their merits, or explain why they are
so admirable. But designers will soon discover that
their apparent simplicity is the result of real power;
their gay and harmonious colour the evidence of an
inborne sense of beauty. Above all, as I have said,
they preserve the best traditions of the art, and yet
never directly imitate earlier work; and therefore
it is possible to praise them very highly, without
once over-stating the case, and still less without
regarding them patronisingly as a woman's work.
It is pleasant to remember that they chance to
be for a craft which has been pre-eminently the
province of women from time immemorial; but
they may take their place as examples of well-
applied art, with no question of sex, and no
attempt to evade criticism by a spurious chivalry
which is often but a covert form of insult.

2. FRA

Fra. H. Newbery, 'An Appreciation of the Work
of Ann Macbeth', *The Studio: An Illustrated
Magazine of Fine and Applied Art*, vol. XXVII,
no. 115, October 1902, pp. 40–49

The association of the needle is with the woman's
hand, and though the sewing machine may have
robbed the expression of much of its truth and of
all its sentiment, it may still be said, to paraphrase
the words of a well-known dictum, that 'the hand
that holds the needle beautifies the world.' And by
this no disparagement is intended of that vast army
of tailors whose office it is to clothe mankind. For
the dress of the modern Occidental man knows
no art in its composition, nor can decoration,
however added, redeem it from its state of sad
monotony. But happily the work of the needle
is not solely confined to the manufacture, or even
the decoration, of garments, and in the hand of the
woman it makes its appeal in poetry and has its place
in art. As the plough to the peasant or the pen to
the writer, so the needle lives in our sentiments
as a personal effect of the woman – part of her
physical belongings, as it were, and without which
life would be incomplete, and the world a loser of a
form of art which is almost coeval with the existence
of mankind. And the needle bears with it a dignity
of labour that, if it be not greater than the plough,

is yet one that puts it into the same category of
absolute necessities. For man, if he cannot live
without the plough, can equally as little do without
the labour of the needle. And to make another
comparison, much of the poetry which comes from
the pen is not for a moment to be compared with
those harmonies of form and colour which owe
their origin to the art of embroidery – the art by
instinct of the woman. And this instinct, whether
primitive or inherited, remains with some women
as a constant quality – an artistic expression ever
seeking outlet. And among such artists is Miss
Ann Macbeth… With no one is the association
of the needle and the hand more close or the results
more precious than with her, and she may fairly be
said to belong to that class of workers who claim
companionship with Penelope and find themselves
at home in the company of those Mediaeval artists,
whether ecclesiastical or lay, whose needles have
made history and whose efforts are to be met with
in the sacristy of the church, among the treasures
of the castle and house, or more fully given to the
world as forming part of the collections of our
various museums.

But we have in these latter days lost sight somewhat of that traditional use of the needle which in
not very remote days brought a personal element to
bear upon the beauty of household surroundings.
The domestic supply that existed so fruitfully has
been supplanted by the art needlework emporium.
Formerly no young girl's education was judged to
be completed until she had worked her sampler and
had thus added her share to the accepted tradition
of needlework, and carried it a generation farther on.
For the sampler was a purely traditional piece of art
needlework, whose stitches and ornament were a
heritage transmitted from mother to daughter;
it was rarely ugly, oftentimes was very beautiful,
and bore on its face a standard of artistic value that
makes it today one of the sought-for treasures of the
antique collector. And the skill thus attained by the
young worker was an abiding one, and her needle
found employment in a hundred ways that today
are either forgotten or are relegated to the shop
or to the machine.

The pride of the bride used to be in her napery.
Her dower chest was gifted her, that she might
store those productions of the loom and needle that
should beautify the bed whereon she was to sleep
and the table at which she was to preside; and much
of genius and a great deal of skill was brought to bear
upon articles alike of use and for ornament, so that
the everyday handlings of life were broidered with
beauty and enhanced by art, even as the flowers of
the hedgerow, the traveller's joy, and the vagrant
honeysuckle, the hop, and the bryony broider
the hedges of the English highroads. And no one
questions the joy that comes from an environment
of household wares that, compelled by use, are
enhanced by art in their making. If the magic of

beauty, the effect of temperament, can be added to the things we needs must have, must needs use, the having and using give sensations of absolute pleasure. And if this be possible, as indeed it is, then the objection that beauty is rare, and therefore dear, and, as a quality, must always remain a possession for the few, must be met and combated. Beauty is not for the few, but for the many, and that it is costly is no valid objection. It costs no more to create a beautiful object than it does to produce an ugly one, and ugliness incarnate is oftentimes dearer than beauty, although less may have been paid for the former. The price of the material in an ugly production is oftentimes more than that contained in a beautiful object. The purchaser of a picture does not pay merely for the tubes of colours used nor for the canvas employed, nor even for the mere time of the artist; he pays for that power that transmutes both pigments and time into beauty. And nowadays there is far too much money invested in the painted side of beauty, and not nearly enough given for that art that expresses itself through the table-cloth that covers our table or the towel upon which we dry our hands. Adam Smith, in his *Wealth of Nations*, left out of account those priceless treasures which we possess in our pictures – wealth that makes poor nations rich, and without which wealthy nations are poor. How much more wealth could he have attributed to nations had he taken into consideration that inexpressible and untold value which the application of art to common things brings alike to maker and to user! And if this honour can be given to the articles that are thus treated, how much greater is the credit due to the worker who produces them!

And to Ann Macbeth every commendation can be paid for the part she is taking in this addition of beauty to our daily surroundings. With her, the art of the needle is at once the object of her life and a means for the fullest expression of a nature that teems with artistic sentiments and ideas. And she has no false pretences as to the value of the good she may possibly be doing in the world. She is content simply to be a worker, doing practical and useful work, and finding for it a place in the market and by it a subsistence for herself. Coming of artistic stock, and bearing a name that figures in more than one list of Royal Academicians, Ann Macbeth began life, if heredity counts for anything, with helpful instincts. But unlike so many art workers of the present day, who start designing before they draw, and claim credit for novelty of idea where workmanship would have been more desirable, Miss Macbeth kept her design aspirations in the background until she had made herself a competent draughtswoman, and had mastered the art of drawing, without which design is as lifeless as a body without a soul. Like old Italian masters she arrived at a knowledge of ornament through the practice of drawing from the figure: and when

at length she turned her attention to traditional ornament, she found herself in a position to ignore it, and to start where the mediaeval ornamentists did – namely, at and with Nature. By her education she had placed herself in the position of being a creative artist, instead of a follower of tradition, and this gave her a distinct advantage over the old sampler worker. For unless tradition in art be added to, be made to live, and be brought up to date as a living entity, there is a fear that it must die of sheer inanition, and history repeats this lesson. Ornament, to be worthy of the name, must be more than an aggregation of conventional forms to be used on occasion, like recipes taken from a cookery book. It must be a personal belonging, and have a distinct relation not only to the *ego* of the creator, but also to the period in which it was created. But this presupposes power to transform, talent to adapt, and, above all, genius to create; and herein comes the good of a sound education, such as Miss Macbeth possesses. To be original in any sense of the word is, first, to find out what has been done, and then to learn the further possibilities both of material and of treatment. Otherwise originality becomes a travesty, and creation (so-called) merely a borrowing. But the instinct that can trace the hieroglyphical forms on a Persian carpet back to the nature from which they were adapted can start again with that nature, and end at a point beyond that, it may be, which the Persian reached. And, what is more, the worker may finish with that touch of nature which the Oriental never had, and thus make a deeper appeal to our senses, because of the added comparison we are able to make between means and ends.

But with the possession of such power comes the application, and Miss Macbeth, instead of producing work which, though beautiful in itself, should, like the painted picture, be unrelated to ordinary surroundings, set herself steadfastly from the very first to execute work which should enter into daily life and have an interest because it was a part of our everyday surroundings. And in this endeavour she is much helped by her own very practical outlook on things. Thus, how dress and personal adornment could be simplified and at the same time beautified, early made a strong appeal to her. How stuffs, plain, yet of sound quality and of good colour, could be beautified by the addition of embroidery or other aids to decoration, led her to essay the art of appliqué and to endeavour to mosaic upon a ground an ornamental treatment in another colour, which should enhance the dress as a possession, without adding much to the original cost. Not that there is anything new in this. The dresses of the mediaeval Italian women, as depicted by artists like Ghirlandaio or Botticelli, glow with appliqué and embroidery; but whereas precious materials, gold, silver, and jewels, entered into their making, with Miss Macbeth the setting of one piece of coloured cloth upon another, and the putting of a border of sewn thread or silk around it, gave the added piece all the appearance and value of a precious metal or of a jewel set among its surroundings. Further, these spots of colour, thus superimposed, are connected, and the design made into a whole, by spots and lines of colour or by ornament, chiefly floral, characteristically conventionalised from Nature. This class of work she applies with success to almost every article where its use is possible and permissible; and the plenishings of the drawing-room, the dining-room, and the bedroom have all received attention. But she has not entirely confined her energies to the decoration of articles of mere necessity. Her knowledge of the figure has enabled her to grapple with the possibilities of its use in design; and various needlework panels of figure subjects, some of which have already been illustrated in *The Studio*, are the fruits of her work in this direction. Notably, also, a coloured reproduction of one side of the British Association banner for the Glasgow meeting of 1901, and which appeared in *The Studio* for January, 1902, is a charming example of how heraldry may be utilised for the purposes of pageantry.

Another fruitful field for art work – namely, designs for sewed book-covers, for which a tradition once existed in England – owes some progress to Miss Macbeth. And the attitude she stands in to her work is shown by her treatment of it. She does not feel that it is enough to merely design and let others execute. She believes that the artist who produces the design is generally the person best fitted to carry it out, and most pieces of work for which she is responsible owe their execution, either in part or the whole, to her own needle. And this is the true artistic position. To completely know how to design for any material, it is necessary to be a worker in that material. For there should be no real fixity of idea in a design that is being produced by hand. It should be possible to make any change of intention as the work proceeds, and it may be that the best design is, in the long run, the one whose general scheme is understood from the beginning, but whose details are studied and carried out as the work proceeds. By such means artistic instinct is always kept on the alert, and the opportunity left open for the attainment of the best possible result.

And to show that this work of Ann Macbeth's is one that by its influence is likely to improve current taste in embroidery, it should be mentioned that she is in touch with a world-known London firm, who have given a special name to her work, and are willing to take as much of it as she cares to send them. That she is kept busy in the supply is a practical testimony to the success of her efforts. As a further addition to her powers, Miss Macbeth possesses in no small degree the art of imparting instruction to others; and as one of the teachers in the Embroidery Class of the Glasgow School of Art she has found another channel whereby the influence of her work is extended. Glasgow decorative art is known outside the city on the Clyde, and a steady progress in the work of the class, especially in the branch of appliqué, has been noticeable since Miss Macbeth's accession to the staff of the school. It is by the cultivation of an all-round appreciation of the application of art to our common surroundings that we may hope for any raising of the standard of that curious quality called public taste. For if beauty be seen and felt in things lowly, there exist the possibilities of its further appreciation in higher things; and a city, whose citizens have beautiful things in their houses, may hope to exact from civic authorities a recognition of the truth that, as the house is, so shall the city be.

APPENDIX 3
KATHLEEN MANN: DESIGNS FROM YUGOSLAVIA AND ROMANIA

From: Kathleen Mann, *Design from Peasant Art* (London: A.& C. Black, 1939), pp. 18 and 54

'Floral Motive on Blue and White Material'
The floral motive around which this design plays is from Yugoslavia. Once more the design was planned with hardly any drawn preparation; the flower and the circular motives in red spots were positioned by the use of three circular pieces of paper. These were pinned to the material and marked round with a round of tacking. From the three tacked circles the design was worked spontaneously on a background of blue and white shirting. Black, red and white are the only colours used in carrying out the design. The black is a stranded cotton, the red is filoselle and the white a mallad [sic] floss. These three differently textured threads add a quality to the work which could not be obtained by the use of all dull threads, or all shiny ones. The flower is worked in chain and satin stitch. The stem is in several rows of plain stitch, and buttonhole stitch in groups of three. Small leaf shapes grouped in two's [sic] follow the line of the main stem on the left, and are worked in black Rumanian stitch. The white leaves on the left of the stem, and in the top left-hand corner, are also in Rumanian stitch. Chain and stem stitch are used for the leaf and scrolls on the left of the design. Groups of spots in the bottom left-hand corner, and top right-hand corner, are detached chain stitches with small stitches radiating from them. The spotted circles are worked in red French knots. To the right of the design is a wavy line in fine stem stitch. Black Vandyke braid forms the pointed border down each side of the design.

'A Panel on Net'
The idea for this panel came from a Rumanian icon painted on glass; a sketch of this will be seen on page 23. In the design of the embroidered panel the mass form of the Virgin is simpler than in the original, and much less detailed. The drooping curves of the figure are further emphasised by the thin curved lines worked in white across the design; stability and dignity are gained by the perpendicular lines in the cross, and masses worked in the background.

The Virgin's head-dress and robe, and the shapes in the background, are closely darned on hexagonal net. The threads of white net give a delightfully broken quality to each mass of colour or not as required. The top left-hand mass has been darned to form diagonal lines, while the mass of the gown has been darned irregularly in order to break up the surface unevenly. The solid darned shape of the head-dress and robe are further broken up by red and blue French knots and detached chain stitches. The chain stitches are worked in a more shiny thread than the rest of the design, to give an added sparkle to the finished effect.

The white cross on the right and the zig-zag border on the left are worked in a thicker thread and stand out in slight relief. The crosses patterning the green shapes in the background are worked in four-legged knots also in the thicker thread. White material cut to the shape of the hands and face is tacked to a greenish fawn background material and then the embroidered net stretched over it. The white curved lines crossing over the design are worked through the net and through the background material, thus serving two purposes – to hold the net and the fawn material together, and to help the design by introducing further white, so that the mass of the white face and hands should not seem too sudden. It will be noticed that the masses produced by close darning have a very different quality from the applied masses in the plate opposite [a bird design on red flannel based on a German tile]. The colours are not dull, but have a certain sombreness which is in keeping with the subject.

APPENDIX 4
GABRIEL MILLET: 'L'ART DECORATIF ET INDUSTRIELS DANS LE ROYAUME SHS 1925'

From: *Exposition Internationale des Arts Décoratifs et Industriels Modernes: Section du Royaume des Serbes, Croates et Slovènes. Catalogue Officiel,* (Paris: Girard et Bunino, 1925), pp. i–v

Visitons l'Exposition. Nous partons des Invalides, nous arrivons au Grand Palais, un peu troublés, par certaines architectures étranges. Nous cherchons une oeuvre solide et bien équilibrée, qui nous repose: prenons à gauche, dépassons les Soviets, arrêtons nous au pavillon yougoslave.

L'extérieur est simple: une cube sévère que la verdure masque et semble adoucir, et, sur l'un de ces murs, nus et clairs, se détache en vigueur un portail de chêne, robuste, une architrave sur des faisceaux de piliers, où le ciseau de M.V. Branis, volontairement fruste, a fait grimper en zigzag un plante géante. Puis nous entrons et nous voilà saisis par les effets d'ombre et de lumière. L'architecte, M.S. Hribar, a su les ménager au moyen de vitraux. Il disposait de vitraux très simples, larges plaques sans modelé. Au centre, dans la pénombre de l'escalier, des tons riches, vert, jaune, sépia, donnent un jour discret. Sur les côtes, au contraire, des couleurs claires et légères, le bleu pâle du ciel, le jaune vert des collines, encore le bleu plus soutenu des personnages, nous font un hall lumineux. Et dans le detail aussi, dans l'éclairage et l'arrangement des vitrines, dans la salle du haut, presque blanche avec sa lumière tamisée, et au Grand Palais et dans cette charmante coupole qui semble faite d'un marbre translucide, partout s'accuse un art consommé de la présentation et de l'effet décoratif.

D'où viennent ces artistes habiles? Quel est donc ce peuple si bien doué? Nos souvenirs d'écoliers ne nous rapportent pas le nom des Yougoslaves. Mais, aux heures d'épreuves, nous avons appris à aimer les Serbes, à admirer leur héroisme, et nous savons que notre victoire commune a réalisé leur rêve, les a réunis, après de longs siècles d'isolement, à leurs frères de race. En effet tous les Slaves qui peuplent le nouveau royaume ont la même origine: leurs dialectes, que les linguistes groupent en trois classes, diffèrent peu les uns des autres. Les Serbes et les Croates se sont donné une même langue littéraire, dont le Slovène se rapproche de plus en plus. Tous vivent sur une même tradition: coutumes, légendes, musique, ornementation se ressemblent. Le célèbre épopée serbe de Kosovo a pénétré jusque dans le Karst, jusque dans les coins les plus reculés du pays yougoslave.

Le passé pourtant leur a laissé son empreinte, à chacun une empreinte particulière, et nous devons observer ces caractères distinctifs, pour bien comprendre le sens et la portée de la présente exposition.

Le relief même du sol les partageait en deux groupes, orientait les uns vers l'Europe centrale et L'Italie, les autres vers Byzance: les uns vers le Catholicisme, les autres vers l'Orthodoxie. Les premiers de bonne heure ont perdu leur indépendance. Dès le IXe siècle, les Slovènes sont opprimeés par les Allemands; en 1102, les Croates s'unissent aux Hongrois; au XVe siècle, les Dalmates deviennent les sujets de Venise. Les Serbes au contraire restent libres et fondent, au XIIIe et au XIVe siècle, un puissant État. Les uns et les autres connurent, au Moyen Age, les bienfaits d'unde haute culture. Les Dalmates et les Serbes nous ont laissé les plus beaux monuments et l'on sait aujourd'hui que les églises serbes, au XIVe siècle, forment le groupe plus riche de l'Orient chrétien. Dans les temps modernes, la Destinée les sépare encore, tous alors subissent la servitude, mais ceux du Nord et de l'Ouest ont des maîtres civilisés et suivent le cours normal de la vie européenne: ils luttent par l'action politique et par l'effort de la pensée. Ceux de l'Est et du Sud, les Serbes, tombent sous les coups de vainqueur barbare et combattent avec le fer et le plomb. Pareille épreuve leur donne d'autres habitudes, d'autres pensées, une autre trempe.

Ces hommes sont des poètes et leurs oeuvres portent le reflet de leur histoire. Aux Serbes, cette vie de combat a donné la noblesse et la magnanimité. Elle a développé en eux le sens de l'épopée. Leurs trouvères célèbrent, sur la guzla, les héros de Kosov avec un art robuste et sobre, qui s'élève aux plus hautes pensées et touche au plus profond des sentiments humains. Les Slovènes, pour défendre leur langue, leurs traditions, leur âme, se sont repliés sur eux-mêmes, ils ont puisé leurs forces dans la profondeur de leur coeur, dans leur foi religieuse, dans l'amour du sol natal. Ils s'abandonnent volontiers au rêve, à la mélancolie, au mysticisme. Leur grand poète, qu'on me dit être le plus grand poéte yougoslave, Fr. Preseren (1800–1849), est un lyrique. Les Croates et les Dalmates, affinés par l'aisance, par les facilités de la vie urbaine, par la culture européenne, aiment le drame et y excellent. Ainsi tous ensemble, unissant leurs forces et leurs dons, font au jeune État yougoslave le plus beau des patrimoines littéraires.

Ils s'unissent aussi pour lui faire un patrimoine artistique, ils apportent chacun leurs spécialités. Les Serbes, avec les Bosniens, ont leurs tapis aux effets puissants et les anciennes techniques byzantines: le filigrane, le cuivre ou l'argent ciselé. Les Slovènes se distinguent par le travail de la dentelle. Les Croates, mieux organisés, ont fait de Zagreb un véritable foyer d'art décoratif. Le grand sculpteur Mestrovic y réside et y exerce son influence. On y travaille le cuir, le bronze, le cuivre et le bois. On y fait de la céramique, on y produit la plus riche et la plus belle des broderies.

Dans tout cet ensemble, nous distinguons une double inspiration: les uns interprètent la tradition nationale et populaire, les autres suivent le courant européen qui les porte vers un art nouveau.

L'ornementation populaire est encore vivante. Elle nous donne ici dentelles (Hvar), des ceintures tissées (Prizren), de la céramique (Sarajevo), des oeufs de Pâques (Ljubljana). Mais, comme partout, elle est menacée par les produits industriels, elle a besoin d'un soutien. Les Yougoslaves, attachés à leur passé, ont fait un bel effort pour conserver aux paysans le goût et le sens de l'art décoratif. Pareille tâche incombait tout d'abord à l'État, à ses écoles, dont les travaux sont exposés au premier étage du Grand Palais, principalement aux Écoles d'arts et métiers (Obrtna skola) et aux écoles professionelles de femmes (Zenska strucna skola) – il s'en trouve dans toutes les grandes villes. – Elle incombait aussi à ses ateliers, surtout à Sarajevo, à la Filature nationale (Drzavna tkaonica i vezionica) et à l'Atelier national des arts appliqués (Zemaljska radionia za umetne zanate). Ce haut devoir de solidarité sollicitait aussi, et surtout, l'initiative privée. Dans toute les grandes villes, les femmes se sont groupées. Voici, à Belgrade, le 'Cercle des soeurs serbes' (Kolo srpskih sestara); à Zagreb et dans d'autres villes croates, 'l'Association pour conserver et répandre l'art populaire croate et les métiers' (Udruga za ocuvanje i promicanje Hvatske pucke umjetnosti i obrta). A Ljubljana, ces bonnes volontés se groupent dans un établissement officiel (Drzavni osrednji zavod za zenski domaci obrt).

Chacune des grandes régions historiques a sa tradition et c'est cette tradition particulière que, dans chacune des grandes villes, les écoles et surtout les associations s'efforcent de conserver et de répandre. Ainsi, le Cercle de Belgrade fait broder les manches pour les paysannes de Kosovo et de Pec. L'Association de Zagreb fait dessiner sur des manteaux de luxe les motifs dont les paysannes de Sisak ornent leurs fichus de mousseline, et les dentelles de Ljubljana sont conçues dans le même esprit. Ainsi va s'accuser une différence très nette entre les produits croates ou slovènes et ceux des Balkans, même de la Dalmatie. Les premiers rappellent les semis de fleurs des tapis persans de Kerman, les autres reproduisent les motifs géométriques ou les fleurons en lignes brisées, légués par Byzance ou par l'Orient. Zagreb s'opposera donc à Belgrade: dans les formes et les couleurs se marqueront les caractères qu'un passé différent a imprimé dans l'âme des hommes.

Les femmes croates ont beaucoup donné, dans presque toutes les vitrines, et notre oeil s'habitue bien vite à reconnaître leur manière. Elles travaillent sur fond blanc et couvent presque entièrement la surface qu'elles se proposent de décorer. Leur dessin est très simplifié. Les fleurs et les branches des tapis persans ont perdu leurs contours précis et ne donnent plus qu'un assemblage de formes rondes, courbes ou sineuses, larges et lourdes. Les couleurs sont aussi simples. L'ensemble est d'un effet riche et plein. D'ordinaire une couleur domine, ave quelques notes différentes qui la font vibrer. Voici deux coussins (Pavillon, nos 240 et 248), d'un même dessin, l'un en jaune d'or, avec un peu de vert-gris et de vieux rose, l'autre en violet pâle, ave du bleu indigo, du vert émeraude et du jaune clair; ou bien encore un châle de crêpe de chine (no. 238), où quelques touches de vert pâle, de jaune d'or ou de bleu indigo adoucissent l'éclat du vermillon foncé. Le chef d'oeuvre du genre est une superbe robe blanche qui a sa vitrine particulière au premier étage du pavillon (no. 216). Dans cette broderie serrée, on se perd à compter les nuances du ton dominant qui est le bleu: bleu pâle, plusieurs bleus gris, bleu ardoise, bleu indigo. Un peu d'or et de rouge ajoutent à l'effet, qui est incomparable.

Les Slovènes tiennent une place discrète, mais
ils laissent un souvenir exquis, celui de leur chambre,
au premier étage du Grand Palais, de leurs meubles
élégants et fermes, taillés en angles, et blancs comme
les admirables dentelles ou les soie brodée du ciel de
lit, des couvertures, des coussins et des déshabillés.
Sur toutes ces étoffes, nous reconnaissons les fleurs
ou les branches stylisées de Croatie. Mais les motifs
sont bien dégagés et produisent une impression
plus ferme.

Venons maintenant à Belgrade. On y préfère
les lignes brisées. Nous y trouvons aussi de beaux
rouges nuancés, mais avec des verts vigoureux qui
font une opposition tranchée (Pavillon, no. 276).
Voici mieux encore: une autre robe de grand style
(no. 275), singulièrement sévère, noir sur blanc. Le
contraste est saisissant. Et ce n'est point un produit
du hasard, une trouvaille heureuse. C'est l'expression
d'une pensée profonde. Passons en effet au Grand
Palais, examinons les tapis, ces tapis aux dessins
anguleux, aux oppositions franches, si différents
de ce que nous montrent, dans la salle voisine,
les marchands d'Anatolie. Il existe deux centres
de fabrication, l'un en Bosnie, l'autre dans la Serbie
orientale: Sarajevo et Pirot. Là, une fabrique d'État,
outillée pour une large production industrielle, ici
des particuliers et le travail à la main. Ceux de Pirot,
plus drus, inusables, sont aussi plus riches et plus
beaux. Ils ont plus d'oppositions et produisent plus
d'effet. L'un d'eux (Palais, no. 162), sur un fond
rouge profond, a des tiges noires et des motifs
bordés de noir. L'autre (Palais, no. 154) est noir
et blanc, comme notre robe: un semis de triangles
blancs tâche le fond noir. Rien de plus émouvant.
Les paysans qui ont conçu ce décor de haut style
semblent porter encore le deuil de Kosovo.

Il y a plus de personnalité dans les fleurs
exotiques, éclatantes – rouge vermillon et jaune
d'or – de Mme Nelly Geiger, plus encore dans la
céramique de M. le professeur T. Krizman, un des
artistes les plus féconds de cette exposition. Celui-ci
nous donne tantôt des vase à fond de couleur ornés
de rinceaux d'or, tantôt des porcelaines blanches ou
un large ruban d'or entoure des bleus ou des roses,
tendres et dêgradés. Le motif complexe, formé de
plantes aux tiges brisées, aux feuilles aigües, parfois
renflées comme celles du décor turc, exprime avec
force, me semble-t-il, l'anxiété douloureuse de notre
âge troublé.

La figure humaine a sa place marquée dans une
exposition d'art décoratif. Mais elle ne sort point
de la tradition populaire. Les Yougoslaves ont, en
fait, une brillante école d'art moderne. Le maître
de cette école, Mestrovic, sur un bouclier de bronze,
a ciselé, avec une rare vigueur d'accent, une frise
antique de cavaliers, de puissantes encolures, des
croupes rebondies, de longues échines pliant sous
les jarrets nerveux. Voici encore, à l'entrée du
Pavillon, un autre oeuvre de style, deux porte-
flambeaux en chêne de Slavonie, semblables à des
Caryatides, où M. Krsinic a sculpté un éphèbe et
une jeune fille, élancés et droits, un peu stylisés
avec leur torse étroit et long et leurs jambes fortes,
mais stylisés par un bel artiste qui a senti la grâce
pénétrante du corps virginal. Ce trait de style, torse
haut, jambes fortes, caractérise aussi les céramiques
vernissées et les bronzes de M. Hinko Juhn (Dans-
euse, Pavillon, no. 62), tandis Mme Radka Sagara,
dans ses cuivres ciselés nous fait parfois songer aux
vases antiques. A toute cette école de Zagreb, qui
cherche, par la stylisation, des formes expressives,
s'oppose le robuste réalisme d'un sculpteur de
Belgrade, M. Palavicini (Maturité, Pavillon, no.
170). Elles s'opposent aussi aux figures de rêves,
légères, insaisissables, dont M.B. Jakac a illustré un
livre de poésie slovène, les 'Pisma' de A. Gradnik.

A bien prendre les choses, cette exposition nous
révèle un centre remarquable d'art décoratif: Zagreb.
Belgrade a produit moins. A Zagreb, ville ancienne,
épargnée par la guerre, revient l'honneur de savoir
embellir la vie des hommes par les grâces d'un art
souple et riche. A Belgrade incombe une tâche plus
haute. Elle a relevé ses ruines. Déjà ses architectes
dessinent le plan de la grande capitale qu'elle sera
demain. Cette immense ville, la Section d'architecture nous la montre en raccourci. Nulle ambition
n'est plus légitime. Le nouveau royaume a reçu des
dieux, enfin cléments, la plus insigne faveur, celle
de commander aux deux grandes artères, celle du
Danube et de la Save, qui viennent s'unir pour
emporter les richesses de la vieille Europe vers
l'Orient. Belgrade est au carrefour, comme
Constantinople fut autrefois, sur la Corne d'Or,
au croisement des routes commerciales de l'ancien
monde. Une brillante destinée l'attend aussi. Dans
le domaine de l'art, Zagreb, aujourd'hui, semble
l'éclipser, comme autrefois, au IVe et au Ve siècle,
Alexandrie et Antioche, vieilles cités, chargées d'un
glorieux héritage, éclispsèrent la ville nouvelle de
Constantin. Mais un jour viendra où les forces art-
istiques qu'elle tient en réserve s'épanouiront à leur
tour en une magnifique floraison.

APPENDIX 5
LENA YOVITCHITCH'S SERBIA

Excerpts from: Lena Yovitchitch, *Pages from Here and There in Serbia* (Belgrade: S.B. Cvijanovich, 1926) [p. nos in brackets]

[79] There is nothing savouring of the commonplace about going to the market in Belgrade. The tremendous abundance; the fine vegetables; the various types of men and women in peasant costume; the kaleidoscopic display of foodstuffs, and every other kind of goods …

Those perhaps seeking in vain for a note of the Orient, or some picturesque touch of the East, will be disappointed with the streets of Belgrade, but in the market place there is all the colour and animation, all the bustle and stir, including the confusion of many voices, which seem at last to fit the picture one looks for in the Balkans. Here are groups of peasants, the women with their bright coloured aprons, sandled feet and curious headdresses …

[80] In the height of the summer and right on to late autumn, the brilliant colourings at the market are worthy of a painter's brush …

[81] The only fear is that the charm of this ancient institution will vanish when it is removed to the new premises. Splendid concrete buildings will replace the quaint old wooden booths, but will that make up for the loss of the picturesque old market?

[82] At present, the shops in Belgrade are undergoing wonderful changes. It is as though a campaign for the general improvement of the shops, – for modern fronts, plate glass windows for the display of goods, and enlarged premises, had swept over the town, involving large and small firms in a great competition and endeavour to realise a higher standard …

[91–93]
'Exhibition of Yugoslav Art in Belgrade 1924'. An exhibition of pictures and sculpture held this winter in Belgrade, marks an epoch in the annals of Yugoslav art. It may be considered as the first exhibition of the kind entirely devoted to the contemporary art of this country, and is a step in the right direction.

Lovers of art in Belgrade have formed a Society under the name of 'Tzvieta Zuzurich', and owing to their efforts, this praiseworthy enterprise has been made possible. In passing, it may be stated that 'Tzvieta Zuzurich' was the name of a beautiful and very talented girl, who lived in Ragusa in the 16th century, and around whom many a sonnet was woven in those days. The present Society is dedicated to her memory and its members gather, as acolytes, at the altar of their ideal.

In organizing this exhibition, the Society had two objects in view. Primarily, they wished, as far as their means would allow, to contribute towards the development of Yugoslav art; to bring it before the public. On the other hand, their aim was to start collecting funds, in order that some day Belgrade might have a permanent art gallery.

The building in which the exhibition was held, served as offices for the Ministry of Foreign Affairs up till a short time ago.* Unfortunately, the rooms are all rather small and do not lend themselves very well to the hanging of pictures, or to the exhibition of sculpture. However, the walls were all covered in grey canvas, which provided an unobtrusive and satisfactory background.

Altogether 202 pictures and sculptures were on view, the work of some 34 artists.

All the world over, one may almost say that artists can be divided into two groups: those who express joy and happiness in a riot of colour, and in rhythm of movement incidental to thought uplifted to reach the glad things of life, or those who seek to portray the tragic problems of every-day existence, in a vague attempt to find a solution to them through their art … However that may be, the pictures under consideration bear witness to a variety of styles. The layman may be pardoned for not understanding modern art, but it is equally mystifying to be confronted by imitations of the old Masters, which give the impression of having been produced at the cost of sacrificing all originality, and fall very far short of the glories of ancient art.

But there are many exhibits which show great talent and augur well for the future. Some wooden panels carved in relief, the work of Thomas Roksandich and Sreten Stoyanovich, are beautiful examples of art inspired by the spark of genius, and wrought according to the traditions of the past.

Among the pieces of sculpture there are many interesting studies. The most prominent in the collection is the figure of a stooping angel, by T. Roksandich, destined for the tomb of a well-known statesman.

Peter Dobrovich has many striking pictures on view, which attract attention on account of their straightforwardness and depth. One or two paintings depict incidents from the War, and have an interest on their own, apart from their artistic value. But this brief account is far from intended to criticise, in any way, the works of art at the exhibition, which were indeed presumption for anyone outside the 'magic circle' of artists.

Previous to the exhibition being opened to the public, a private view-day was held, and the most distinguished members of Belgrade society assembled for the occasion. A number of foreigners and representatives of various countries were also present.

At the end of February the picture gallery was closed, and it may be considered to have been a great success.

This house belonged to Mr Yovan Ristitch, twice Regent, Prime Minister, Statesman, Historian under the Obrenovitch dynasty.

[99] An important section of the Ethnographical Museum is set aside for the exhibition of national dress. The costumes are representative of all parts of the kingdom; they come from Bosnia, Hertzegovina, Croatia, Dalmatia, Montenegro, Banat, Old Serbia etc. There is striking variety among them, and all are most picturesque. Some of the costumes have already fallen into disuse, and one regretfully realises that, sooner or later, with the advance of progress, they are bound to disappear althogether. Alas! Progress so often deprives us of things that are really beautiful.

[100] Weaving done on hand looms, and embroidery, are the chief industries among the Serbian peasant women. The perfect workmanship, and the beauty of the colourings and designs, of the old embroideries exhibited at the museum, prove this branch of needlework to have been made into a fine art.

[105] The National Museum in Belgrade includes a picture gallery, containing works of art from the 17th and 18th centuries. Among them are some fine portraits and a number of pictures dealing with historical subjects. The Yugoslav sculptor, Ivan Mestrovitch, who began life as a peasant lad and climbed the ladder of fame, has presented several of his statues to the museum. Although the majority of them are plaster casts, they are good examples of his style of art and are a valuable asset.

[112–113] Belgrade … Beograd – White City, – Town of Contrasts is thy name! There are no half measures here; only the two extremes: it is the law of opposites which prevails, *and triumphs*, and can be traced in all that concerns the Serbs.

Fashionable civilians, and officers in their smart uniforms, rub shoulders with the peasant in his home-spun clothes; luxurious motor cars drive side by side with the ox-cart; giant modern buildings tower above the quaintest little houses in striking incongruity. Thus new and old, high and low, rich and poor, all mingle together, forming a 'tout ensemble' which can only be appreciated by those who have some inkling of Serbia's history.

[135] … we passed numbers of peasants, sometimes on foot, sometimes on donkeys or ponies, all making for Peć, for tomorrow was market day. In Old Serbia it is quite the exception to see western clothes, and there is something very novel and delightful about being in the midst of a people who all wear national dress. The costumes are very rich and picturesque, varying according to the districts. Men, women and children, including donkeys, oxen and ponies, carry an amulet in the shape of a blue bead. This is adopted in order to ward off the evil eye, still firmly believed in by these simple folk.

[138] Distaff and spindle accompany the women wherever they go. As they gossip with each other, or trudge along the high road, they are forever spinning wool, afterwards to be woven into materials on hand looms. The process is slow and laborious, but all the apparel of the peasants is produced solely by these means. Hand woven garments (luckily for the women!) last for many a year, and no upsetting fashions disturb these good folk.

No western clothes mar the harmony of the scene in Southern Serbia, for one and all wear national dress, which is very fascinating to the eye of the stranger. On market days, the costumes are particularly gorgeous – rich both in colouring and design, supplying subjects for 'pictures' in legion enough to rejoice the heart of any artist.

[158–159] Now and again, high up in the hills [author: on the way to 'Kosieritch'], we would spy small groups of houses, forming what are known as 'Zadrugas'. There is no exact equivalent for this word in English; a 'Zadruga' is a kind of settlement where several generations live together under one jurisdiction, the domain being handed down from father to son. These large family communities live contentedly together, working on the land or looking after the cattle. We noticed the peasants, both men and women, in their white homespun clothes, bending to their task in the fields. They all work in a row, as though to emphasize their system of co-operation. Some of the women were spinning wool by the wayside, looking very picturesque and far removed from modern civilization.

Excerpts from: Lena Yovitchitch,
Yugoslavia (London: A. & C. Black, 1928)
[p. nos in brackets]

[7–9] Belgrade, the capital of Serbia, has been
completely rebuilt within the last eight or nine
years. Strangers who knew the place long ago
cannot recognise it to-day.

The city was heavily bombarded and set on
fire during the European War, so that when the
inhabitants eventually returned to their homes they
found nothing but a heap of ruins. Some of the
houses which had escaped, as though by a miracle,
from being shattered to pieces, had been emptied
of all their contents. Furniture, linen, pots and pans,
everything of any use, had been carried off by the
enemy. The shops had not a thing left in them, and
consequently there was nothing to be had for love
or money. In those days you were lucky if you could
buy sewing-cotton by the yard! People went about
in strange garments made out of blankets or old
curtains. Belgrade was like a dead city. Everyone
seemed dazed and unequal to grappling with the
situation …

However, the need to make the place habitable
was so great that building quickly became the city's
chief concern …

The inhabitants of new Belgrade now erected
huge tenements, five or six floors high… Building is
still going on apace … I have heard Belgrade called
'The Concrete City', which is a rather descriptive
name for it…

Serbs do not go for long walks in the country
as one may do in England. They go out for a little
stroll in the evening, when the *corso*, or principal
street, is thronged with an animated crowd, all
bent on taking some exercise and meeting friends.
Everyone is dressed in the latest fashion, and ladies
use quite as much, if not more, powder and paint
than in Paris. The feminine mind is taken up with
the question of clothes to about the same extent as
the masculine mind is absorbed by politics. Women
spend a great deal of time and money on dress-
makers, and in the buying of beautiful materials,
silk stockings, dainty shoes and such like. They
would rather go without other things than be
behind in fashion. From this you must not think
that they are empty-headed. Far from it. At the
Belgrade University there are nearly as many girls
as young men studying for various careers.

[13] The peasants make very little distinction
between clothes for children and for grown-up
people. Tiny tots are dressed like miniature men
and women and look very quaint sometimes …

In Serbia there are neither very rich nor very
poor people, and class distinction does not exist
as in other countries. This is an agricultural land,
and the educated peasant can rise to practically
any position.

[19–22] A girl's life in Serbia is quite different from
that of a boy. For one thing, women are not put on
the same level as men, and the education of [author:
peasant] girls has been sadly neglected. Given no
opportunity to better herself, the Serbian woman
has up till now resignedly accepted this unfair state
of things, but the day of her awakening is not far
off. Energetic women have founded societies in
order to try to obtain emancipation for their sisters
in this country. It will no doubt take time before
results can be expected, but the work has begun
and will surely succeed in the end …

From their earliest days girls are imbued with the
idea of domesticity, and brought up to prepare for
marriage as their only aim in life. The great necessity
for a girl is to be a good housewife – to know how to
cook and sew, how to sweep and dust and to be able
to do every kind of work in the house. If, including
all this, she can paint a little and do embroidery, she
has all the qualities that could possibly be wished for.
While still a child she begins to prepare things for
her 'bottom drawer', so that when the time comes
for marriage her trousseau is ready…

At the end of the day the Serbian woman enjoys
a good gossip with her neighbour across the way.
She takes her knitting with her, and all the time
she is talking her needles fly in and out; socks and
stocking must be supplied for all the family, which
always keeps mothers and daughters busy.

When they are through with their work, young
girls love to tidy themselves up and go for a stroll
down the village street …

[23–24]
'A Sketch of Life in Macedonia or Old Serbia'
To make a trip into Old Serbia is to find yourself
suddenly transported into a world which you have
hitherto only seen in pictures. It is to be in the
heart of the Orient, where all the charm of the
East is undisturbed by Western civilisation.

The people in this land all wear national dress,
and travellers in modern clothes seem quite out of
place and attract the attention of the natives. Most
of the towns and villages down south can only be
reached by carriage or motor transport, for there
is but one short railway line in the whole district.
Consequently these folk live quite in a world of
their own, cut off from outside influences and
events. This explains their simple, indeed primitive
way of living, and how it is that they still wear the
picturesque clothes of their forefathers. They are
entirely dependent upon what they can produce
with their own hands. The materials out of which
their garments are made are all woven on hand
looms, and afterwards beautifully embroidered
by hand. You would be surprised at the fineness
of the embroidery done by the women in these
parts. They do not grudge time or trouble, but the
costumes worn here last for generations. This is
fortunate for the women, who spend long winter

days making and stitching these works of art.

The colouring of the landscape in Old Serbia, combined with the picturesque costumes, somehow reminds one of biblical scenes, as depicted on canvas by the brush of an artist. It is perhaps the absence of all modern inventions, the perfect simplicity and extraordinary dignity of the natives, which put one in mind of pictures from the Old Testament or the New.

Travelling in this country, one frequently passes men and women on the road whose striking carriage cannot fail to attract attention. You will see women on their way to market, carrying a bundle balanced on their head, and as they walk along their fingers are busy with spindle and distaff. You will see men leading stout black water buffaloes, harnessed to primitive carts with wooden axles. Or, again, you will come across a caravan of peasants, trudging alongside their donkeys or mules laden with brushwood. Sometimes, at the end of the day, the owners straddle their beasts of burden and ride home on them at a trot. Wherever you look, there is a picture.

[31–33] 'Zagreb'

In all Croatia, Zagreb is the greatest centre for trade and business. It is likewise the home of many well-known artists, sculptors and writers, who live in a secluded world of their own …

In the lower part of the town is a fine square, named after Ban Jelačić, with a statue of the famous governor of Croatia erected in the middle. This is the most picturesque spot in Zagreb, for it is also where the chief market is held. The little stalls, decked with fruit and vegetables, are each surmounted by a huge white umbrella, which acts as a protection against rain or sunshine. On Sundays and holidays the peasants all come bustling into market in their national dress, and there is a splendid display of gay colourings and wonderful designs in men's and women's clothing. You would smile to see the men in very wide trousers of white homespun cotton material, some looking as if they were accordion pleated! Others are clad in sheepskin cloaks, which reach from top to toe and are very bulky and voluminous. No doubt these wraps must be very warm and delightful in winter, but I have always wondered how the wearer does not suffocate when the collars are turned up, covering the mouth and nose, with only the eyes peeping over the top. And it is very strange that these cloaks should be worn in summer *and* winter, you must admit! The Croatian peasant women wear very attractive costumes. They usually have huge, billowy sleeves, like sails, of white cotton, and pretty coloured ribbons float from their aprons which half cover the wide pleated skirt beneath.

APPENDIX 6
ETHEL MAIRET'S BALKAN WEAVING

From: Ethel Mairet, *Hand-Weaving To-Day: Traditions and Changes* (London: Faber & Faber, 1936), pp. 52–54 [1949 edition]

In almost every country there is still some peasant weaving. Though it is rapidly dying out the tradition still survives and in many countries it is being carried over into modern work. The most cultured peasant weaving of Europe is found in Jugoslavia, especially in the intricate and restrained work of the south – in Macedonia. The Balkan countries are the frontier between Asia and Europe and they have kept the qualities native to frontier countries. From early times the culture and civilization of Greece, Egypt, and the East have reached Europe through the Balkans. In the remote valleys of these southern countries an aesthetic understanding and a technical quality of weaving has been preserved that has not been reached anywhere else in Europe. There is a restraint and simplicity of design and colour with an understanding of material which is unsurpassed. There is also a comprehension of the aesthetic born of long ages of struggle – the instinctive acceptance and knowledge of beauty

as a necessity. Where this southern weaving technique was evolved is only to be conjectured. In its designs it is reminiscent of early Crete and Egypt and probably was left in these remote valleys of the south when influences from farther East came into Europe through the Balkan countries.

Peasant weaving is usually very simple, relying on stripe effects and tapestry technique, done on the simplest of looms, with a hard-wearing quality. The best local materials are employed and colour is strictly limited – often only two or three colours, white and red as in Croatia, white and blue as in some early Swedish weaving, very brightly striped materials as in Estonian skirts, tapestry woven aprons as in Dalmatia. Only direct colouring with very few colours and no shading. The quality is always good and the design always simple. In the Macedonian weaving there is a different quality from the ordinary European peasant weaving. It has the qualities of both East and West; the intricate delicate design with incredible technique (entirely un-European) is expressed with great restraint of colour. It is comparable only to the finest weaving of India and the Far East.

NOTES

Introduction

1. Henceforth, where appropriate and in order to avoid confusion, I use preferred first names rather than surnames to identify the Newberys. Fra was commonly used by Francis, though to Jessie, and presumably close acquaintances, he was Frank.

2. As Jessie Rowat, Jessie had enrolled as a student at the Glasgow School of Art in the same year as Fra took up his appointment, i.e. 1885 (see George Rawson's publications, for eg his *Francis Henry Newbery and the Glasgow School of Art*, PhD thesis, University of Glasgow, 1996, p. 134). Her life dates are 1864–1948, his 1855–1946. Concerning Jessie, see Liz Arthur, 'Jessie Newbery', in Jude Burkhauser (ed.), *Glasgow Girls: Women in Art and Design 1880–1920* (Edinburgh: Canongate, 1990), pp. 147–151.

3. Margaret H. Swain, 'Mrs J.R. Newbery 1864–1948', *Embroidery*, vol. 24, no. 4, 1973, p. 105. Ailsa Tanner has confirmed Jessie's interests, noting that 'throughout her life she collected textiles from Italy, Russia, and the Balkans', 'Glasgow Girls (*act.* 1880–1920)', *Oxford Dictionary of National Biography*, Oxford University Press, 2004; online edition, January 2010, at http://www.oxforddnb.com/view/article/73660 (accessed 31 August 2017).

4. The exhibition ran from 28 January to 14 March 1931. A black-and-white photograph of *Serbian Women* introduced the exhibition to readers of (presumably) the Glasgow newspaper *The Bulletin and Scots Pictorial*, 29 January 1931. See copy in *Glasgow School of Art Press Cuttings*, 1927–1932, p. 222 (Glasgow School of Art archives). The headline of the notice ran 'Serbian Women seen through an Artist's Eyes'. It may also have been exhibited at the Royal Glasgow Institute in the autumn of that year, as *Serbian Folk* (see below).

5. 'Guthrie Pictures. Paisley Art Institute. Annual Exhibition', *The Scotsman*, 28 January 1931, p. 15.

6. Private collection. Emphasis in bold mine. See appendix 1 for transcriptions of all known relevant letters and postcards sent by Jessie and Fra in the 1920s and early 1930s. The first letter is to Elsie, the second to Mary. Elsie (Margaret Elliot) Newbery [*married*: Lang] (1890–1977) and Mary Newbery [*married*: Sturrock] (1892–1985). The reference to Alick is to Mary's husband, the painter Alick Riddell Sturrock. The reference to 'Rodier' fabric implies a material and style connection with the French fashion house Rodier, which in the 1920s was renowned for its invention and experimentation, based on tradition, not least those of the French colonies.

7. While widely recognised as Yugoslavia (land of Southern Slavs), until 3 October 1929 the official name of the country was the Kingdom of Serbs, Croats and Slovenes.

8. J. Gleeson White, 'Some Glasgow Designers and Their Work – iii', *The Studio: An Illustrated Magazine of Fine and Applied Art*, vol. 12, no. 55, October 1897, p. 48. White's essay comprises an important contemporary appreciation of Jessie's artistry, and includes extensive quotations from her concerning her design 'beliefs', which may be considered her creed (see appendix 2 and chapter 7).

9. Fra. H. Newbery, 'An Appreciation of the Work of Ann Macbeth', *The Studio: An Illustrated Magazine of Fine and Applied Art*, vol. xxvii, no. 115, October 1902, pp. 40–41. This article, which is included in appendix 2, can be taken as Fra's creed (see chapters 3 and 7).

10. Concerning Newbery's early Glasgow masques, see George Rawson, *Francis Henry Newbery and the Glasgow School of Art*, PhD thesis, University of Glasgow, 1996, pp. 268–272. Despite the gendering in Newbery's statement he was a successful advocate for advancement in the arts by both sexes (see chapter 7).

11. The Mackintoshes visited the Newberys in Dorset in 1920, i.e. very soon after the Newberys had moved to Corfe Castle on the Isle (peninsula) of Purbeck.

12. Without mentioning any of our artists or the Balkans, Kassia St Clair has recently drawn attention to the intrinsic value of fabric creation for human culture. Her examination of practices and languages of spinning and weaving means that she understands not just the material importance of the transfiguration of fibres into thread but also the 'blessing' and 'blight' of the 'age-old kinship between women and cloth', as well as the 'interwoven' character of linguistic and textile communication: 'The words "text" and "textile" share a common ancestor: the Latin "*texere*", to weave. Similarly, "*fabrica*" – something skilfully produced – birthed both "fabric" and "fabricate" … The language of textiles is like the ticking of a clock in a room: inescapable once noticed … From language to fairy tales, technology and social relations, our lives are woven through with the threads of fabric production.' Kassia St Clair, *The Golden Thread: How Fabric Changed*

History (London: John Murray, 2019), pp. 13–18.
13. Mira Crouch, 'Death and Images of Womanhood and Manhood: The Case of Serbian Epic Poetry', in Asa Kasher (ed.), *Dying and Death: Inter-Disciplinary Perspectives* (Amsterdam, New York: Rodopi, 2007), p. 54. Through her analysis of Serbian epic poetry's female/male distinctions Crouch elucidates and anticipates the wider gender roles that are a main concern of this book, with the distaff (female) side possessing an often under-appreciated fundamentality which acts as a contrasting counterpart to the otherwise more conspicuous, intermittent doings of the spear (male) side.
14. Fanny S. Copeland, *The Women of Serbia* (London: Kossovo Day Committee/Faith Press, 1916), p. 16. Concerning Edinburgh-raised Copeland (1872–1970) and her Yugoslav vocation, see Richard Clarke, Marija Anteric, 'Fanny Copeland and the Geographical Imagination', *Scottish Geographical Journal*, vol. 127, no. 3, 2011, pp. 163–192.
15. Copeland, op. cit., pp. 3, 8, 12.
16. Srgjan Pl. Tucić (Fanny S. Copeland, trans.), *The Slav Nations* (London: Hodder & Stoughton, 1915), pp. 190–191.
17. Clarke, Anteric, op. cit., p. 171; Eric Percival, 'Fanny Susan Copeland 1872–1970', *The Copeland Family*, at https://www.ericpercival.co.uk/Copeland/Fanny%20Copeland.htm (accessed 20 August 2020); J.L. Flanner, 'Meet the People: Fanny Copeland – Linguist, Alpinist, Promoter of Slovenia & Resident of Hotel Slon, *Total Slovenia News*, 4 February 2019, at https://www.total-slovenia-news.com/meet-the-people/2980-meet-the-people-fanny-copeland-linguist-alpinist-promotor-of-slovenia-resident-of-hotel-slon (accessed 20 August 2020). The architecture in the background of the Copeland photograph suggests Zagreb, Croatia, rather than Ljubljana.

Chapter 1 | **Interweaving**

1. Conversation with Mirjana Menković, Director, and Vjera Medić, Senior Curator, at the Ethnographic Museum in Belgrade, 15 March 2017; and cf. H. Th. Bossert, *Volkskunst in Europa* (Berlin: Verlag Ernst Wasmuth, 1926), plate 85. Concerning the term 'Old Serbia', see below.
2. Concerning Macedonian, Serbian and Croatian national (and urban) dress, see, for example: Angelina Krsteva, *Macedonian Folk Embroidery* (Skopje: Institute of Folklore, 1975); Jasna Bjeladinović, *Serbian Ethnic Dress in the Nineteenth and Twentieth Centuries* (Belgrade: Ethnographic Museum, 2011); and relevant entries in Joanne B. Eicher, Djurdja Bartlett, *Berg Encyclopedia of World Dress and Fashion: East Europe, Russia, and the Caucasus*, vol. 9 (London, 2011), pp. 460–473, 509–533, 100–140. Names for the clothing items vary from region to region, hence those given here, while common, should not be considered as wholly standard.
3. Diane Waller, *Textiles from the Balkans* (London: British Museum Press, 2010), pp. 11–12.
4. The back of the postcard indicates that Jessie wrote it (not mentioning Zara) on 11 October 1929 while further down the Dalmatian coast, in Split (which, despite her calling it by its Italian name, Spalato, was then part of the Kingdom of Yugoslavia). This and four other postcards discussed below were discovered and scanned by Ilay Cooper, Dunshay Manor, Dorset. Their whereabouts are now unknown. Ilay Cooper, email correspondence with author, 9 March 2017 and 16 July 2021. Mary Spencer Watson's dates are 1913–2006.
5. Surviving hand-tinted versions of the postcard; available at various internet sites, e.g. https://deutsche-schutzgebiete.de/wordpress/projekte/oesterreich-ungarn/oesterreich/dalmatien/zara (accessed 27 May 2020) show the embroidery as mainly red, while the skirts and apron vary between being predominantly green and predominantly red.
6. The 'Carretto', 'Piana dei Greci' and King William II cards have been passed down to the Newberys' descendants.
7. This card was published by Carrère, a Rodez printer and bookshop.
8. The dog in question was a seventeenth-century hunting hound. Stuffed and dressed in its armour and fine trappings it was mounted on a pedestal in the Royal Armory. Early twentieth-century postcards of its 'proud', 'pet'-like, bearing existed: see, for example, 'armadura para perro de caza'; at http://ceres.mcu.es/pages/SimpleSearch?index=true (accessed 22 July 2021). Jessie's Spanish cards to the Spencer Watsons were found, and scanned, by Ilay Cooper.
9. The painting remains in the Museo Nacional del Prado, Madrid and is dated *c.*1665. Working

closely with her daughter, Hilda Spencer Watson (1879–1952) was an exceptional performance artist, dancer and producer. She established her own barn-style theatre at her Dunshay Manor home, five kilometres from Corfe, in late 1929, having previously located it on the nearby coast at Studland and Swanage in the 1920s. She was also a regular performer on stages across southern England; see Ilay Cooper, *Purbeck Arcadia: Dunshay Manor and the Spencer Watsons* (Wimborne Minster: Dovecote Press, 2015). Fra's high appreciation of the Spencer Watsons and his patronage of their performance art is witnessed in a letter from 1931 where he not only refers to Hilda as 'Gentilissima Madonna' but to the 'genius' of both mother and daughter (see appendix 1).

10. On their reverse the cards have the caption 'Union Postale Universelle. Carte Postale' accompanied by Japanese *kanji* characters and a patterned border that dates them to between 1898 and 1912.

11. Fra and Jessie also purchased original *ukiyo-e* prints, at least five of their collection being handed down to successive Newbery generations. Four of the five are full-figure close-ups of women in beautiful dress, while the fifth features four women, a man (possibly Urashima Tarō) and a turtle within a landscape. Four very similar *ukiyo-e* prints survive from Mary Spencer Watson's collection, though whether Fra and Jessie were instrumental in her acquiring these is unknown (information courtesy of Toby Wiggins).

12. Concerning the development of Górale costume and music, see chapters 5 and 9 in Jan Gutt-Mostowy, *Podhale: A Companion Guide to the Polish Highlands* (New York: Hippocrene Books, 1998), pp. 47–53 and 87–95.

13. See Peyton Skipwith, 'The Early Years', in Annette Ratuszniak et al., *Mary Spencer Watson: Sculpture* (Salisbury: R&R Publications, 2004), p. 56.

14. The cards were published by Drava, Zagreb. Kirin (1894–1963) was based in London for several years after the First World War. During that period he worked as a graphic artist, illustrating, among others, Oscar Wilde, Edgar Allan Poe and Ivana Brlić-Mažuranić, the last's *Croatian Tales of Long Ago* appearing in English (London: George Allen & Unwin) from 1922. It is, therefore, not impossible that the Newberys knew of him before arriving in Zagreb in 1929.

15. Published in 1926. The original watercolour reproduced on the card is signed by Tomerlin, with the place indicated as Saint Simeon (Sv. Šimun), this being a church and its parish in the southern Medvednica foothills, a few kilometres north of Zagreb in the vicinity of Šestine and Gračane. Tomerlin (1892–1981) had studied painting at the Prague Academy of Arts. He settled in Zagreb from 1921, dedicating himself to local landscape and folklore subjects.

16. Tomerlin's example in this range hints at the wide scope for a separate study on the subject.

17. Another card in the set shows Vanka's similarly stylised *Blessing of the Grain* (Blagoslov žita), its fulsome rustic-peasant Catholic imagery being complemented by the ribboned motto 'To Us the Field Yields More' (Da bi nam, polje rodilo bolje). Both cards are dated 1928. Vanka's dates are 1889–1963. He died in Mexico, having emigrated to the USA in 1935.

18. Oil on canvas, 180 x 205 cm, Old City Hall, Zagreb.

19. Vukomerec is six kilometres east of Zagreb city centre.

20. Berger (1858–1934) exhibited his wares at international exhibitions, including in London (e.g. 1908). He promoted his products by way of publishing his own company picture postcards and magazine advertisements featuring women in national dress and, often, spinning fibre. Such an advertisement is seen here – a half-page in *The Studio* magazine's special-edition book *Peasant Art in Austria and Hungary* (ed. Charles Holme, 1911, p. vi).

21. Sertić's life dates are 1899–1986. A graduate of the painting department of Zagreb Academy of Fine Arts, she worked for the Ethnographic Museum until 1959, being acting director 1939–41.

22. Borelli's watercolour is dated 1928, the card being published by S. Marković, Zagreb, 1929. Zoe Borelli Vranski-Alačević lived 1888–1980.

23. H. Th. Bossert, *Volkskunst in Europa* (Berlin: Verlag Ernst Wasmuth, 1926), p. x.

24. A.S. Levetus, 'Austria' and 'Croatia and Slavonia' in Charles Holme (ed.), *Peasant Art in Austria and Hungary* (London: The Studio, 1911), pp. 1–14 and 51–54.

25. Ibid., pp. 3–6.

26. Ibid., pp. 9–10, 52–54.

27. The postcards are reproduced among the digitised Rojc documents of the Croatian Academy of Science and Art, at https://dizbi.hazu.hr/a/?pc=i&id=93744 (accessed 5 June 2020). They bear witness to Rojc's affiliation with the 'Zagreb Colourful School' initiated by Vlaho Bukovac in the late nineteenth century. Rojc's dates are 1883–1964. Her father, Milan Rojc, was a prominent Croatian lawyer and politician, a member of the Croatian-Serbian Coalition who twice served as head of the Department of Religious Affairs and Education in Zagreb. In his second term (1917–20) his advocacy led to the establishment of several higher education institutions as well as Zagreb's Ethnographic Museum. Rojc was brought up on the family estate at Gudovac, central Croatia and at a private girls' school in Graz. At Gudovac she played an active part in the physical labour of agriculture. She enjoyed a long artistic training, in Zagreb, Vienna, Munich and Dachau, as a result of which she became a highly proficient and stylistically eclectic painter as well as a sculptor and photographer.

28. Rojc played an active role in Zagreb's art

societies, including, in 1928, founding the Zagreb
Fine Art and Women Artists' Clubs. Having
designed her own studio house in Zagreb around
1919, from the early 1920s her partner was Alexandrina Onslow, who had arrived in the Balkans to
work for the Scottish Women's Hospitals for Foreign
Service during the First World War. Together with
Onslow, Rojc visited Britain for a number of extended stays during the 1920s. Based at Stratfield
Saye Rectory near Reading, the couple explored a
great deal of the British Isles while Rojc continued
to maintain her artistic relations with Croatia. She
exhibited sixty works (paintings and sculptures)
at Gieves Art Gallery, London, in 1926. As with
Kirin and Vanka one may speculate whether the
Newberys were acquainted in some way with Rojc.
29. The card of the Sokobanja girl was published
by Rajković & Ćuković, a pioneering Serbian
bookshop, publishing house and printer of the
era (with a particular renown for its advance of
textbooks and children's titles). Šantel's card was
one of a set depicting Yugoslav dress, published
by Edition Čaklović, Zagreb, in the 1920s. Šantel
(1883–1945) was a versatile Slovenian artist, violinist,
composer and teacher.
30. Iosif Berman (1892–1941) was a Romanian
Jewish photographer renowned for his images
of Romanian life that appeared in numerous
newspapers and journals of the era.
31. The use of the term 'spinster' in this book is,
in keeping with its reinvention-of-tradition thread,
to allow that which has become regarded as archaic
to reacquire its original denotation in order to move
forward afresh once more. Hence spinster means
a girl or woman who spins yarn. It has nothing to
do with its corrupted modern, often derogatory,
signifying of an unmarried woman.
32. Concerning Denis Galloway (1878–1957),
see publications by Tekla Tötszegi, e.g.: *Satul
tradiţional văzut prin obiectivul lui Denis Galloway
(Transilvania, Partium, Banat, Bucovina)* (Cluj-
Napoca: Edition Argonaut, 2008). Galloway was
to live in Romania until 1950, when he returned
to London. The Ethnographic Museum of
Transylvania holds an extensive archive of his work.
33. Concerning the concept of fractals as applied to
the anthropology of art, see chapter 6 and Alfred
Gell, *Art and Agency: An Anthropological Theory*
(Oxford: Clarendon Press, 1998), pp. 137–140.
34. George Oprescu, *Peasant Art in Roumania*
(London: The Studio Ltd, 1929), p. 65. The Romanian
art historian George Oprescu (1881–1969), was then
secretary of the League of Nations' International
Committee on Intellectual Cooperation. He possessed a great collection of Romanian folk textile
art, much of it reproduced in his *Studio* volume.
35. Reproduced in L.W. Rochowanski, *Columbus in
der Slovakei* (Bratislava: Eosverlag, 1936), opp. p. 380.
The watercolour was in the collection of educationalist Rudolf Kratochvil, Bratislava. Having trained in

Prague, Jan Hála (1890–1959) settled permanently
in Važec, just south of the Tatra mountains, in 1923.
The village was almost totally razed to the ground
by a fire in 1931. Hence by the time of publication,
Hála's *Woman from Važec, Spinning* was, for all its
representation of long-standing rural type, already
an essay on the fragile existence of folk culture.
36. The card was a New Year's greeting card, one of
'McIan's Highland Series' published in Great Britain
by D.B. & S. Robert Ronald McIan (1803–1856)
wasa Scottish actor, artist and nationalist based
in London for much of his professional career.

Chapter 2
Materialising Balkanic Dorset and more

1. A.S. Levetus, 'Croatia and Slavonia', in Charles
Holme (ed.), *Peasant Art in Austria and Hungary*,
(London: The Studio, 1911), p. 54.
2. George Rawson, *Fra H. Newbery: Artist and Art
Educationist* (Glasgow: Foulis Press of Glasgow
School of Art, 1996), p. 18.
3. For a visual survey of most of these, and other
Newbery paintings, see https://artuk.org/discover/
artworks/search/actor:newbery-francis-henry-1855
1946/page/2 (accessed 10 June 2020). The most
detailed and useful research into Newbery has
been conducted by George Rawson. See Rawson,
*Francis Henry Newbery and the Glasgow School of
Art*, PhD thesis, University of Glasgow, 1996; *Fra
H. Newbery: Artist and Art Educationist*, op. cit.; and
Fra H. Newbery: A Dorset Artist (Bridport: Bridport
Heritage Forum, 2008). *My Lady Greensleeves* is a
portrait of Jessie.
4. Margaret Swain, 'Mrs Newbery's Dress', *Costume*,
vol. 12, no. 1, 1978, pp. 64–73. Significantly, Swain
found out about the dress having seen it first in
Fra's *Daydreams* (ibid., p. 73).
5. Ibid., pp. 69–71.
6. The whereabouts of the painting are currently
unknown. Anna (1870–1961), wife of architect and
design reformer Hermann Muthesius, had moved
to London in 1896 when her husband was appointed
cultural attaché at the German Embassy. Thereafter the couple established strong links with the
progressive leaders of the Glasgow School of Art.
In 1904 Anna gave birth to her son Eckart, whose
two godfathers became Fra Newbery and his
designer for the new building of the Glasgow
School of Art, Charles Rennie Mackintosh.
7. The painting was shown at the summer exhibition
of the Munich Secession in 1903. It was owned by
Muthesius.
8. Swain observed that Muthesius 'is shown wearing
a dress of Batik-printed cotton material in blues and
greens – an unheard-of material at that time for a
European dress, but in line with her taste for unusual
design in materials'. She also noted the painting was
created at Walberswick, Suffolk, where the Newberys often spent their summers. See Swain, 'Mrs

Newbery's Dress', op. cit., pp. 68 and 73.

9. A painting which Fra then titled *Serbian Folk* was shown at the Royal Glasgow Institute annual exhibition, which opened on 1 October 1931. The work has not been traced, leaving the possibility that it could also be *Serbian Women*. Rawson has indicated that when shown at Paisley, *Serbian Women* was priced at £75, while *Serbian Folk* in Glasgow was £150 (unpublished *Catalogue of Newbery's Paintings*, 1931 entry). Whether this indicates two different works or that Fra toyed with title and price remains unclear. In any case, *Serbian Women* remained unsold – an indication, perhaps, of Fra being 'out-of-step' with the market (no bad thing).

10. Rawson (from Mary Spencer Watson), *Francis Henry Newbery*, op. cit., pp. 284 and 301.

11. I am grateful to Vesna Zorić of the Ethnographic Museum, Zagreb, Vlasta Sabić of the Museum of Slavonia, Osijek, and Mirjana Menković and Vjera Medić of the Ethnographic Museum in Belgrade, for help in identifying Brynley's costume.

12. Brynley (1902–1981) lived with his partner, baritone Norman Notley, at Little Woolgarston Cottage. The painting was first exhibited as *A Serbian Musician* at the Royal Glasgow Institute exhibition in late 1928, yet when it moved to the Paisley Art Institute in early 1929 it was given the title *David*. Brynley made amateur films of Corfe life in the 1930s, fragments of which appear on 'Corfe Castle, Its Life and Its People in 1937', *Purbeck on Film*, DVD (Windrose Rural Media Trust, 2018). The film is accompanied by Mary Spencer Watson's commentary and features the Corfe society of which the Newberys were an integral part.

13. A very similar example of the budding circle motif is reproduced in H. Th. Bossert, *Volkskunst in Europa* (Berlin: Verlag Ernst Wasmuth, 1926), plate LXXXIV, where it is described (p. 20) as marking the lower hem of the back of a woman's jacket of loden cloth from Graněsina village, ten kilometres northeast of Zagreb. The jacket was in the collection of the Zagreb Ethnographic Museum.

14. Anon., 'Art and the Crafts. Scottish Artists' Society Exhibition', *Aberdeen Press and Journal*, 15 December 1928, p. 4.

15. An image of *Lucy* can be found in the Archive and Image Library of 'Peter Nahum At The Leicester Galleries', at https://leicestergalleries.com/archive (accessed 30 November 2021).

16. The darkness of the painting in the background and the fact that it is obscured by the woman and her distaff makes identification difficult. Its horizontal 'landscape' format, ornate gilded frame and smudges of a seemingly seated pair of figures, suggest a genre scene. The Newbery family have preserved one of Fra and Jessie's gate-leg tables and the jug. The latter has the date 1912 prominently moulded onto its face

above a sprig of green leaves. Descendants of Fra and Jessie believe it was brought back to Dorset from one of their Balkan trips.

17. Fra designed and published a detailed programme of the event: Newbery, *Sanctus: Edwardus. West: Saxonum. Rex: Martyr* [1927] (copy in Corfe Castle Town Trust collection). It contained the full order of proceedings, names and roles of participants, plus the lyrics of Fra's three songs and four orations. See also Rawson, *Francis Henry Newbery*, op. cit., pp. 288–289.

18. This hypothesis was suggested to me by George Rawson, email correspondence, 7 March 2017.

19. The church is now known as the Church of the Holy Spirit and St Edward.

20. For a close analysis of the commission, as realised by Fra, Jessie and their assistant Neil Thomas, between 1924 and 1930, see Rawson, *Francis Henry Newbery*, op. cit., pp. 285–291 and 299–301. Rawson notes 'it forms the most complete decorative scheme produced by him, rendered even more significant by the fact that he was architect of the sanctuary that included it and that Jessie also had a share in the work' (ibid., p. 285).

21. Concerning potential references and meanings for Fra's spinning Virgin, see Florentina Badalanova Geller, 'The Spinning Mary: Towards the Iconology of the Annunciation (between Christian Iconography and Slavonic Ethno-Hermeneutics', *Cosmos*, vol. 20, 2004, pp. 211–260. She can also be associated with the twelfth-century Byzantine icon of the Annunciation belonging to St Catherine's Monastery of Mount Sinai, Egypt.

22. Jessica Sutcliffe, *Face: Shape and Angle. Helen Muspratt Photographer* (Manchester: Manchester University Press, 2016), pp. 38–39. Two of the portraits were published in *The Professional Photographer*, December 1930. Helen Muspratt's life dates are 1907–2001. Much of her archive is now in the Bodleian Library, Oxford. Sutcliffe also reproduces a solarised photograph by Muspratt of Mary Newbery (Sturrock), who became her lifelong friend (p. 75), and numerous photographs of Hilda and Mary Spencer Watson, at least two of which from *c.* 1933 (pp. 69 and 73) appear to show them in embroidered dress inspired by Jessie's 'Serbian' turn. Muspratt, as Helen Dunman, published a posthumous appreciation of Fra in which she described his and Jessie's life in Dorset, including: 'Every autumn, when Nine Barrow Down turned brown, the Newberys would travel to France and Italy, and especially Yugoslavia, where the peasant art and costumes interested them. Both over 70, they would go by train and stay in small hotels. They spoke a little German, French, Italian and Spanish. They returned home in October to the Isle of Purbeck.' Helen Dunman, 'Artist of Corfe Castle', *Dorset: The County Magazine*, no. 63, May 1977, p. 8.

23. Ewen (1862–1942) was an engineer from Forfarshire who had worked on the construction of the Forth Bridge before becoming an H.M.

Inspector of Schools (Aberdeen and Glasgow). In 1930 Fra prepared at least two cards for him featuring the *Annunciation*. See Glasgow School of Art Archive, reference code GSAA/DIR/5/38/7/5 and 6.

24. Sutcliffe, op. cit., p. 40.

25. Jessica Sutcliffe collection, Swanage (from 2020 the Bodleian Library, Oxford).

26. Anon., 'Art in Glasgow', *The Aberdeen Daily Journal*, 25 September 1915, p. 4.

27. Concerning the organisation of the Meštrović exhibition, and the vexed question of the sculptor's national identity and allegiance, see Flora Turner-Vučetić, Eric Turner, 'Meštrović and the Victoria and Albert Museum', *Sculpture Journal*, vol. 25, no. 2, 2016, pp. 161–176. The whole *Sculpture Journal* issue comprises a reappraisal of Meštrović and includes other studies of the exhibition.

28. In addition, in keeping with British war-time interest in stoking Serbian nationalism so that the Kingdom of Serbia could expand and become a strong buffer to prevent the Central Powers' moves for rival Middle Eastern control, two monographs on Meštrović were published. The first, *Mestrovic and Serbian Sculpture* (1916), was a minor piece of naked political propaganda (by Abdullah Yusuf Ali). The second, *Ivan Meštrović* (1919), edited by Milan Ćurčin, was a major visual, critical and biographical survey from a group of authors led by John Lavery.

29. Anon., 'Royal Scottish Academy. Concluding Notice. Past and Present-Evolution and Continuity', *The Scotsman*, 1 June 1918, p. 4.

30. The reciprocal exhibitions were organised by the Friends of Great Britain in Yugoslavia and the Yugoslav Society of Great Britain, these friendship societies being one of the positive outcomes of the British-Yugoslav allegiance during the First World War. The Belgrade display of contemporary British artists opened, with considerable fanfare, on 3 February 1929. Artworks comprised paintings, sculptures and graphic art, the variety possessing a fair breadth of stylistic and genre range. Artists included: William Reid Dick, Frank Dobson, Paul Drury, J.D. Fergusson, Roger Fry, Jacob Epstein, Alfred Frank Hardiman, Iain Macnab, Paul Nash, William Nicholson, Walter Sickert and Ethelbert White.

31. The Yugoslav Embassy in London and the British Council organised the 'Yugoslav Exhibition' at the Royal Academy of Arts, London in 1944.

32. A particularly detailed and extensive visual survey was published in the German periodical that most favoured the work of the Newberys and the Glasgow Style: Josef Strzygowski, 'Ein Grabkirche von Ivan Mestrovic', *Deutsche Kunst und Dekoration*, vol. 52, June 1923, pp. 126–172. For a more recent overview, with summaries in English, see Lida Roje Depolo, Ljiljana Čerina, *Ivan Meštrović. Gospa od Anđela Mauzolej obitelji Račić u Cavtatu* (Zagreb: Glipoteka-Hrvatska Akademija Znanosti i Umjetnosti, 2008). The mausoleum is known as the Chapel of Our Lady of Angels. Meštrović designed and built it for the tragic Račić family between 1920 and 1922. It is located in the Adriatic coastal village of Cavtat in southeast Dalmatia, fifteen kilometres from Dubrovnik (Ragusa), where Fra and Jessie were staying.

33. Kineton Parkes, 'The Sculpture of Mestrovic', *Artwork: An Illustrated Quarterly of the Arts and Crafts*, vol. 1, no. 1, 1924, p. 7.

34. Rawson, *Francis Henry Newbery*, op. cit., p. 292. Dunman was to include a chapter on Yugoslavia in his book *Agriculture: Capitalist and Socialist* (London: Lawrence & Wishart, 1975).

35. See Ilay Cooper, *Purbeck Arcadia: Dunshay Manor and the Spencer Watsons*, (Wimborne Minster: Dovecote Press, 2015), pp. 159. She travelled with Rachel Lloyd, daughter of the art historian Sir Herbert Cook; Cook's Dorset estate at Studland was just a few kilometres from Corfe. Before moving on to Greece, the pair were particularly drawn to the frescoes, architecture and stonework of the Serbian and Macedonian churches they sought out.

36. Ibid., p. 157.

Chapter 3 | Threads of Legacy

1. Information about the frame of *The Spanish Shawl* (*c*. 1916, private collection) was provided by George Rawson. Gibson established his practice in 1900. I have been unable to discern when his workshop closed.

2. Margaret H. Swain, 'Mrs J.R. Newbery 1864–1948', *Embroidery*, vol. 24, no. 4, 1973, pp. 105–106.

3. A most valuable, succinct account of Newbery's transformative impact is given in Elizabeth Cumming, *Hand, Heart and Soul: The Arts and Crafts Movement in Scotland* (Edinburgh: Birlinn, 2006), chapters 1 and 2.

4. Concerning his views on the machine, as well as the Arts and Crafts movement and politics, see George Rawson, *Francis Henry Newbery and the Glasgow School of Art*, PhD thesis, University of Glasgow, 1996, pp. 114–146.

5. Anon., 'Ornamental and Decorative Art', *The Dundee Courier*, 16 January 1892, p. 2. This report indicates that Fra admonished pervasive poor decorative design in modern housing, the craze for Japanese art, and recent coin and postage stamp design.

6. Anon., 'The Principles of Ornament and Decoration', *The Dundee Advertiser*, 16 January 1892, p. 6.

7. Ibid.

8. In his address, the Provost used the occasion of Fra's lecture to call for a school of design in Dundee, as an artistic impetus to industry and so that skill in design may serve to raise the quality of jute fabric production to compete with that of Austria (ibid.).

9. An online copy of this can be found in the 1892–95 press-cutting album of Henry Taylor

Wyse. See the Wyse website at https://htwyse. info/HTW/press-cutting-albums/1892-95 (accessed 13 June 2020). I am grateful to Elizabeth Cumming for drawing my attention to this.

10. Elizabeth Cumming, Heather Jack, *Henry Taylor Wyse: Artist, Teacher, Craftsman* (Glasgow: Arberbrothock Imprints, 2016), p. 17f. This book and the associated website dedicated to Wyse (1870–1951, see previous footnote), provide a very useful basis for understanding at least some aspects of the Newberys' Scottish legacy and context.

11. See Oleg Grabar, *The Mediation of Ornament* (Princeton: Princeton University Press, 1992).

12. See: Anonymous, 'Technical Education in Dundee. Chairman's Speech', *Journal of Decorative Art*, vol. 12, no. 5, May 1892, pp. 75–77; Murdo Macdonald, 'The Patron, the Professor and the Painter' in Christopher A. Whatley et al. (eds), *Victorian Dundee: Image and Realities* (Dundee: Dundee University Press, 2001), pp. 197–216; and Matthew Jarron, *Individual and Individualist: Art in Dundee 1867–1924* (Dundee: Abertay Historical Society, 2015), pp. 48–91.

13. Anonymous, 'Here and There', *Dundee Evening Telegraph*, 1 February 1900, p. 2.

14. Anonymous, 'Here and There', *Dundee Evening Telegraph*, 28 March 1900, p. 4.

15. Anonymous, 'Piper's Portrait Gallery. no. 713 – Mr John Duncan', *The Piper O' Dundee*, May 1900, pp. 336–337. If Fra had not seen the murals in person, he may have seen sketches or reproductions.

16. Stenberg was a New Zealander. His dates are 1919–2017.

17. The president was Barclay Lockhart, a linen manufacturer.

18. Anon., 'Kirkcaldy Home Arts and Industries Exhibition', *The Fife Free Press*, 9 May 1903, p. 2.

19. Concerning the origins, early activities, structure and objectives of the HAIA, see Janice Helland, '"Good Work and Clever Design": Early Exhibitions of the Home Arts and Industries Association', *The Journal of Modern Craft*, vol. 5, no. 3, 2012, pp. 275–293. One group associated with the HAIA was the Haslemere (Surrey)-based Peasant Arts Society, later the Peasant Art Guild. Besides encouraging weaving, from the first decade of the twentieth century it also formed a collection of European peasant crafts, including Balkan textiles. See David Crowley and Lou Taylor (eds), *The Lost Arts of Europe: The Haslemere Museum Collection of European Peasant Art* (Haslemere: Haslemere Educational Museum, 2000).

20. Anon., 'Kirkcaldy Home Arts and Industries Association', *The Fife Free Press*, 7 May 1904, p. 2.

21. Concerning both Jessie and Macbeth (1875–1948), see, for example, Fiona C. MacFarlane and Elizabeth F. Arthur, *Glasgow School of Art Embroidery 1894–1920*, (Glasgow: Glasgow Museums and Art Galleries, 1980). Besides being a useful commentary on Jessie's pedagogy

(pp. 4–5) this exhibition catalogue provides the most detailed catalogue of her work to date (pp. 37–44). For Macbeth, see: pp. 5–7 and 17–26 of this catalogue; Fra H. Newbery, 'An Appreciation of the Work of Ann Macbeth', *The Studio*, vol. XXVII, 1902, pp. 40–49 [and this book's appendix 2]; and Liz Arthur, 'Ann Macbeth', in Jude Burkhauser (ed.), *Glasgow Girls: Women in Art and Design 1880–1920* (Edinburgh: Canongate, 1990), pp. 152–157.

22. For a black-and-white reproduction of an embroidered Elizabeth panel designed and sewn by Macbeth, see *The Studio Yearbook of Decorative Art*, 1914, p. 66.

23. Margaret Swanson, Ann Macbeth, *Educational Needlecraft* (London: Longmans, Green & Co., 1911), p. 2. Swanson had gained needlework teaching certificates from the Glasgow School of Art during Jessie's period as head of embroidery.

24. Ann Macbeth, *The Country Woman's Rug Book* (Leicester: Dryad Press, 1929), pp. 21–22.

25. Ibid., p. 54.

26. Ann Macbeth, May Spence, *School and Fireside Crafts* (London: Methuen & Co., 1920), p. 60.

27. Ibid., p. 53.

28. Ibid., p. 53.

29. Ibid., pp. 67–68.

30. Ann Macbeth, *Embroidered and Laced Leather Work* (London: Methuen & Co., 1924), pp. 37–38.

31. Ibid.

32. Ibid.

33. Ibid., p. viii. Unsurprisingly, Macbeth omits the second clause of the Ecclesiastes (King James Bible Version) sentence: 'for there is no work, nor device, nor knowledge, nor wisdom, in the grave, whither thou goest'.

34. Ann Macbeth, *The Playwork Book* (London: Methuen & Co., 1918), pp. 2–4. She repeated the claim at the end of the foreword she wrote for *An Embroidery Book* (London: A.& C. Black, 1920, p. xi), a teaching manual by Anne Knox Arthur, the Glasgow School of Art colleague who replaced her as head of embroidery in the 1920s.

35. In her book, *School and Fireside Crafts* (London: Methuen & Co., 1920), co-authored with May Spence, Macbeth used some of the same images as Anne Knox Arthur in her contemporary *An Embroidery Book* (London: A.& C. Black, 1920). Figs 3.9 and 3.10 are reproduced from the latter since there they appeared in colour, whereas in Macbeth and Spence (op. cit., pp. 66 and 74) they are reproduced in black and white.

36. Burkhauser, op. cit., p. 163. Dewar's dates are 1878–1959.

37. Anon., 'Yugoslavia', *The Motherwell Times*, 30 September 1932, p. 6.

38. Dewar may well have participated in other Balkan fieldtrips of the Le Play Society, including visits to Bulgaria (August 1935) and northern Albania (summer 1938). These excursions, like most others, were not followed by published Le Play reports (in fact only eight reports were published, two of them by student groups, three of them with Dewar's artwork). Dewar did give a Harkness House lecture on her participation in a Le Play study trip to Somerset in spring 1932.

39. In L. Dudley Stamp (ed.), *Slovene Studies* (London: Le Play Society, 1933), p. 7. Mackinder became president of the society following Geddes' death in 1932.

40. Concerning Geddes' regional survey concept for the society, and its derivation from Frédéric Le Play's methods of sociological survey, see S.H. Beaver, 'The Le Play Society and Field Work', *Geography*, vol. 47, no. 3, July 1962, pp. 225–240. The article also gives some detail as to the countries in which the excursions took place (some seventy-one overseas and ten in the British Isles in the thirty years of the society's existence). Besides Yugoslavia and Romania, in the 1930s fieldwork was also undertaken in Albania and Bulgaria, Beaver lamenting (p. 237) that these failed to result in direct publications.

41. Ibid., p. 231.

42. For a detailed study of Copeland's input, as well as consideration of the Slovenian fieldtrip as a key model for Le Play Society enquiry, see Richard Clarke, Marija Anteric, 'Fanny Copeland and the Geographical Imagination', *Scottish Geographical Journal*, vol. 127, no. 3, 2011, pp. 173–179. The authors mention the society's hope that the excursion would lead to increased collaboration between British and Yugoslavian intellectuals.

43. Stamp, op. cit., p. 20.

44. In the 2020s, the shed remains a centrepiece for marketing Gradišnik as a 'tourist farm'.

45. See, for example, Borut Juvanec, 'Slovene Architecture Kozolec', at https://www.ijs.si/kozolci (accessed 16 October 2020). I am grateful to Ana Lipovsek for drawing my attention to the significance of the *kozolec*. Many comparative historic examples of *kozolci* have been recorded by the Slovenian Ethnographic Museum, at https://www.etno-muzej.si/en/digitalne-zbirke/kljucne-besede/kozolec (accessed 16 October 2020).

46. Baron Meston, 'Foreword', in H.J. Fleure and R.A. Pelham (eds), *Roumania: East Carpathian Studies* (London: Le Play Society, 1936), pp. 5–6.

47. P.M. Roxby, 'Foreword', in H.J. Fleure and E. Estyn Evans (eds), *Roumania II: South Carpathian Studies* (London; Le Play Society, 1939), p. 5.

48. H.J. Fleure and R.A. Pelham (eds), op. cit., pp. 63–64.

49. Ibid., pp. 66, 72, 76.

50. Ibid., opp. p. 13.

51. Anon., 'An Outpost of Western Civilisation – Travels in Roumania', *The Bellshill Speaker*, 6 October 1933, p. 8. The reference to the Prince of Wales (the future Edward VIII) arose due to his visit to Harkness House a few months earlier, on which occasion it was noted that: 'Pausing at the embroidery table the Prince took up the articles and examined them for himself. "I am highly delighted with this style of embroidery" he told Mrs Eliz. Paterson. "In fact", he said, "I do this kind of work myself". He wished to know how many strands of thread were in it and about the different stitches. He did that kind of work himself and found it very soothing and restful.' Anon., 'Bellshill Welcomes the Prince of Wales', *The Bellshill Speaker*, 31 March 1933, p. 1.

52. Anon., 'An Outpost of Western Civilisation – Travels in Roumania', p. 8.

53. Luminiţa Machedon, Ernie Scoffham, *Romanian Modernism: The Architecture of Bucharest, 1920–1940* (Cambridge, Mass.: MIT Press, 1999), pp. 248–249. The Gaz Electra Rest House was one of the first projects of Octav Doicescu, who went on to become one of Romania's most important modern architects.

54. Anon., 'A Splendid Experiment – Harkness House', *The Bellshill Speaker*, 9 October 1931, p. 6. Macbeth had semi-retired in 1920, though she maintained her Glasgow School of Art connection, and influence, as 'visiting instructress', until 1928. Anne Knox Arthur replaced Macbeth as head of needlework at the school from 1920 until 1930, her place then being taken by Kathleen Mann (see below).

55. Anon., 'Social Centre for Bellshill', *The Bellshill Speaker*, 23 October 1931, p. 6. Katherine Dewar also brought various examples of textiles to the inaugural meeting of the centre, indicating various ways in which fabric may be worked, repaired and embellished.

56. H.J. Fleure and E. Estyn Evans, (eds), op. cit., pp. 24, 31 and 26.

57. Ibid., p. 25. In fact the picturesque church is regarded as the potters' church and is dedicated to the Assumption of the Virgin. Dating from the late seventeenth century, the exterior frescoes were added in the late 1860s.

58. Beaver, op. cit., p. 239.

59. Concerning Kathleen Mann (1908–2000), see, for example, Liz Arthur, 'Kathleen Mann Crawford', in Burkhauser, op. cit., p. 183. Mann's concern with peasant dress derived from her student days in London in the late 1920s. Liz Arthur has noted that she got her *Peasant Costume in Europe* book commission upon the 'instigation' of Randolph Schwabe, principal of London's Slade School of Art (Arthur in Burkhauser, op. cit., p. 183). Schwabe, his wife Gwendolen and daughter Alice were close acquaintances of the Newberys. Schwabe had influence in Glasgow (he helped his son-in-law, Harry Barnes, to get appointed as assistant master in painting and drawing in 1944). Hence, while we can only speculate at present, he may well have also recommended Mann to lead the embroidery department, perhaps in consultation with Fra and Jessie. In a sign of a return to depressed and repressive times, Mann was, in 1935, forced out of her job by a post-Newbery era regulation requiring married women to resign (this after her marriage to the painter Hugh Adam Crawford). She remained living in Glasgow and devoted herself to raising a family and continuing her needlework and publishing independently.

60. The Modern Embroideries Society was founded in Edinburgh in 1921. It held biennial exhibitions through to at least the late 1930s. The Needlework Development Scheme was established in Scotland in 1934 and ran until the Second World War. Organised through the art schools of Aberdeen, Dundee, Edinburgh and Glasgow, the aim was to develop embroidery education and practice, and through these contribute to improved standards of design.

61. Kathleen Mann, *Peasant Costume in Europe* (London: A.&C. Black, 1968) [a one volume edition], p. 5. Mann also has illustrations of Hungarian and Romanian costume, though in the central European rather than Balkan section.

62. Kathleen Mann, *Peasant Costume in Europe*, (London: A.& C. Black), vol. 2, 1936, pp. 90–109.

63. While the man wears the '*belodreshna nosiya*' (white costume) typical of northern Bulgaria, but without typical girdle and vest, the woman's 'pinafore' is more typical of the Thracian lowlands of southern Bulgaria and the central Balkans, but without typical apron. My thanks to Rada Georgieva for her insights on the dress.

64. Ibid., p. 91.

65. Ibid., p. 91.

66. Kathleen Mann, *Design from Peasant Art*, (London: A.&C. Black, 1939), p. 11.

67. Ibid., p. 18. For Mann's full analysis of this and her Romanian-inspired work, see appendix 3. The book contains no bibliography, instead just loosely acknowledging 'members of a number of embassies, legations and societies who have assisted greatly by suggesting sources of information' (p. 5).

68. Ibid., p. 54.

69. Mann's sketch was reproduced, with that of another Romanian glass icon (of The Lamentation), ibid., p. 23. The two sketches were derived from the first two artworks reproduced within Oprescu's introduction to his monograph, op. cit., p. 8. The caption of the Mother of Sorrows icon photograph indicates that it is a work from Nicula in the collection of Ion Muşlea (a leading Romanian folklorist at the University of Cluj-Napoca). This means the original is from the glass-icon-painting workshop of the Greek-Catholic Monastery at Nicula, northern Transylvania. The National Museum of Transylvanian History at Cluj-Napoca has three similar but not identical icons from Muşlea's collection. It remains possible that the icon survives in the Transylvanian Museum of Ethnography, Cluj-Napoca, since a part of Muşlea's collection is held there. Mann does not acknowledge her sources, yet her use of Oprescu's *Studio*-published monograph for the fabric icon is symptomatic of the main kind of publications she trawled.

70. Mann, *Design*, p. 54.

71. Ibid., p. 11. She notes that 'Many contemporary artists have found inspiration in the study of such work', while giving the example of the French artists Paule and Max Ingrand, who she contends may have borrowed from Russian icons in an altar panel painted on glass (ibid., pp. 11–12). She does not specify further, but her placing of Paule before her husband Max Ingrand is noteworthy, given the second place often accorded to Paule in the spousal artistic partnership.

72. Ibid., p. 13.

73. Ibid., p. 15.

74. Ibid., p. 13.

75. Ibid., p. 14.

76. See H. Th. Bossert, *Volkskunst in Europa* (Berlin: Verlag Ernst Wasmuth, 1926), p. 19 and plate LXXVII, nos 1–3.

77. I am grateful to Danijela Velimirović and Davor Petrović of the Department of Ethnology and Anthropology at Belgrade University for their help in identifying the possible origins of a number of the Newberys' artefacts and costumes.

78. Concerning Denise Findlay's work, see, in particular, her website: https://www.denisefindlay.com.

Chapter 4 | Cross-stitching

1. George Rawson, *Francis Henry Newbery and the Glasgow School of Art*, PhD thesis, University of Glasgow, 1996, p. 282. It is known that Jessie made use of Baedeker's travel guide books when planning and travelling, her copy of *Austria-Hungary with Excursions to Cetinje, Belgrade, and Bucharest* (Leipzig: Karl Baedeker, 1911 edition) being handed down through different generations of the family.

2. Reproductions of several of these can be found in Rawson, ibid., and at https://artuk.org/discover/artworks/search/actor:newbery-francis-henry-1855 1946 (accessed 30 June 2020).

3. Besides *The Nimbus of Toil* illustrated here a second version is discussed and illustrated in Rawson, ibid., pp. 121, 261–262 and 394. I am grateful to Keith Roberts for drawing my attention to the relationship between Fra's and Borelli's works.

4. Jack Dunman, *Agriculture: Capitalist and Socialist* (London: Lawrence and Wishart, 1975), pp. 215–216.

5. Ibid., p. 13. In contrast to the Yugoslavian statistics concerning agricultural labour, in 1920 when Britain's population numbered around forty million, just under 1,700,000 were employed in agriculture (by 1931, when the UK population had reached 46 million, this had declined to under 1,400,000). Hence instead of nearly 80% the UK had around 4%, reducing to around 3%.

6. Fra. H. Newbery, 'An Appreciation of the Work of Ann Macbeth', *The Studio: An Illustrated Magazine of Fine and Applied Art*, vol. XXVII, no. 115, October 1902, p. 41 (See appendix 2 and chapter 7 for more on Fra's evaluation of needlework's significance).

7. Anon., 'Royal Scottish Academy', *The Aberdeen Daily Journal*, 12 May 1916, p. 4; Anon., 'Royal Scottish Academy', *The Scotsman*, 22 May 1916, p. 7. The whereabouts of both works are unknown.

8. Selwyn Image, Letter, *The Times*, 30 June 1915, p. 9.

9. Rawson, *Francis Henry Newbery*, p. 308.

10. Anon., 'The Lace-Making Industry', *North-Eastern Daily Gazette*, 20 October 1916, p. 6. The lace exhibition at which Fra spoke was dominated by work from the Loch Fyne and Kintyre Lace Association. Buckinghamshire and East Devon Lace Associations were also represented. The exhibition was held in the showrooms of Daly's department store, Sauchiehall Street, Glasgow.

11. Hereafter just the year and correspondence item number from appendix 1 will be given.

12. Jessie's observations on Niš dress, customs and East-West identity were anticipated by Mary Edith Durham in a short chapter on the town that she included in her first Balkan book, *Through the Lands of the Serb* (London: Edward Arnold, 1904), pp. 170–181.

13. Anon., 'Uddingston Literary Society', *The Hamilton Herald*, 9 October 1903, p. 7.

14. Fra's connection with Hardie may have gone back to his Glasgow days, when he certainly would have known his uncles, the painters Charles Martin Hardie and John Pettie.

15. See appendix 1, 1926: 3. For Woods' important role as a conduit between British and Turkish interests, see Geoffrey R. Berridge, *British Diplomacy in Turkey, 1583 to the Present: A Study in the Evolution of the Resident Embassy* (Leiden: Brill-Nijhoff, 2009), pp. 162–163.

16. Brooklyn Museum Press Release, 1927, 053 (though 54 appears on the original typed copy). See http://cdn2.brooklynmuseum.org/labels/ PUB_Press_releases_1927_053.JPG (accessed 25 September 2020). Ismailovitch (1890–1976) was from Satanov, a small, predominantly Jewish, town on the border between the Austrian and Russian empires. Being anti-Bolshevik, he had emigrated to Istanbul in 1919. Thereafter, he became an active member of the 'Union of Russian Artists in Constantinople'. He spent much of the next seven years studying and copying the city's Byzantine art, his work on Kharie Djami comprising his most significant project. He worked for the 'Russian Archaeological Institute in Constantinople' and received at least part of the Kharie Djami commission from Gardiner Howland Shaw, the secretary of the US Embassy in Turkey. He held an exhibition at the private American Robert College in Istanbul in late October 1926, just after the Newberys' visit. At that time his work was seen by Edith Wilson, the widow of President Woodrow Wilson, who, becoming his Maecenas, helped facilitate his travel to the USA, exhibitions and patronage. Upon the invitation of the Soviet Byzantinist Viktor Lazarev, Ismailovitch wrote a lecture on the Kharie Djami mosaics and frescoes, his research informing various studies of Byzantine art, both Russian and Western. I have been unable to ascertain the present whereabouts of his Kharie Djami work.

17. Eric Maclagan, 'Prefatory Note', Muriel Clayton, *Mosaics and Frescoes in the Kahrié-Djami Constantinople Copied by Dmitri Ismailovitch* (London: Victoria and Albert Museum, 1928), p. 2 (the small, illustrated catalogue of the London exhibition). Coincidentally, Maclagan had been a major supporter of Meštrović, facilitating, then as Keeper of Sculpture, his Victoria and Albert Museum exhibition in 1915, and having his portrait bust (now in the V&A, London) made by the Croatian sculptor around 1919.

18. P.G. Konody, 'Byzantine Art of the Fourteenth Century', *The Observer*, 22 July 1928, p. 14.

19. Paul A. Underwood, *The Kariye Djami*, vol. 1 (London: Routledge & Kegan Paul, 1967), p. 252. For a visual survey of the scheme of martyr saints, see Underwood, op. cit., vol. 3, pp. 474–475, 492–504.

20. See Underwood, op. cit.: vol. 1, frontispiece, pp. 27f. and 39–43; vol. 2, pp. 12–13, 17–19 and 26–29 for an analysis of the church panels, their place in the programme and layout, and reproductions.

Chapter 5 | Stitch-ups

1. See, primarily, Eugene Michail, *The British and the Balkans: Forming Images of Foreign Lands 1900–1950* (London: Continuum, 2011); Vesna Goldsworthy, *Inventing Ruritania: The Imperialism of the Imagination* (London: C. Hurst, 2013); chapter four of Maria Todorova, *Imagining the Balkans* (Oxford: Oxford University Press, 2009). While none of these deal with the paradigms in terms of the visual arts, Goldsworthy comes closest, through her insightful deconstruction of the creative literary elements of the paradigms.

2. For a huge tranche of documents revealing recent/current British interventionist policy, supported by the UK government Conflict, Stability and Security Fund (CSSF) and, in part, provided by intelligence cutouts designed to 'capture the information space' through 'black propaganda', such as ZINC Network, Albany Associates and the Media Diversity Institute, see the three parts of: Matthew Doer, 'OP. HMG Trojan Horse. Part 5: Fracturing the Balkans', 5 July 2021, at https://telegra.ph/ OP-HMG-Trojan-Horse-Part-5-Fracturing-The-Balkans-I-07-05 (accessed 1 August 2021). See also the so-called Stabilisation Unit's final report (March 2019) titled 'Western Balkans Rule of Law Initiative Scoping', published at https://ufile.io/ pxonxk1j (accessed 1 December 2021).

3. Goldsworthy, op. cit., p. xvii.

4. Ljiljana Blagojević has offered a useful introduction to the 'noble savage' approach adopted by

Le Corbusier towards that which he took from the Balkans, which combined with his disapproval of the signs of 'Europeanisation' that he encountered. See her *Modernism in Serbia: The Elusive Margins of Belgrade Architecture 1919–1941* (Cambridge, Mass.: MIT Press, 2003), pp. 3–8.

5. *Exposition Internationale des Arts Décoratifs et Industriels Modernes: Section du Royaume des Serbes, Croates et Slovènes. Catalogue Officiel* (Paris: Girard et Bunino, 1925).

6. Gabriel Millet, 'L'Art Decoratif et Industriels dans le Royaume SHS 1925', ibid., pp. iii–iv.

7. An album of photographs of the Yugoslavian section is in the collection of the Museum of Applied Arts, Belgrade. I am grateful to Bojana Popović, curator at the museum, for supplying me with reproductions relevant to this enquiry and discussed here.

8. Blagojević, op. cit.; Jelena Bogdanović, Lilien Filipovitch Robinson and Igor Marjanović (eds), *On the Very Edge: Modernism in the Arts and Architecture of Interwar Serbia (1918–1941)* (Leuven: Leuven University Press, 2014); Nikola Ivanović, *Identity(ies): Representations of Women in Serbian Painting (1918–1941)* (Novi Sad: Galerija Matica srpska, 2021). The last is a bilingual English-Serbian edition.

9. Blagojević's modernist tack is complemented by that offered by Snežana Toševa in her exhibition catalogue: *Serbia and Britain: Cultural Contacts at the Beginning of the 20th Century* (Belgrade: Museum of Science and Technology, 2007). In this we are introduced to more varied forms of cultural interchange stretching back into the late nineteenth century, with the section on architecture and urbanism being particularly significant, not least for its outlining of the distinct contributions of four Scots to the fields of planning and design: Francis Harford Mackenzie, Hugo and Edward McClure and Katherine MacPhail.

10. Lilien F. Robinson, 'From Tradition to Modernism: Uroš Predić and Paja Jovanović', in Bogdanović et al., op. cit., p. 34. In fact the girl in Predić's painting is Marija Mica Predić, his twelve-year-old niece and future wife of Serbian composer (and collector of folk songs) Stevan Mokranjac. Significantly, she is knitting socks for her brother, after their mother had died.

11. Zenit translates as Zenith; Oblik is best translated as Oblique, since it implies an askance approach to form, shape, feature, figure, fashion.

12. Ivanović, op. cit., p. 48.

13. Ibid., p. 76.

14. Ibid., p. 46.

15. The fullest study to date of Vukanović (1872–1972), who studied in Munich (most significantly at the atelier of Slovene Anton Ažbe (1892–96)), is Vera Ristić, *Beta Vukanović* (Belgrade: TOPY, 2004).

16. Bogdanović, op. cit., p. 22.

17. Lidija Merenik, *Nadežda Petrović: Projekat i Sudbina* (Belgrade: Topy, 2006), p. 168. A good selection of photographs of Petrović are reproduced across the book. Petrović (1873–1915) studied at the Munich studios of Anton Ažbe and Julius Exter, 1898–1902. She died of typhus having contracted it while working as a Serbian army nurse during the First World War.

18. See Jasna Jovanov, *Nadežda Petrović: Sobe strane objektive* (Novi Sad: Spomen Zbirka Pavla Beljanskog, 2012).

19. Golubović (1888–1961) studied at various European art schools. From the 1920s he taught art in Belgrade and was a member of the Lada society as well as other groups.

20. Jovanović's dates are 1886–1914. Concerning her art and biography, see Jasna Jovanov, *Danica Jovanović* (Belgrade: Topy, 2007); and Jasna Jovanov, *Danica Jovanović. Unverwirklichte Träume/Neostvareni Snovi* (Beška-Karlshuld: Stara Beška-Stiftung Donaumoos, 2020).

21. Antonov was born in Provadia, east Bulgaria, in 1868 (death date uncertain). He was awarded a stipend by Bulgaria's then Prince Ferdinand to study at the Academy of Fine Arts, Munich c. 1887–90. Thereafter he became a secondary school art teacher in Bulgaria, interrupting his career with a subsequent state grant to further his own art education in Munich (with Franz von Lenbach), Paris, Rome and other European centres (1896–98). See *Милена Георгиева, Съюзът на Южнославянските Художници «Лада» (1904–1912). Българкото Изкуство на Южнославянските Изложби* [*The 'Lada' Society of Southern Slav Artists (1904–1912). Bulgarian Art at the Southern Slav Exhibitions*] (Sofia: PSSA, 1994), p. 202

22. V. Antonoff, *Bulgarien vom Beginn seines Staatlichen Bestandes bis auf unsere Tage (679–1917)*, (Berlin: Georg Stilke, 1917), p. 60. *A Macedonian Slave* is preceded in the book by reproductions of two less allegorical, but similarly ethnographic, paintings by Antonov: *Bulgarian Woman from North Bulgaria* (1900) and, mentioned below and shown here, *Bulgarian Woman from West Macedonia* (1899). The formation of an ethnic Macedonian community identity only occurred after the establishment of the Socialist Republic of Macedonia within post-Second World War socialist Yugoslavia.

23. Eudoxia (1898–1985) was Bulgaria's first lady until her brother King Boris married in 1930. Nadezhda (1899–1958) became Duchess of Württemberg in 1924. Their mother, Princess Marie Louise of Bourbon-Parma, had died after giving birth to Nadezhda. In dressing his children in Bulgarian attire, Ferdinand was mirroring the use of tartan by his aunt and uncle, Britain's Queen Victoria and Prince Albert (with whom he stayed at Balmoral), as a way of expressing London's control over Scotland.

24. Caption from Lena A. Yovitchitch, *The Biography of a Serbian Diplomat* (London:

Epworth Press, 1939), facing p. 257.

25. Draginja Maskareli, email correspondence with author, 21 July 2020. For comparisons with a mix of modern urban and folk Serbian fashion see Draginja Maskareli, *Fashion in Modern Serbia* (Belgrade: Museum of Applied Arts, 2019). This provides a useful overview of the diversity and development of Serbian dress, including its incorporation of Ottoman, Jewish and western European elements. The well-illustrated text includes a selection of photographs by Milan Jovanović. Through text and image, the process of the tradition-inventing construction of Serbian national costume is outlined.

26. With these attributes the photograph resembles that of the three women in national costume in Aranđelović's Niš postcard discussed and illustrated in the previous chapter [fig. 4.3].

27. Natalia and Lena seem never to have married. Mara married David Halyburton Low in 1912 and thereafter lived in Scotland until shortly before her death in Westport, Connecticut, USA in 1962. She made a considerable contribution to the translation of the epic southern Slav *Ballads of Marko Kraljevic* attributed to her linguist husband (Cambridge: Cambridge University Press, 1922). Natalia died in Edinburgh in 1937. Lena died there in 1969. A younger sister Persida, along with their parents, died in Belgrade between the world wars. Their brother Milan was an officer in the Serbian army.

28. Lena A. Yovitchitch, *Pages from Here and There in Serbia*, (Belgrade: S.B. Cvijanovich, 1926).

29. Lena A. Yovitchitch, *Yugoslavia* (London: A.&C. Black, 1928).

30. Marcovitch (née Goninan, 1897–1991) was an Australian artist married to a Yugoslav diplomat, Radoje Marcović. I have been unable to trace B.E. Brown.

31. The previously mentioned exhibition of contemporary British art was shown in the Zuzorić exhibition building in February 1929.

32. 'Изложба савремених париских сликара', Илустровани лист ['The Exhibition of Contemporary Parisian Artists'], *Илустрованн Лист* [*Illustrated Newspaper*], no. 41, 10 October 1926, p. 31; B.P. [V.R.], 'Изложба савремених париских сликара', Политика ['The Exhibition of Contemporary Parisian Masters'], *Политика* [*Politika/Politics*], 29 September 1926, p. 5. Of the nine artists mentioned in the review four (including Sonia Delaunay) were émigrés from the former Russian empire, while Foujita was Japanese. Zadkine's *Woman* looks akin to his known nudes in wood from the early 1920s. Lhote's *Les Rugbymen* appears to be the 1920 work sold as Lot 148 at Christie's Paris 'Art Moderne' auction, 20 October 2017 (or a very similar version). Robert Delaunay's *Eiffel Tower* appears to be the 1911 version now in the Solomon R. Guggenheim Museum, New York. The exhibition should be considered a major milestone in terms of introducing French avant-garde work directly to a Balkan audience and as such deserves investigation in its own right.

33. B.P., op. cit.

34. I have been unable to definitively identify the Picasso. It appears very similar to his early Cubist work (1910–13), including his etchings for Max Job's *Saint Matorel* (Paris, 1911), as well as various studies of musicians, nudes and seated women. It seems to be signed and dated bottom right, though the date (191?) is cropped in the published photographs. The *Политика* [*Politika*] review (op. cit.) noted that Picasso had sent 'three things, one small nude with perfectly clean lines and an interesting drawing'.

35. В. [V.], 'Изложба слика г-ђе Соње Ковачић' ['The Exhibition of Paintings by Ms Sonja Kovačić'], *Политика* [*Politika*], 27 October 1926, p. 5. Kovačić (1894–1968) followed Lhote's example in her choice of an academic-style Cubism. Retaining the figure and a sense of illusionistic space, she added elements of geometricisation. The review held her up as a potential role model for others, noting her ability with oil and pastel.

Chapter 6
Wrapping anew the age-long hidden spark

1. Fra and Jessie's 1926 stay in Belgrade coincided with the city hosting a congress of the International Council of Women, chaired by its Scottish/British president Ishbel Hamilton-Gordon, Lady Aberdeen. See, for example, А.К.Б. [A.K.B.], 'Леди Абердин', Политика ['Lady Aberdeen'], *Политика* [*Politika*], 25 October 1926, p. 4; and, А.К.Б. [A.K.B.], 'Конгрес Женског Народног Савеза' ['Congress of the National Council of Women], *Политика* [*Politika*], 26 October 1926, p. 4. More research on the Balkan effects of this women's rights group, and its Yugoslavian representation, is needed. Autumn 1926 also saw the creation of a British-run orphanage in Niš, Lena Yovitchitch, Florence Maw and Una Moffet being among those responsible. Other British philanthropists active in the Balkans in 1926 included Dr Isabel Emslie Hutton and Arthur Headlam, Bishop of Gloucester.

2. My conception of the fractal derives mostly from Alfred Gell, *Art and Agency: An Anthropological Theory* (Oxford: Clarendon Press, 1998). Gell seems to have been the first to have proposed a theory of the art object as person, with enquiry into its nature and relations being a form of biography. It seems particularly appropriate to apply such a concept to the Newberys' Serbian works since their inter-relations offer much little-explored, yet rich, territory for investigation/understanding.

3. Another important advocate, particularly of Albania, and who was also a collector of Balkan textiles, was Mary Edith Durham (1863–1944). The illustrated catalogue of her collection, with its emphasis on Albanian, Bosnian, Montenegrin and

Dalmatian work, provides a useful counterpart to the textiles and postcards collected by Jessie. See: Laura E. Start and M. Edith Durham, *The Durham Collection of Garments and Embroideries from Albania and Yugoslavia* (Halifax: Calderdale Museums, 1939).

4. Талица [Talitsa], 'Наш ратни друг Ана Дикинсон – Дикица' ['Our Wartime Friend Anna Dickinson – Dikitsa'], *Жена и свет* [*Woman and the World*], no. 1, 1928, p. 14. Published in Belgrade, the illustrated, moderate feminist and fashion magazine had been founded in 1925. Its appearance further belies the identification of 'Serbian women' solely with peasant dress and its making.

5. 'Scotland's Aid to Serbia: Cause Pleaded at Dundee', *Dundee Evening Telegraph*, 23 October 1918, p. 3. Dickinson (1864–1953), together with her brother Baron Willoughby Dickinson, was an early proponent of the League of Nations, even creating in the 1920s, with her Bosnian students, a chairperson's 'peace' chair for the Palais Wilson in Geneva.

6. F. May Dickinson Berry, 'Captivity', in James Berry, F. May Dickinson Berry et al., *The Story of a Red Cross Unit in Serbia* (London: J. & A. Churchill, 1916), pp. 259, 261. See also 'Pepelyouga', in Woislav M. Petrovitch, *Hero Tales and Legends of the Serbians* (London: Harrap, 1914), pp. 224–230. Pirot carpets were kilims woven in the region of Pirot in south-east Serbia. With vibrant designs, often of geometric forms (frequently rhomboidal) on red bases, the kilims were woven by women and became national Serbian symbols: see Marina Cvetković, *Two Faces: The Catalog of Pirot Kilims in the Ethnographic Museum, Belgrade* (Belgrade: Ethnographic Museum, 2016). Judging from photographs of the Dickinson sisters they looked alike, hence it may be that their identification should be vice versa to that stated here.

7. Bojanna Popović published her rediscovery of Dickinson in her catalogue: *Primenjena Umetnost i Beograd 1918–1941* [*Applied Art and Belgrade 1918–1941*] (Belgrade: Museum of Applied Arts, 2011), pp. 24–25 and 231.

8. Anon., 'Miss A.J. Dickinson. Artist and Social Worker', *The Times*, 8 August 1953, p. 8.

9. Tanya Harrod, 'Primary Text/Commentary', *The Journal of Modern Craft*, vol. 8, no. 1, March 2015, p. 72. Harrod's text introduces the publication of Mairet's first Yugoslavian journal (op. cit., pp. 77–86). Her second journal, from her 1930 visit, is a remarkably rich resource, complete with quick sketches of various textile, ceramic and wooden articles, yet it remains unpublished. A telling excerpt of the latter, relating to her visit, with Dickinson, to a Bosnian peasant weaver, are reproduced in Margot Coatts, *A Weaver's Life: Ethel Mairet 1872–1952* (Bath: Crafts Council, 1983), p. 86. This journal also records various other significant meetings and encounters, including with Lena and Natalia Jovičić, their mother, 'Madame Yovitchitch. Old Scotch lady',

and 'Two Miss Browns from England staying [with them]'. Both diaries are in the collection of the Crafts Study Centre, Farnham.

10. Harrod, op. cit., p. 65. See also Margot Coatts, op. cit., the fullest biography of Mairet to date.

11. Ethel Mairet, *Hand-Weaving To-Day: Traditions and Changes* (London: Faber & Faber, 1936), pp. 52–54 (1949 edition). See appendix 6 for full transcript.

12. See Mairet's work reproduced on the Visual Arts Data Service (VADS) website, home page https://vads.ac.uk, and also on the V&A's digitised collection website, home search page https://collections.vam.ac.uk/search.

13. Ethel Mairet, 'Yugoslavian Journal May 4 –May 30, 1927', *The Journal of Modern Craft*, vol. 8, no. 1, March 2015, pp. 77–86. Besides observing Balkan craft conventions for her own art's sake, Mairet also bought numerous examples of work on this and her subsequent trip to resell in Britain.

14. See: Rosemary Edmonds, Muriel Rose, 'The Work of Jean Milne', *Quarterly Journal of the Guilds of Weavers, Spinners and Dyers*, no. 9, March 1954, pp. 264–265. This accompanied a death notice (ibid., p. 262) and announcement of a posthumous exhibition (ibid., p. 274). Very little has been published on Milne, though Harrod (op. cit., pp. 66 and 74) has noticed the significance of her Balkan experience. Her dates are 1875–1953.

15. Harrod, op. cit., p. 66.

16. Milan Ćurčin, *Ivan Meštrović: A Monograph* (London: Williams and Norgate, 1919), p. 75. Ćurčin also noted Kljaković's drawing represented 'a modern "Maiden of Kossovo" or "Mother of the Jugovići", or a widow in the sense of Meštrović'. The Croatian Kljaković was subsequently one of the artists of the stained glass panels of the Yugoslav pavilion at the 1925 Paris exhibition. The following verses by Milne appear on p. iv.

17. Ibid.

18. Reproduced in *The Studio: Yearbook of Decorative Art* (London: The Studio, 1909), p. 58.

19. Edmonds, Rose (op. cit., p. 265) indicate that 'Starting with only a rough sketch on a fairly large scale but with a clear mental image, she wove her rug, working out the pattern as materials and technique suggested and without further recourse to paper.'

20. Ibid., p. 264. Jean Milne's will of 24 June 1952 indicates that at that time she had 'seven pieces of Bushongo woven work, two pieces of Coptic tapestry, one piece of Pre-Conquest Peruvian tapestry, two North African bast woven round salvers', which she left, along with all her weaving-related work, drawings and tools, to Edmonds and Rose for their use or purposeful disposal. Both the V&A in London and the Crafts Study Centre, Farnham, currently possess four rugs by Milne.

21. Anon., 'Obituary. Miss Jean Milne', *The Times*, 4 January 1954, p. 8.

22. Jean Milne, 'Basis of Art Teaching', *The Listener*,

7 December 1939, p. 1134.

23. Seamus O'Malley, *Making History New: Modernism and Historical Narrative*, Oxford Scholarship Online: November 2014, DOI: 10.1093/acprof:oso/9780199364237.001.0001, p. 175.

24. Rebecca West, *Black Lamb and Grey Falcon: A Journey through Yugoslavia* (Edinburgh: Canongate, 2006), pp. 637, 640, 647, 673, 1099, 1127–1128. The first edition was published in 1942.

25. O'Malley, ibid., p. 158.

26. Ibid., p. 171.

27. Ibid., p. 158 (from West, op. cit., p. 785). O'Malley, somewhat disingenuously, then omits West's subsequent observation (ibid., p. 785).

28. West, op. cit., p. 785.

Chapter 7 | Towards a conclusion

1. J. Gleeson White, 'Some Glasgow Designers and Their Work – III', *The Studio: An Illustrated Magazine of Fine and Applied Art*, vol. 12, no. 55, October 1897, pp. 50–51.

2. Ibid., p. 48.

3. Margaret H. Swain, 'Mrs J.R. Newbery 1864–1948', *Embroidery*, vol. 24, no. 4, 1973, p. 105.

4. Ibid.

5. Fiona C. MacFarlane, Elizabeth F. Arthur, *Glasgow School of Art Embroidery 1894–1920* (Glasgow: Glasgow Museums and Art Galleries, 1980), p. 4.

6. The cushion cover is in Glasgow Museums Collections (E.1953.53.c). The curtain (whereabouts unknown) was exhibited at the Glasgow International Exhibition, 1901.

7. Jessie's other works with quotations included: a cushion cover (*c.* 1916) with 'We are such stuff as dreams are made of [sic: 'on' in Shakespeare]' (from Prospero in William Shakespeare's *The Tempest*); a tablecloth (*c.* 1902), with 'Into this Universe, and Why not knowing, Nor Whence like Water willy-nilly flowing …' (Quatrain XXIX of *Rubaiyat of Omar Khayyam*, Edward Fitzgerald translation, 1859); a church pulpit fall (*c.* 1900), with 'Be ye doers of the word and not hearers only' ('Letter from James', 1:22, the Bible: King James Version). One of her earliest known cushion covers (*c.* 1900, V&A, London) has a central panel embroidered with the capitalised Latin saying (derived from an Italian sun-dial): 'SENSIM SED PROPERE FLUIT IRREMEABILIS HORA: CONSULE NE PERDAS ABS QUE LABORE DIEM' ('Gently but swiftly flows on the hour that can never return: Consider well, that thou lose not the day without its work').

8. Swain, op. cit., 1973, p. 106.

9. The tunics are now in Glasgow Museums Collections (E.1985.162.11 and E.1985.162.10). Together with a third costume (E.1985.162.12a, b), which consisted of 'a gently gathered skirt suspended from a sleeveless silk bodice … over which is worn a straight tunic, cut in rectangles like a peasant smock', they are briefly analysed by Margaret Swain (Swain, 'Mrs Newbery's Dress', *Costume*, vol. 12, no. 1, 1978, pp. 71–73).

10. Rozsika Parker, *The Subversive Stitch: Embroidery and the Making of the Feminine* (London: Bloomsbury, 2019), pp. 187 and 193 (originally published 1984).

11. MacFarlane and Arthur, op. cit., p. 42. It dates from 1896 and was apparently made by Edith Rowat, Jessie's cousin. It is in the collection of the Glasgow School of Art.

12. Diane Waller, *Textiles from the Balkans* (London: British Museum Press, 2010), p. 10.

13. Gleeson White, op. cit., p. 51.

14. Ibid., p. 48.

15. George Rawson, *Francis Henry Newbery and the Glasgow School of Art*, PhD thesis, University of Glasgow, 1996, pp. 136–139.

16. Ibid., pp. 137–138.

17. Fra. H. Newbery, 'An Appreciation of the Work of Ann Macbeth', *The Studio: An Illustrated Magazine of Fine and Applied Art*, vol. XXVII, no. 115, October 1902, pp. 41–42.

18. Milan Ćurčin, *Ivan Meštrović: A Monograph* (London: Williams and Norgate, 1919), p. iv.

19. Ibid., p. 45.

20. The Faculty of Arts Gallery was at 10 Upper John Street, London. It held exhibitions of Yugoslav peasant embroidery and Sidney Gausden's Balkan watercolours and woodcuts in mid-1924. Gausden (1892–1947) held an exhibition entitled 'Balkan Men and Ways' at Gieves Art Gallery, 22 Old Bond Street, London in autumn 1923. It included 'clever portraits and pictures of picturesque people and scenes in the Balkans … and furniture designs' (Anon., 'More Art Shows', *Western Daily Press*, 3 November 1923, p. 5). After art school in London, Bernard Rice (1900–1998) taught furniture design in a craft school in Bosnia from 1922 (a connection with Annie Dickinson should not be ruled out). With a break for further studies in London in 1926–27, he lived in Bosnia until 1929. He created many woodcuts of Bosnian rural life and landscapes.

Epilogue

1. Mira Crouch, email correspondence with the author, 18–19 June 2020.

2. Mira Crouch, *War Fare: Sustenance in Time of Fear and Want (A Memoir of Belgrade 1941–1945)* (London: Fisher, 2008), p. 86. Embroidery, *vezanje*, is actually masculine, though embroiderer, *vezilja*, is feminine and signifies woman embroiderer.

3. Ibid., pp. 103–104. See also Mira Crouch, 'Reading *Anna Karenina*, Considering the Holocaust', *Quadrant*, November 2012, pp. 85–89.

LIST OF ILLUSTRATIONS

Modernes au XXème Siècle (Paris: Exposition Internationale des Arts Décoratifs et Industriels Modernes, 1925, vol. 6), plate LXXII

5.7 | Stained glass panels (design by Milo Milunović, Marijan Trepše, Maksimilijan Vanka, Zlatko Šulentić, Jozo Kljaković; executed by Ivan Marinković atelier, Zagreb), Kingdom of Serbs, Croats and Slovenes national pavilion, Paris Exposition Internationale des Arts Décoratifs et Industriels Modernes, 1925; from album of photographs of Yugoslav sections, © Museum of Applied Arts, Belgrade

5.8 | Vladimir Becić, *Kolo*, staircase mural, Kingdom of Serbs, Croats and Slovenes national pavilion, from *Encyclopédie Internationale des Arts Décoratifs et Industriels Modernes au XXème Siècle* (Paris: Exposition Internationale des Arts Décoratifs et Industriels Modernes, 1925, vol. 2), plate XCVI (photograph by H. Thibaud)

5.9 | Vladimir Becić, *Kolo*, staircase mural in situ, Kingdom of Serbs, Croats and Slovenes national pavilion; from album of photographs of Yugoslav sections, © Museum of Applied Arts, Belgrade

5.10 | Paja Jovanović, *Preparation of the Bride*, 1888, oil on canvas, 96.5 x 135 cm; National Museum in Belgrade

5.11 | Uroš Predić, *Industrious Little Hands*, 1887, oil on wood, 27 x 15.5 cm; National Museum in Belgrade

5.12 | Beta Vukanović, *Woman Spinning*, c.1920–25, oil on canvas, 87 x 65 cm; private collection

5.13a | Nadežda Petrović in nurse's uniform, Prizren, 10 April 1913; The Pavle Beljanski Memorial Collection, Novi Sad

5.13b | Nadežda Petrović in modern folk dress, 1908; private collection

5.14 | Nadežda Petrović, Anđa Petrović, c.1907–8, Kolarž family collection.

5.15 | Nadežda Petrović, *Two Peasant Women*, 1905, oil on card, 66 x 96 cm; National Museum in Belgrade

5.16 | Nadežda Petrović, *Shepherd Playing a Pipe*, 1906, oil on card, 78 x 49 cm; private collection

5.17 | Miloš Golubović, *Spinster*, c.1930, oil on board, 55 x 47 cm; private collection, courtesy Madl' Art Auction House, Belgrade

5.18 | Miloš Golubović, *Girl*, c.1925, oil on canvas, 68 x 58 cm; private collection, courtesy Madl' Art Auction House, Belgrade

5.19 | Danica Jovanović, *Peasant Woman with Woven Bag*, c.1913, oil on canvas on cardboard, 44 x 27 cm; private collection

5.20 | Danica Jovanović, *Peasant Woman*, c.1913, oil on canvas on cardboard, c.22 x 20 cm; private collection

5.21 | Danica Jovanović, *Peasant Woman with Distaff*, c.1913, oil on canvas on cardboard, 22.5 x 20 cm; private collection

5.22 | Valcho Antonov, *Macedonian Woman [A Macedonian Slave]*, 1905; from V. Antonoff,

Bulgarien vom Beginn seines Staatlichen Bestandes bis auf unsere Tage (679–1917) (Berlin: Georg Stilke, 1917), plate 39

5.23 | Valcho Antonov, *Bulgarian Woman from West Macedonia*, 1899; from V. Antonoff, *Bulgarien vom Beginn seines Staatlichen Bestandes bis auf unsere Tage (679–1917)* (Berlin: Georg Stilke, 1917), plate 38

5.24 | Princesses Eudoxia and Nadezhda of Bulgaria, c.1914; from V. Antonoff, *Bulgarien vom Beginn seines Staatlichen Bestandes bis auf unsere Tage (679–1917)* (Berlin: Georg Stilke, 1917), plate 28

5.25 | Milan Jovanović, Mara, Lena and Natalia Jovićić, 1907; from Lena A. Yovitchitch, *The Biography of a Serbian Diplomat* (London: Epworth Press, 1939), opp. p. 257

5.26 | Milan Jovanović and Lena Jovićić, 1907; from Lena A. Yovitchitch, *Pages from Here and There in Serbia* (Belgrade: S.B. Cvijanovich, 1926), frontispiece

5.27 | B.E. Brown, Kosovan shepherd, pre-1926; from Lena A. Yovitchitch, *Pages from Here and There in Serbia* (Belgrade: S.B. Cvijanovich, 1926), opp. p. 136

5.28 | Alfreda Marcovitch, Jelačićev Square market, Zagreb, pre-1928; from Lena A. Yovitchitch, *Yugoslavia* (London: A.&C. Black, 1928), opp. p. 10

5.29 | Cvijeta Zuzorić Association, members, c.1925; Lada Association Archive

5.30 | Milan Jovanović, 'Ana Marinković', photograph, c.1906; Museum of Applied Arts, Belgrade

5.31 | Ossip Zadkine, *Woman*, n.d.; from 'Изложба савремених париских сликара', *Илустрованн Лист*, no. 41, 10 October 1926, p. 31; National Library of Serbia

5.32 | André Lhote, *Portrait of a Woman*, pre-1926; from, 'Изложба савремених париских мајстора', *Политика*, 29 September 1926, p. 5; National Library of Serbia

5.33 | Pablo Picasso, drawing, n.d.; from 'Изложба савремених париских сликара', *Илустрованн Лист*, no. 41, 10 October 1926, p. 31; National Library of Serbia

5.34 | Sonja Kovačić (Tajčević), *Portrait of a Girl*, c.1926; from 'Изложба слика р-ђе Соње Ковачић', *Политика*, 27 October 1926, p. 5; National Library of Serbia

5.35 | Sonja Kovačić (Tajčević), *Girl's Head*, c.1926; from 'Изложба слика р-ђе Соње Ковачић', *Политика*, 27 October 1926, p. 5; National Library of Serbia

6.1 | Textile cover, c.late 1920s (by anon.); Ethel Mairet Source Collection (record 153, 2004.203.120), Crafts Study Centre, Farnham, © Estate of Ethel Mairet

6.2 | Fancy dress party, Vrnjačka Banja Red Cross Hospital, January 1916; from James Berry, F. May Dickinson Berry et al., *The Story of a Red Cross Unit in Serbia* (London: J. & A. Churchill, 1916), opp. p. 256

BIBLIOGRAPHY

CONTEMPORARY PUBLICATIONS

Periodicals and newspapers

The Aberdeen Daily Journal, Aberdeen Press and Journal, Artwork: An Illustrated Quarterly of the Arts and Crafts, The Bellshill Speaker, Deutsche Kunst und Dekoration, The Dundee Advertiser, The Dundee Courier, Dundee Evening Telegraph, Жена и свет [*Woman and the World*], *The Fife Free Press, The Hamilton Herald, Илустрованн Лист* [*Illustrated Newspaper*], *Journal of Decorative Art, North-Eastern Daily Gazette, The Observer, The Piper O' Dundee, Политика* [*Politika*], *The Scotsman, The Studio: An Illustrated Magazine of Fine and Applied Art, The Studio: Yearbooks of Decorative Art, The Times, Western Daily Press.*

Selected articles/event programme

Gleeson White, J., 'Some Glasgow Designers and Their Work – III', *The Studio*, vol. XII, 1897, pp. 47–51.

Levetus, A.S., 'Austria' and 'Croatia and Slavonia', in Charles Holme (ed.), *Peasant Art in Austria and Hungary* (London: The Studio, 1911, pp. 1–14 and 51–54).

Milne, Jean, 'Basis of Art Teaching', *The Listener*, 7 December 1939, p. 1134.

Newbery, Fra. H., 'An Appreciation of the Work of Ann Macbeth', *The Studio*, vol. XXVII, 1902, pp. 40–49.

—, *Sanctus: Edwardus. West: Saxonum. Rex: Martyr* [1927, event programme for pageant at Corfe Castle] (copy at Corfe Castle Town Trust).

Strzygowski, Josef, 'Ein Grabkirche von Ivan Mestrovic', *Deutsche Kunst und Dekoration*, vol. 52, June 1923, pp. 126–172.

Taylor, J., 'The Glasgow School of Embroidery', *The Studio*, vol. 41, 1910, pp. 124–135.

Monographs

Antonoff, V., *Bulgarien vom Beginn seines Staatlichen Bestandes bis auf unsere Tage (679–1917)* (Berlin: Georg Stilke, 1917).

Arthur, Anne Knox, *An Embroidery Book* (London: A.&C. Black, 1920).

Berry, James, and F. May Dickinson Berry et al., *The Story of a Red Cross Unit in Serbia* (London: J.&A. Churchill, 1916).

Bossert, H. Th., *Volkskunst in Europa* (Berlin: Verlag Ernst Wasmuth, 1926).

Clayton, Muriel, *Mosaics and Frescoes in the Kahrié-Djami Constantinople Copied by Dmitri Ismailovitch* (London: Victoria and Albert Museum, 1928).

Copeland, Fanny S., *The Women of Serbia* (London: Kossovo Day Committee/Faith Press, 1916).

Ćurčin, Milan, *Ivan Meštrović: A Monograph* (London: Williams and Norgate, 1919).

Durham, Mary E., *Through the Lands of the Serb*, (London: Edward Arnold, 1904).

Encyclopédie Internationale des Arts Décoratifs et Industriels Modernes au XXème Siècle (Paris: Exposition Internationale des Arts Décoratifs et Industriels Modernes, 1925).

Fleure, H.J., and E. Estyn Evans (eds), *Roumania II: South Carpathian Studies* (London: Le Play Society, 1939).

—, and R.A. Pelham (eds), *Roumania: East Carpathian Studies* (London: Le Play Society, 1936).

Holme, Charles (ed.), *Peasant Art in Austria and Hungary* (London: The Studio, 1911).

Macbeth, Ann, *The Playwork Book* (London: Methuen & Co., 1918).

—, *Embroidered and Laced Leather Work* (London: Methuen & Co., 1924).

—, *The Country Woman's Rug Book* (Leicester: Dryad Press, 1929).

—, and May Spence, *School and Fireside Crafts* (London: Methuen & Co., 1920).

Mairet, Ethel, 'Yugoslavian Journal May 4–May 30, 1927', *The Journal of Modern Craft*, vol. 8, no. 1, March 2015, pp. 77–86; available at https://doi.org/10.2752/174967715X14213400209999.

—, *Hand-Weaving To-Day: Traditions and Changes*, (London: Faber & Faber, 1939).

Mann, Kathleen, *Peasant Costume in Europe* (London: A.&C. Black, 2 vols, 1931 and 1936; and a one-volume edition, 1968).

—, *Design from Peasant Art* (London: A.&C. Black, 1939).

Millet, Gabriel (co-author), *Exposition Internationale des Arts Décoratifs et Industriels Modernes: Section*

*du Royaume des Serbes, Croates et Slovènes.
Catalogue Officiel*, Paris: Girard et Bunino, 1925.
Moore, W.A., et al., *The Balkan States Exhibition,
1907, Official Guide & Catalogue* (London:
Gale & Polden, 1907).
Muthesius, Anna, *Das Eigenkleid der Frau*
(Krefeld: Kramer & Baum, 1903).
*Official Catalogue of the Bulgarian Section, Balkan
States Exhibition* (London: J.C. König &
Ebhardt, 1907).
Oprescu, George, *Peasant Art in Roumania*
(London: The Studio Ltd, 1929).
Petrovitch, Woislav M., *Hero Tales and Legends
of the Serbians* (London: Harrap, 1914).
Stamp, L. Dudley (ed.), *Slovene Studies* (London:
Le Play Society, 1933).
Start, Laura E., and M. Edith Durham, *The
Durham Collection of Garments and Embroideries
from Albania and Yugoslavia* (Halifax: Calderdale
Museums, 1939).
Swanson, Margaret, and Ann Macbeth,
Educational Needlecraft (London: Longmans,
Green & Co., 1911).
Tucić, Srgjan Pl. (Fanny S. Copeland, trans.),
The Slav Nations (London: Hodder & Stoughton,
1915).
West, Rebecca, *Black Lamb and Grey Falcon:
A Journey through Yugoslavia* (Edinburgh:
Canongate, 2006; first published 1942).
Yovitchitch, Lena A., *Pages from Here and There
in Serbia* (Belgrade: S.B. Cvijanovich, 1926).
—, *Yugoslavia* (London: A.&C. Black, 1928).
—, *The Biography of a Serbian Diplomat* (London:
Epworth Press, 1939).

SECONDARY SOURCES

Arthur, Elizabeth F., 'Glasgow School of Art
Embroideries, 1894–1920, *The Journal of the
Decorative Arts Society 1890–1940*, no. 4, 1980,
pp. 18–25.
Arthur, Liz, *Textile Treasures at the Glasgow School
of Art* (London: A.&C. Black, 2005).
Badalanova Geller, Florentina, 'The Spinning Mary:
Towards the Iconology of the Annunciation'
(sub-sect. 'Between Christian Iconography and
Slavonic Ethno-Hermeneutics'), *Cosmos*, vol. 20,
2004, pp. 211–260.
Beaver, S.H., 'The Le Play Society and Field Work',
Geography, vol. 47, no. 3, July 1962, pp. 225–240.
Bjeladinović, Jasna, *Serbian Ethnic Dress in the
Nineteenth and Twentieth Centuries* (Belgrade:
Ethnographic Museum, 2011).
Blagojević, Ljiljana, *Modernism in Serbia: The
Elusive Margins of Belgrade Architecture 1919–1941*
(Cambridge, Mass.: MIT Press, 2003).
Bogdanović, Jelena, Lilien Filipovitch Robinson
and Igor Marjanović (eds), *On the Very Edge:
Modernism in the Arts and Architecture of Interwar
Serbia (1918–1941)* (Leuven: Leuven University
Press, 2014).
Burkhauser, Jude (ed.), *Glasgow Girls: Women in Art
and Design 1880–1920* (Edinburgh: Canongate,
1990).
Clarke, Richard, and Marija Anteric, 'Fanny
Copeland and the Geographical Imagination',
Scottish Geographical Journal, vol. 127, no. 3, 2011,
pp. 163–192.
Coatts, Margot, *A Weaver's Life: Ethel Mairet
1872–1952* (Bath: Crafts Council, 1983).
Cooper, Ilay, *Purbeck Arcadia: Dunshay Manor
and the Spencer Watsons* (Wimborne Minster:
Dovecote Press, 2015).
Crouch, Mira, 'Death and Images of Womanhood
and Manhood: The Case of Serbian Epic Poetry',
Asa Kasher (ed.), *Dying and Death: Inter-
Disciplinary Perspectives* (Amsterdam, New York:
Rodopi, 2007), pp. 41–56.
—, *War Fare: Sustenance in Time of Fear and Want
(A Memoir of Belgrade 1941–1945)* (London:
Fisher, 2008).
—, 'Reading *Anna Karenina*, Considering the
Holocaust', *Quadrant*, November 2012, pp. 85–89.
Crowley, David, and Lou Taylor, (eds), *The Lost
Arts of Europe: The Haslemere Museum Collection
of European Peasant Art* (Haslemere: Haslemere
Educational Museum, 2000).
Cumming, Elizabeth, *Hand, Heart and Soul:
The Arts and Crafts Movement in Scotland*
(Edinburgh: Birlinn, 2006).
—, and Heather Jack, *Henry Taylor Wyse: Artist,
Teacher, Craftsman* (Glasgow: Arberbrothock
Imprints, 2016).
Cvetković, Marina, *Two Faces: The Catalog of Pirot
Kilims in the Ethnographic Museum, Belgrade*

(Belgrade: Ethnographic Museum, 2016).

Čorak, Željka, 'The Yugoslav Pavilion in Paris', *The Journal of Decorative and Propaganda Arts*, no. 17, Fall 1990, pp. 36–41.

Dunman, Helen, 'Artist of Corfe Castle', *Dorset: The County Magazine*, no. 63, May 1977, pp. 8–9.

Dunman, Jack, *Agriculture: Capitalist and Socialist* (London: Lawrence & Wishart, 1975).

Edmonds, Rosemary, and Muriel Rose, 'The Work of Jean Milne', *Quarterly Journal of the Guilds of Weavers, Spinners and Dyers*, no. 9, March 1954, pp. 264–265.

Eicher, Joanne B., and Djurdja Bartlett, *Berg Encyclopedia of World Dress and Fashion: East Europe, Russia, and the Caucasus*, vol. 9 (London, 2011).

Gell, Alfred, *Art and Agency: An Anthropological Theory* (Oxford: Clarendon Press, 1998).

Милена Георгиева, *Съюзът на Южнославянските Художници «Лада» (1904–1912). Българкото Изкуство на Южнославянските Изложби* [*The 'Lada' Society of Southern Slav Artists (1904–1912). Bulgarian Art at the Southern Slav Exhibitions*] (Sofia: PSSA, 1994).

Goldsworthy, Vesna, *Inventing Ruritania: The Imperialism of the Imagination* (London: C. Hurst, 2013).

Grabar, Oleg, *The Mediation of Ornament* (Princeton: Princeton University Press, 1992).

Gutt-Mostowy, Jan, *Podhale: A Companion Guide to the Polish Highlands* (New York: Hippocrene Books, 1998).

Harrod, Tanya, 'Commentary', *The Journal of Modern Craft*, vol. 8, no. 1 (March 2015), pp. 65–76; available at https://doi.org/10.2752/174967715X14213400209953.

Helland, Janice, '"Good Work and Clever Design": Early Exhibitions of the Home Arts and Industries Association', *The Journal of Modern Craft*, vol. 5, no. 3, 2012, pp. 275–293.

Howard, Jeremy, *East European Art* (Oxford: Oxford University Press, 2006).

Ivanović, Nikola, *Identity(ies): Representations of Women in Serbian Painting (1918–1941)* (Novi Sad: Galerija Matica srpska, 2021).

Jarron, Matthew, *Individual and Individualist: Art in Dundee 1867–1924* (Dundee: Abertay Historical Society, 2015).

Jovanov, Jasna, *Danica Jovanović* (Belgrade: Topy, 2007).

—, *Nadežda Petrović: s obe strane objektive* (Novi Sad: Spomen Zbirka Pavla Beljanskog, 2012).

—, *Danica Jovanović. Unverwirklichte Träume/ Neostvareni Snovi* (Beška-Karlshuld: Stara Beška-Stiftung Donaumoos, 2020).

Кадијевић, Алексанар, *Један век тражења националног стила у Српској Архитектури (средина XIX–средина XX века)* (Belgrade: Грађевинска књига, 1997).

Kadijević, Aleksandar, 'Echoes of Medieval Architecture in the Work of Master Builder Andreja Damjanov', *Зограф*, no. 27, 1998–99, pp. 167–176.

Krsteva, Angelina, *Macedonian Folk Embroidery* (Skopje: Institute of Folklore, 1975).

MacFarlane, Fiona C., and Elizabeth F. Arthur, *Glasgow School of Art Embroidery 1894–1920* (Glasgow: Glasgow Museums and Art Galleries, 1980).

Machedon, Luminiţa, and Ernie Scoffham, *Romanian Modernism: The Architecture of Bucharest, 1920–1940* (Cambridge, Mass.: MIT Press, 1999).

Mansbach, S.A., *Modern Art in Eastern Europe: From the Baltic to the Balkans, ca. 1890–1939*, (Cambridge: Cambridge University Press, 1999).

Maskareli, Draginja, *Fashion in Modern Serbia* (Belgrade: Museum of Applied Arts, 2019).

Merenik, Lidija, *Nadežda Petrović: Projekat i Sudbina* (Belgrade: Topy, 2006).

Michail, Eugene, *The British and the Balkans: Forming Images of Foreign Lands 1900–1950* (London: Continuum, 2011).

Moriarty, Catherine, Jon Wood and Peter Dent, (eds), *The Sculpture Journal* (special issue on Ivan Meštrović), vol. 25, no. 2, 2016.

Novakov, Anna, *Diplomatic Ties: Pavle Beljanski, Patronage and Serbian Women Artists* (San Francisco: Fibonacci Academic Press, 2012).

O'Malley, Seamus, *Making History New: Modernism and Historical Narrative*, Oxford Scholarship Online, November 2014, DOI: 10.1093/acprof:oso/9780199364237.001.0001.

Parker, Rozsika, *The Subversive Stitch: Embroidery and the Making of the Feminine* (London: Bloomsbury, 2019).

Popović, Bojanna, *Primenjena Umetnost i Beograd 1918–1941* (Belgrade: Muzej Primenjene Umetnosti, 2011).

Ratuszniak, Annette, et al., *Mary Spencer Watson: Sculpture* (Salisbury: R&R Publications, 2004).

Rawson, George, *Fra H. Newbery: Artist and Art Educationist* (Glasgow: Foulis Press of Glasgow School of Art, 1996).

—, *Francis Henry Newbery and the Glasgow School of Art*, PhD diss., University of Glasgow, 1996 (online edition http://radar.gsa.ac.uk/5419).

—, *Fra H. Newbery: A Dorset Artist* (Bridport: Bridport Heritage Forum, 2008).

Ristić, Vera, *Beta Vukanović* (Belgrade: TOPY, 2004).

Roje Depolo, Lida, and Ljiljana Čerina, *Ivan Meštrović. Gospa od Anđela Mauzolej obitelji Račić u Cavtatu* (Zagreb: Glipoteka-Hrvatska Akademija Znanosti i Umjetnosti, 2008).

St Clair, Kassia, *The Golden Thread: How Fabric Changed History* (London: John Murray, 2019).

Sutcliffe, Jessica, *Face: Shape and Angle. Helen Muspratt Photographer* (Manchester: Manchester University Press, 2016).

Swain, Margaret, 'Mrs Newbery's Dress', *Costume*,

vol. 12, no. 1, 1978, pp. 64–73.

Swain, Margaret H., 'Mrs J.R. Newbery 1864–1948', *Embroidery*, vol. 24, no. 4, 1973, pp. 104–107.

Tanner, Ailsa, 'Glasgow Girls (*act.* 1880–1920)', *Oxford Dictionary of National Biography* (Oxford University Press, 2004; online edition, January 2010).

Taylor, Lou, *Establishing Dress History* (Manchester: Manchester University Press, 2004).

Todorova, Maria, *Imagining the Balkans* (Oxford: Oxford University Press, 2009).

Toševa, Snežana, *Serbia and Britain: Cultural Contacts at the Beginning of the 20th Century* (Belgrade: Museum of Science and Technology, 2007).

Tötszegi, Tekla, *Satul tradiţional văzut prin obiectivul lui Denis Galloway (Transilvania, Partium, Banat, Bucovina)* (Cluj-Napoca: Edition Argonaut, 2008).

—, *Port* și Culoare. Imagini autocrom din colecția Galloway a Muzeului Etnografic al Transilvaniel (1931–*1933)* (Cluj-Napoca: Argonaut, 2018).

—, and István Pávai, *Music, Dance, Tradition: Dennis Galloway's Romanian Photographs, 1926–1932* (Budapest: Hagyományok Háza, 2010).

Troy, Virginia Gardner, *The Modernist Textile: Europe and America 1890–1940* (Aldershot: Lund Humphries, 2006).

Underwood, Paul A., *The Kariye Djami*, vols 1–3 (London: Routledge & Kegan Paul, 1967).

Vintilă-Ghiţulescu, Constanţa (ed.), *From Traditional Attire to Modern Dress: Modes of Identification, Modes of Recognition in the Balkans (xvith–xxth Centuries)* (Newcastle-upon-Tyne: Cambridge Scholars Publishing, 2011).

Waller, Diane, *Textiles from the Balkans* (London: British Museum Press, 2010).

Whatley, Christopher A., Bob Harris and Louise Miskell (eds), *Victorian Dundee: Image and Realities* (Dundee: Dundee University Press, 2001).

ACKNOWLEDGEMENTS

Inevitably, this book owes much to many. It has been enabled by generous giving of time and material from an array of folk with whom it has been my pleasure to interact. The range is extensive, but in the first place, I owe most debt of gratitude to the descendents of Fra and Jessie Newbery, who have furnished me not just with the main fabric of my enquiry but with a welcome that was truly warm and encouraging. Secondly, but equally vitally, come the remarkable colleagues, collectors and friends, whether employed by institutions or freelance, who embraced my seemingly eccentric project, interests and requests, and supplied me with answers and directions no others could have provided, all so openly and without hint of reservation. Thirdly, I express my deep gratitude to all those who enabled the provision and use of images.

I pay particular tribute to George Rawson (1946-2022) and Mira Crouch (1932-2021), two of my wisest counsellors for this book, both of whom departed this life in the period between completion of the manuscript and publication. Without their unstinting magnanimity, guidance and respective sharing of abundant Newbery and Serbian knowledge, this tome would have been a shadow of what it became. I deeply feel their loss and hope, in some small way, *Balkan Fabrications*, can be my testament to them.

What follows is a list of many individual helpers, with apologies to anyone who should be there that I've missed out in error. What it doesn't mention is my family and friends who allowed me the space to recognise and source my fibre and then spin my yarn – thanks are due all round.

In appreciation to: Nicole and Keith Roberts, Vivien and Denise Findlay, Judith Witts, Erica and John Kerr; Andrew and Stephen Allberry; Elisabeth Guilloson; Ian Robertson; Tess Dickinson; Jessica Sutcliffe; Mirjana Menković and Vjera Medić of the Ethnographic Museum in Belgrade; Draginja Maskareli, Bojana Popović, Marijana Petrović of the Applied Arts Museum, Belgrade; Lazar Rančić of Madl'Art, Belgrade; Jasna Jovanov; Tamara Butigan of the National Library of Serbia; National Museum in Belgrade; The Pavle Beljanski Memorial Collection, Novi Sad; Vesna Zorić of the Ethnographic Museum, Zagreb; Vlasta Sabić of the Museum of Slavonia, Osijek; Daniel Zec of the Museum of Fine Arts, Osijek; Danijela Velimirović, Davor Petrović, Aleksandra Ilijevski, Nenad and Svetlana Makuljević, Lidija Merenik, Aleksandar Kadijević of Belgrade University; Miloš Kolarž; Gvozden Perković; Darko Tanasković, Tamara Ognjević; Florentina Badalanova Geller; Gruiţă Ioana of the National Museum of Transylvanian History, Cluj-Napoca; Tötszegi Tekla of the Transylvanian Museum of Ethnography; Breda Gradišnik of Tourist Farm Gradišnik; Lili Bartholomew, Anna Robertson, Susan Keracher, Bruce Pert of the MacManus Art Gallery & Museum, Dundee; Barry Sullivan, D.C. Thomson & Co Archive; Elizabeth Cumming of Edinburgh University; Helen Scott of the City Arts Centre, Edinburgh; Liz Arthur; Purbeck residents Ilay Cooper, Toby Wiggins, Carole Brown, Susan and David Lansbury, Louise Haywood, Tony Bryan and the Corfe Castle Town Trust; Fathers Timothy Lewis and Paul Keys, Church of the Holy Spirit and St Edward, Swanage; Simon Parvin of Swanage Photographic Society; Camilla King, Dorset County Museum; Greta Bertram and Shirley Dixon of the Crafts Study Centre, Farnham; Paul Deaton and Clara Hudson of Sansom & Company; Ann Kay, editor; Ian Parfitt of E&P Design; Rada Georgieva, Shona Kallestrup, Alex Chiriac of the University of St Andrews.

Appreciation for financial support is due to the University of St Andrews and The Marc Fitch Fund.

INDEX